MEMORIES OF LOYANG

*Yang Hsüan-chih and
the lost capital (493–534)*

BY
W. J. F. JENNER

CLARENDON PRESS · OXFORD
1981

Oxford University Press, Walton Street, Oxford OX2 6DP

OXFORD LONDON GLASGOW
NEW YORK TORONTO MELBOURNE WELLINGTON
KUALA LUMPUR SINGAPORE HONG KONG TOKYO
DELHI BOMBAY CALCUTTA MADRAS KARACHI
NAIROBI DAR ES SALAAM CAPE TOWN

*Published in the United States
by Oxford University Press, New York*

British Library Cataloguing in Publication Data
Jenner, William John Francis
  Memories of Loyang.
  1. Lo-yang, China—History
  I. Title
  951'.18   DS796.L57   80-41307

ISBN 0-19-821568-1

*Printed in Great Britain
at the University Press, Oxford
by Eric Buckley
Printer to the University*

Preface

We are fortunate in knowing the extraordinary Northern Wei capital of Loyang, which within forty-one years went from desolation to a great metropolis with over half a million inhabitants and back to desolation, from the full account of it written by one of its former court officials, Yang Hsüan-chih. Yang's memoir, a guide-book for the mind, allows us to look on the city through the eyes of a high-born Han gentleman. It also tells us much more about Northern Wei Loyang than any surviving source does about any earlier Chinese city.

This study is an attempt to marry a modern European view of the origins, history, function, and nature of the city with a translation of Yang's 'Record of the Monasteries of Loyang', our main source of information on it. It will come as no surprise to those familiar with Chinese literature to find that what appears to be no more than nostalgia turns out to contain comment on the grave crisis of 547 to 550, the years when it was conceived and written.

This study and translation have been long in gestation. Work on them began in 1962 at the invitation of David Hawkes, who over the years has offered invaluable encouragement and advice. In turning a thesis into a book I have reduced my commentary to Yang's 'Record' to about one-ninth of its former size, leaving the sinological barbed-wire entanglements to lie in the Bodleian Library. One part of this earlier commentary, almost totally excised from these pages, deals with Yang's account of the journey across central Asia to the Buddhist lands of Udyāna and Gandhāra in what is now Pakistan made by the diplomat Sung Yün and his monkish companions Hui-sheng and Tao-jung in 518. (Yang's account has been retained in order not to mutilate the original; it is, besides, a good story.) Another omission, both from Yang's 'Record' and from this study, is any detailed consideration of Buddhist thought and scholarship in Loyang: that would have called for another book as long as this.

In romanizations (on modified Wade–Giles principles) hyphens have been omitted from modern place-names, to distinguish them from earlier ones, in which they are retained, except in the case of Loyang itself. Hyphens have also been omitted from the names of peoples and people who were in Wei eyes foreign, except in the account of Sung Yün's journey. Chinese sources are cited by full or abbreviated titles, modern works by author and date only.

Among other debts that it is a pleasure to acknowledge are those to two other teachers, T. L. Zinn and Wu Shih-ch'ang; and to the editors of the two best editions of Yang's 'Record', Fan Hsiang-yung and Chou Tsu-mo, whose commentaries and critical apparatus have been indispensable guides and inexhaustible mines. I am deeply grateful to the Delegates of the Press for agreeing to publish a book of this nature, and in the interests of economy I have kept to the minimum use of Chinese characters. The greatest debt has been to my wife Eileen.

Contents

Abbreviations

AM	*Asia Major*
ASBIHP	*Academia Sinica, Bulletin of the Institute of History and Philology*
BEFEO	*Bulletin de l'École Française de l'Extrême Orient*
BMFEA	*Bulletin of the Museum of Far Eastern Antiquities* (Stockholm)
BSOAS	*Bulletin of the School of Oriental and African Studies*
CHSC	Chung-hua shu-chü
Chou	Chou Tsu-mo, or his *Lo-yang ch'ieh-lan chi chiao shih*
CMYS	*Ch'i min yao shu*
Fan	Fan Hsiang-yung, or his *Lo-yang ch'ieh-lan chi chiao chu*
HHS	*Hou Han shu*
HJAS	*Harvard Journal of Asiatic Studies*
HKSC	*Hsü kao seng chuan*
K	Bernhard Karlgren's reconstruction of 'ancient' (*c.* AD 600) pronunciation of Chinese as given in *Grammata Sinica Recensa* (Stockholm, 1964), reprinted from *Bulletin of the Museum of Far Eastern Antiquities*, (Stockholm) 29, 1957)
LSYC	*Li-shih yen-chiu*
LYCLC	*Lo-yang ch'ieh-lan chi*
PCS	*Pei Ch'i shu*
PS	*Pei shih*
SCC	*Shui ching chu*
SKC	*San kuo chih*
SS	*Sui shu*
TCTC	*Tzu-chih t'ung-chien*
TPYL	*T'ai-p'ing yü-lan*
TT	*T'ung-tien*
WS	*Wei shu*, original unreconstructed parts
WSa	*Wei shu*, parts reconstructed from *Pei shih* and other sources by Sung editors

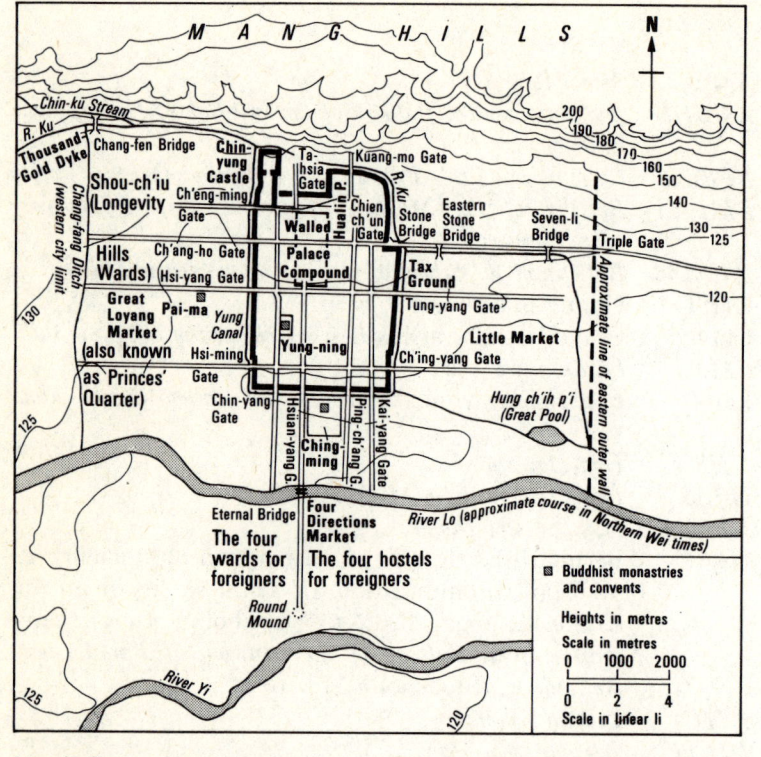

Map I. Greater Loyang around the years 520–530 (freely adapted from the map accompanying Su Pai's article in *Wen wu*, 1978.7). With the use of the sketch-map most of the places mentioned in Yang Hsüan-chih's account of the city can be approximately located. The lines of most of the walls and roads of the inner city have been established by modern surveys (see Map II). The lines of watercourses and of the roads outside the inner city are more speculative. It should be remembered that some of Yang's distances appear to be inclusive: thus, 'seven *li*' may mean within the seventh *li*.

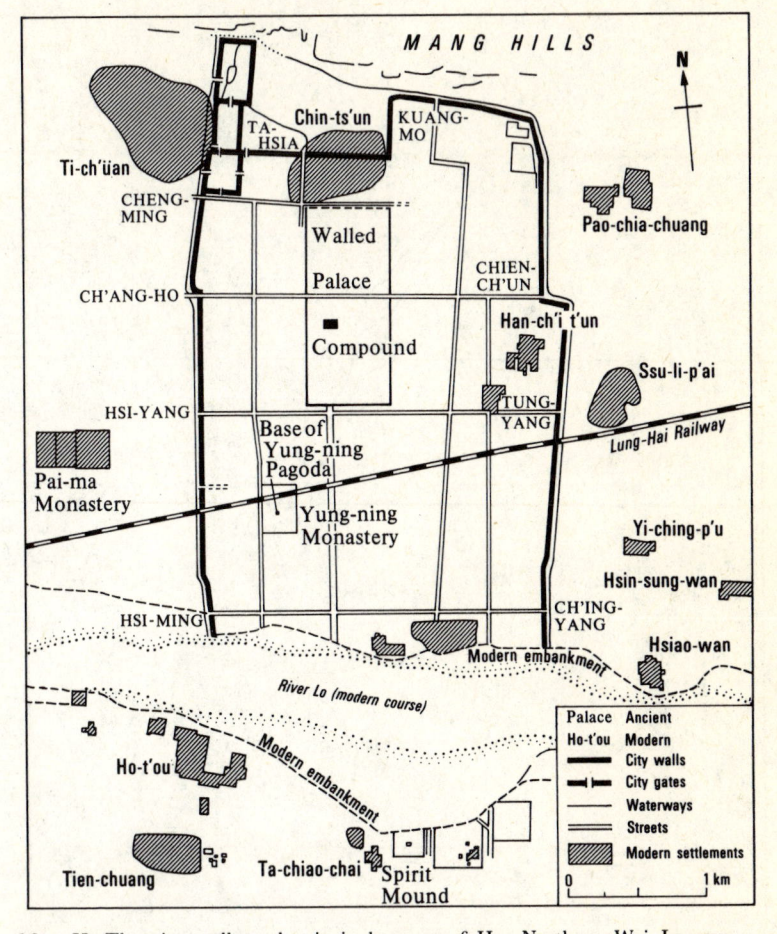

Map II. The city walls and principal streets of Han-Northern Wei Loyang as surveyed in the early 1970s (from *K'ao-ku*, 1973:4, p. 199).

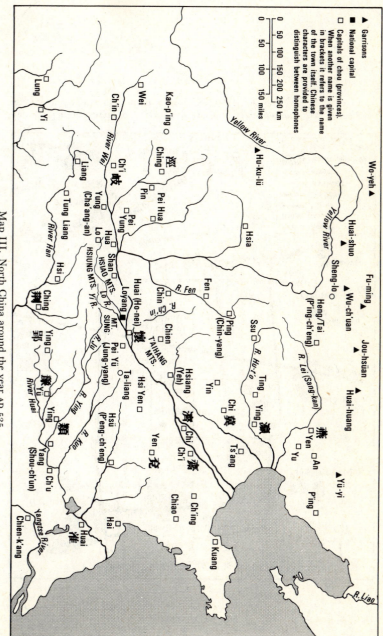

Map III. North China around the year AD 525.

Part I

Chapter 1

Memories of Loyang: Yang Hsüan-chih and the lost capital

An official passing in AD 547 through the empty ruins of Loyang, the great capital whose splendour and decline he had observed, was moved by the sight to write a memoir of the lost metropolis. The Loyang Yang Hsüan-chih knew had been an extraordinary city. Founded, or rather refounded, on a historic but largely deserted site at one man's bidding in 493, it had grown within thirty years to hold some half a million people, only to be abandoned and depopulated with its surrounding countryside at three days' notice on another man's orders in 534. Such rapid urban growth, so sudden a beginning and end to the short life of so huge a capital, are hard to parallel in history before the industrial revolution. Nor had Loyang been a mere shanty-town. The magnificence of its secular and religious buildings can still dazzle the imagination.

The book written by that official with profound and loving regret, the lost city he celebrated, and its origins, years of prosperity, and disastrous end, are the subject of this study. Yang's *Lo-yang ch'ieh-lan chi*, or 'Record of the Monasteries of Loyang', is the earliest substantial account of a Chinese city to survive, and this gives it a general value to the historian extending beyond the mass of evidence it gives us on city, state, and society as the Northern Wei regime slid from apparently unbounded wealth and power to humiliating impotence. As a document of the decades immediately following Loyang's destruction it is also a reflection of, and commentary upon, a profound crisis for the Han-Chinese aristocratic culture that had flourished there. If the evidence that Yang's book offers in such abundance is to be evaluated its political message has first to be decoded; and that message is essentially concerned with the events of 547 to 550, the time when the book was conceived and written. We must therefore begin our recovery of Loyang with a brief look at that crisis

3

and at the little that can be known or surmised about Yang Hsüan-chih.

At a first reading of the 'Record' such an exercise might appear to be unnecessary. It appears to be no more than a guidebook to the memory; indeed, at a casual glance the original, free as it generally is of indications of tense, might be taken as an account of a living city. Its five chapters—one for the area within the inner wall of the cities and four for the extensive suburbs outside this wall—are made up of topographical entries organized around the city's principal Buddhist monasteries and nunneries, fleshed out with the sort of anecdote one might expect in a guide-book of the more discursive kind, telling us about people and events associated with these establishments, many of which had been the houses of princes or aristocrats until their secular owners perished in the disorders of Loyang's last years. Some of these anecdotes are inconsequential gossip about social snobbery or supernatural events (though they bring the city back to life for us with an immediacy not to be found in the more formal historical texts of the period); but darker, more serious themes run through the book, conveying the feeling that the city, its way of life, and the dynasty that had created it were doomed.

What are less immediately apparent to the modern reader of Yang's book than the shadows of the city's terrible final years falling across the remembered splendour are the sharp comments on the issues of the late 540s, when the same political forces that had ended Loyang seemed to be destroying nearly all that remained of Han-Chinese aristocratic power and influence under the Northern Wei's successor regimes. Praise and blame are handed out liberally in Yang's pages; and in many cases his admiration and hatred are given extra force by their relevance to the crisis of the late 540s. Without going so far as to present the 'Record' as simply a thinly disguised attack on the enemies of Wei legitimacy and the Han aristocracy in 549, it can be argued that this aspect of the book was most important to its author.

For he wrote at a time when some of the dismal events of Loyang's last years were being played out again in the new capital, Yeh, to which nearly all the old capital's inhabitants had been moved. As before, a puppet Wei emperor was trying

and failing to assert his authority against that of a powerful non-Han subject who controlled the military. As before, the Han aristocrats and high officials around the throne were resisting the rise of a new style of government in which ability rather than birth was the main qualification for office. Some of the characters in the new drama had also acted in the earlier one; and others could be identified by birth, function, or association with performers in the Loyang tragedy.

With that tragedy—and the word is not inappropriate to describe events in which pride led to catastrophe—later chapters of this study and Yang's own book will deal at length. Let us consider here the politics of Yeh.[1] Kao Huan, the northern-frontier soldier who had risen through his martial and political abilities from obscurity to become the dominant figure of Loyang's last three years, had strengthened his position still further by moving the capital eastwards to Yeh in 534. Here he had kept a boy on the throne as his puppet Wei emperor, to whom he carefully observed the forms of respect due to a sovereign while maintaining real control of the state from his military headquarters at Chin-yang (Taiyuan). He did have his trusted apointees in key positions in Yeh, but he allowed the young emperor and his court a measure of dignity; and he did keep the high-born Han bureaucrats at the capital and the non-Han soldiers and tribal leaders out of each others' way as far as possible. He used the youthful emperor as a focus of loyalty.

Kao Huan's elder son, however, had other ideas. On Kao Huan's death in 547 Kao Ch'eng succeeded his father as dictator; but at twenty-six to the emperor's twenty-three he could not bring himself to treat the monarch as his superior. He sent subordinates to spy on him, ordered him to be struck, and insulted him publicly. The emperor, unable to bear the humiliation, recited a verse with which the poet Hsieh Ling-yün had once justified his revolt against an upstart regime in southern China.[2]

---

[1] On the politics of the Eastern Wei regime and its replacement by the Kao family see *PCS*, *PS*, and *TCTC*; Miao Yüeh (1963), pp. 78–94; Hamaguchi Shigekuni (1966), 2, pp. 685–736; Tanigawa Michio (1971), part 3, ch. 2; and the general histories of Lü Ssu-mien, Wang Chung-lo, and Okazaki Fumio.

[2] *PCS* 3, pp. 36–7; *TCTC* 160, pp. 4958–60.

The hint was taken by a number of Wei princes and Han officials, who conspired with the emperor in an unsuccessful attempt to kill Kao Ch'eng. Some conspirators were executed; many members of the royal family died;[3] and the emperor was imprisoned in the palace.

Although Kao Ch'eng successfully foiled that attempt to reassert Wei imperial power, he was not to enjoy his victory for long. In the seventh month of 549 he was killed by a kitchen slave, the captured son of a Liang provincial governor. The emperor saw this as the fulfilment of the will of heaven and a presage that the Wei house would recover its lost power.[4] But Kao Yang, the cooler and younger brother of Kao Ch'eng, succeeded to his dictatorship. In the fifth month of 550 he forced the emperor formally to abdicate in his favour. A new dynasty, the Ch'i, now ruled.

While the Wei state was undergoing this final crisis in the east, the puppet emperor at Ch'ang-an in the west was also on the point of being deposed. Meanwhile the troubles of the whole of north China were spreading to the south. Loyang's southern counterpart and rival Chien-k'ang (Nanking) was sacked by armies under Hou Ching, a barbarian (in both senses of the word) and renegade general who earlier had contributed to Loyang's miseries; and Chien-k'ang had been an even greater city and centre of Han aristocratic culture than Loyang.[5] Now that Chien-k'ang was being engulfed in the rising tide of barbarism, men such as Yang Hsüan-chih had every reason to feel that civilization itself was going under.

When we bear these developments in mind it becomes clear that Yang's lament for the old capital was much more than an expression of nostalgia; we understand why imperial legitimacy is so great a concern in his pages, and why the misfortunes of the last emperors who reigned in Loyang are dwelt on at such length. It would have been perfectly obvious to Yang's contemporaries that he was commenting on events in Yeh through his treatment of two Loyang officials who died

---

[3] Over sixty of them, according to Hou Ching: *TCTC* 160, p. 4968.

[4] *PCS* 3, pp. 37–8; *TCTC* 162, pp. 5026–7.

[5] On Chien-k'ang see Okazaki (1967 repr.), pp. 58–109; on Hou Ching and the sack of Chien-k'ang see the excellent popular account in Yoshikawa Tadao (1974), pp. 3–87.

after the attempt on Kao Ch'eng's life in 547. Hsün Chi, whom Yang described as a 'famous gentleman of untrammelled nature whose lofty perception and refined understanding distinguished him from his contemporaries', was either boiled or burned alive in the market-place at Yeh for his part in the conspiracy.[6] Wen Tzu-sheng (known to posterity principally as one of the leading writers of the age) is mentioned four times in the 'Record', most dramatically for helping the emperor Chuang-ti to steady his nerves before killing the dictator Erhchu Jung in the place at Loyang in 530.[7] Yang did not need to remind his readers that in 547, on suspicion of being involved in the similar plot against Kao Ch'eng, this most eminent man was starved to death in the jail at Chin-yang, and his whole household enslaved.[8] Merely to name these two well-known public figures was a political act when Yang wrote; and he drives his point home by attributing to both of them derogatory comments about 'men of Ch'i'. Ostensibly they were discussing the inhabitants of what is now Shantung; but as Kao Ch'eng had arranged for himself the title 'prince of Ch'i' in 548 as a step towards taking the throne, it seems obvious that Yang was using the dead men's words to condemn the Kao family's disloyalty to the house of Wei.

Yang's positive characters in his account of Loyang are the unfortunate emperors tossed aside or killed at a dictator's whim, and the princes and well-born Han officials who supported them; for these were the groups whose position was most gravely threatened by the new state system of the Kao family. His villains are low-born favourites, dictators, and others who challenge legitimacy. His most outspoken attacks are on members of the frightful Erhchu clan, the tribal chieftains from northern Shansi who massacred most of the court and the aristocracy in 528, then sacked the city in 530 to avenge the death of Erhchu Jung in the palace, before strangling the emperor.

Whereas Yang felt able to use violently abusive language about the Erhchu, he had to be more discreet in his criticisms of Kao Huan and, by extension, his sons. Partly he does this by

[6] See ch. 2 of the 'Record'; *KHMC* 7, pp. 1a–7a; *PS* 83, p. 2786.
[7] See pp. 187, 209, 229 and 248 below.
[8] *WSa* 85, pp. 1874–7; *PS* 83, pp. 2783–6.

the striking omission of any direct reference to Kao Huan, although he dominated Loyang's last three years. He includes none of the anecdotes found in such pro-Kao books as the toadying *Wei shu* to suggest that Kao, when associated with the Erhchu, had tried to restrain them from their worst excesses. Nor does he praise Kao for freeing China from the Erhchu yoke, another theme familiar in other sources. Instead he uses silence and innuendo to convey to informed readers that the Kao were not so much the opponents as the heirs of the Erhchu. By leading up to a brief statement that 'the emperor was deposed and died'[9] with an account of the sinister omen that preceded the event—the growth of hair on the brow and scalp of a golden statue—he reminds his contemporaries of the circumstances in which prince Kung of Kuang-ling, an Erhchu puppet ruler who had stood up to his masters on some minor issues, was deposed when Kao Huan returned to the capital in 532 as the military master of north China and conqueror of the Erhchu. The prince died soon afterwards in the Palace Bureau; and the *Pei shih*, compiled long after the demise of Kao power, states explicitly that he was killed.[10] If that was so, it is more than likely that Kao Huan was responsible. Yang's hint would have been eloquent enough.

That is one part of the message of Yang's 'Record'. Another part is harder to decode. Ostensibly it is a book about Buddhist religious institutions; it is included in the Chinese and the Japanese Buddhist canon; and Yang is listed in *Hsü kao seng chuan*, the biographical compendium of famous Buddhist monks.[11] If those indications point towards the book as a work of pious intention, the only other piece of his writing to survive (albeit in summary form) is to be found in the seventh-century compilation of writings on Buddhism, *Kuang hung ming chi*:

Yang Hsüan-chih, a man of Pei-p'ing, was Keeper of the Palace Archives (*mi-shu chien*) in the last years of the Wei. Having seen the splendour of the monasteries, the waste of treasure, the contention among princes and nobles, and the fleecing of the common people, he wrote the *Lo-yang ch'ieh-lan chi* to demonstrate how little pity was shown for ordinary folk.

---

[9] See p. 206 below.
[10] *PS* 5, p. 169.
[11] *HKSC* 1, pp. 16a–16b.

Later he submitted a memorial maintaining that Buddhism was empty nonsense. For all the useless expenditure on it, its [adherents] carried no arms to defend the country, while cold and hunger could be read on the people's faces. It supported corvée shirkers, servants, and menials, who turned to Buddhism not from real piety, but as a comfortable escape from their sufferings. The Buddha's words were untrue, and all just products of the imagination.

Some of the clergy who had a deep understanding of Buddhist principles refuted his accusations.

In [another] memorial he cited many examples of begging for wealth and of relentless avarice and accumulation. He also complained that those who studied Buddhist sutras were honoured as if they were royalty, and accused the master-painters who portrayed the Buddha of having no proper respect whatever. He requested that the Buddhist clergy be laicized, as were Confucians and Taoists, and recorded all this in the national history. He begged that all those whose actions were very frivolous or subversive should be placed under severe constraint. Only when the true was distinguished from the false could the Buddha's law be honoured. When there was no longer an excess of teachers and believers those shirking military service could be sent back to their duties, the country would be rich, its armies would be strong, and the world would be a much happier place.[12]

Although this passage presents some difficulties of translation and interpretation, its general drift is unmistakable. It shows Yang as an objector to the extravagance and avarice of the Buddhist church and the damage it did to the interests of the state and the people. In one part of it he rejects Buddhist ideas as such; in another he is a severe critic of parts of the faith while apparently seeking to preserve its true essence. Perhaps this seeming discrepancy could be explained if we had the full texts of the two memorials and knew the circumstances in which they were written. But even with this unsolved problem in it, the passage definitely puts Yang in the anti-Buddhist camp.

Or so it would seem. Shih Tao-hsüan (596–667), the compiler of *Kuang hung ming chi*, includes it as an example of the attacks made on the religion under successive dynasties. The section from which it is taken, 'Arguments against delusion',

[12] *KHMC* 6, pp. 12a–12b.

appears to have been lifted more or less completely from an anti-Buddhist work, *Kao shih chuan*, a collection of biographies of outstanding supporters and opponents of Buddhism compiled by the Taoist Fu Yi (554/5–639). In this work, which survives only in quotations, Yang was listed as one of the eleven 'men of high understanding' in Chinese history who opposed the religion.[13] Shih Tao-hsüan seems to have followed Fu Yi's assessments wholesale, simply reversing Fu's approval of the anti-Buddhists, and not asking whether Fu Yi had distorted the position of his heroes for the sake of polemical simplicity.

Certainly Fu, followed by Shih Tao-hsüan, distorts the religious message of the 'Record' in the brief account he gives of it. Yang explains in his preface that the Buddhist faith had flourished in Northern Wei Loyang as never before, that high-born and humble alike had given of their wealth for the religion, and that the capital's temples had been many—over a thousand—and magnificent. His intention in writing his book was simply to record all this lost splendour for posterity. If this is the authority on which *Kuang hung ming chi*, following *Kao shih chuan*, asserts that the 'Record' was meant 'to demonstrate how little pity was shown for ordinary folk', that part of the case for seeing Yang as an anti-Buddhist collapses.

Nor does the rest of his book show him as an enemy of the faith. He built his reconstruction of the city round its monasteries and nunneries although no precedent required or encouraged it, and his descriptions of them seem to be marked more by nostalgia and regret for their loss than by disapproval of the immense expenditure involved. His local pride is evident in his account of how the western monk Bodhidharma—in his own lifetime already well on the way to becoming a legendary figure—marvelled at the 'divine construction' of the Yung-ning Pagoda, declared that its equal was not to be found in the Buddhist world, and chanted 'namah' in admiration for days on end.[14]

He describes with evident relish the splendid processions in which Buddha statues were carried through the streets of the

---

[13] *KHMC* 6, pp. 1a–1b.
[14] See p. 151 below.

city accompanied by musicians and acrobats to celebrate Śākyamuni's birthday. He appears to approve of the piety of the gentlefolk and commoners of the Chien-yang ward who supported ten convents and monasteries.[15]

But if the author of the 'Record' appears as no enemy of Buddhism, no more does he appear to be a fervent supporter of the religion as such. He tells us much less about the spiritual life of Loyang than about its buildings, and his lack of interest in doctrinal matters is apparent. He passes on a good story about the judgements on five Loyang monks at the underworld throne of King Yama as observed by a sixth monk, Hui-ning of the Ch'ung-chen Monastery, who returned to life after the discovery of an infernal bureaucratic error.[16] But even if he sympathized with the condemnation of the monks for extracting funds from the people for their holy works, he refers elsewhere with evident delight to the praise Bodhiruci, another western immigrant, showered on a third condemned one, T'an-mo-tsui.

On the surviving evidence it is hard to reconcile the basically neutral attitude to Buddhism of the 'Record' with the fierce partisanship attributed to Yang in *Kuang hung ming chi*, though we can dismiss his inclusion in *Hsü kao seng chuan* as of no significance, and may remember that the Buddhist canon is a very unexclusive compilation in its various East Asian forms. Could it be that after writing the 'Record' he became much more hostile to the religion? Or that, just as the *Kuang hung ming chi* interpretation of the 'Record' is distorted, his later memorials were not as hostile as they are there represented? The question remains open.

What appears to count much more than Buddhism to Yang are the political values discussed earlier and the high culture of the educated aristocrats and gentlemen whose Chinese learning he describes with admiration. Undoubtedly these traditions were a source of pride and identity to the great families that alone had enjoyed the means to keep them alive in the troubled centuries since the fall of an earlier Loyang in 311; and study of this heritage seems to have been a fairly safe way

---

[15] See p. 178 below.
[16] See ch. 2 of the 'Record' below.

in which to assert a compensatory superiority to make up for
the racial, political, and military subordination to non-Han
rulers during the ensuing centuries in north China. Han-
Chinese culture (for which the epithet 'Confucian' is too
narrowly specific) was thus the vehicle for pride of clan, class,
and race. It had been in the ascendant at court for a few
decades in the late fifth and early sixth centuries, and most
spectacularly so in Loyang until 525, where Han-Chinese
aristocrats and officials could feel that they were reliving the
splendour of the Eastern Han and the Chin Loyangs, and the
Hsienpei rulers were doing all they could to play down their
barbarian origins. But racial feelings were most safely expressed
only with distorted violence against the rival court and capital
south of the Yangtse at Chien-k'ang. Contempt for the
Hsienpei could not be expressed openly with impunity.

Yang also gives some signs that he had inclinations of a
philosophical Taoist kind. The long 'Prose-poem on the
Pavilion and the Mountain', which he copied into his second
chapter, is permeated with a Taoist spirit, and its author
appears to have been a gentlemanly Taoist recluse. We also
find in his fifth chapter the Wei envoy to the far West citing
Lao Tzu, Chuang Tzu, and others with Taoist associations, as
well as Confucius and the Duke of Chou, as great men who
proved that the country which produced them was a Buddha-
land; the diplomat mentions no Buddhists in his list.[17] Other
hints of the sort can be found in the book; but they are not
sufficient for us to label Yang as a committed Taoist sectarian.

The reader will be able to get the feeling of Yang's
personality from the translation of his book that follows later.
It remains here to put in order the few pieces of information we
have on his life.[18]

Even the form of his surname is uncertain. Its pronunciation, Yang, is established, but it is written variously 楊,
陽, and 羊. The last of these has the weakest authority and
may be rejected.[19] The first is used in all surviving editions of

---

[17] See p. 262 below.

[18] On Yang Hsüan-chih and his possible family connections see the useful study by
Osawa Terumichi, 1963.

[19] This form is used by Liu Chih-chi in this late seventh or early eighth century *Shih-
t'ung*, and by a few of the Sung, Yüan, and Ming scholars who refer to the 'Record'.
(See the citations on pp. 358–60 of Fan.)

the 'Record', in at least one edition of *Kuang hung ming chi*, and in most pre-Ch'ing references to the author of the 'Record'.[20] The second form is backed by fewer citations, but it offers the possibility of identifying him beyond reasonable doubt as a member of a distinguished if not aristocratic family, that of Yang Ku.[21]

Yang Ku (465–523), a youthful reprobate who became a Confucian in his middle years, was appointed magistrate of Loyang county in 517.[22] In the power struggles of the period he was associated with Yuan I, prince of Ch'ing-ho and one of the three regents for the young Su-tsung/Hsiao-ming-ti until his murder by Yuan Yi in 520.[23] Yang Ku dared to mourn his patron in public, and justified his reputation for financial integrity by dying a poor man. He had three sons according to *Wei shu*, five according to *Pei shih*.[24] The eldest was Yang Hsiu-chih (509–82), who rose to quite high office under the Northern Wei and later served the Eastern Wei, Northern Ch'i, and Sui. He was among other things an official historian, helping to compile the 'Diaries of activity and repose' (*ch'i chü chu*) for the last emperors of the Northern Wei.[25] A younger brother of his, Ch'en-chih, chose the western regime after the fall of the Northern Wei.[26] A younger brother still, Chün-chih, was less distinguished than Hsiu-chih both as official and as writer; but his 'coarse and crude' hexasyllabic verses known as 'Yang the Fifth's Friend' (*Yang Wu pan-lü*) were widely quoted and sold in Yeh as the work of an ancient worthy.[27] Another brother, Ch'üan-chih, was murdered when young by a retainer.[28]

There are several arguments for seeing Yang Hsüan-chih as a member of this family, and only one objection, the confusion

---

[20] See Fan, loc. cit.

[21] Some editions of *KHMC*; *Hsin T'ang shu* 59; *Yüan Ho-nan chih*. (Fan, loc. cit.)

[22] *WS* 72, p. 12; *PS* 47, pp. 1720–4.

[23] See the glowing account at the beginning of ch. 4 of the 'Record'.

[24] Five is the more likely number, as we have the names of four sons (not counting Hsüan-chih), and the Chinese numerals 3 and 5 are easily confused in transmission.

[25] *WS* 72, p. 1612; *PS* 47, pp. 1724–8; *PCS* 42, pp. 560–64. *PCS* 30, p. 408, shows he was no Wei loyalist: he prepared the documents for the Wei abdication to Ch'i.

[26] *PS* 47, p. 1728.

[27] Ibid.

[28] *WS* 72, p. 1612.

over the form of his surname, which is less of a problem than it might seem: another Yang mentioned in the 'Record' has his surname given in the same three forms as Hsüan-chih's.[29] The positive arguments are these: Yang Ku's family was from Pei-p'ing; so, according to *Kuang hung ming chi*, was Hsüan-chih. According to population figures from the 540s, Pei-p'ing had only 1,836 registered inhabitants belonging to 430 house-holds.[30] Even allowing that this frontier prefecture may have been several times as populous before the troubles of the 520s and 530s, it is almost inconceivable that it could have produced two unrelated clans of central officials and writers with homophonous surnames and apparently related personal names—Hsüan-chih is in just the form one would expect for another brother or cousin of Hsiu-chih—both connected with palace records and privy to court secrets. Hsüan-chih quotes from several palace documents in his book,[31] and appears to have known much about what happened at court.[32] His age, inasmuch as we can guess it from his presence at court in 529 as a court guest (*feng ch'ao ch'ing*),[33] would have been about right for a younger brother or cousin of Hsiu-chih. The case for a family connection with Yang Ku is further helped by the evident partiality of the 'Record' towards Yüan I, prince of Ch'ing-ho, and hostility towards the dictator Yüan Yi who caused his death.

The fragmentary information we have on Yang's career can be briefly summarized. In the years *yung-an* (528–30) he was a court guest, a post involving few substantive duties which offered an apprenticeship in court life for the well-born young and carried the junior seventh grade. Assuming that his appointments moved steadily up the grading scale, the next

[29] The second chapter of the 'Record' refers to a Yang Wen-yi with the first form of the surname. In *WS* 10, p. 268, and 41, p. 936, it is written in the third form, as it is in a text of the 'Record' that no longer survives. (See textual note in Fan, p. 108.) The *TCTC* passage evidently derived from this part of the 'Record' gives the second form. (*TCTC* 155, p. 4800.)

[30] *WS* 106/1, pp. 2496–7.

[31] e.g. the exchange of edicts and memorials between the princes of Ch'ang-kuang and Kuang-ling when the former abdicated to the latter in 532 in ch. 2 of the 'Record'; or Yüan Hao's letter to Chuang-ti in ch. 1.

[32] See his account of the killing of Erhchu Jung in chs. 1 and 4 of the 'Record'.

[33] See the end of ch. 1 of the 'Record'.

post we know that he held was prefect of Ch'i-ch'eng,[34] which must have been before that prefecture (in Piyang county, southern Honan) was lost to the Western Wei in 538.[35] This would have carried the fifth grade (lower) or sixth grade (lower).[36] We next see him as the second assistant to a general (*fu-chün fu ssu-ma*), in the fifth grade (upper).[37] He reached the third grade as keeper of the Palace Archives,[38] in which post he would have had access to the state documents on which he drew in writing his memoir of Loyang.

This was compiled between 547, when he visited the site of Loyang on a mission for the Eastern Wei regime, and late 549 or early 550. There is no good evidence to show that he served the Ch'i dynasty that came to power;[39] even the reference in the problematical *Kuang hung ming chi* to memorials written after the 'Record' does not necessarily mean that they were written under the new dynasty. Indeed, given his fervent Wei loyalism, it seems unlikely that he would have held office under the house of Kao which he hated. It would have been appropriate for his career to end with the old dynasty, a career broadly typical of the educated Han-Chinese gentleman of his time: court appointments interspersed with provincial administration. He was intimate with power, but he did not share it; he was an observer rather than a doer.

What lifts Yang from obscurity is his book, and his book alone. As it takes much knowledge of Northern Wei Loyang's short history for granted, and as that city was the previous Wei capital uprooted from the far north and transplanted, there is much to be investigated before we can appreciate Yang's memoir.

---

[34] *Li-tai San-pao chi* 9, *Ta T'ang nei-tien lu* 4 and *Fa-yüan chu-lin* 119 cited in Fan, p. 356. *HKSC* 1 p. 16a reads Ssu-ch'eng, evidently a corruption of Ch'i-ch'eng.

[35] Fan, p. 356.

[36] *WS* 113, pp. 2997, 2999.

[37] *WS* 113, p. 2997. This is the title he carries at the beginning of all editions of the 'Record'.

[38] *KHMC* 6, p. 12a; *WS* 113, p. 2995.

[39] Yen K'o-chün (1762–1843), the indefatigable compiler of the *Ch'üan shang-ku san-tai Ch'in Han San-kuo Liu-ch'ao wen*, states that Yang died in the service of the Ch'i during the years *t'ien-pao* (550–9), but gives no authority for this. (*Ch'üan Pei Ch'i wen* 2, p. 3835.)

Chapter 2

Loyang's predecessor P'ing-ch'eng and the sinification of the Northern Wei state before 493

The capital to which Yang Hsüan-chih looked back with longing and regret had been deliberately located at the very centre of the Chinese world by a young emperor, Kao-tsu/Hsiao-wen-ti, resolved to destroy every possible 'barbarous' element in the state and society he ruled. The Loyang that arose from 493 onwards had few direct, practical connections with the earlier and impeccably Chinese Loyangs that had stood on or near its site. Most of the population of the new Loyang were brought down from the old capital in northern Shansi, P'ing-ch'eng, as were many of the institutions and values that shaped it. Northern Wei Loyang was both a negation of P'ing-ch'eng and P'ing-ch'eng transplanted; and it is with P'ing-ch'eng that a study of Northern Wei Loyang should begin, just as it is with the revenge of the slighted and neglected north that the story ends.

The Hsienpei, a people whose language seems to have combined Turkic and Mongol elements, were long known to the Chinese as herdsmen in eastern Mongolia north of the Shiramuren River. During the second century AD they conquered or absorbed many groups who had formerly belonged to the Hsiungnu federation and became dominant in Mongolia from the Liao River in the east to the Kansu corridor in the west. There was no regular Hsienpei state strong enough to survive the death of a great war-leader such as T'an-shih-huai, the second-century chief; and although the Hsienpei were able to profit from the collapse of Chin rule in north China at the beginning of the fourth century and conquer parts of the Chinese frontier regions, they did not do so as a united force.

16

They were always divided among themselves, and their regimes in China were at odds more often than in alliance.[1]

One Hsienpei clan established its dominance in the central region of the northern frontier: the T'opa (or Tabgach, as they were known to the Turks). The centre of their power in the third century was the Yin Shan range in Inner Mongolia, and at the beginning of the fourth century they occupied northern Shansi.

The 'sinification' of the T'opa and their state is a process that has been much discussed.[2] The process was not uniform, steady, or complete. The Hsienpei of the fourth and early fifth centuries belonged to two worlds: inner Asia and sedentary China. By now their pastures north and west of the Gobi had been abandoned to rawer nomadic confederacies, the Joujan and the Kaoch'e;[3] they were now increasingly dependent on the rich, agriculturally based economy of China. They were no longer on the outside looking in, but on the inside, casting anxious eyes out across the steppe. To the Han people of north China they were probably barbarians, but they were inner rather than outer barbarians; to the Joujan they doubtless seemed to be softies. The leaders of the T'opa confederacy, from the monarch to the elders of the thirty-six 'nations' (*kuo*) and ninety-nine lineages (*hsing*) of which it was composed, were drawn by the material advantages to be had from controlling a subject peasantry; and from the middle of the fourth century they began to imitate some of the bureaucratic

[1] On the early history of the Hsienpei see Uchida Gimpu (1975), pp. 1–94; Ma Ch'ang-shou (1962); and Lin Lü-chih (1967).

[2] The literature on the origins and early sinification of the Northern Wei state is extensive. See especially T'ang Chang-ju (1955), pp. 193–249, (1959), pp. 132–54; Uchida Gimpu (1936); Kawachi Jūzō (1953); Sun T'ung-hsün (1962); Koga Noboru (1965/1); Kaneko Hidetoshi (1960); and the general histories of Wang Chung-lo, Lü Ssu-mien, and Okazaki.

On P'ing-ch'eng see Lu Yao-tung (1968); and Mizuno Seiichi (1936).

[3] On the Joujan see the references in n. 37 to ch. 3 of the 'Record'. The Kaoch'e or Ch'ihle (also T'iehle, Tili, and Tingling) were Turkish tribes living between Lake Baikal and the Aral Sea. Caught between Wei and Joujan power, several hundred thousand of them were moved south of the deserts in the fifth century to man the Wei frontier. A revived Kaoch'e state north of the deserts was smashed by the Ephthalites in or around 516. In the seventh century the Huiho (Uighurs) arose from among them to become a central-Asian power. (See *Sui shu* 84, pp. 1879–80; *PS* 98, pp. 3270–77; Liu Mau-ts'ai, 1958, vol. 2, pp. 496–8; Ts'en Chung-mien, 1958, vol. 2, pp. 662–91; Colin Mackerras, 1968.)

forms of the Chin state, instituting a rudimentary legal code to replace or supplement the customary unwritten law that had hitherto prevailed.

THE CAPITAL AT P'ING-CH'ENG

The need for a capital was first felt by the T'opa tribal rulers in the middle of the third century AD, when the high chief Li-wei made a headquarters at Sheng-lo (near Holinkoerh, inner Mongolia).[4] In the following century his grandson Yi-lu reunited the confederacy of northern-steppe peoples, won recognition from the moribund Chin government as duke of Tai, and made two capitals, a northern one at Sheng-lo and a southern one at P'ing-ch'eng. The former was in the heartland of T'opa power and the latter was well placed to control the lands newly conquered as the Chin regime lost its grip of the north. We may doubt whether there was much of a city at either place, though Yi-lu did move 100,000 families to increase the population of his base area around Sheng-lo, then built another P'ing-ch'eng (perhaps no more than a stockaded or earth-walled camp) 100 *li* further south on the north bank of the Lei (Sangkan) river, where he placed a garrison under his eldest son to control the southern part of his territories.[5]

During the next seventy years or more the T'opa confederacy enjoyed changing fortunes and little stability. Capitals—for thus did later historians, wanting to make the Northern Wei dynasty's ancestors look like respectable Chinese rulers, designate the temporary headquarters of T'opa power—were generally in the Yin Shan area till in 376 the conqueror of north China, Fu Chien, defeated the T'opa and drove their leader Shih-yi-chien to flee and die north of the mountains.[6] When the short-lived domination of north China by Fu Chien collapsed after the defeat of his invasion of the south in 383, T'opa power recovered under Shih-yi-chien's grandson T'opa Kuei, known posthumously as T'ai-tsu or Tao-wu-ti (reigned 386–409). For eleven years after he inaugurated his state in 387 he had no permanent capital. He

---

[4] *WS* 1, p. 3.

[5] *WS* 1, pp. 7–8. This southern P'ing-ch'eng must have been somewhere near the confluence of the Yü and Sangkan rivers.

[6] On his reign see *WS* 1, pp. 11–16.

made the headquarters of his rudimentary government wherever the needs of war took him. The annals show him always on
the move, fighting enemies on all sides, holding court in the
towns (perhaps really stockades or walled encampments) or
beside the rivers of the area where his power was based—
northernmost Shansi and the adjacent parts of inner Mongolia.
We are told that in 386 he stayed at Sheng-lo, where he
encouraged agriculture; and most of the place-names in the
Wei annals for 386–96 are in the Yin Shan region. We do not
know where the first 'palace'—the Ho-nan-kung built in 391—
was located, but war with his rivals left little time or resources
for the building of cities, and the palace was probably nothing
magnificent by later standards.[7]

In 398 the power of the state now called Wei or Tai was
established in north China. The rival nomad powers of the
steppe, the Joujan and the Kaoch'e, had been repulsed; to the
west the Hsiungnu state that controlled the Ordos and
northern Shensi had been destroyed; and the rich agricultural
area of central Hopei had been wrested from the Yen state of
the Mujung clan, a branch of the Hsienpei more sinicized than
the T'opa. T'opa Kuei had assumed the imperial title in 396,
and the wealth of himself and his followers had grown
enormously through the plunder of war.[8] With the formation
of a semi-sinified monarchy the old tribal structure of the
T'opa confederacy was abolished, and tribesmen became
registered subjects of the new state. They were allocated land
and compelled to settle on it. Nomadism was henceforth
forbidden them.[9]

The capture of the Mujung capital at Yeh in 398 fired T'opa
Kuei with the ambition to build a splendid capital for himself.
The site he chose was the old strategic centre at P'ing-ch'eng,
which was well placed to control the Yin Shan, northern
Shansi, central Hopei, and the Ordos with the huge cavalry
armies that were the essence of Wei power. Here he created a
new capital by compulsion and violence. In 398 he brought

---

[7] See the outline narrative of these years in *WS* 2, pp. 20–8.

[8] T'opa Kuei's wars in these years are chronicled in *WS* 2, pp. 20–31; and *TCTC*
106–9, pp. 3360–460. One campaign alone brought in over 4,000,000 cattle, sheep,
and goats as well as some 300,000 horses. (*WS* 110, p. 2849.)

[9] *WS* 113, p. 3014; *PS* 80, p. 2672.

back from his campaigns in Hopei some 360,000 officials, commoners, T'uho tribesmen, Koreans, and 'assorted barbarians' (*tsa-yi*) as well as over 100,000 'skilled craftsmen in various trades' to 'fill out the capital'.[10] The immigrants were allocated ploughing oxen and land within the imperial domain (*chi-nei*), an area of about 1,000 square kilometres occupying much of Shansi north of the Luya Shan and Heng Shan ranges.[11] Here can be seen two essential features of all the Northern Wei capitals: forced movement of population, and a broad belt of agricultural land under state control to grow some at least of the capital's food. Forced migrations to the capital continued during T'opa Kuei's reign, the largest being of over 90,000 prisoners from a campaign against the Kaoch'e in 399.[12]

We do not know much about the kind of capital T'opa Kuei had built. The annals refer to the construction of palaces, ancestral temples, and ceremonial altars in 398. That same year the emperor ordered the organization of the imperial domain, the suburbs of the capital, and the streets and wards (presumably of the capital). The next year the Kaoch'e prisoners were used to create a huge deer-park near P'ing-ch'eng with canals running from the Wuch'uan river (probably the modern Wuchouch'uan) through the park to the palace compound.[13] As T'opa Kuei's reign continued more palaces were built in P'ing-ch'eng and elsewhere;[14] but as a city it can only have been embryonic, as in 403 the emperor was toying with the idea of building a new capital south of the Lei River. In 406 the palace south of the Lei was actually built, with markets, wards, roads, and a wall 20 *li* square built by all the adult males from the eight divisions within 500 *li*.[15] Was

---

[10] *WS* 2, p. 32. *WS* 110, pp. 2849–50 gives another version of the list with 'over 100,000 families'. *TCTC* 110, p. 3463, makes it 'over 100,000 heads'. A critical note in the Chung-hua shu-chü *WS* compares the *WS* 2 passage with ones in *PS* and *Ts'e fu yuan kuei* evidently derived from it and decides that the 100,000 should refer to people, not families; but the editors take no account of the evidence of *WS* 110.

[11] *WS* 110, p. 2850.

[12] See the table of forced migrations until 472 on pp. 416 ff. of Kawachi, 1953.

[13] *WS* 2, pp. 33, 35.

[14] Palaces in 400, 401, 403, 404, and 406. (*WS* 2, pp. 36–42.)

[15] The planned new capital or palace, *WS* 2, p. 41; its building in 406, pp. 42–3.

this the P'ing-ch'eng modelled on Yeh, Loyang, and Ch'ang-an of which Mo T'i superintended the construction, using several million trees in the process?[16] We cannot be sure, but we are left with the impression of an uneasy compromise between Hsienpei and Han cultures.[17]

The unsympathetic account of his northern neighbours compiled by the south-Chinese historian Hsiao Tzu-hsien (d. 537) from the records of the previous dynasty has some remarks on the Wei capitals which, though blatantly biased, suggest that P'ing-ch'eng did not add up to much at this time. 'When Shih-yi-kuei [i.e. T'opa Kuei] first made a capital at P'ing-ch'eng they still moved around following water and pasture and had no city walls. Mu-mo [i.e. T'ai-tsung/Ming-yüan-ti] was the first to settle there permanently.'[18]

Even in T'ai-tsung/Ming-yüan-ti's reign (409–24) P'ing-ch'eng's existence was precarious. In 415 several years of frost and drought resulted in a famine so bad that a move of the capital to Yeh on the rich Hopei plain was strongly advocated, to be rejected on grounds not economic but strategic when the north-Chinese aristocrat and official Ts'ui Hao pointed out that the Wei cavalry armies would lose their air of mystery and terror if they lived among the plainsmen, while the Yin Shan–P'ing-ch'eng base area would be dangerously exposed to Kaoch'e and Joujan attack if the Hsienpei abandoned it. He urged that the poorest and most hungry—presumably from among the agricultural population of the domain—should be allowed to go east in search of food; the new grass of the coming spring would provide dairy products which together with vegetables and fruit could feed those who remained until the millet harvest of the coming autumn.[19]

Evidently the early Northern Wei rulers could not support a capital city of any size at P'ing-ch'eng until they controlled

---

[16] *WS* 23, p. 604.

[17] On the 'barbarism' of P'ing-ch'eng, see the southern accounts cited below. Signs of T'opa Kuei's policy of limited sinification were his wooing of the Han landed classes of Hopei, his collection of Chinese books, and his creation of a somewhat Chinese state structure with which to rule his Chinese subjects.

[18] *Nan Ch'i shu* 57, p. 984.

[19] *WS* 35, p. 808.

north China and could tax efficiently the agricultural wealth of the great Hopei plain. Plunder could furnish animals and slaves for the traditional pastoral economy of the Hsienpei in northern Shansi. Forced settlements of farmers could provide grain to the capital when the climate permitted, and *ad hoc* conscriptions of labour could build palaces and wall off hunting parks; but the state could not make enough rain fall regularly in the Sangkan valley to feed a city, or create waterways to bring grain to the north-Shansi uplands from the Hopei plain. An enlarged hunting park with a new wall 40 *li* long around it[20] was a much cheaper and more practical undertaking than the creation of a city; and to the first emperors of the Northern Wei it was probably also far more attractive.

It was not until about 440 that the Wei, having eliminated their rivals in north China,[21] could afford to divert some of the resources now under their control to building and supporting a city at P'ing-ch'eng. Shih-tsu/T'ai-wu-ti resisted pressures from his officials until nearly the end of his reign (423–52) to create a more splendid metropolis with new palaces,[22] struck by the folly of his defeated neighbour Hsia in wasting its people's labour to build a great triple-walled capital city which was taken only fourteen years after its construction.[23] He was not, however, averse to forced population movements to P'ing-ch'eng and the domain, which brought with them the urban

---

[20] Such a one was built by 6,000 conscript labourers from the area of the capital in 421. (*WS* 3, p. 61.)

[21] Hsia in the north-west was crippled in 427 and destroyed in 431; the petty states of the Kansu corridor had all fallen by 439; to the east the Northern Yen was smashed in 436; and to the south the Yellow River valley was seized from the Sung. (The campaigns are summarized in *TCTC* 119–24 and *WS* 4.) In 429 a huge expedition across the northern wastes dealt a heavy blow to the most dangerous rival of all, the Joujan. Over 300,000 families of Joujan and Kaoch'e prisoners and immigrants, as well as animals by the million, were brought back to be settled along the frontier. (*WS* 4/1, p. 75; *WS*a 103, p. 2293; *WS* 35, pp. 815–16; *PS* 98, p. 3253.) When the Joujan recovered heavy losses were inflicted on them once again by another attack in 449. (*WS* 4/2, p. 103; *WS*a 103, pp. 2294–5; *PS* 98, p. 3255.)

[22] *WS* 4/2, p. 107. *TCTC* 120, pp. 3796–7, places this with the events of 427.

[23] On the building of the Hsia capital T'ung-wan and Shih-tsu/T'ai-wu-ti's comments after taking it, see *TCTC* 120, p. 3795. The massive ruins of the city, whose walls still rise ten metres high in places, are described and illustrated in the Shan-pei wen-wu tiao-ch'a cheng-chi tsu's 1957 article.

cultures of west China and the Yangtse valley;[24] and in 450 he finally succumbed to large-scale palace building.[25]

Shih-tsu/T'ai-wu-ti's outburst during his last two years was not followed up during the first years of his grandson and successor Kao-tsung/Wen-ch'eng-ti (r. 452–65). A new palace was started in 438, abandoned for a while when it was pointed out that the project would involve the labour of 20,000 men for six months during the farming season, and completed later in the year.[26] The short reign of Hsien-tsu/Hsien-wen-ti (465–71) was made wretched by successive years of drought and famine,[27] and during it another group of forced migrants—this time from the newly conquered Ch'ing and Ch'i *chou*—were settled in the domain or given as slaves to officials,[28] but palaces were not built in his reign or in the years between his nominal abdication in favour of his three-year-old son in 471[29] and his suspiciously sudden and early death in 476, which cleared away the last obstacle to the complete dominance at court of his father's widow, the empress dowager Feng. Before we look at her attempt to transform P'ing-ch'eng, let us consider what sort of city it was during the seventy years since T'opa Kuei's building programme.

Essentially it was a palace and court complex combined with a military headquarters. It was precariously fed by unfree

[24] In 426, 10,000 families from T'ung-an, of whom only two-thirds survived the journey. (*WS* 4/1, p. 71; *TCTC* 120, pp. 3789, 3791.) In 439, 30,000 households from Liang-chou. (*WS* 4/1, p. 90.) In 446, 2,000 families of skilled artisans from Ch'ang-an. (*WS* 4/2, p. 100.) In 447, 3,000 families of Tinglin (i.e. Kaoch'e) from Hopei. (*WS* 4/2, p. 102.) In 448, over 5,000 families from Hsi-ho. (*WS* 4/2, p. 102.) In 449, possibly, some of the prisoners from the victory over the Joujan. In 451, over 50,000 households captured in the war with Sung and settled in the domain. (*WS* 4/2, p. 105.)

[25] *WS* 4/2, p. 104.

[26] *WS* 5, pp. 116, 117; 48, p. 1073. The palace, the T'ai-hua kung, was pulled down in 492 (*SCC* 13, p. 3/11.) Kao-tsung's architect Kuo Shan-ming is the earliest one of the Northern Wei period whose name has been preserved.

[27] *WS* 5; *WS* 110, p. 2852.

[28] See Tsukamoto Zenryū (1942), pp. 171–5, on these P'ing-Ch'i households, some members of which, bringing with them the high culture of the Yangtse valley, were to be prominent in Loyang.

[29] As the boy was born when his supposed father was only thirteen, his parentage is open to question; except that a conversation between Kao-tsu and some Han-Chinese advisers on the advisability of providing his son with women at the age of twelve or thirteen may imply that so early a sexual initiation had previously been a T'opa custom. (*WSa* 22, p. 589; *PS* 7, p. 741.)

peasants and herdsmen forcibly settled in the extensive royal domain around it, and guarded to the north from the tribesmen across the deserts by a broad frontier zone manned by Hsienpei and people of other races, some detribalized, others not.

Supercilious observers from south China who visited the city in the reign of Shih-twu/T'ai-wu-ti were struck by the huge palace complex.[30] The emperor lived in three palaces of more than one storey, and the heir apparent had a separate one, built of brick. The palace women all lived in buildings of stamped earth. The palace was a hive of economic activity. Over 1,000 slaves wove fine silks (plain silk being produced by peasant women and levied as tax), traded, brewed and sold liquor, raised sheep, pigs, cattle, and horses, and grew vegetables for the market. Metal and wooden goods were made in palace workshops. The palace was also a granary—eighty grain-pits could each hold 4,000 bushels (*hu*) of millet—and an arsenal, having forty units of building filled with arms.

South of the palace complex ran the city wall, enclosing an area divided into walled wards (*fang*), each of which held between sixty and 500 households and opened during approved hours into lanes (*hsiang*). Doubtless many of the ward-dwellers were soldiers and their households; the southern visitors noted that a special official was put in charge of all people living within 3 *li* of the palace who were not on the military rolls. Despite regular searches of the wards and curfew regulations, government control was not always effective: in 454 all the capital's gates were closed for a three-day search in which hundreds of 'evildoers and desperadoes' were arrested;[31] and four years later the gentlemen and commoners were thought so quarrelsome and vociferous on affairs of state when in their cups that the brewing, selling, and drinking of liquor was forbidden on pain of death, a ban not lifted until 465 or 466.[32]

---

[30] *Nan Ch'i shu* 57, pp. 984–6, draws on several southerners' descriptions of P'ing-ch'eng, including one going back to the reign of Shih-tsu/T'ai-wu-ti.

[31] *WS* 5, p. 113.

[32] *WS* 5, p. 116; 111, pp. 2875–6. The ban was a serious one: a woman who risked brewing some millet beer for her sick grandmother despite it was for that act alone mentioned in the dynastic history for her outstanding virtue. (*WS* 92, p. 1980.)

One has the impression from the sparse evidence that the P'ing-ch'eng palace was·like the villa at the centre of a huge *latifundium*, making for itself what the domain's peasants and stockbreeders could not provide. The residential wards were a larger version of the quarters for the servants, stewards, guards, and hangers-on of a villa. Although the palace went in for some trade, both locally and internationally across inner Asia, merchants and artisans were only palace dependants, and the economy managed without its own coinage until after the move to Loyang.[33]

The city's culture was, to southern eyes, barbaric: oxen and horses were sacrificed to heaven in Hsienpei style while mounted musicians galloped round the altars; officials had outlandish, un-Chinese titles and the empress dowager showed her face to the world when she went out with an escort of armoured cavalrywomen. Whereas civilized people knelt, P'ing-ch'eng sat.[34] Later Wei accounts emphasize the 'civilized aspects' of early P'ing-ch'eng. No doubt the first Northern Wei rulers wanted to have·it both ways; and they were realistic enough to keep their capital from getting too big.

In the matter of religion, they did not abandon their ancestral shamanistic cults; to these they added Buddhism, well established throughout their realms even before the conquests, which T'opa Kuei brought under control through an innovation to be of great importance in preventing the emergence of a powerful and independent Buddhist church: a state-appointed hierarchy, which treated the emperor as an incarnation of the Tathāgata.

Buddhism was an established part of P'ing-ch'eng life well before Shih-tsu/T'ai-wu-ti turned violently against it in 446 with a persecution whose intended savagery was frustrated by his heir apparent; and after his death the religion revived with new vigour. Once again the emperor was identified with the Buddha and under the influence of the formidable hierarch T'an-yao the first of five cave temples were carved in the cliffs overlooking the Wu-chou river, each with a huge stone

---

[33] P'ing-ch'eng's trade with Central Asia is thoroughly treated in Maeda Masana's 1955 and 1972 articles. On trade and industry in general under the Northern Dynasties see the useful survey in Han Kuo-p'an (1962), pp. 167–201.

[34] *Nan Ch'i shu*, loc. cit.

Buddha-statue of between 8 and 15.6 metres in height. Even before this a stone Buddha had been carved in one of P'ing-ch'eng's monasteries with all the monarch's moles; and it is likely that the images in the cave temples were in fact idealized representations of the four Wei emperors and one former heir apparent. The Indian tradition of cave temples, which had come through central Asia, coincided with the T'opa tradition of cutting rock shrines for their pre-dynastic rulers. The emperors returned the compliment by observing the central-Asian custom of scattering flowers over Buddha-statues from the palace gates on the Śākyamuni's birthday. At this stage P'ing-ch'eng's Buddhism was still on a modest scale.[35]

This, like so much else about the city, was to be changed by the formidable empress dowager Feng, whose influence at court was strong after the death of her husband Kao-tsung/Wen-ch'eng-ti in 465 and paramount from the sudden death of his successor in 476 until her own life ended in 490.[36] The great changes in the city and the whole Wei polity from the 470s onwards were essentially the product of her will. Her step-grandson Kao-tsu/Hsiao-wen-ti let her decide everything during her life, and continued her programme after it.

Feng's hostility to Hsienpei tradition must have gone back to the time when, as a young girl of an aristocratic Han-Chinese house, she and the other women of her family were forced into the imperial seraglio after the execution of her father. In 466 she disposed of the Hsienpei chief minister, Yi Hun, and from

[35] On P'ing-ch'eng's Buddhism see Tsukamoto Zenryū (1942), especially pp. 62–164, and his 1961 study of *WS* 114, the *Wei shu*'s chapter on Buddhism. An important essay from the former is translated by Sargent in Tsukamoto (1957); and an annotated English version of *WS* 111 based on the latter is to be found in Leon Hurvitz (1956). Other very useful studies include K. Ch'en (1973), ch. 6; Ochō Enichi on pp. 11–27 of the 1970 volume he edited; and T'ang Yung-t'ung (1963 repr.), ch. 14.

On the cave temples at Yün-kang, there are the 32 volumes of Mizuno Seiichi and Nagahiro Toshio's monumental 1951–6 work; Mizuno's 1939 book; and the earliest but still serviceable Chavannes compilation published from 1911 onwards. The essence of the cave's sculptures can be found in the booklets prepared by the Shan-hsi Yün-kang Ku-chi pao-yang-so in 1957 and the Shan-hsi Yün-kang shih-k'u wen-wu pao-kuan-so in 1973. The 1977 album compiled jointly by the Shan-hsi-sheng wen-wu kung-tso wei-yüan-hui and the Shan-hsi Yün-kang pao-kuan-so is the best single volume album of Yün-kang photographs. Lo Ch'ia-tzu (1955) is a useful introduction to these and other cave temples of the Northern Dynasties. On the periodization of the cave temples see Su Pai (1978/1).

[36] See her biographies in *WS* 13, pp. 328–31, and *PS* 13, pp. 495–7.

then on advanced Hans to the highest office. She was also a devout, perhaps even fanatical, Buddhist, favouring her co-religionists in civil appointments, and encouraging the rapid growth of the state-supported church. Most of the datable monasteries and pagodas of which we know were built during her tenure of power, as were most of the Yün-kang cave temples. It was during the same period that church authorities were given their own means of support by an indulgent state: a dependent population. 'Saṅgha households' (*seng-ch'i-hu*) were half-free peasants who supplied large amounts of grain to the church instead of tax grain to the state; although this grain was supposed to be held for distribution in famine years, monasteries and monks sometimes treated it as their own. The unfree dependants, 'Buddha households' (*Fo-t'u-hu*), were convicted criminals given to the church as slaves instead of being executed.[37] It is also likely that other families attached themselves to monasteries.

These measures were to bear their full fruit in the following century. P'ing-ch'eng still had only a hundred or so monasteries and convents with some 2,000 monks and nuns in 476.[38] This was no great burden on the state, any more than were the demands for corvée labour for building the Yün-kang temples, or for the construction of the mausoleum for Feng herself north of the city at Fang-shan (which still rose 22 metres high in the present century, but was never used, as her remains were buried near Loyang).[39] In the words of Li Tao-yüan, a writer on antiquarian topography of the following century: 'The Buddha's Law flourished in the imperial capital; sacred images and handsome stupas were crowded together. This was the highest point reached since the Wheel of the Law rolled east.'[40]

Few rulers in history have made more thoroughgoing attempts to change their subjects' lives than did the dowager and her step-grandson Kao-tsu/Hsiao-wen-ti. The effects of the

[37] On these dependants see Tsukamoto (1942), pp. 165–213; K. Ch'en (1964), pp. 154–8, and Jacques Gernet (1956), pp. 96 ff. The *seng-ch'i-hu*'s annual payment of 60 *hu* a year would have been a large proportion—more than half, perhaps—of a peasant family's grain output.

[38] *WS* 114, p. 3039.

[39] *WS* 7/1, p. 147. On the mausoleum see A. G. Wenley (1947), and Ta-t'ung-shih po-wo-kuan and Shan-hsi-sheng wen-wu kung-tso wei-yüan-hui (1978).

[40] *SCC* 13, p. 3/13.

series of decrees from 472 till her death in 499 on China for the next three centuries were to be immeasurably great. Precedents for many of the reforms can be found earlier in the Northern Wei period or under previous regimes in north China, and some of them were disastrous failures; but instead of the gradual process of sinification of the Northern Wei state and society in response to specific problems that arose in ruling an overwhelmingly Han-Chinese population, the T'ai-ho reforms (as they may be called after the reign-title of the years in which most of them were enacted) were a conscious and deliberate attempt to bring the country closer to the dowager's and the young emperor's ideal of a Han-Chinese, Confucianized bureaucratic monarchy ruling an ordered, aristocratic society.[41] To this end Hsienpei ways had to be rejected as far as possible. These motives are clearly expressed in surviving decrees and records of the palace conferences at which the empress dowager and Kao-tsu discussed policy with their leading advisers. It was as part of this willed process that P'ing-ch'eng had to be first transformed, then transplanted; and the changes to the whole capital cannot be separated from the reforms as a whole.

Some of the measures taken before the move of the capital to Loyang may be set out chronologically thus:

Reform measures in Kao-tsu/Hsiao-wen-ti's reign before the change of capitals

472   'Witches and wizards' (*nü-wu yao-hsi*—probably Hsienpei shamans) forbidden to take part in sacrifices at temple of Confucius (*WS* 7/1, p. 136).
Monks forbidden to leave their monasteries and wander among the people (*WS* 7/1, p. 137; *WS* 114, p. 3038).
Artisans, merchants, 'miscellaneous households' and

---

[41] A brief selection from the voluminous secondary literature on the reforms may be found useful. A good summary is given in pp. 376–408 of Wang Chung-lo's general history; and Sun T'ung-hsün (1962), may also be consulted, as may several other of the works listed in n. 2, p. 17 above. The two groups of topics on which the most useful work has been done are (1), land, local government, and taxation, and (2), the bureaucratic structure and the genealogical classification of the aristocracy.

On (1), much can be learned from the following: Hori Toshikazu (1962 and 1965, included in revised form with other related studied in his 1975 volume); Ikeda On

performers permitted to take up farming (*WS* 7/1, p. 138).

Triennial assessments of the performance of officials introduced (ibid.).

473 Farming households owning more than one ox ordered to share with others who have none (ibid.).

Officials in charge of counties and prefectures to be rewarded for suppressing banditry in their territories by grant of more territories to govern and draw income from (ibid.).

Punishment of leading local inhabitants who criticize local officials during inquiries into their performance ordered to be ended (*WS* 7/1, p. 139).

Ten commissioners sent out to find households missing from official registers (ibid.).

474 Reduction of number of offences for which penalty is to be extermination of offender's whole family (*WS* 7/1, p. 140).

475 Henceforth all *fu* and *tiao* taxes to be collected by county authorities, then checked and sent to capital by prefect and *chou* governors on pain of dismissal (*WS* 7/1, p. 141).

Decree orders better methods for promoting and demoting officials (ibid.).

476 Officials asked to suggest measures to 'benefit the people and the state' (*WS* 7/1, p. 142). Later in the year invitation extended to commoners (ibid., p. 143).

477 Decree announces new reign period *t'ai-ho* ('great harmony') (ibid.).

Local officials ordered to encourage agriculture, rewarding the diligent, punishing slackers, and limiting the demands for forced labour (ibid.).

(1963); Koga Noboru (1965/2); Matsumoto Yoshimi (1956); Nishimura Genyū (1968), pp. 92–155; Sogabe Shizuo (1953), especially pp. 66–106; and the articles by various hands in the 1957 volume edited by the *Li-shih yen-chiu* pien-chi-pu.

On (2), see Miyazaki Ichisada (1956); Koga Noboru (1965/1); Cheng Ch'in-jen (1965); Mao Han-kuang (1966); and Yen Keng-wang (1948). Two interesting studies in English of the Chinese upper class that refer to this period are David Johnson (1977), and Patricia Ebrey (1978).

After epidemic killing most draught oxen in previous years, authorities in charge of agriculture to ensure that those with oxen work harder and those without hire more than in years of surplus. Each adult male (*fu*) to work 40 *mu*, secondary adult male (*chung fu*) to work 20 *mu* (*WS* 7/1, p. 144).

478 Extravagant weddings and funerals to be brought within legal limits. Members of royal family and others reminded that they are not allowed to marry those not of their own kind (*WS* 7/1, p. 145).
Local officials reproved for slackness and corruption (*WS* 7/1, p. 146).

479 Several hundred constables (*chin-chih-che*) appointed to prevent fighting in the streets (of P'ing-ch'eng presumably) in place of corrupt *hou-chih* (*WS* 111, p. 2877).

481 New legal code (*lü-ling*) in 832 clauses introduced after revisions of old one by Kao Lü and others (*WS* 111, p. 2877).

483 Hsienpei nobles forbidden to marry people of same surname (*WS* 7/1, p. 153).

484 Introduction of regular, graduated official salaries, to be paid out of extra tax (*WS* 7/1, pp. 153–4; 110, p. 2852).
Draconian penalties for official corruption introduced afterwards (*WS* 111, p. 2877).
Emancipation of merchants (*WS* 7/1, p. 154).
A further request for reform proposals from officials and private citizens (ibid.).

485 Strict ban on apocryphal literature (*t'u-ch'en, mi-wei*) on pain of death; also on invocation of deities and prophecies by mediums and back-alley soothsayers (*WS* 7/1, p. 155).
System of *chün-t'ien* land allocation promulgated throughout Wei realm; land allocated for each peasant, slave and ox, some of which (*sang-t'ien*, mulberry plantations) was a permanent grant, some of which was only for working life of recipients (*WS* 110, pp. 2853–5; 7/1, p. 156; 53, p. 1176).
Another request for reform proposals (*WS* 7/1, p. 155).

486 Introduction of better system of controlling population and levying taxes through organizing households into groups of 5, 25, and 125, each with a head responsible for delivery of tax and forced labour in his group; together with a new tax system (*WS* 7/2, p. 161; 110, pp. 2855–6; 53, p. 1180).

487 As harvest fails (in domain) officials ordered in seventh month to compile registers of those who may go out through the passes in search of food and those who must remain. In ninth month compilation of fresh registers ordered (*WS* 7/2, p. 162; 110, p. 2856).
Instruction in morality to be carried out in countryside during winter (*WS* 7/2, p. 163).
State weavers of brocade and gauze 'released'; population now allowed to make these textiles (ibid.).

488 Proposals by Li Piao that two-ninths of the tax grain and silk collected by *chou* and prefectures and the surplus grain in the capital be used to build up reserves to be sold in famine years; and that one tenth of households under *chou* and prefectures be turned into colonists (*t'un-min*) near good land and water communications, each man to be required to produce 60 *hu*. This measure prevented famine in later years (*WS* 110, pp. 2856–7; 62, pp. 1385–6).
Land to be irrigated along northern frontier and in the domain (*WS* 7/2, p. 164).

491 After court discussions, Northern Wei adopts Water as its dominant element in order to show itself as successor to Chin dynasty (*WS* 108/1, pp. 1144–7).
New scheme for grading of officials settled in outline (*WS* 7/2, p. 168; 113, pp. 2976–93).
Assessment of *chou* governors and of prefects (*WS* 7/2, p. 168).

492 Sacrifices to legendary Chinese emperors of antiquity; many of the (barbarian) ceremonials of the sacrifice to heaven in the western suburb abolished (*WS* 7/2, p. 169).
New legal codes promulgated (ibid.).

This is a formidable list. Although we do not know precisely what each measure involved and how effectively it was carried out, the nature of the Northern Wei state was being drastically altered, as was its ideological basis. The monarchy, no longer primarily concerned with conquest despite its continuing struggle with the southern regimes, was extending its effective control over the countryside through a Confucianized bureaucracy intended to draw its income from regular salaries instead of the spoils of office, subject to regular assessments, and working within a formalized career structure. The peasantry were to be organized into groups of households under officially appointed headmen responsible for delivering the tax grain and silk as well as the forced labour they were required to supply in return for the land allocated to them according to circumstances and rank; they were even expected, during the winter, to attend indoctrination courses in Confucian morality. One-tenth of their number were ordered to be turned into virtual state serfs as colonists, required to hand over each year an amount of grain that might be estimated at somewhere around two-thirds of the output of a peasant couple in normal years.

In addition to these institutional changes and the revival of Buddhism, there was a new surge in secular building activity at P'ing-ch'eng. Within months of taking power in 476 the dowager had two new palace buildings put up, to be followed by six more in the next two years, and another two in 488.[42] In 492 some of the older palaces were demolished for a new Palace of the Great Ultimate (T'ai-chi tien) to be built.[43] Li Tao-yüan, whose remarks on the city's Buddhist splendour have been cited, also tells of the buildings of Confucian cosmological significance: the Ming-t'ang (Bright Hall) surmounted by a Ling-t'ai (Spirit Tower), with a Pi-yung, a circular structure with water flowing round it, below. These, like the stone embankments shaded by many trees which channelled the waters of the river round them, were built between 486 and 491.[44] We have little information on private building at this time.

[42] *WS* 7/1, pp. 143, 144, 146; *WS* 7/2, p. 164.
[43] *SCC* 13, p. 3/11.
[44] Ibid.

Along the northern frontier the emphasis was changing from the aggressive and effective policy of sending powerful forces on destructive raids against the Joujan to one of wall-building, static defence, appeasement, and bribery through allowing Joujan 'tribute missions' to make frequent and presumably profitable visits to P'ing-ch'eng.[45] The effects of neglecting the northern frontier after Kao-tsu's reign were to be most disastrously seen a quarter of a century after his death, when the frontier garrisons rose in the rebellion that brought down the whole Northern Wei system. In the short term, too, appeasement endangered the capital, and only served to encourage Joujan attacks, which happened almost every year between 485 and the decision to abandon P'ing-ch'eng in 493.[46]

We know too little about the organization and life of the city of P'ing-ch'eng and the surrounding domain to be able to make any secure assessment of the effect of the reforms. But as the question is crucial to any understanding of how P'ing-ch'eng and Loyang worked as cities, it is worth setting out what can be established.

The policy of forced immigration to the imperial domain was abandoned during the 480s, evidently because it did not work.[47] Instead the peasants of the domain were allowed to leave in the famine year of 487 for the richer lands of Hopei.[48] The new emphasis was on bringing food from the areas producing a surplus to the hungry capital and northern frontier, and on increasing the fertility of the dry northern soil through irrigation projects. Attempts had been made to feed the capital through tax grain in earlier reigns, most notably by Hsien-tsu, who had tax-paying households classified into nine grades and required those in the three wealthiest categories to

---

[45] See, in addition to the general references in n. 37 to ch. 3 of the 'Record', the report of a court conference on Joujan policy at which appeasement apparently carried the day in *WS* 54, pp. 1202–3.

[46] *Jou-jan tzu-liao chi-lu*, pp. 176–84.

[47] See the table on pp. 416–18 of Kawachi Juzō (1953), to which should be added 30,000 southern captives sent to the capital in 481. (*WS* 7/1, p. 150.)

[48] *WS* 7/2, p. 162; 110, p. 2856. This was probably the authorities trying to regulate what had been happening for many years, as may also be implied by the edict ordering that new population registers be compiled.

deliver their grain direct to the capital.[49] For all its appalling—
and, to the authorities, appealing—simplicity, it is unlikely
that this system can have worked well, given the cost and
difficulty of moving grain by land and water across Hopei and
by bad roads into northern Shansi. Even after the Ling-ch'iu
road was made by 50,000 corvée labourers in 482[50] the
fundamental logistical problems remained insoluble.

There is no way of measuring the combined effects on the
capital of the reforms of the 480s. No doubt they must have
reduced the difficulties of feeding P'ing-ch'eng and the
frontier; and we are told that after 488 famine—a drearily
frequent entry in the annals of the preceding years—was
avoided.[51] But while these measures must have improved the
supply of food, the location of P'ing-ch'eng still cramped Kao-
tsu/Hsiao-wen-ti's style, both economically and politically.

While the capital and domain could not be self-sufficient
unless greatly reduced in population, the supply problem was
made worse by peasants leaving the land for the more lucrative
employments of the capital. As one so often finds in attempts to
uncover Chinese social history, the best evidence on what was
actually happening are decrees intended to change some state
of affairs. In this case, there is a decree of 492 demanding that
the many 'vagabonds' (*yu-shih-che*) of the capital be sent back
to the land under supervision.[52] There must have been a living
for the 'vagabonds' to make in the capital and we may wonder
whether the capital's merchants took advantage of the permission given to them—as it was to the artisans, miscellaneous
households, and performers—to switch to farming in 472. Four
years earlier the stern Confucian critic Han Ch'i-lin had
maintained that some two-thirds of the common people of the
capital (here presumably including the domain) did not till the
soil and urged that these non-producers be allocated land and
compelled to work it. He was also shocked by the contrast
between the wealth of the city—where even the slaves of the
rich wore fine silk, and merchants and artisans ate and dressed
well—and the destitution of the hungry, half-naked

[49] *WS* 110, p. 2852.
[50] *WS* 7/1, p. 151.
[51] *WS* 110, p. 2857.
[52] *WS* 7/2, p. 170.

peasantry.[53] The segregation by social orders—one might almost say castes—which had been a feature of P'ing-ch'eng in its early decades as capital was breaking down by now, to the regret of Han Ch'i-lin's son Hsien-tsung, who found it shocking that singers and dancers could live next door to scholars, and urged Kao-tsu to restore the old system when planning the new capital at Loyang.[54] The tantalizingly cryptic statement in the *Wei shu* that in 484 Kao-tsu *pa chu shang-jen*, which may be rendered 'emancipated the merchants',[55] has given rise to much speculative interpretation;[56] it may mean that they were now allowed to operate on their own account, instead of as agents of officials. This would be compatible with the decision taken in 487 to close the palace's brocade and gauze workshops and permit anyone to weave these textiles, hitherto reserved for the throne's servile craftsmen. But the growth of commerce should not be overestimated. P'ing-ch'eng was still a city without a coinage of its own.

All these indications point to a changing P'ing-ch'eng, which despite the continuing difficulties of food supply was becoming larger (at the expense of the domain around it), less rigidly segregated by caste, more sinified, more splendid, and also, perhaps, more unruly. This last feature made necessary the creation of the new police force in 479; and it found most notable expression in the conspiracy led by the Buddhist monk Fa-hsiu, in which both officials and slaves were involved, and which was bloodily suppressed in 481.[57]

It would appear that the domain was no longer expected to feed the capital once reasonably effective control had been established over the peasantry of the whole of north China through the new administrative, tax, and agrarian systems. It is also likely that state control of the peasantry of the domain was weaker than it had been at the beginning of the dynasty. By now they were perhaps more of an economic liability than an asset.

What proportion of the peasantry in the domain were slaves,

---

[53] *WS* 60, pp. 1332–3.
[54] *WS* 60, pp. 1340–1.
[55] *WS* 7/1, p. 154.
[56] Notably in Koga (1965/1).
[57] On which see Tsukamoto (1942), pp. 256–60.

serfs, and other dependants of the officials and monasteries of the capital? Under the Northern Dynasties slavery flourished, justified by both Hsienpei and Han tradition.[58] Although it is unlikely that slaves made up a large proportion of the whole working population, they were one of the principal forms of wealth for the rich and powerful; and the state encouraged this form of exploitation both by example—holding its own slaves, and giving them to meritorious generals and officials—and by granting land to slave-owners proportionately to the number of their slaves without any upper limit in the *chün-t'ien* regulations.

Slaves and other unfree people would have staffed the princely, noble, and official households of P'ing-ch'eng, toiled in many of the palace's workshops, done much of the menial work in the monasteries, and tilled the estates of the aristocrats, officials, and monasteries in the domain. We may guess that during P'ing-ch'eng's century as capital the proportion of slaves belonging to private individuals and institutions in the city and the domain increased, while the numbers of state slaves and serfs went down. If this happened, it would help to explain why many of the leading metropolitan officials, both Han and Hsienpei, accepted the decision to move the capital to Loyang, where the land allocated to them in respect of their slaves would have been much more productive than the same amounts of land near P'ing-ch'eng.

The extraordinary efforts of Kao-tsu and the dowager Feng to sinify the capital and the whole state from P'ing-ch'eng were not as successful as they had wished. In the short term, they could only change the style of P'ing-ch'eng to a certain extent, as is most vividly shown by the contents of the tomb of Ssuma Chin-lung, a descendant of the Chin emperors whose family had held high office under the Wei for generations. He was buried in 484, when the reform programme was well under way, and as the scion of a Chinese royal house he would presumably have been one of the city's stronger adherents of Han-Chinese culture. But apart from a magnificent and now unique specimen of lacquer panel-painting which is entirely Chinese in its subject-matter and style, most of the tomb

---

[58] On slavery see Wang Yi-t'ung (1953), and Miyakawa Hisayuki (1960).

objects symbolize a more barbaric way of life: of the human models, the majority are of infantry and cavalrymen in Hsienpei clothing, mostly wearing armour. There are no models of kitchen equipment or grain-processing machinery: instead there are camels and pack-horses.[59]

Perhaps the death of the dowager Feng in 490, to which Kao-tsu reacted with extravagant displays of grief which went far beyond the exacting demands of ritual, increased his impatience with P'ing-ch'eng and determination to move. The only motives that can be directly attributed to him are two: frustration at the impossibility of carrying through his civilizing mission from P'ing-ch'eng, and the absence of water transport between P'ing-ch'eng and the north-China plain.[60] The reason for leaving P'ing-ch'eng that impressed southern observers was its climate, with bitterly cold winters, frequent dust-storms, and snow in midsummer.[61] There may also have been military considerations in Kao-tsu's mind—he was more interested in the southern frontier than the northern one. But even if P'ing-ch'eng would sooner or later have had to be abandoned as capital, given the way the Wei state was developing, no compelling practical reason made Loyang the inevitable site for the new capital. The reasons for the choice, the organization of the move, and the construction of the new metropolis will be discussed in the next two chapters. P'ing-ch'eng, meanwhile, did not cease to exist, as is still to be seen from the cave temples its inhabitants went on creating at Yün-kang: the last dated inscription is from 524.[62]

---

[59] Shan-hsi-sheng Ta-t'ung-shih po-wu-kuan and Shan-hsi-sheng wen-wu kung-tso wei-yüan-hui (1972).

[60] See ch. 3 below.

[61] *Nan Ch'i shu* 57, p. 990.

[62] See the references in n. 35, p. 26 above.

Chapter 3

The Decision to Move and the Building of the New Capital

In the seventh month of 493 the young emperor Kao-tsu/Hsiao-wen-ti announced a great expedition against his southern rival, the state of Ch'i, in preparation for which he had ordered a bridge to be thrown across the Yellow River and held a military review. The next month he left P'ing-ch'eng with an army claimed to be 1,000,000 strong and travelled south, crossing the Yellow River.

Two months of unceasing rain pushed the expeditionary force's morale ever lower until the emperor's senior officials prostrated themselves before his horse, begging him to abandon a campaign that the weather was making impossible and was not wanted by anybody in the world but His Majesty himself. When the emperor angrily rejected the protests of the Confucian gentlemen who had, he said, repeatedly obstructed his plans to unify China, several princes of the royal house added their tearful pleas. He then offered them all a choice: either the doomed expedition would continue, or else they had to agree that the capital should be moved to the place where they were now encamped, Loyang. Not surprisingly, they accepted the latter alternative.[1]

The whole performance had probably been arranged beforehand. Earlier in the year the emperor had told one of his confidants that he wanted to abandon P'ing-ch'eng. 'This is a place from which to wage war,' he said to Prince Ch'eng of Jen-ch'eng, 'not one from which civilized rule can come. It would be very hard indeed to change the way of life [here].' He went on to explain that his real intention in launching the southern expedition was to 'make a brilliant home on the

---

[1] *WS* 7/2, p. 172; *WS* 53, pp. 1182–3. According to *TCTC* 138, p. 4335, the army was only 300,000 strong.

Central Plain,' where 'the Hsiao mountains and Han pass make a royal residence, and the Yellow and Lo rivers form a kingly domain.' The prince said that such a move would be popular among the masses as 'the central region of the Yi and Lo is the support of the world and just the place from which to rule the Chinese (Hua-Hsia) and pacify the empire.' The emperor's reply was more realistic: 'The northerners are fond of their roots, and when they hear the unexpected news of a move they are bound to be alarmed and upset.'[2]

We do not know who else was told in advance of the real purpose of the southern expedition. It is unlikely that Li Ch'ung, for example, one of Kao-tsu's most trusted officials, played the leading role in the performance described above unprompted; and Kuo Tso, a Northern Han-Chinese aristocrat, was later rewarded with a title for agreeing to the plan.[3] The evidence points towards a conspiracy to force an unwanted upheaval on a powerful minority in the state, the non-Han northerners. Two decades of reform had not changed them enough for Kao-tsu; and it was inconceivable that those of them who did not stand to benefit from generous land allocations around the new capital would accept with enthusiasm what had been forced on them. As it happened, Kao-tsu's own son was to lead the resistance to the move. Just over thirty years later the north was to rise in rebellion on a much larger scale; and a decade after that it was to destroy the metropolis it hated and despised.

THE CHOICE OF LOYANG

Why Loyang? What other capital might Kao-tsu have chosen?[4] The strongest candidates were Ch'ang-an, Chinyang, Loyang, and Yeh. Only a few scraps survive of the records of the conferences in which Kao-tsu and his closest advisers discussed the choice, and of the memorials weighing the merits of the various possible sites submitted by officials. We can, however, make some conjectures as to why the emperor chose Loyang.

---

[2] *WS* 19/2, pp. 464–5.

[3] *WS* 64, p. 1422.

[4] The following paragraphs drawn on two studies of the principal cities of north China at this period: Lao Kan (1960); and Miyakawa Hisayuki (1956), pp. 473–533.

Ch'ang-an was perhaps too remote from the Yangtse valley to which Kao-tsu's ambitions were turned; as it also was from the power-base of the T'opa; and although Ch'ang-an and its environs had thoroughly respectable cultural associations from antiquity, it was half a millennium since it had been the seat of a Han-Chinese dynasty. Several non-Han regimes had reigned there in the century before it fell to the Wei armies in 430. It was to be a capital again for a number of strong dynasties after 534. But Kao-tsu rejected it.

Chin-yang (modern T'aiyüan) had advantages as a military headquarters from which cavalry armies could dominate the Yellow River valley and the north-China plain. As such it was later put to good use by the Erhchu tribal chieftains, followed by Kao Huan and his successors, and in the seventh century by the T'ang rulers who made it their northern capital. But it was not the place for a large city, as neither the water-transport links with the rest of China nor the local agricultural resources were adequate for one; and in cultural prestige it was no match for Loyang, Ch'ang-an, or Yeh. There is a hint that when the decision to abandon P'ing-ch'eng became known some of the less sinified Hsienpei would have preferred Chin-yang.[5] If that is so, no wonder Kao-tsu rejected it.

Of all the other rivals to Loyang, Yeh was the best placed economically, being at the edge of the fertile north-China plain, then the most populous and wealthy agricultural area of China, and connected with it by natural and man-made waterways.[6] Although strategically easily accessible to the Wei power-base in northern Shansi, its natural defences were not good. Its history was rich in cultural associations. The Yeh region, which straddled the borders of modern Honan and Hopei provinces, had been the centre of the later Shang-Yin power; during the Han period the local prefecture, Wei, had been one of the most populous in the empire; and with the collapse of the Loyang-based Eastern Han regime the warlord Yüan Shao made Yeh his headquarters in 191, followed by Ts'ao Ts'ao in 204. That Ts'ao Ts'ao's son moved his capital to Loyang in 220 may partly explain why his Ts'ao-Wei dynasty

---

[5] Lao Kan (1960), pp. 258–9.
[6] On Yeh see ibid., pp. 247–9.

did not last long. In the fourth century the Chieh tribesman Shih Lo moved the capital of his Chao dynasty there, to be followed by the Former and the Southern Yen regimes of the Mujung, a Hsienpei clan like the T'opa but less sinified.

Yeh's palace architecture and general splendour made a deep impression on its Northern Wei conquerors at the end of the fourth century. It was the main Wei logistical base in the fighting against the Sung regime to the south in the middle of the fifth century. Around 415 Yeh had been considered as an alternative capital to P'ing-ch'eng; but the suggestion was rejected.[7] During the fifth century Yeh was often included in the itinerary of imperial tours;[8] and during the transition from P'ing-ch'eng to Loyang it was the temporary capital, with a palace specially built in 493.[9] Kao-tsu spent much time in Yeh between 493 and his death in 499.[10] Evidently the lure that Loyang had for him could not outweigh Yeh's practical advantages.[11]

Why then was Yeh not chosen when on practical grounds it was preferable in almost every way to Loyang? Apart from Loyang's cultural and historic claims and the hold they had on Kao-tsu—to which we shall return—Yeh had the overwhelming disadvantage of its association with the 'barbarian' regimes of Shih Lo and the Mujung. As Kao-tsu said when the Censor Ts'ui Kuang urged him during a visit to Yeh in 494 to make that city his capital, 'Yeh is not a place for permanence. First Shih Hu fell there, and later the Mujung. These states were wealthy and their monarchs extravagant; sudden success was followed by rapid decline.'[12] He went on to list some local place-names that struck him as un-Confucian, inauspicious, and ill suited to imperial dignity. The evidence of all the time he spent at Yeh after P'ing-ch'eng was abandoned and this tantalizing fragment of argument as late as 494 both suggest

---

[7] See ch. 2 above.
[8] Lao Kan (1960), pp. 250–4.
[9] *WS* 7/2, p. 173.
[10] See the summary of Kao-tsu's movements in *WS* 7/2, pp. 172/85.
[11] Lao Kan (1960), p. 256.
[12] *T'ai-p'ing yü-lan* 161, p. 782 (quoted by Lao Kan on p. 257 of his article) citing the lost *Hou Wei shu*, which may be the work of this title by the Sui writer Wei Tan (biography, *SS* 58, pp. 1416–20) listed in the *Sui shu*'s bibliographical treatise (33, p. 956).

strongly that Yeh had still not been finally rejected even after
Kao-tsu ordered the move to Loyang. And it was to Yeh that
Kao Huan took the Wei court when Loyang became untenable
in 534.

The practical grounds for choosing Loyang were strong but not
overwhelming.[13] Although it had mountains to south, east, and
west, and the broad and swift-flowing Yellow River behind the
Mang hills to the north, if it was to be defended from attack a
number of passes and a river crossing within a couple of days
march of the city all had to be held. At this time the Yellow
River could be conveniently crossed only by the pontoon
bridge at the Meng Ford, except when the water was low
enough for it to be waded across. But even if the city's natural
defences were not as good as those of P'ing-ch'eng, Chin-yang,
or Chang-an, they were better than those of Yeh. Anyone
wanting to control north China had to hold the Loyang area as
it lay across the easiest line of communication between the
great plains north and south of the Yellow River's lower
reaches and the Wei valley of the north-west. Though the area
was strategically vital, for military purposes a well-garrisoned
strongpoint in it was all that was needed. During the wars that
ebbed and flowed across the Loyang area during the century
before its incorporation into the territories of the Northern
Wei, as in the strife-torn decades after Loyang ceased to be the
Northern Wei capital in 534, the only part of the city that
survived and functioned was the Chin-yung Castle, a fortress
in the north-west corner of the city walls; and it can be argued
that it was the only absolutely necessary feature of Loyang.

Loyang lies in an alluvial plain created by the rivers and
streams that flow from the mountains and hills surrounding it.
The principal rivers are three. The largest, the Lo, which rises
in the Hua-shan mountains in the west, divides the Hsiao from
the Hsiung-erh ranges, and flows south of the ancient and
modern sites of Loyang (thus giving the city its name 'North of

---

[13] On the historical topography of the Loyang region see Li Chien-jen (1936).

the Lo') to join the Yellow River some kilometres below the Northern Wei capital. The Yi comes from the Hsiung-erh mountains, forcing its way through the Yi-ch'üeh gorges (now known as the Lungmen) to join the Lo to the east of Loyang. The Chien, in its upper reaches called the Mien, comes from the Hsiao range and has its natural confluence with the Lo to the west of the Northern Wei city. This river was known in antiquity as the Ku; and when the Eastern Han capital was built it was dammed and its waters led along artificial channels under the southern slopes of the Mang hills where they were joined by the Ch'an, a stream rising in the north, before they approached the city from the north-west and were skilfully divided to fill the network of canals that flowed round and through Loyang. They rejoined the Lo to the south-east.[14]

This alluvial plain is fertile and well watered, but there is not enough of it to provide sufficient food and cloth for a big city. Yeh and Ch'ang-an both had much more grain and cloth locally available. A big city at Loyang was therefore mainly dependent on grain brought in from outside its immediate vicinity. This was more easily done than it had been for P'ing-ch'eng, which had to be supplied from the Hopei plains, up long and difficult tracks, probably by pack animals for the most part. Although the Wei valley produced more surplus food than the Loyang region, the difficulties of feeding an over-large Ch'ang-an by imported grain were greater than for Loyang, as was shown by the long and frequent moves of the T'ang court from Ch'ang-an to Loyang in the seventh and eighth centuries.[15]

The waterways connecting Loyang with those of the north-China plains were not reliable, but they could sometimes be used. Moreover the existing rivers and canals of Honan meant that grain could always be brought much closer to Loyang by boat than had been possible for P'ing-ch'eng. The greater convenience of Loyang for water transport is one of the very few reasons for leaving P'ing-ch'eng and making the new capital at Loyang that can be directly attributed to Kao-tsu. 'In our view', he declared, 'it was because there are no

[14] On the hydrography of Loyang see Li Chien-jen and *SCC* 15 and 16, pp. 3/45–82.
[15] D. C. Twitchett (1970), pp. 86 ff.

waterways in Heng and Tai that the people of the [old] capital were impoverished. The capital is now being moved to the Yi and Lo rivers in order to have transport links with all four quarters.' He went on to explain why he had to make a journey up the Yellow River from Shantung back to Loyang by water. 'Now that the Yellow River is in spate, fording it would be very difficult for everyone. That is why I must go by water in order to lighten the people's worries.'[16] Unfortunately there is an ambiguity in this text: were the worries about the dangers of fording the river, or of sailing on it?

The condition of some of the waterways joining Loyang and the north-China plain left much to be desired. When Kao-tsu ordered the building of boats and oars to take him to Yeh from Loyang in 493 or 494 there was no problem about the timber, huge quantities of which had been assembled for the construction of the new capital. He allowed himself to be dissuaded on a number of grounds, among them the long-neglected state of the towpaths and the great hardships that would be caused to the people required to tow the boats.[17]

But the possibility of making the journey, however troublesome it might have been, evidently existed; the north-China plain's network of rivers and canals developed in the second and third centuries by Ts'ao Ts'ao and his successors[18] must still have been there, even if in bad condition. The Northern Wei topographer Li Tao-yuan refers to the vital link, the Pai Kou, that connected the Huan Ch'i and Yellow rivers as if it still existed.[19] But Li is not always clear on the distinction between past and present; his evidence cannot be relied on as referring to conditions in his time.

We must therefore distinguish clearly between the possibility of direct links by water with the principal food-surplus areas of China as one of Loyang's attractions for Kao-tsu, who also dreamed of having a system of waterways leading from Loyang to the Huai war zone,[20] and the actual situation both during his

---

[16] *WS* 79, p. 1754.

[17] *WS* 62, pp. 1400–1.

[18] See Wang Chung-lo (1961), pp. 84–6; Shih Nien-hai (1963), pp. 145 ff.

[19] *SCC* 10, p. 2/82. The system is mapped in Yang Shou-ching (1903), 'Pei-Wei ti hsing t'u', *nan* 1/*hsi* 1, and *nan* 2/hsi 1.

[20] *WS* 53, p. 1185.

reign and afterwards. It seems that Loyang was linked with the waterways of the rest of China not by boat but by cart. The digging of the necessary canals was left to the Sui and T'ang regimes.

Perhaps the strongest attraction that Loyang had for Kao-tsu were cultural and symbolic. The area of the Three Rivers—the Lo, the Yi, and the Chien/Ku—had been celebrated in the written traditions of Chinese high culture as the very centre of civilization. To found a capital on the banks of the Lo was an act heavy with cultural and historical associations.

The name of Loyang had a ring to it that conjured up images of splendour and high civilization even during the long periods when it was not a great capital but only a country town, a frontier fortress, or an extensive ruin. Like Jerusalem or Rome, Loyang was as much a symbol as a real place; and the symbol outlasted the reality. Loyang's past was also a challenge. Kao-tsu, drawn by Loyang's past glory, longed to conquer south China and found a unified Chinese empire from the same capital as the Eastern Chou, Later Han, and Chin dynasties.

Loyang had been at the centre of the Chinese world since long before the beginning of recorded history. The long sequence of neolithic cultures in the Loyang region[21] would have meant nothing to Kao-tsu even had he known about them; but the traditions associating the Yi and Lo rivers with the legendary Hsia dynasty, the earliest in Chinese historical tradition, would have mattered much more.[22] Whether the

---

[21] For summaries of the neolithic archaeology of the Three Rivers see Chung-kuo k'o-hsüeh-yüan k'ao-ku yen-chiu-so (1961), pp. 11–12, 15–16, 43–45; and Chang Kwang-chih (1977), ch. 3. Some relevant carbon datings are given on pp. 485 and 510–11. The local sequence is Miaotikou I–II–Honan Lungshan (about 2,000 BC). Sun Ping-ch'i (1965), however, regards the Loyang area as the home of a Yangshao culture distinct from both the Panp'o and the Miaotikou types.

[22] *Chan kuo ts'e* 22, p. 782, gives the Yi and the Lo as the southern boundary of the territories of the last Hsia ruler; and king Wu of Chou is said to have regarded the north of the Yi and Lo as the dwelling place of Hsia. (*Shih chi* 4, p. 129; see also p. 145.) In the 'Wu tzu chih ko' of the *Shu ching* a Hsia ruler who goes hunting for a hundred days beyond the Lo is deposed, while his family remain north of the river. On place-names later associated with Hsia see Hsü Hsü-sheng (1959). The archaeological evidence for the Loyang area as Hsia territory is summarized in Wu Ju-tso (1978); and Chang (1977), pp. 258–9. See also Yin Wei-chang (1978).

Hsia rulers ever established a settled capital, near Loyang or elsewhere, remains to be established; but their successors, the Shang kings, built several, of which one of the earliest, Po, is traditionally associated with the area of modern Yenshih county next to Loyang.

That Northern Wei scholars were aware of this is shown by a line in an ode written by Ch'ang Ching between 518 and 520 in which the Lo river is said to 'flow through Chou and water Po'.[23] Some archaeologists believe that the impressive remains at Erhlit'ou, just 4 kilometres south of Northern Wei Loyang's city wall across the Lo river, are indeed those of Po. The extensive site contains the stamped-earth foundations of what is almost certainly a palace compound, a remote but direct ancestor of the Northern Wei palace built on the other side of the river nearly 2,000 years later. It has been dated by radiocarbon (corrected by the tree-ring method) to between 1590 and 1300 BC.[24]

Loyang itself appears to have been only a regional centre in the later part of the Shang dynasty, when capitals were created at Chengchou and then Anyang. This area has not left much mark on the surviving literary traditions of the Shang, which are weighted towards the dynasty's last two centuries, although the Shang remains at Loyang and Yenshih approach those at Chengchou and Anyang in extent.[25]

Loyang begins to feature in literary records in Chou times; and the Chou cities at Loyang are probably the earliest ones of which Kao-tsu was aware. At some time in the eleventh century BC, after the Chou conquerors had overthrown the Shang state, their legendary leader the duke of Chou decided to found a subsidiary capital in the Loyang area. This followed the suppression of a rebellion by the three Shang princes who had been set over the former Shang subjects as Chou vassals.[26]

---

[23] See ch. 3 of the 'Record' below.

[24] On this site see the 1974 report by the Chung-kuo k'o-hsüeh-yüan k'ao-ku yen-chiu-so Erh-li-t'ou kung-tso-tui, and Chang Kwang-chih (1977), pp. 218–29 and 258–9.

[25] On Shang remains at Loyang and near Loyang see Cheng Te-k'un (1961), pp. 26, 60–1, 115, 142, 196; and previous note.

[26] The traditionally accepted story is well told in *Shih chi* 4, pp. 132–3. See also H. G. Creel (1970), pp. 72, 89, 84, 90, 128, 310–11.

The literary traditions concerning the founding of Chou's 'New Great City' or 'New City Lo' directly influenced the refounding of the city in AD 493; the relevant exhortations in the *Shu ching* would have been known to Kao-tsu and his leading Chinese advisers since their schooldays.[27] In siting his capital at Loyang Kao-tsu would have been consciously imitating the Duke of Chou. Something of the aura that still radiated from the site as a result of its illustrious past can be seen in Ch'ang Ching's *Ode to the North Bank of the Lo* which Yang Hsüan-chih included in the third chapter of his account of the city.

Labour for building the duke of Chou's city was conscripted within the former Shang domains;[28] and some at least of the inhabitants of the last Shang capital were evidently compulsorily moved there.[29] In Northern Wei times the potters' quarter was known as the place where the Shang people had once lived and was accordingly called the Shang-Shang ('Honouring the Shang') ward.[30]

After its founding the New City Lo fades into the general obscurity of Western Chou history. There were two Chou cities on the north bank of the Lo, one on or about the site of the Northern Wei capital and the other, Wang-ch'eng, the 'Royal City', several kilometres to the west of it on the east bank of the Chien/Ku river; but the relationship between the two sites and the various names of cities in the area known from texts and bronze inscriptions is highly problematical.[31]

With the decline in Chou power after Loyang was made its main capital in the eighth century, the area's ritual and political significance shrank as Loyang became increasingly important as a commercial centre. The merchants of the Chou domain were famous throughout China for their business

---

[27] 'K'ang kao', 'Shao kao', 'Lo kao', and 'To shih'. The opening section of 'K'ang kao', referring to the city, probably belongs to 'Lo kao'. See the edition of Juan Yuan, pp. 202–17; and Bernhard Karlgren (1948, (1949), and (1950).

[28] 'Shao kao'.

[29] 'To shih'.

[30] See the beginning of ch. 5 of the 'Record'.

[31] For a good attempt to sort out the problem of Chou Loyang's dual cities (which were, perhaps, a Chou characteristic) see Gotō Shimpei (1961). On the Chou sites at Loyang see Chang Kwang-chih (1977), pp. 312–16, 321–4; Cheng Te-k'un (1963), pp. 23–5, 94–106, 186, 210, 212, 216–19; Paul Wheatley (1972), pp. 136 ff.

acumen and zeal;[32] and the 'people of Chou'—that is, of Loyang—continued in Western Han times to set the standard by which devotion to commerce and the pursuit of profit were to be judged.[33] Pan Ku, summing up the shortcomings of the same population with the prejudices of a Han Confucian, wrote:

The failings of the Chou people are these: they are cunning and deceitful in pursuit of profit; they honour riches and hold moral duty in contempt; they respect the rich and despise the poor: they love being traders and dislike serving in public office.[34]

The commercial side of Chou and Western Han Loyang would not perhaps have seemed as exciting to Kao-tsu as the prescriptions for an idealized (but not purely imaginary) royal capital contained in that intriguing text, the 'K'ao kung chi' of the *Chou li*. Although the date of this work is open to discussion, it was regarded in Han times and after as laying down an antique standard of what a capital city should be like. It was to be square with walls 9 *li* long, and nine roads, each nine chariot-axles wide, running from north to south and east to west. The palace compound was to be south of the main market, and so on. Whatever the relationship between the city described in 'K'ao kung chi' and any city that ever existed, this text undoubtedly affected the planning of Kao-tsu's capital both directly and indirectly.[35]

The Loyang that Liu Hsiu laid out on a grand scale to be the capital of the revived Han dynasty in the first century AD was probably of more interest to the Northern Wei rulers than its rather mercantile predecessor of the earlier Han period.[36] Its city walls (to be followed by the Chin and Northern Wei capitals later built on the site) enclosed a roughly rectangular

[32] See *Shih chi* 69, p. 2241, for a local woman's pride in the Chou people's commitment to trade and industry.

[33] *Shih chi* 129, p. 3279.

[34] *Han shu* 35, p. 1650. On Loyang and other Western Han cities see Utsonomiya Kiyoyoshi (1967).

[35] The 'K'ao kung chi' is § 12 of the *Chou li*. On it see Wheatley (1972), pp. 411 and 415, where a reconstruction of this text's ideal city is reproduced from *Yung-lo ta tien*.

[36] On Eastern Han Loyang see Hattori (1966), pp. 85–91, 201–16; and especially Hans Bielenstein (1976).

area measuring some 3,800 metres from north to south and 2,500 from east to west. The magnificence of this capital as seen through the eyes of courtiers is described with extravagant rhetoric by Pan Ku in his *Prose-poem on the Eastern Metropolis* (*Tung tu fu*) and by Chang Heng in his *Prose-poem on the Eastern Capital* (*Tung ching fu*), two versions of a legendary city whose imperial splendour must surely have dazzled the young Kao-tsu. They gave an image of the city as essentially a huge palace compound, graced with every rare and splendid thing imaginable, set amid parks in the centre of the universe.[37]

This was not the only memory of the Eastern Han capital to influence the founding of the Northern Wei city on its site; to judge from Yang's book the *Hou Han shu* was well known to educated readers and its many anecdotes about the dominant personalities of that earlier Loyang helped to form a view of what a capital should be like and how its senior officials should behave.

Kao-tsu must have been uncomfortably aware of Han Loyang's wretched end in 190, when the warlord Tung Cho abandoned the city under pressure from his military rivals, taking the court and emperor west to Ch'ang-an. When he left Loyang

Tung Cho's men burned everything within 100 *li* [some 50 kilometres]. Tung himself saw to the destruction of the northern and southern palaces, the ancestral temples, the government offices, the storehouses, and the homes of the people. Within the city walls the devastation was total.[38]

The destruction left its mark, both in the development of the Loyang district as it can be seen from archaeological evidence[39] and in the imagery of literature, as in a poem of Ts'ao Chih's, written in or about 211, which includes some lines on the desolation of Loyang seen from the Mang hills:

[37] These specimens of Han baroque literature can be found in *Wen hsüan* 1, pp. 15–24, and 3, pp. 47–72; parts are translated in E. R. Hughes (1960).
[38] Hua Ch'iao's *Han shu* (now lost) quoted in the commentary to *SKC*, Wei 6, pp. 177–8.
[39] See especially Huang Chan-yüeh (1957).

> How desolate is Loyang,
> Its palaces burned down,
> The walls fallen in ruins,
> As brambles climb to the sky . . .
> There are no paths to walk,
> Unworked fields have to run to waste . . .
> Lonely is the countryside,
> A thousand *li* without one smoking hearth.[40]

There was to be a city at Loyang for much less than half of the following 260 years; during that time it was to be rebuilt and destroyed twice more on the same site, the interval between building and destruction growing shorter each time.

Loyang remained abandoned for three decades after its destruction in 190 while rival warlords fought for control of China. One factor in the success of the victor, Ts'ao Ts'ao, was his choice first of Hsü (Hsüch'ang, Honan) then of Yeh as his headquarters, both situated in rich farming country which could feed them through the system of state serfdom;[41] while the area of Loyang remained so utterly desolated and cut off from food supplies that when the pathetic Han court tried to return there in 196 some of the emperor's entourage starved to death.[42] The decision of Ts'ao Ts'ao's son, the first emperor of the (Ts'ao-) Wei dynasty, to make Loyang his capital required enormous efforts in 220 before it could be put into effect. The surrounding countryside was so badly overgrown that an official, the director of farming for Loyang (*Lo-yang tien-nung*), had to be appointed to get the land cleared and back into cultivation. Such directors were appointed for the rest of the dynasty, and at least a part of the land was worked by state serfs.[43] Some of the immigration to the deserted region was involuntary.[44]

The rebuilt Loyang, created from 220 onwards on the site of the Eastern Han capital, enjoyed decades of prosperity and even brilliance which reached a climax after the Ts'ao-Wei regime gave way to the Chin dynasty in 265, only to be

---

[40] 'Sung Ying-shih' in *Ts'ao Tzu-chien shih-chu*, p. 8.
[41] On the *t'un-t'ien* system of state serfdom see Nishijima Sadao (1956).
[42] *HHS* 9, p. 379.
[43] *SKC*, Wei 27, p. 744; Nishijima (1956), pp. 8, 22–4.
[44] See e.g. *SKC*, Wei 13, p. 393.

The decision to move 51

dragged into the misery of wars between Chin princes from 291 to 306 then to be sacked by barbarians in 311.[45] This was the Loyang, also known as Chung-ch'ao, that the early rulers of the T'opa had visited in the third century; and for the north-Chinese aristocracy it was the lost capital whose memory was preserved through the generations of upheaval that followed its fall, and whose personalities—such as the poet Hsi K'ang and the extravagantly rich Shih Ch'ung—they admired. It seems likely that both Kao-tsu and his leading Chinese advisers were in many ways consciously trying to recreate the Chin city. They emulated rather feebly the art of 'pure talk' (ch'ing t'an) which had been so fashionable in that earlier Loyang; and renewed the Chin attempt to regularize an aristocracy graded by birth rather than talent.

After Loyang was put to the torch in 311 it disappeared as a city of any importance. It was briefly the southern capital of the Chieh rulers Shih Lo and Shih Hu around 336; in the middle of the century it came again under the rule of the Chin, now re-established at Chien-k'ang, only to be taken first by the Former Yen regime of the Mujung branch of the Hsienpei and then by their Ti rivals, the Former Ch'in. Another short spell under southern rule was ended in 399 by the Later Ch'in state of the Ch'iang. An expeditionary force from the south under the general Liu Yü restored Han-Chinese rule in 416 until Loyang fell to the Northern Wei armies in 423.[46] Throughout these upheavals the city was essentially the Chin-yung Castle.

The northern Wei general Yü Li-ti was made governor of Yü-chou with his headquarters at Loyang.

Although Loyang had been a capital for many reigns, it had long been on the borders. City walls and ceremonial gateways were in ruins, and there was no sign of life in the countryside around. Li-ti cleared the brush, settling those who came there, and greatly winning the hearts of the people through his good government.

At this time a pontoon bridge was thrown across the Yellow

---

[45] For a narrative of these gloomy events see *TCTC* 84–6; Wang Chung-lo (1961), pp. 138–41, and Lü Ssu-mien (1948), pp. 43–60, offer succinct accounts. The fall of Chin Loyang is admirably described in Arthur Waley's essay on pp. 47–55 of his 1963 volume.
[46] This period of Loyang's history is ably summarized on pp. 508–10 of Miyakawa (1956).

River, linking Loyang more firmly to the Wei territories north of the river.[47]

A renewed northern drive by the Sung forces of Tao Yen-chih forced the Wei garrison to abandon the city in 430. But what with the disrepair of the walls of the Chin-yung Castle and the lack of food the city was recaptured by Wei forces later that year.[48] For the next sixty-three years Loyang was to be a strategically important base for the southern wars but little else; as a city it amounted to very little, least of all a potential capital.

But practical considerations were only secondary in choosing Loyang. After all, it was not just where some of the great capitals of China had stood in the past; it was also the centre of the world. This was a belief based not only on Loyang's cultural area, but also by the movement of the shadow cast by the sun at the summer solstice at Yang-ch'eng, about 75 kilometres south-east of Loyang, which had long been thought to mark the earth's centre.[49]

When he reached the historic site in the ninth month of 493 Kao-tsu made an inspection of the ruined foundations of the city's former palace, wept at the decline of Chin which had resulted in its ancestral shrines being so badly ruined, visited the site of the imperial university, and examined the standard texts of the classics that had been inscribed on stone.[50] It was a clear statement of his determination to make himself an authentic Chinese monarch ruling the civilized world from its very centre, and a truer expression of his feelings than the performance that was to be enacted for the benefit of the army a few days later.

THE MOVE AND THE BUILDING OF THE NEW CAPITAL

The decision to make Loyang the capital, announced in the ninth month of 493, did not take effect immediately. The new city had to be built, and the apparatus of court and state, together with much of the population of P'ing-ch'eng, brought south. The resistance from the north had to be overcome, for

[47] *WS* 31, pl 736; *TCTC* 119, pp. 3751, 3756.
[48] *WS* 4/1, pp. 76–7; *TCTC* 121, pp. 3818, 3821–2.
[49] Lao Kan (1960), pp. 238–9; Joseph Needham (1954), 3, pp. 284 ff.
[50] *WS* 7/2, p. 173.

the time being at least. It was not until the autumn of 495 that all the palace women and civil and military officials completed the move to Loyang, and it was seven years more before the new capital had its systems of wards built.

The site chosen for the new city was that of the Ts'ao-Wei and Chin capital, the line of whose walls was followed closely. The arrangement within the walls was, however, different.[51] The planning of the city was influenced by several models. In 491 Chiang Shao-yu, a southern-aristocratic captive who had risen from low military status through his skill as a sculptor and painter to be one of Kao-tsu's leading experts in the design of ceremonial objects from court costumes to palace buildings, was included on an embassy to the Ch'i capital, where it was felt by some southerners that in spying out the imperial architecture for the sake of a barbarian dynasty he was guilty of cultural *lèse-majesté*. He played a big part both in the rebuilding programme in the last years at P'ing-ch'eng and in the construction of the walls, palaces, and water system for Kao-tsu's Loyang, to the distress of the cultured northern friends who felt he should have confined his efforts to writing.[52] He has been taken by Ch'en Yin-k'o as representing the southern branch of the traditions of Han, Ts'ao-Wei, and Chin in the formation of Northern Wei Loyang.[53]

The branch of these traditions that had flourished in the far west was represented by Li Ch'ung (a leading actor in the performance described at the beginning of the chapter), who as chancellor was entrusted with the building of the new capital together with the Hsienpei elder statesman Mu Liang and the high artificer Tung Chüeh.[54] As Ch'en Yin-k'o has shown, Li Ch'ung was the key figure in the city's planning, and he may have been responsible for one aspect of the city's design for which there was neither canonical approval nor Han, Ts'ao-Wei, or Chin precedent—the location of some of the markets south of the main palace compound instead of to the

---

[51] On the differences between the Ts'ao-Wei/Chin and the Northern Wei cities see Miyazaki Ichisada (1961), pp. 66 ff.; and Hattori Katsuhiko (1965), pp. 54 ff.

[52] *Nan Ch'i shu* 57, p. 990; *WS*a 91, pp. 1970–1 (after *PS* 90, pp. 2984–5).

[53] Ch'en Yin-k'o (1963 repr.), p. 67.

[54] *WS* 7/2, p. 173; 53, pp. 1183–4. According to *WS*a 105/4, p. 2427, Tung's personal name was Mi, and they were ordered to build the palaces.

north of it. This arrangement had been a feature of Liang-chou (or Ku-tsang) as an independent capital in the fourth and early fifth centuries; and Li Ch'ung was of a western family. The arrangement was besides convenient as it made the main markets directly accessible by water. Li Ch'ung took a close interest in architecture, supervising work himself and even holding tools in his own hands.[55]

The scant information on how the capital was built points to military and civilian forced labour. Kao-tsu was urged not to visit Yeh or the Shantung area in the summer of 494 in order to reduce the burden of corvée that royal tours or campaigns imposed on the people, and thus speed up the building of Loyang with all efforts concentrated on it.[56] No doubt the large armies already assembled at Loyang for the southern campaign were put to work; many civilian labourers were brought in as well. Thus it was that 'civilians and soldiers were moving tens of thousands of logs every day' for the building of the palaces, and having to endure the misery of wading through the waters of the Yi and Lo until pontoon bridges were provided.[57] In 495 the builders of the city were men too weak to be of any use in the wars on the southern frontier.[58]

Apart from the soldiers already encamped at Loyang, many of whom would have become residents of the new city, other people were obliged to move there from Tai in 493 or 494. Their wretched situation in the autumn of 494 was used by prince Ch'eng of Jen-ch'eng as an argument against launching a big campaign in the south. He maintained that as they had just brought their families with them, had nowhere to live, and had virtually no stocks of grain, they should be working in the fields, instead of going unwillingly to fight.[59] It is not clear whether he was referring to people transferred from the city of P'ing-ch'eng or from its surrounding countryside, though his mention of farming implies the latter. If so, they would seem to have been moved to the countryside around Loyang rather than the city itself. As there were no major campaigns in the

[55] Op. cit., pp. 34–5, 62–9. Li Ch'ung's biography is in *WS* 53, pp. 1179–89.
[56] *WS* 60, p. 1338.
[57] *WS* 79, pp. 1754–5.
[58] *WS* 40, p. 912.
[59] *WS* 19/2, p. 466.

earlier part of 494, these families might have been brought back by members of the 493 expeditionary force sent north to fetch their dependants. Many of the inhabitants of P'ing-ch'eng and its surrounding countryside were probably ordered to move *en masse* in 494, just as they or their descendants were sent to Yeh in 534. In the twelfth month of 494 the households transferred from Tai were remitted three years' grain and cloth tax.[60] The following year they were all reclassified as people of Loyang; and even in death were required to leave their bones south of the Yellow River.[61]

The new inhabitants of the Loyang area had been so badly exhausted by the long, hard journey south, losing their cattle and much of their property, that in the first decade of the new century 'farmers had not yet accumulated two years' reserve and people had only built a few rooms for their houses', according to a memorial urging the new emperor to abstain from the military adventures in which Kao-tsu had indulged to the end of his life. Li P'ing argued that the move had cost the rich most of their wealth, with consequences for the poor that could be imagined. The new settlers should be left alone and the metropolitan area allowed to get rich.[62] A decree of 502 was intended to ease the capital's agricultural problems.[63]

The implied complaint about how the new settlers had been treated by the unrelenting Kao-tsu was well founded. Unable to resist the temptation to exploit the weaknesses of a decaying dynasty in the south, he nearly always had armies of several hundred thousand men in action on the frontier from the end of 494 until his death. His ambition was to be the ruler of the whole of China, and he did not care unduly about the price his subjects had to pay.

Officials and the many inmates of P'ing-ch'eng's palaces were given longer than the mass of the population in which to make the transfer: it was not until the ninth month of 495 that they all reached Loyang.[64]

The monastic population of P'ing-ch'eng also had to be

---

[60] *WS* 7/2, p. 176.
[61] *WS* 7/2, p. 178.
[62] *WS* 65, pp. 1451–2.
[63] *WS* 8, p. 195.
[64] *WS* 7/2, p. 178.

dealt with. Although Buddhist activity there did not come to a halt with the end of the city's role as a capital, as the continued work on the Yünkang cave temples after 493 shows, there can be no doubt that most of the monks followed their patrons south. Two who are known to have taken part in the move are Shih Tao-pien and the *dhyāna* master Fo-t'o.[65] Kao-tsu ordered that no monasteries were to be allowed in Loyang apart from the Yung-ning in the inner city and a nunnery outside the wall, though after his reign this ruling was flouted.[66] If other monastic establishments existed in the city no record of them survives.

It was not only people that had to move. The new city needed horses for war, oxen for agriculture and transport, and sheep and cattle for the mutton and dairy products that made up a good part of the diet of the inhabitants of Loyang, Han, and non-Han alike.[67] The royal herds had to be shifted; and at the request of Yüwen Fu, who was given the job of moving them, a strip of land 10 *li* wide along the north bank of the Yellow River from Shih-chi (below where the Ch'in joins the Yellow River)[68] in the east to Ho-nei (modern Wuchih) in the west was set aside as grazing land for the capital's military reserve of 100,000 horses. The Ho-hsi grazing lands, which continued to be the main royal pastures, sent horses south, moving them gradually so as to accustom them to the terrain and water, thus avoiding sickness; such concern was not shown for the welfare of the people who were forced south. Other animals were also moved south to new pastures which are not identified. Some at least of them must have been closer to the capital than the horse-grazing lands if unnecessary transport costs for meat and dairy products were to be avoided.[69] Private

---

[65] *HKSC* 7, p. 15a; 19, p. 5a.

[66] *WS* 114, p. 3044; Tsukamoto Zenryū (1961), pp. 281 ff.

[67] On mutton and dairy products in Loyang's diet see ch. 3 of the 'Record' and notes 19 and 20 to it.

[68] *SCC* 4, pp. 1/82–3.

[69] *WS* 44, p. 1000; 110, p. 2857; *TCTC* 139, p. 4369. The figure of '10 *li*' is from *TCTC*, which is much more plausible than *WS* 44's '1,000 *li*', an evident corruption. On the royal grazing lands see Han Kuo-p'an (1962), pp. 38–9; on the unfree or half-free herdsmen see T'ang Chang-ju (1955), pp. 209–16. The vast herds were administered by the Livestock Office (*T'ai p'u ssu*), on which see *TT* 25, p. 150; the livestock minister generally made a fortune from this post.

herds, particularly those of the aristocrats who moved to Loyang,[70] must also have been moved.

From the beginning of the building work to the achievement of what could be regarded as a reasonably complete city took nine years from the order to start work in the tenth month of 493. Labour gangs were on the job that winter. By the eighth month of 495 a palace was ready in the Chin-yung Castle; at the beginning of the next year the emperor was hearing lawsuits in a pavilion of the capital's Hua-lin Park which was often used for official occasions thereafter;[71] and there are references to ceremonies held in the Kuang-chi Hall from 495 and the Ch'ing-hui Hall from 497.

How much of his new capital did Kao-tsu see built before his death in 499? He was not idle during his last years, as is shown by the records of his almost incessant campaigns in the south, his progresses round the country, and the continuing succession of decrees which took the process of sinification further than had been possible at P'ing-ch'eng. But there is very little evidence of building, apart from that just cited, and there are some indications that the new capital was still more of a project than a functioning city when its founder died. Kao-tsu was in Loyang for most of 496, but he spent barely a quarter of the rest of the time between the decision to move and his death in his new capital.[72]

According to a complaint made by Lu Jui in 495 there were still no buildings in which the departments of government could function, and the officials themselves were becoming ill as the result of having nowhere to live.[73] Few of the many buildings mentioned in the pages of Yang's 'Record' are said to have been built in Kao-tsu's time.

In chapter 2 the principal reform measures of the *t'ai-ho* era taken at P'ing-ch'eng were set out. The same can usefully be done for Loyang's first three years.

---

[70] Prince Hsi of Hsien-yang had, among many other properties, grazing lands at Hung-ch'ih shortly after the move. (*WS* 21/1, p. 538.) If this is the same place mentioned in Chang Heng's *Tung ching fu* it was only 30 *li* east of the capital.

[71] *WS* 7/2, p. 179. This park is described at the end of ch. 1 of the 'Record'.

[72] Calculated from the information on his movements in *WS* 7/2.

[73] *WS* 40, p. 912.

Reform measures, 494 to 496

494   Intention to move the capital to Loyang publicly proclaimed (*WS* 7/2, p. 174).

Sacrifice to heaven in western outskirts [of P'ing-ch'eng] abolished (ibid; *WS* 108/1, p. 2751).

Triennial assessment (*k'ao*) of officials instituted (*WS* 7/2, p. 175).

Wearing of Hsienpei clothes banned (*WS* 7/2, p. 176).

495   Northern (i.e. non-Han) languages banned at court, on pain of dismissal from office for those under thirty (ibid. 177; 21/1, p. 536).

Transferees to Loyang to be buried south of the Yellow River; all transferees from Tai to be registered as people of Loyang (ibid., p. 178).

Units of length and volume revised according to *Chou li* (ibid.).

150,000 warriors recruited as Forest of Wings and Tiger Guards (ibid.).

Provincial governors required to evaluate their subordinates (ibid.).

Tai (i.e. Hsienpei) families classified and ranked to match Han-Chinese aristocracy (*WS* 113, pp. 3014–15).

Decree institutes the division of official posts into nine grades (*p'in*) and the 'great selection' of officials (to fit them to posts suited to their rank) (*WS* 7/2, p. 178; 59, pp. 1310–11).

The dynasty coins money for the first time (*WS* 110, p. 2863).

Court clothing issued to officials (*WS* 7/2, p. 179).

496   Royal family's surname changed from T'opa to Yuan (*WS* 7/2, p. 179).

Hsienpei surnames given single-syllable equivalent (*TCTC* 140, p. 4393).

Decree orders strict supervision of agriculture in imperial domain (*WS* 7/2, p. 179).

All men transferred from Tai made Forest of Wings and Tiger Guards (ibid. p. 180).

After 496, when northern resistance to the reforms became open and violent, the pace of change was finally relaxed. Short of exterminating the majority of the Hsienpei, there was little else Kao-tsu could have done. Another policy of great importance that was energetically pursued during these years but cannot be precisely dated was the careful classification of the status of all Han-Chinese families and the integration of the Han and non-Han aristocracies into what was intended to become a single system.[74] Families were graded according to the offices held by their ancestors, and officials were not supposed to rise above the official rank to which their birth entitled them. It was evident from some of the objections made to his selection of officials on birth alone rather than ability, and from Kao-tsu's half-hearted acceptance of such criticism, that he believed the aristocratic principle to be fundamental to the maintenance of Chinese civilization,[75] and regarded the distinction between the higher, 'pure', grades and the rest as vital.[76] To this end he was careful in his choice of the provincial *chung-cheng* whose main function was to assess the standing of the local lineages. The result of these efforts was an official classification of nobility which was to be influential for centuries.[77] Intermarriage between the highest ranking four (or five) Han-Chinese lineages and the princes of the royal house was also enforced at this time.[78] To complete this policy a new grading of official posts which had been carried out with much advice from the southern aristocrat Wang Su was introduced right at the end of Kao-tsu's reign.[79]

Not only did this series of measures do much to consolidate the power of the leading Han-Chinese families in the provinces

[74] On the grading of officials the work of Miyazaki Ichisada, 1956, especially pp. 41–7 and 390 ff., is fundamental. See also David Johnson (1977), and Patricia Buckley (1978), for broader English-language studies of the medieval aristocracy (or, as Johnson prefers, oligarchy).

[75] *WS* 60, pp. 1343–4, reports some of the objections to selection on birth alone and Kao-tsu's replies.

[76] See his conversation with the southern refugee Liu Ch'ang in 496. (*WS* 59, pp. 1310–11.)

[77] Although the surviving Wei documentation is poor, Liu Fang's T'ang account is preserved in *Hsin T'ang shu* 199. Ssuma Kuang outlines the policy in *TCTC* 140, pp. 4393–5. The best modern treatment is in Johnson, 1977.

[78] *WS* 21/1, pp. 534–5.

[79] *Nan Ch'i shu* 57, p. 998; *TCTC* 142, p. 4457.

and to integrate them with the chosen few among the Hsienpei
into a single élite, but it also changed the nature of the Wei
state and thus of the Wei capital for as long as it lasted. The
city Yang Hsüan-chih described for us was undoubtedly an
aristocratic one whose dominant values he shared. But the
system could not work for long once the political will to enforce
it was gone; and within a quarter of a century of Kao-tsu's
death it was in disarray, just as the city he founded went
beyond the limits he had planned for it.

In the short term, however, he succeeded in dealing with
some strong opposition to the move and the other upheavals
associated with it. The tactics used to force the choice on the
men of the southern expedition were hardly the ones to win
wholehearted enthusiasm. The soldiers on the northern frontier and the Hsienpei remaining in the old capital were
doubtless even further from accepting Kao-tsu's decision.
Anticipating difficulties, he had sent his half-brother prince Yü
of Kuang-ling in the summer of 493 to remove the doubts of the
northern-frontier garrisons about the southern campaign and
to hold special powers over the old capital with duke P'i of
Tung-yang.[80] When the news of the move came out, Kao-tsu
sent his trusted confidant prince Ch'eng of Jen-ch'eng back to
P'ing-ch'eng to assess the reaction of the officials there and in
the frontier garrisons. The prince succeeded in calming some of
the initial alarm;[81] and it was doubtless on his advice, as well
as that of Li Ch'ung,[82] that the emperor returned to P'ing-
ch'eng in the spring of 494 to bring a potentially dangerous
situation under control.[83] Meanwhile the northerner Yü Lieh,
whose own feelings about the move were mixed, was sent back
to garrison P'ing-ch'eng.[84] Prince Yü of Kuang-ling was also
instrumental in keeping P'ing-ch'eng calm during this difficult
period.[85]

Reports of the court conferences that followed the emperor's

[80] *WSa* 14, pp. 358–9; *WS* 21/1, p. 546; *PS* 15, p. 554.

[81] *WS* 19/2, p. 465.

[82] Who had advised him to go north immediately the decision to move was
announced. (*WS* 53, pp. 1183–4.)

[83] *WS* 7/2, p. 174.

[84] *WS* 31, p. 736.

[85] *WS* 21/1, p. 546.

return to the north give some of the objections of the Hsienpei nobles to the move. One felt that the military dangers to the north, east, and west were still too great to permit a move and referred to the difficulty of breeding horses at Loyang. Kao-tsu replied that horses could still be raised in the north. Another protested that the people were used to Tai and would not move; a third wanted the decision tested by divination. The emperor argued that there were good T'opa precedents for changing capitals. Finally he divided the northerners between those who were to stay and those who were to move,[86] ruthlessly dismissing from office any dissenters.[87] That his support was limited is indicated by the rewards of title and income he gave to one prince simply for approving of the move.[88] During the summer and autumn of 494 Kao-tsu toured the northern frontier, doubtless to bring the military into line.[89]

In 496, however, Mu T'ai (who had once stopped the dowager Feng from dismissing the future Kao-tsu as heir apparent) led a rising in the north in which a number of the leading Hsienpei nobles and generals took part.[90] It was quickly put down, but it might easily have been much more dangerous: only one of the leading northern clans had not been involved.[91]

Although opposition to the move and the other policies associated with it did not take so violent a form among the Hsienpei transferred to Loyang, it was not entirely overcome. Its most dramatic expression was the attempt by the emperor's son and heir Hsün to leave Loyang, where he was held against his will, and return to the north; he thoroughly disliked the changes his father was imposing. He was stripped of his position as crown prince and forced to kill himself in 497.[92] This was not just a personal disaster for Kao-tsu; it also meant

---

[86] *WS* 21/1, p. 546; *PS* 15, pp. 554–5; *WSa* 14, pp. 359–60; *TCTC* 139, pp. 4351–2.
[87] *WS* 79, p. 1754.
[88] *WS* 19/3, p. 494.
[89] *WS* 7/2, p. 174.
[90] *WS* 19/2, pp. 468–9; 27, p. 663; 40, p. 913; *WSa* 14, pp. 359–61; *PS* 15, pp. 554–5; *TCTC* 140, pp. 4402–3.
[91] *WS* 31, p. 738.
[92] *WSa* 22, pp. 588–9; *PS* 19, pp. 713–14.

that when he died unexpectedly young his new crown prince was a sixteen-year-old, so that the state was exposed to the perils of a regency. A more trivial sign that the emperor's will was not all-powerful was that the women of Loyang continued to wear 'barbarian' clothing right up to the end of his reign.[93] On the whole, however, Kao-tsu succeeded in founding a sinified city at Loyang as the most visible symbol of his determination to change the whole structure of the Northern Wei state.

Perhaps in response to local discontent, or perhaps as an unprompted gesture of Confucian concern, Kao-tsu instituted a welfare system for the city in 497. The elderly without families to support them were to be fed and clad, while four physicians and free medicine were to be provided for the poor and disabled.[94]

It was not until 501, the second full year of the reign of his young son Shih-tsung/Hsüan-wu-ti, that the city's 220 walled residential wards were built, a measure designed to strengthen the state's control of the capital.[95] As a force of 55,000 conscripts took forty days on the job, there would have been an average of 10,000 man-days spent on each ward; and this would have allowed them to make the 1,200 *pu* (2,130 metres) of wall round each ward substantial and solid.[96]

Loyang's palaces were basically finished in 502,[97] and Kao-tsu's initial building programme was now complete. The major construction that continued thereafter was no longer primarily of palaces, government offices, or walls, but of magnificent residences for aristocrats, leading officials, favourite eunuchs, imperial in-laws, and rich merchants; and of monasteries and convents on which they showered their patronage.

[93] *WS* 19/2, p. 469.

[94] *WS* 7/2, p. 192; *PS* 3, p. 118.

[95] This is the number of wards in all editions of the 'Record' at the end of ch. 5. *WS* 8, p. 194 makes the number 323. *PS* 4, p. 132; 16, p. 616; and *WSa* 18, p. 428, all give 320. Ho Ping-ti (1966, pp. 66–70) shows that of these three figures 220 is the only one consistent with the known dimensions of the wards and the inner and outer walls of Loyang. Su Pai (1978/2), p. 51 n. 1, also accepts 220.

[96] In 484 it was argued that ten men could built 1 *pu* of northern frontier wall in a day (*WS* 54, pp. 1201–2); the builders of walls for Loyang's wards had a daily quota one-fifth shorter. However, each length of the massive Han city walls of Loyang had required hundreds of times as much labour. (Ho Ping-ti (1966), pp. 78–80.)

[97] *WS* 8, p. 195; *TCTC* 145, p. 4527.

Chapter 4

Flawed prosperity

Loyang enjoyed twenty or so years of peace and prosperity before the neglected northern garrisons began to mutiny in 523. Five years later Erhchu Jung led his heavy cavalry across the Yellow River and massacred the élite of the court and the city. After another six years Loyang was abandoned. Before dwelling on the melancholy decline and death of the great city, it is worth looking at the flawed magnificence of its splendour.

As the whole nature of the city was determined by the court we must focus in this chapter mainly on palace politics between the death of Kao-tsu in 499 and the Ho-yin massacre of 528. Some of Kao-tsu's policies and methods of imposing them may have been ill considered; but during his reign, both in the earlier part when the dowager Feng held power, and later, when he asserted his own will, the state was under firm and effective control from the centre. In pushing through their thoroughgoing reform measures they had imposed great strains on the political structure of the state, particularly by alienating many of the military. Had Kao-tsu enjoyed another twenty or thirty years of vigorous life he might have achieved his dream of uniting the whole of China under a strong, centralized, aristocratic, sinified regime ruling at Loyang, using the martial prowess of the northern peoples from which his dynasty had sprung while at the same time depriving them of many of their privileges. But what might just have been possible for a strong and determined emperor in full control of the state machine was beyond the capacity of the weak and divided regime he left to his heirs. There was no lack of perceptive diagnoses of the state's problems in the years after his death; but at no time during the rest of the dynasty was power in the hands of a ruler firmly enough established to be able to act for the greater good of the state rather than for narrow personal or sectional interests.

When Kao-tsu's young heir Shih-tsung/Hsüan-wu-ti came to the throne his father had thoughtfully arranged for his empress Feng to be made to kill herself after his death to save the boy from being inflicted with a domineering dowager empress as he had been.[1] The new emperor was entrusted to a regency council dominated by princes Hsieh of P'eng-ch'eng and Hsi of Hsien-yang,[2] when a better choice might have been prince Ch'eng of Jen-ch'eng, who seems to have been the most wise politically of the royal princes. Rivalries within the imperial clan became even more acute when the young emperor formally took power into his own hands in 501.[3] Prince Hsi of Hsien-yang, a half-brother of Kao-tsu's, was alarmed at the influence of the emperor's humbly born advisers and he attempted a rising that was crushed.[4] It was a bloody and inauspicious beginning to the new emperor's reign.

The men to whom Shih-tsung turned belonged to the category known to conventional historiography as 'favourites' (*en-hsing*): officials in his personal service who did not belong to the great aristocratic families or the higher ranks of the bureaucracy or the army and were felt by their detractors to have won their advancement by sycophancy. Such men as Wang Chung-hsing, K'ou Meng, Chao Hsiu, and Ju Hao displaced both Hsienpei and Han aristocrats in the emperor's confidence, building themselves vast fortunes in the process.[5] They were men of the palace, and the growth of their influence was regarded by the conservative Sung historian Ssuma Kuang as marking the beginning of the dynasty's political decline.[6] While the rewards of imperial favour could be very great, jealous rivals were always watching for a chance to strike down those who depended on nothing more substantial than their master's confidence. The unsuccessful rebellion of prince Hsi of Hsien-yang was followed in 503 by the downfall and death of Chao Hsiu, one of the 'favourites' who had profited from the

---

[1] *WSa* 13, p. 334; *PS* 13, pp. 500–1.
[2] *WS* 21/2, pp. 575–6; 21/1, p. 537.
[3] *WS* 8, p. 193; *TCTC* 144, pp. 4482–4.
[4] *WS* 8, p. 193; 21/1, pp. 538–9; *TCTC* 144, pp. 4487–8; *Nan Ch'i shu* 57, p. 999.
[5] For hostile biographical notes on the first four of these see *WS* 93, pp. 1996–2002.
[6] *TCTC* 144, p. 4483.

prince's fall.[7] The next year Ju Hao and another prince, prince Hsiang of Pei-hai, lost both royal favour and their lives.[8] The new palace favourite, who had engineered their fall, was a Korean, Kao Chao, the emperor's maternal uncle, and he lasted until the end of the reign. As a foreigner and a relative of the imperial house through marriage Kao was doubly objectionable to later historians. According to an extremely hostile biographical sketch, he stopped at nothing in his determination to keep power.[9] It was even rumoured that he and the empress Kao brought about the death of one of the emperor's sons as well as of an empress of the Yü (originally Wanniuyü) clan in order to prevent the emergence of a rival clique of imperial in-laws. Although he was able to get a niece of his made empress in her place, the only son she produced died young.[10]

Another royal consort, a woman of the powerful Han-Chinese Hu family from Lin-ching in the north-west, had produced a boy, disregarding advice to lose the child lest she receive the usual Northern Wei treatment for mothers of heirs to the throne—death. She succeeded in keeping both him and herself alive.[11] How she did this we do not know, but it shows that by the time of her husband's fatal illness in the first month of 515 she had mastered the deadly game of palace politics.

The heir, a boy of four, later known as Su-tsung/Hsiao-ming-ti, was put on the throne in a hasty, midnight ceremony almost as soon as his father had expired.[12] He began his reign with inauspicious sobs. The empress Kao and Kao Chao, who was far from the capital leading an expeditionary force to the attempted conquest of Szechuan, had deliberately not been consulted. The officials who carried out this rapid move to

---

[7] *WS* 93, pp. 1999–2000; *TCTC* 145, pp. 4535–6.

[8] *WS* 21/1, pp. 561–3.

[9] *WSa* 83/2, pp. 1829–31; *PS* 80, pp. 2684–6.

[10] *WSa* 13, pp. 336–7; *PS* 13, p. 502; *TCTC* 146, p. 4575.

[11] On her family see *WSa* 83/2, pp. 1833 ff., after *PS* 80, pp. 2689–90. The biography of her in *WSa* 13, pp. 337–40, is from *PS* 13, pp. 503–6. Her personality pervades the 'Record'. See also the study by Jennifer Holmgren (1978).

[12] On the coup see *WS* 31, pp. 742–3; 67, p. 1491; *WSa* 83/2, pp. 1830–1; *PS* 80, pp. 2685–6.

forestall any Kao plot to enthrone some prince of the blood who would be amenable to them were a mixed group. Ts'ui Kuang, originally one of Kao-tsu's bright young men from a family fallen on hard times since the conquest of Shantung, was now an elder statesman.[13] Yü Chung, a member of the Wanniuyü clan whose great-grandfather Yü Li-ti had conquered Loyang for the Wei in 423, had long served at court and had a personal reason for hating the Kao family: the late empress Yü had been his sister.[14] Hou Kang, also of non-Han origin, rose to high office in the palace guard from being a waiter at the royal table:[15] his control of the security forces was vital to the success of the plan. Hou Kang, Yü Chung, and Ts'ui Kuang also helped to foil the attempt of the dowager empress Kao to have her rival Hu killed off, a scheme in which the eunuch Liu T'eng played a vital part by warning Hou Kang of the danger and hiding the lady Hu away until it was passed,[16] thus opening the way for a period of strong eunuch influence in the court and the city.

During the months that followed the new emperor's mother, the lady Hu, took advantage of a situation in which nobody else had an unquestionable claim to political dominance in order to take power for herself. For a short time it looked as though Yü Chung, one of the leaders of the 515 coup, might succeed in establishing his own domination. He lost no time in installing the weak prince Yung of Kao-yang as regent, with prince Ch'eng of Jen-ch'eng as controller of the Chancellery.[17] In the second month of the year Kao Chao returned to the capital to be granted the favour of suicide after he had been strangled by the palace guards.[18] Within days his niece, the dowager empress Kao, was forced to become a nun and leave the palace for the Yao-kuang Convent.[19]

---

[13] See n. 52 to ch. 2 of the 'Record'.

[14] Yao Wei-yüan (1962), pp. 54–6; biography, *WS* 31, pp. 741–7.

[15] *WS* 93, pp. 2004–6.

[16] On the scheme to save the Lady Hu see *TCTC* 148, p. 4612; on Liu see *WS* 94, pp. 2027–8, and ch. 1 of the 'Record'.

[17] *WS* 9, p. 221; 31, p. 742. On prince Yung see *WS* 21/1, pp. 552–7. By trimming he survived until the Ho-yin slaughter. On his extravagance see ch. 3 of the 'Record'.

[18] *WSa* 83/2, p. 1831; *PS* 80, p. 2685; *WS* 9, p. 221.

[19] *WS* 9, p. 221; *WSa* 13, p. 337; *PS* 13, p. 506.

Shortly before this the lady Hu had been raised to the rank of *huang t'ai fei*, dowager consort. In the eighth month she obtained for herself the highest rank possible at that stage, becoming empress dowager;[20] this followed an attempt by the aristocratic Han officials P'ei Chih, Kuo Tso, and others, to mount a coup against Yü Chung—a move largely inspired by resentment that a mere 'barbarian' should outrank Han aristocrats—that was ruthlessly put down.[21] There is no doubt that Yü Chung was one of those behind the request from the corps of officials that Hu should take power herself, which she did formally in the ninth month.[22]

Thus began the empress dowager Hu's first spell of personal rule, five years that coincided with the beginning of the decade or so that was the most prosperous and magnificent of Northern Wei Loyang's short life. This was the time when the drastic administrative changes of the *t'ai-ho* period were perhaps yielding their greatest benefits to the state as they had not yet been undone by the decay of central control and Confucian morality. The highly productive agriculture of the north-China plain yielded handsome surpluses in grain and cloth which filled the public and private granaries and storehouses of the city's rulers. The country knew a few years of comparative peace between the virtual abandonment from about 516 onwards of serious efforts to destroy the Liang state in the south—for a while the profits of trade replaced the losses of war—and the outbreak of mutinies in the north. In Yang Hsüan-chih's words, 'in those days the state was rich and its treasuries and storehouses filled to overflowing' and 'incalculable quantities of coins and silk were piled in the open.' The dowager could think of nothing better to do with some of this public wealth than to lavish it on her officials, who were allowed to carry away as much as they liked.[23] Some of the rest was used by her for the building of monasteries and nunneries of unusual magnificence, and for the carving of cave-temples which still adorn the outskirts of Loyang.

[20] *WS* 9, pp. 221–2.
[21] *WS* 9, p. 222; 64, p. 1426; 71, pp. 1570–1.
[22] *WS* 9, p. 222.
[23] 'Record', ch. 4, followed by *TCTC* 149, p. 4646. Another version of the story is in her *PS* 13 and *WSa* 13 biography.

There was also immense private wealth in the hands of royal princes, eunuchs, other palace favourites, some of the aristocracy, and the leading merchants. This can be attributed in part to the dowager's generosity to her supporters (or connivance in their corrupt practices); but to a much greater extent it was the product of the *t'ai-ho* reforms, which ensured that the mighty were allocated all the land their slaves and dependents could use. They also used their power to seize more sources of wealth for themselves. How else could the immense establishments described by Yang Hsüan-chih, particularly in the aristocratic suburbs to the west of the inner city wall known as the 'Princes' Quarter', have been supported? Yang, whose accounts of them are written with evident admiration, look back with regret on the time when

all within the seas was peaceful, everywhere men followed their occupations, historical records were all full of good events, and there were no natural disasters. The common people prospered and rich harvests brought joy to the masses. Widows and unmarried men did not have to know the taste of dogs' and pigs' food;orphans did not have to dress like oxen or horses. Princes and nobles of the imperial clan, princesses and the emperor's relations through marriage seized for themselves the wealth of mountains and seas as well as the bounty of forest and rivers. They competed in building gardens and mansions, boasting to each other of their achievements . . .[24]

His description of the style in which the rich, particularly the richest princes, lived almost beggar belief. Prince Yung of Kao-yang, who became regent in 520, had a residence which rivalled the imperial palace. 'His wealth embraced mountains and seas'; and it may well be true that 'no prince from Han and Chin times onwards was his equal in extravagance.' When he rode out the imperial highway was cleared by horsemen for his huge procession of musicians and attendants carrying the insignia of his rank. He spent tens of thousands of cash on a single meal, and had musicians play in turns all through the day and the night.[25] Prince I of Ch'ing-ho, the most powerful of the princes from 515 till his murder in 520, had a mansion even more splendid, with a tower in the corner of his fine

[24] 'Record', ch. 4.
[25] 'Record', ch. 3.

gardens from which you could see the whole of the capital.[26] Prince Shen of Ho-chien, said to be the richest of the royal princes, competed in extravagance not only with his contemporaries but also with the richest men of Chin-dynasty Loyang. As he put it, 'Although he was a commoner, Shih Ch'ung of the Chin dressed in clothes made from the feathers on pheasants' heads and the fur of foxes' armpits. The eggs he ate were painted and his firewood was carved. So why shouldn't I, a heavenly prince of the Great Wei, be extravagant?' Even his brother princes envied him the Persian horses and rare cups and bowls in gold, silver, crystal, agate, glass, and red jade he imported from the West, and his storehouses full of textiles of every kind and of money.[27]

Liu T'eng, the eunuch who was one of Hu's leading supporters during her first period of personal rule until he helped to end it in 520, also lived in royal style. His house filled a whole ward of the inner city and was modelled on the imperial palace itself; it was said to exceed in magnificence even the houses of the imperial princes.[28] His wealth was derived from 'skinning the Six Garrisons [of the northern frontier] and engaging in frontier trade [probably with the prosperous south], bringing in huge profits every year'.[29] Liu was not the only rich eunuch: during the dowager Hu's years of power 'the eunuchs were very much in her favour and their households grew extremely wealthy', to the disgust of the regular bureaucracy.[30] The dowager's relations also prospered, as Yang observed in the passage quoted just now; and they too put some of their new-found wealth into the building of Buddhist institutions.[31]

More of the city's datable Buddhist monasteries and nunneries which were originally planned as religious institutions (rather than being secular mansions turned into temples after their owners deaths) were built during this decade than in any

---

[26] 'Record', ch. 4.
[27] Ibid.
[28] 'Record', ch. 1.
[29] *WS* 94, p. 2028.
[30] 'Record', ch. 1.
[31] e.g. one of the Ch'in T'ai-shang monasteries ('Record', ch. 3), and the Hu-t'ung Convent ('Record', ch. 1).

other. According to a memorial of 518, Kao-tsu's strict limit of one monastery (the Yung-ning)[32] within the inner walls of the city and one nunnery within the outer walls still had effect in the first years of his son's reign. From 506 it began to be relaxed; from 509 it virtually ceased to apply; and ten years later over 500 monasteries and nunneries were said to take up a third of all the area within the city, not counting sites designated for such purposes but not yet built up.[33] No doubt this contrast is exaggerated—temples were built outside the inner wall of Loyang before 506—but there can be no mistaking the repeated descriptions of huge and splendid monasteries and nunneries dating from the dowager's years of power that are to be found throughout Yang Hsüan-chih's book.

This was the time when the most spectacular structure of the city, the Yung-ning Pagoda, which by the most sober accounts rose 400 Northern Wei feet, with in addition a 90-foot high mast above it (making a total of 145 metres), was erected.[34] South of the inner city wall the dowager Hu and a relative founded two monasteries to bring blessings to her late father that each had pagodas '500 feet high' and their inmates were supported in grand style.[35] Yet another of the dowager's spectacular pagodas was constructed in the grounds of Ching-ming Monastery between 520 and 525.[36] She also had a large monastery, the Ch'in T'ai-shang-chün, built for her mother's benefit.[37] The eunuchs also celebrated their wealth and power by building convents and monasteries to perpetuate their collective or individual glory: of the six they are known to have

[32] 'Record', ch. 1, and n. 1 thereto.

[33] So it was argued in 518 (*WS* 114, pp. 3044–5). However, though we only know of the Yung-ning being built in the inner city before 506, the 'Record' lists others in the suburbs that were definitely founded by then, including the Cheng-shih (ch. 2); Ching-ming, Pao-te, and Cheng-chüeh (ch. 3); and Ling-hsien (ch. 4). On this question see Shigenoi in Ocho Enichi, ed. (1970), pp. 420–1. (He also dates the Lung-hua and Chiu-sheng to before 506, but this is doubtful; and it is most unlikely that the Ning-yüan was built then as its founder, the eunuch Chia Ts'an, was powerful and wealthy much later.)

[34] 'Record', ch. 1. Yang makes it over twice as high, which strains belief.

[35] 'Record', ch. 3.

[36] Ibid.

[37] 'Record', ch. 2.

founded,[38] most were probably built in this period. Officials built with less enthusiasm.[39] The imperial princes, however, did it with more style: prince I of Ch'ing-ho endowed three establishments that were among the capital's finest;[40] prince Huai of Kuang-p'ing, who died in 517, gave two splendid houses, perhaps posthumously.[41] No doubt the great majority of the temples were humble: even young butchers got together in threes and fives to found little temples amid the noise and stench of the slaughter-house.[42] Certainly merchants prospered during these years: not only the remarkable builder of a business empire, Liu Pao, but also many other craftsmen, merchants, and men of property who lived around the great western market and were now so rich that they flouted the sumptuary regulations denying them the right to wear gold, silver, or embroidered silk issued between 518 and 520.[43]

While this was happening in the capital itself, magnificent cave temples were being carved outside the city limits. In the Yi-ch'üeh (Lungmen) gorges to the south of Loyang the city's faithful had been dedicating statues of various sizes since before it was made capital; and there is no great variation in the rate at which datable inscriptions were carved in the first three decades of the sixth century. Between 500 and 523 the state managed to devote 802,366 work-days of corvée labour to the carving of huge cave-temples to the glory of Shih-tsung's mother and Shih-tsung himself.[44] The many humble images and inscriptions in the Lung-men caves are rather more informative about the religious feelings of the clergy and laity of Loyang than are Yang's descriptions of the splendours of the

[38] The Ch'ang-ch'iu and Chao-yi (ch. 1); the Wei-ch'ang and Ching-hsing (ch. 2); the Wang Tien-yü (ch. 4); and Ning-hsüan (ch. 5).

[39] Shigenoi (op. cit., p. 428) attributes eight foundations to officials; of which some were posthumous gifts after the Ho-yin massacre, at least one was from the Erhchu, and at least two date from before this decade.

[40] The Ch'ung-chüeh and Jung-chüeh (ch. 4) and the Ching-lo (ch. 1). The first of these was his own house, given after his death.

[41] They became the P'ing-teng (ch. 2) and Ta-chüeh (ch. 4).

[42] *WS* 114, pp. 304–5.

[43] On Liu and other traders, see ch. 4 of the 'Record'. Sumptuary regulations: *WS* 21/1, p. 556.

[44] See the table on p. 372 of Tsukamoto (1942). On these remarkable caves see the end of ch. 5 of the 'Record' and the references in n. 50 to it.

great monasteries and convents; but as they have less to tell us about the city, this is not the place to discuss them.

It is very likely that four of the five cave-temples at Hsiao-p'ing Ford, opposite the modern town of Kunghsien on the finger of land between the Lo and Yellow rivers, were built on the dowager Hu's orders. They are thought on stylistic grounds to have been begun around 517. Cave-temple I was finished around 523, II was uncompleted, and III and IV were finished in or about 528. These dates correspond so closely with the dowager's period of power, and the donor shown among the bas-reliefs on the walls is so clearly a royal lady, that these impressive excavations may be regarded as the principal surviving relics of the dowager Hu's building programme.[45]

But the prosperity was shallowly based, being founded not on the capital's own economic activity, but on the success of the state and its leading subjects in diverting wealth from the countryside to Loyang, through public tax and forced labour, through the private holding of land, slaves, and other sources of wealth by its richest members, and through the corruption of many of the officials.

It is striking that the Han-Chinese peasantry of the north-China plain, free, semi-servile, and enslaved, did not rise against Loyang except in the years 515 to 517, when the great millenarian Ta-sheng (Mahāyāna) rebellion flared up in Hopei. This was an uprising in which monks broke away from the state-controlled church and joined with peasants to proclaim the beginning of a new *kalpa* with the slogan, 'A new Buddha is born: Away with all the old demons.' Progressive stages of bodhisattva-hood were awarded according to the number of enemies killed; and wherever the rebels went they destroyed official monasteries and nunneries, slaughtering their inmates. A hundred thousand horse and foot were needed to put them down in Chi-chou in 515, and there were enough survivors to rise again in 517.[46]

As had generally happened for the previous 700 years, what

[45] See the introduction to the album by the Ho-nang-sheng wen-hua-chü wen-wu kung-tso-tui (1963), for dating, and the association with the dowager, who is probably represented in pls. 15 and 205.

[46] On this rebellion see the excellent study in Tsukamoto (1942), pp. 269–84.

drove peasants to the desperate measure of rebellion was not regular demands for taxes and local labour but long periods of corvée and military service away from home. During the last century of the Northern Wei the cause of unrest lay in the protracted campaigns against the Ch'i regime and its Liang successor in the south, involving an enormous waste of life, labour, and material. With comparative peace from late 516 onwards, the burden of the peasantry was reduced. They may not have liked Loyang, but they do not appear to have resisted it after 517. There was a short-lived rebellion in the hills to the south and the east of the city by the *yao-tsei* (religious rebel) Li Hung in 528, but he seems to have been a Man tribal chieftain, not an ordinary peasant.[47] Peasant opposition was not, as far as we can tell, a major factor in the city's agony and end. The causes of the city's fall must be sought elsewhere. The external ones will be examined in the next chapter; our concern here is with the city itself.

In the first place, the attempt to create a united, multi-racial aristocratic ruling class with a shared Confucian culture had enjoyed only limited success. Certainly such a culture did flourish in some circles in Loyang: this is the aspect of the city on which Yang dwells with most loving attention and undisguised admiration. He clearly appreciated the courage of men willing to speak their minds at the risk of their lives, such as Liu Hsüan-ming who was beheaded for opposing the will of the empress dowager;[48] those who encouraged and helped the emperor Chuang-ti to kill Erhchu Jung, such as Hsün Chi, Wen Tzu-sheng, and prince Hui of Ch'eng-yang;[49] or Liu Chi-ming, who dared to berate Erhchu Shih-lung in 531.[50] He also approved of scholars, particularly if, like Ch'ang Ching, they were also incorrupt and therefore poor;[51] and he shared the general upper-class admiration for the Yang family which supposedly achieved the ideal of an extended family living

[47] *WS* 44, p. 1004; 54, p. 1475.
[48] 'Record', ch. 2, and n. 16 thereto.
[49] On whom see 'Record', ch. 4, and n. 6 thereto.
[50] 'Record', ch. 2, and n. 73 thereto.
[51] 'Record', chs. 1 and 2, and n. 14 to ch. 1. Among other scholars Yang praised were Liu Pai-t'ou and Hsing Tzu-ts'ai.

together in ordered harmony.[52] No doubt such men served the state well, putting the public good as they saw it before their personal interests. But honest officials were unusual enough to be worth remarking on. It was not they who set Loyang's style, but the princes, eunuchs, and other officials who took advantage of their precarious hold on power or favour to grab and spend as much wealth as they could.

Chinese high culture also had serious drawbacks as a set of values for drawing together the Han and the Hsienpei when pride of birh played so large a part in it, and when it was so objectionable to most of the non-Hans in the Wei state. Kao-tsu's belief in the value of a good pedigree may have pleased the few families deemed to be the most distinguished; but among the Han Chinese it narrowly restricted the supply of talent available to the regular public service, so that when the empress dowager, for example, picked her own administrators from among the eunuchs and lower officials they could not be expected to feel any identification with a system from which they were excluded by birth. Kao-tsu's infatuation with Han-Chinese aristocracy may not have done the state much harm in his own time, but to his successors it was a terrible, perhaps even fatal, legacy. There could be no *carrière ouverte aux talents* even for most of the literate minority of the Han Chinese; and by turning the majority of the non-Hans into subjects of the second, third, fourth, fifth, or even lower classes the Northern Wei rulers were to alienate them from the polity they had once thought of as their own.

The most serious consequences of this were to develop in the north; but even in Loyang members of the capital's guard armies—men of the Hsienpei military families settled in and around Loyang by Kao-tsu—were infuriated by the proposal made by the Han official Chang Chung-yü that the grading system be tightened up to exclude all soldiers from posts carrying the higher, 'pure' grades (*ch'ing-p'in*). In the second month of 519 placards appeared in the city's streets calling on the soldiery to exterminate the family of the offending

---

[52] On this family see ch. 2 of the 'Record' and pp. 275–89 of Tanigawa Michio's 1970 article. The family was not perfect, even by Confucian standards: Yang Ch'un was convicted of illegally cultivating 3,400 *mu* of state pasture land and for irregularly conscripting forced labour to build monasteries. (*WS* 58, pp. 1286–7).

bureaucrat. About 1,000 rioters gathered, and after hurling abuse, tiles, and stones at the Chancellery they burned down the Chang house, fatally wounding Chung-yü's father and killing his brother. Although eight guardsmen were executed as ringleaders, most of the rioters were amnestied. Some observers regarded this as a sign of weakness which heralded the state's decline; and the soldiers won the right to high office.[53] Among them was the man who was later to order the city's end.

Apart from the princes of the blood, who appear with few exceptions to have been thoroughly assimilated into Han-Chinese culture, and a small number of other families designated as aristocratic in Kao-tsu's time,[54] few Hsienpei can be detected among the élite of Loyang society as portrayed by Yang Hsüan-chih. And those who did have a place within the charmed circle included few models of devotion to public duty. True, there was prince Ch'eng of Jen-ch'eng, whose memorials submitted over three decades show him to have been a perceptive analyst of the state's problems; but whether the well-read and elegant princes Yü of Lin-huai and Lüeh of Tung-p'ing or the Taoistically inclined prince Ching-hao of Ch'en-liu contributed much to the general well-being is open to doubt.[55] Moreover the aspects of Han-Chinese culture that seemed to appeal most to the powerful were its material ones, just as much of the Buddhism in Loyang seems to have been worldly. For all the shortcomings of the Confucian approach to government and political morality, there can be little doubt that the prevailing values of Loyang in its years of prosperity were far worse for the state than Confucian ones would have been, as can be seen by returning to the story of palace politics.

The dowager's first period of personal rule was brought to an end in 520 as unscrupulously as it had begun, when Liu T'eng, her most trusted eunuch, joined with her younger sister's husband Yüan Yi, a distant member of the imperial clan to whom she had given command of the capital's armies, to end her regency and have her put under house arrest in a remote

[53] *WS* 9, pp. 228–9; 64, pp. 1432–3; *TT* 14, pp. 79–80.
[54] For the criteria see *WS* 113, pp. 3014–15.
[55] On these princes see ch. 4 of the 'Record' and its notes.

part of the palace compound. The coup was also aimed at the dowager's leading princely ally (and, it was said, her lover), the regent prince I of Ch'ing-ho, who was felt by Yüan Yi and Liu T'eng to be threatening their position, for which the regent paid with his life, falsely charged with plotting to seize the throne for himself.[56] The new joint regents were prince Yung of Kao-yang (who seems to have been more interested in the splendid trappings and opportunities for enrichment of high office than in the government of the state), and Yüan Yi, who held the real power, and for the next five years was dictator of Loyang, in association with Liu T'eng until Liu's death in 523, and by himself thereafter. As usual the princes were divided. Yüan Yi had the support not only of the prince of Kao-yang, but also of prince Yüeh of Ju-nan, a half-brother of the murdered prince of Ch'ing-ho who had evidently not forgiven the empress dowager for investigating and threatening to punish him for the savage beatings he inflicted on his wife.[57] Other princes tried to resist the coup, including two who rose in unsuccessful rebellion at Yeh.[58]

To judge from the way Yang Hsüan-chih and other contemporaries write about the Yüan Yi/Liu T'eng faction and its opponents, the years from 520 to 525 saw misrule and corruption rather worse than the dowager's.[59] Polite opinion evidently disapproved of the coup and the killing of several princes; and this was the time in which things went seriously wrong for the Wei state. Polite opinion may also have resented Yi's good relations with the officers of the capital and the frontier. Not that this kept the military happy. When one garrison rose in revolt in 523 after a Joujan raid, mutiny spread right along the frontier marches of the north and west. The frontier risings and their consequences will be examined in the next chapter; suffice it to say here that Yüan Yi's dictatorship cannot be held any more respohsible for provoking them than the previous regimes in the capital. While the north and west

---

[56] On the coup see ch. 1 of the 'Record'; *WS* 16, p. 404; 94, pp. 2027–8; *WSa* 13, p. 339; *PS* 13, p. 504. On Yüan Yi see also n. 82 to ch. 1 below.

[57] See n. 94 to ch. 1 of the 'Record'.

[58] See ch. 4 of the 'Record' and n. 56 to it.

[59] e.g. *WS* 16, p. 405; 94, p. 2028.

fell into chaos, the previously quiescent southern front began to crumble as the Liang armies put pressure on their weakened rivals; and the Man tribesmen in the hills south of the capital, never reconciled to Chinese rule, took their chance to raid the imperial domain. Armies and commanders were dispatched from Loyang to the various fronts, nearly all to meet with failure and defeat.[60]

It was in these inauspicious circumstances that the empress dowager succeeded in returning to power. Over the years Yüan Yi became careless, feeling no doubt that his command of the capital's guard armies and control of the administrative machine, combined with the other commands held by his younger brother, made him invulnerable. Thus it was that the dowager Hu managed to re-establish contact with her son, the boy emperor Su-tsung/Hsiao-ming-ti. In the autumn of 524 she told him that as she was being kept apart from him she would withdraw from the world and live as a nun. This threat made the emperor determined to get rid of Yüan Yi when he could; and he used his mother's declared intention (which, if carried out, would have been a humiliating insult to the dictator) to win Yüan Yi's agreement to unrestricted contact between mother and son. The dowager next detached the prince of Kao-yang from Yüan Yi, then used the defection of one of Yi's protégés to Liang to intimidate him into surrendering his command of the capital's armies. The propaganda campaign against Yüan Yi was helped along by the circulation among princes and officials of a violently abusive letter sent from exile by the son of a prince who had died resisting Yüan Yi's coup. The next step was to relieve him of his most important civil office and thus his control over the administration; the day after this the dowager formally resumed power at court. When reports came in that Yüan Yi and others were planning a co-ordinated series of risings involving a new rebellion by former rebels from the northern frontier, attacks on county towns near the capital, and Man raids through the gorges of the Yi river—these charges are reported by a source that is generally hostile to Yüan Yi—the dowager ordered him

---

[60] The troubles of Yüan Yi's last years are well recounted in *TCTC* 149–50; see also the next chapter.

to kill himself, or so the *Wei shu* has it; we may prefer the bald statement by Yang that he was executed.[61]

So began the dowager Hu's second spell of power. Her return had been brilliantly managed as she first threw her opponent off balance, then disarmed him, and finally destroyed him, when her own weapons had been, to begin with, only her cunning and a boy of fourteen. Unfortunately she did not show comparable skill in her handling of the nation's affairs. The rebellions could not be defeated or even contained by the armies that remained loyal to the throne. By 527 the rebels from the northern garrisons controlled virtually the whole of what is now Hopei province, and even the T'ungkuan pass leading to the Wei valley was lost for a while. The dowager Hu contributed to disaster by denying her one successful general, prince Yüan of Kuang-yang, the unified command needed to recover Hopei for fear he would grow too powerful.

Inside the city euphoria gave place to gloom. In 525 the dowager Hu had ordered a halving of taxes;[62] the following year the court tried to raise too much too late. Grain taxes were demanded for six years in advance, and—apparently for the first time—taxes were levied on land in the domain as well as on shoppers and stall-holders in the markets. Discontent was widespread, and some rather trivial economies were made; but with taxable territories rapidly disappearing these measures fell short of meeting the needs of the crisis.[63] Just then the court threw away one of its few remaining reliable sources of income, abolishing the salt tax which was worth 300,000 bolts of cloth each year.[64]

While the state crumbled, court intrigue continued unabated. During her second period of power the dowager relied on an external coalition of princes and high officials and an internal clique of palace 'favourites'. The former had been on the whole more hostile to Yüan Yi than to her; and the latter she found more dependable and more enjoyable than eunuchs,

[61] *WS* 9, p. 240; 16, pp. 405–8; 'Record', ch. 1.
[62] *WS* 9, p. 241; *TPYL* 103, p. 496.
[63] *WS* 110, pp. 2860–1.
[64] *WSa* 25, p. 648; *PS* 22, p. 814.

whom she had not forgiven for their betrayal in 520. Liu
T'eng's remains were exhumed and mutilated.[65] Of her
'favourites' the two best known are Hsü Ho, an able technocrat
who had risen through ability rather than birth but was
despised by the nobility as a mere pen-pusher (a *pi tao hsiao ts'ai*
in the words of one member of the royal clan),[66] and Cheng
Yen, a lover of the dowager's who had great influence during
her last years and ran the affairs of state with Hsü Ho.[67] They
both held appointments as assistant secretaries (*she-jen*), positions of only middling rank that gave their holders great
scope for developing their personal power as they were in effect
private secretaries to the monarch, or in this case to the
dowager.[68] Of the various princes who co-operated with the
dowager in these years, prince Hui of Ch'eng-yang was the one
most closely associated with her personal rule.[69]

By 528 the dowager's clique was facing a threat more
immediate, perhaps, than the great rebellion: the emperor,
now eighteen, was showing signs of wanting to rule and to be
rid of Hsü Ho and Cheng Yen. Never one to let scruples get in
her way, the dowager let it be arranged that her tiresome son
should meet with a sudden and early death, probably through
poison. He left behind him a nine-month-old daughter whom
the dowager had announced to the world as a boy at birth. At
first she put the baby on the throne, only to replace her a few
days later with a two-year-old great-grandson of Kao-tsu. Her
intention must have been to carry on ruling for many more
years, enjoying the even more exalted title of 'grand dowager'.[70] But within two months she and her new infant
protégé were hurled into the muddy waters of the Yellow
River.

[65] 'Record', ch. 1.
[66] *WSa* 19/2, p. 483; *PS* 18, p. 664.
[67] On Hsü and Cheng see the hostile accounts in *WS* 93, pp. 2007–9.
[68] On this vital post see Cheng Ch'in-jen (1965), pp. 95–115.
[69] For an invective against prince Hui's pettiness in high office see *WSa* 18, pp. 431–3, and *PS* 16, pp. 619–20.
[70] *WS* 9, p. 248; 74, p. 1646; 93, p. 2007; *WSa* 13, p. 340; *PS* 13, p. 505.

Chapter 5

Things fall apart

The investigation of Loyang's fall leads from the veiled ruthlessness of court intrigue back to the open violence of the frontier. After 528 the fate of Loyang was no longer primarily determined by palace politics; instead, the city was a helpless prize to be won, lost, and finally destroyed as rival military factions contended for supremacy.

This last period in the city's life is the one to which Yang Hsüan-chih most often returns in his anecdotes, nowhere more effectively than in the long list of disasters associated with the great Yung-ning Monastery whose towering pagoda was one of the world's wonders.[1] As Yang was writing a topographical account of the capital, not a history of the frontier and the military campaigns of those years, and as he also assumed that his readers were generally familiar with the unhappy story of the dying years of the dynasty, we must supply some of what he took for granted. It is also necessary to fill in some of the omissions he had to make because he wrote when the military were all-powerful and on the point of pushing the last Wei emperor off the throne.

The northern frontier's alienation from the Northern Wei state had worsened since Kao-tsu's reforms. Those Hsienpei who moved south seem to have been fairly successfully transplanted, as is suggested by both positive evidence, such as their willingness to fight against northerners during the troubles after 523, and by such negative signs as their loss of the martial qualities on which the whole Wei system was based.

The north, however, lost much and gained little by the way the state was changing. After Kao-tsu's death there was never again a ruler in Loyang willing to take on the trouble and expense of maintaining a well-run army on the frontier. To

[1] 'Record', ch. 1.

some extent this can be attributed to the comparative peace in the north after 485, when Wei diplomacy exploited dissension among the Joujan so skilfully that the full weight of Joujan power was not thrown at the frontier for nearly twenty years.[2] But when at last they struck deep into the Heng and Tai area of northern Shansi in 504, the Wei response was not the massive retaliatory expedition across the Gobi that had been characteristic of Wei strategy before Kao-tsu's reign, but the passive and labour-intensive method of fortifying a series of strongpoints along the frontier, a solution to the problem that would have been rejected in the years of the dynasty's vigour as both ineffective and unworthy of a warrior people. But the advocate of the defence works, himself a veteran Hsienpei general, argued that only they would enable Chinese grain-eating, silk-clad village-dwellers to withstand the onslaught of the incomparably tougher barbarians who dressed in wool and drank blood.[3] An earlier proposal for a wall made in 484 had met with Kao-tsu's approval, but it does not seem to have been built.[4] Once the Joujan grew strong again from 516 onwards the loss of fighting power on the Wei side became very serious.

The problems of the northern frontier went deep.[5] To protect the settled areas of Shansi and the rest of north China a defence line had to be far enough north to prevent attackers from building up the strength of their horses in the grazing lands south of the desert belt, where they could move freely close to the Wei frontier, and strike without warning. An

---

[2] On Joujan–Wei relations since the last years of the P'ing-ch'eng era see *Jou-jan tzu-liao chi-lu*, pp. 20–33 and 167–231; and Uchida Gimpu (1975), pp. 368–89.

[3] *WS* 41, pp. 927–8.

[4] *WS* 54, pp. 1200–2. This is included in *TCTC* 136, pp. 4262–3, with the events of 484.

[5] On the origins and nature of the garrisons see Chou Yi-liang's article reprinted on pp. 199–219 of his 1963 volume. The following studies of the risings are useful: T'ang Chang-ju and Huang Hui-hsien (1964); Ch'en Hsüeh-lin (1962); Hamaguchi Shigekuni on the eastern Ch'i military system in vol. 1 of his 1966 collection; Tanigawa Michio (1958, repr. in his 1971 volume); Wan Shen-nan (1964, a reply to T'ang and Huang); Yang Yao-k'un (1978); and Etienne Balazs (1953), pp. 241–50. Wang Chung-lo (1961), pp. 416–37, offers a good narrative; and *TCTC* is, as always, invaluable. The principal sources of information on northern grievances are the memorials by Yüan Huai (*WS* 41, pp. 926–8); the reports of Wei Lan-ken (*PCS* 23, p. 329); and the memorial by prince Yüan of Kuang-yang (*PS* 16, p. 617, and *WSa* 18, pp. 429–30).

attacking enemy denied these pastures had to make a long and exhausting desert crossing on the way to battle.

To this end a line of garrisons (*chen*) and smaller forts (*shu*) had been set up in the last years of the fourth century and the first half of the fifth century that ran from Yü-yi-chen (north-east of modern Ch'ihch'eng, Hopei) in the east to Wo-yeh-chen (in the Hara Narin Ula range north of Wuyuan in Inner Mongolia), then turned south-west to Kao-p'ing (Kuyuan, southern Ninghsia). A further garrison at Tunhuang was too isolated to play much part in the upheavals of the 520s. The garrisons were originally bases from which counter-strikes could be launched, rather than passive obstacles (such as a wall) that could hinder but not destroy a marauding enemy.

The logistical difficulties of maintaining large armies so far north were great. Attempts had been made during the fifth century to achieve a measure of self-sufficiency for the garrisons by organizing agriculture around them, including the creation of irrigated fields where water was available and the settling of peasant families to work the land. This policy had evidently failed by the first years of the sixth century, when there were droughts for years on end with consequent famine, which was made worse because the garrison commanders and their staff had taken all the irrigated land for themselves.[6] The shortcomings of the northern frontier commanders were remarked on by prince Ch'eng of Jen-ch'eng in or around 516,[7] who also mentioned the collusion of corrupt subordinate officials sent to the frontier as a punishment. Both prince Yüan of Kuang-yang and the stern Confucian Wei Lan-ken emphasized in 523 and 524 the demoralizing effect on the frontier officers of the loss of the prestige that army officers had enjoyed in the past and that their own kinsmen who had moved to the new capital were now enjoying.[8] Nothing brought out the northern frontier's decline in status more clearly than the adoption of the Han-Chinese practice of sending convicts there to serve out their sentences.

To the problems within the garrisons must be added both hatred of the capital and, especially since the largely successful

[6] *WS* 41, p. 926.
[7] *WS* 19/2, p. 476.
[8] *PS* 16, p. 617, and *WSa* 18, pp. 429–30; *PCS* 23, pp. 329–30.

riots of the Loyang guard armies in 519, contempt for the government's weakness. In that year an ambitious junior officer of the Huai-shuo garrison, Kao Huan, made regular visits to the capital carrying official dispatches. Once a civilian official to whom he reported ordered him to be flogged for daring to sit down to eat some meat he had been given. Instead of brooding over his welts he used all his wife's riches to build up a personal following in the garrison, explaining that when a government was so weak as to let the guard armies riot and burn, as he had seen them do with his own eyes, and not punish them afterwards, then nobody could expect to keep his wealth in the chaos that was bound to follow. As the story is told, Kao Huan spent the next few years cultivating his friends through falconry and other pursuits.[9]

The frontier was set ablaze in 523 after a great Joujan invading force had struck across the defence lines, collected 2,000 captives and animals by the hundred thousand, and withdrawn, scarcely touched by the Wei armies 100,000 strong sent across the desert belt in vain pursuit of them.[10] The garrison at Huai-huang-chen (north of Changpei in north-east Hopei) mutinied because its commander refused to issue grain to its starving personnel.[11] During the first months of 524 the mutiny spread from one garrison to the next, involving officers and men of the many different nationalities serving on the frontier; Han, Hsienpei, Hsiungnu, and Kaoch'e among them. Some garrisons stood up to a long siege by the rebels before falling. The targets at first were generally the unpopular and corrupt commanders about whom clear-headed officials had been warning the central authorities in vain. But what hope was there of redress from the capital when one of its most powerful officials, the eunuch Liu T'eng, had grown exceedingly rich by 'skinning the Six Garrisons and trading across the frontier' until his death in 523?[12] The dominant leader to emerge from the general collapse of Wei authority in the north was a descendant of the Hsiungnu royalty, P'oluhan Pa-ling, who rose in a fortress under Wo-yeh-chen, was accepted by

[9] *PCS* 1, p. 2.
[10] *Jou-jan tzu-liao chi-lu*, pp. 30–1, 213–20.
[11] *WS* 31, p. 747; *TCTC* 149, p. 4674.
[12] *WS* 94, p. 2028.

practically all the northern rebels as their overlord, and defeated the Wei forces sent against him.[13]

The revolt in the north sparked off other risings in the west, starting at the garrison of Kao-p'ing (Kuyüan, Ninghsia) where the troops mutinied in response to P'oluhan Pa-ling, made the Ch'ihle (Kaoch'e) chieftain Hu Ch'en their king, and stormed the garrison headquarters. As the troubles spread in the west, the Wei troops in the walled *chou* towns had to decide whether to remain loyal to the governors appointed from the capital, or to capture them and go over to the roving rebel groups that rode up to their walls. The most powerful of these was the force under the Ch'iang leader Moche Ta-ti, succeeded in 524 by his son Moche Nien-sheng, who proclaimed himself emperor.[14] The following year the Wei armies under Hsiao Pao-yin and Ts'ui Yen-po sent to put them down were destroyed with tens of thousands of men lost.[15]

Meanwhile the Liang regime was taking advantage of its neighbour's disarray to push forward all along the line on the southern front, an advance that might have gone all the way to the Yellow River had not a Liang prince defected to the Wei.[16] Liang agents also encouraged a reassertion of independence by the Man tribes, who held most of the high ground from northern Szechuan to the Huai valley and whose various chiefs and princes were able to take appointments and honours from either or both of the sides as it suited them. With the weakening of the capital's armies they were able to raid closer and closer to Loyang, sometimes attacking the Yi gorges. They do not, however, seem to have posed an immediate threat to the capital itself, although a decree issued in the last month of 525 listed them as the first priority among the many threats to the regime to be dealt with.[17]

[13] *WS* 9, p. 237.

[14] See the sources and studies cited in n. 5, p. 81 above; on the *ch'eng-min* see Tanigawa especially.

[15] On this campaign and the capital's feelings about it see the 'Record', ch. 4, and notes 38–42 thereto. On Moch'i Ch'ou-nu, a leading western rebel, see n. 45 to ch. 3. On Hsiao Pao-yin, see ch. 2 and n. 85 to it.

[16] *TCTC* skilfully combines information from north and south in its account of this fighting. On the defecting prince Hsiao Tsung see ch. 2 of the 'Record' with n. 5.

[17] *PS* 95, p. 3151 (*WSa* 101, pp. 2247–8); *WS* 9, p. 242. On the Man rising in 528 see ch. 4 above and especially n. 47, p. 73. On the Man in this period see *PS* 95; Chang Kuan-ying(1957); Chou Yi-liang (1963), p. 170.

In the course of 524 and 525 practically all the ethnic groups in Wei territories either joined with one or other of the rebellions mentioned above, or else raised their own standard of revolt. The Ch'ihle (Kaoch'e) horsemen were mostly with P'oluhan Pa-ling; the Ch'iang and Ti, though disunited, had driven Wei power from the west; the Man controlled the high ground in the south; and some of the Hu tribesmen in various parts of Shansi were setting up independent regimes.

The dynasty's fortunes might just have been retrieved if the remaining forces still loyal to the capital had been effectively used. It was not that the Loyang authorities lacked ruthlessness: they were prepared to call in the Joujan and the T'uyühun, the very foreign powers that the northern and western garrisons had been set up to keep out, to crush the mutineers. The T'uyühun were not particularly effective except in recovering Liang-chou in the far west; but Anakuei, the *k'o-han* (khan) of the Joujan, swept along the frontier from Wu-ch'uan-chen to Wo-yeh-chen, inflicting several defeats on the forces of P'oluhan Pa-ling, which were also attacked by some of the remaining government armies.[18] Had ruthlessness been combined with wise leadership the men of the garrisons who surrendered by the hundred thousand might have been won back to loyalty to the dynasty. But Loyang was too preoccupied with its court politics as the dowager seized back power from Yüan Yi; and she was more concerned to prevent the emergence of a strong general than to reassert the capital's control over the provinces. Her mistake was fatal, because in so doing she prepared the way for the rise of an enemy far more dangerous to herself and the capital.

The chances of pacifying the north became much smaller when the men of the garrisons rose again in late 525 and early 526.[19] Instead of keeping them in the far north after their previous mutinies as their conqueror prince Yüan of Kuang-yang had advised,[20] which would have involved moving much grain over long distances to feed them, the court had foolishly sent most of them south to the three rich agricultural *chou* of Ting, Chi and Ying in search of food. The new round of

[18] *PS* 98 p. 3265 (*WSa* 103, pp. 2302–3); *Jou-jan tzu-liao chi-lu*, pp. 3, 221–4.
[19] *WS* 9, pp. 241, 243; *TCTC* 150, pp. 4706–11.
[20] *PS* 16, p. 618.

mutinies threw up a number of leaders, who killed each other until two of them, Ko Jung and Tu Lo-chou, emerged by late 526 as supreme. The rebels now controlled most of the countryside north of the Yellow River and were taking the walled cities one by one, sometimes with the help of the troops inside them. The threat to the capital's supplies was very serious.

While Hopei was falling to the rebels a rather different situation was developing in Shansi, a region that was ethnically and politically heterogeneous. The northern part of the modern province had fallen to the Joujan, but in the centre and south a tribal grouping neither Hsienpei nor Han was the nucleus round which many who had broken with one or other rebel leader gathered.

The Erhchu (K: ńźie-tśiu) were members of an ethnic group known variously as Chieh, Chieh Hu, and Ch'i Hu.[21] (The modern readings of Chieh and Ch'i conceal medieval pronunciations that were something like Kiat or Kat.[22]) The term Hu in texts of the Six Dynasties period almost invariably refers to people of western origin (generally from India and Indianized central Asia), or with high noses and hairy faces. When the Chao dynasty, a Chieh regime that had governed or ravaged areas of north China for thirty years, was overthrown in 349 some 200,000 of the Chieh were slaughtered by their unappreciative former subjects in the capital, Yeh; and it was by these physical features that they were identified for slaughter.[23]

---

[21] In sixth-century texts 'Chieh' 羯 is used in a way that suggests it was more pejorative than 'Ch'i' when referring to the Erhchu. Compare the hostile or insulting use of 'Chieh' in the 'Record' and *PCS* 21, p. 301, with the more neutral *WS* use of 'Ch'i Hu', all referring to the Erhchu.

[22] Pulleyblank (1962), p. 246, reconstructs the earlier pronunciation of Chieh as Kiat or Kāt. Karlgren does not list the character in *Grammata Serica Recensa*, but the phonetic group to which it would presumably have belonged (no. 313) includes g'iät and γat. The character for Chieh was also used to represent the Sanskrit sounds *ka* and *kha* (see Soothill and Hodous, pp. 344 and 441–2).

Ch'i 契 is reconstructed by Karlgren as K'iei; but he reads the cognate 羯 as K'at, *gāthā* (Ch'en Yin-k'o, cited by Chou Yi-liang (1963), p. 160) and *ka* (Soothill and Hodous, p. 299). The two characters may thus have represented the same sound originally.

[23] The short and chaotic history of the Chao regime is well retold in Wang Chung-lo, pp. 159–73.

The Chieh appear to have been connected with K'angchü or K'angkuo, the Iranian people and state also known as Sogdiana,[24] and were probably a part of the Ta Yüehchih who had allied themselves with the Hsiungnu in Han times and been moved to south-east and east-central Shansi,[25] which was their homeland thereafter.

The Erhchu—the surname was taken from the name of a river—evidently strengthened their position among the Chieh after the disastrous fall of the Chao dynasty; and in 385 Erhchu Yü-chien led 1,700 'Ch'i Hu' warriors to help the rising T'opa power conquer Chin-yang (T'aiyüan) and Chung-shan. For his contribution the Erhchu leader was given a hereditary chieftainship and an enfeoffment of 300 *li* of land along the Hsiu-jung river. The Erhchu grew so wealthy that their cattle, sheep, goats, camels, and horses were divided into herds according to their colour and could be counted only by the valleyful. They provided horses and fodder whenever the Wei emperor launched a military expedition.

The Erhchu were thus outside both the sinified part of the Northern Wei state and the regular military organization of the frontier. They had not belonged to any early T'opa confederacy, but had cast their lot with the newly dominant T'opa power only in the late fourth century. Instead of being regular tax-paying subjects liable to corvée, or holders of bureaucratic or military office, the Erhchu leaders were pastoral chieftains enjoying a direct relationship with the Wei emperor (rather than the Wei state) that was remarkably close to medieval European feudal vassalage. The provision of horses and fodder for war was the due owed for the emperor's grant of a large fief of good stock-raising land within 100 kilometres of the capital at P'ing-ch'eng.[26] These feudal aristocrats of partly Iranian descent would have had many reasons to be unhappy about the move to Loyang. They were now much further from the centre of power; it must have been

---

[24] On the linguistic evidence see Pulleyblank (1962), pp. 246–8. Yao Wei-yüan (1962), pp. 355–70, assembles evidence from Chinese sources to suggest many connections with Sogdiana, including cremation and other customs, physical appearance, and apparent Sogdian place-names apparently transplanted to Shansi.

[25] Yao Wei-yüan, loc. cit.

[26] On the early history of the Erhchu see *WS* 74, pp. 1643–4.

much harder to sell the meat and dairy products of their herds; and their ethnic memories of the near-extermination of their people in 349 cannot have inclined them to sympathize with the court's sinifying tendency. As a concession the chief Erhchu was granted the privilege of attending court at Loyang in winter only, returning to the tribal lands in summer.

The rapid rise of the Erhchu to national prominence began after the outbreak of mutinies along the northern frontier. Just before these broke out the son and successor to Erhchu Hsin-hsing, the white-skinned Erhchu Jung, had taken 4,000 men, many of whom were newly recruited dependants of the Erhchu, to join the unsuccessful retaliatory expedition after the Joujan raid of 523; no doubt this was a useful training exercise for the young chief and his men.[27] The next year the herdsmen on the state's grazing lands at South Hsiu-jung, which lay just south of the Erhchu lands, rebelled; and Erhchu Jung put down both this group and the herdsmen of Ping-chou. Two years later there was another revolt among the herdsmen in the state grazing lands west of the Yellow River in response to the rising at the Po-ku-lü garrison (Lingwu, Ninghsia), and once again Erhchu Jung led the forces of repression.[28]

In the general disorder some of the officials previously in charge of the herdsmen fled to the Erhchu for protection, where they were joined by former officers of the northern garrisons who had either fled from the mutinies at the outset or—and this seems to have been a much larger category—had taken refuge with the Erhchu when the rebel group to which they had belonged was crushed, whether by the government's armies in association with the Joujan or by a rival faction.[29] The Erhchu have been represented as providing an island of reaction in a sea of popular rebellion, and there is justification for this in relation to the herdsmen's rising; but this is open to question as regards the frontier mutinies, which, though fuelled by discontent and hunger among the soldiery, numbered many well-born officers among their leaders, who did

---

[27] On Erhchu Jung's early career see *WS* 74, pp. 1644–6 and the 'Record', ch. 1.

[28] On the herdsmen, (probably state serfs) and their rising see T'ang Chang-ju (1955), pp. 210–16.

[29] T'ang and Huang (1964), pp. 111–13.

not hesitate to join the Erhchu coalition when it suited them.[30] In 527 Erhchu power, now established in most parts of central and northern Shansi not under Joujan occupation, turned towards Hopei, which was under the sway of the former garrison men in open rebellion against the Wei.

By 528 Erhchu Jung commanded the strongest military forces still nominally loyal to the throne, and he was preparing to descend on the rich Hopei plain when, according to one report, the emperor Su-tsung/Hsiao-ming-ti sent word to him asking his help in getting rid of the dowager Hu's henchmen Hsü Ho and Cheng Yen and enabling him to rule in fact as well as in name.[31] Whatever the truth of this story, which met the needs of Erhchu propaganda, when the news of the sudden death of the eighteen-year-old emperor reached Erhchu Jung in the second month of 528 he decided to postpone his eastern expedition and instead to lead his horsemen to the capital.

He gave as his reasons his family's hereditary relationship with the Wei throne, the extremely suspicious circumstances of the emperor's death, and the danger to the state if a baby were allowed to succeed him. Forming a covenant with Yüan T'ien-mu, a distant member of the royal clan who had fought beside him for several years and was now governor of Ping-chou, he used the ancient Hsienpei method of casting bronze figures of all the eligible descendants of some recent Wei monarchs; and, by accident or design, only one prince's statue was a perfect casting. Jung sent his nephew and a slave to Loyang to contact his cousin Erhchu Shih-lung and secure the chosen candidate's consent. Yüan Tzu-yu, the prince of Ch'ang-lo, accepted the offer of the throne, and the Erhchu cavalry armies, clad in mourning white, were soon riding towards Loyang.[32]

The dowager Hu's advisers tried to assure her that Erhchu Jung had no more chance of installing his candidate than a mantis of stopping a cart-wheel; but the analogy would have been better applied to their own attempt to block his advance by holding the vital bridge across the Yellow River with only

---

[30] Reservations about the 'revolutionary' nature of the garrison risings are well argued in Wan Sheng-nan (1964), and replied to in Yang Yao-k'un (1978).

[31] *PCS* 1, p. 3.

[32] 'Record', ch. 1 and notes 28 ff.; *WS* 74, pp. 1646–7.

5,000 men. The defenders of the bridge went over to the attacker when they heard that the prince of Ch'ang-lo was already in the Erhchu camp. On the twelfth day of the fourth month Erhchu Jung was encamped outside the city on the plain of Ho-yin; and it was to Ho-yin that he summoned the officials of the capital to come the next day to pay homage to their new emperor.

The thirteenth was a day of blood. When almost all of the capital's princes, officials, and aristocrats came out of the city to greet the new ruler who was being forced on them, they were rounded up by the Hu cavalry and butchered with the sort of ruthless frontier efficiency normally reserved for defeated enemies.[33] The dowager Hu and her child emperor were hurled into the Yellow River, but not before that redoubtable woman had given Erhchu Jung a piece of her mind.[34] Reports of the numbers killed in the Ho-yin massacre range between 1,300 and 3,000.[35]

It was a catastrophe for the aristocratic Loyang which developed during the previous thirty-five years. Nearly all of the royal family living in the capital was wiped out, and this made a great difference to the city as they had set the city's style, controlled so much of its wealth, and been required to make their permanent homes there, like the other non-Han northerners brought down from P'ing-ch'eng at the end of the previous century. Imperial favourites and palace eunuchs had also made some of the running, and few of them were to be seen after 528. The damage to the Han-Chinese upper classes, who generally kept their family homes in the provinces, was proportionately not so great; of those in office, many were in provincial posts and so escaped destruction, while those out of office would also have been away from the capital. But we only need to read Yang's book to find confirmation that they were profoundly shocked by the massacre, in which many of their number perished. One group that benefited from the slaughter was the clergy. Some of the huge mansions of the princes and other victims of the slaughter were turned into monasteries;

[33] On the massacre see ch. 1 of the 'Record', and sources cited in the notes thereto.
[34] *PS* 13, p. 505; *WSa* 13, p. 340.
[35] 1,300 according to *WS* 74; over 2,000 according to *WS* 10, p. 256; 2,000 or 3,000 in different editions of the 'Record'.

and it is possible that the income needed to support them came from the property, especially lands, slaves, and other dependants, of the dead princes.

Why did Erhchu Jung do it? It appears to have been a calculated act of terror. One of the dowager's Hsienpei generals who defected to him advised mass slaughter in order to intimidate the populous capital and its many officials. Otherwise they might be contemptuous of his small force, only some 10,000 strong, and lack of military triumphs, and rise against him as soon as his back was turned.[36] This advice seems to have been heeded by Jung, who said to a subordinate that the numerous, rich, proud and extravagant gentlemen of Loyang would be uncontrollable unless butchered.[37] The victims themselves were told that they were being punished for their cruel and rapacious misgovernment.[38] Behind these specific motives lay the north's deep hatred for Loyang and what it stood for.

The massacre was a spectacular and horrible ending to Loyang's years of splendour. Little new building took place after 528, and although the city enjoyed interludes of comparative prosperity during its remaining six years the story was mainly one of a succession of disasters. What remained of the policy basis of Kao-tsu's state was openly rejected and destroyed by the Erhchu, although the form of government was maintained, and it continued to function in some parts of the country.

Immediately after the massacre there was a general air of fear and confusion both in Erhchu Jung's camp and in the capital. The emperor-designate tried to decline the throne which was soaked in the blood of Ho-yin, and Jung toyed with the idea of taking it for himself before finding through casting statues and consulting his trusted soothsayer that the omens were unfavourable. Many of Loyang's inhabitants fled the city as news of the massacre was followed by rumours that Jung was planning to move the capital to his headquarters at Chin-yang, and that his troops were to be let loose to do their worst. Jung

[36] *PCS* 20, p. 272.
[37] *WS* 44, pp. 1004–5.
[38] *WS* 74, p. 1648.

was persuaded to keep Loyang as the capital after climbing a high tower and seeing the extent of the great city; and the full fury of the northerners was reserved for a later occasion. When the new emperor (Chuang-ti or Hsiao-chuang-ti) entered his palace, only one official turned out to greet him. Erhchu Jung now adopted a somewhat conciliatory line, having extravagant posthumous awards heaped on his victims, whom he now maintained were unfortunates caught in the middle of a battle whose deaths had been somehow accidental.[39]

Although he enjoyed himself accumulating honours and behaving badly at court, Erhchu Jung could not linger there as the threats to his power in the provinces were growing stronger than ever. The various forces of former garrison mutineers had been brought under the control of Ko Jung, who was by now threatening the great city of Yeh and sending parties of scouts to explore the approaches to Loyang.[40] He could no longer be ignored. In the ninth month of 528 Erhchu Jung prepared to meet the forces of Ko Jung, claimed to be 1,000,000 strong and probably to be numbered by the hundred thousand; and with great daring he chose to meet the challenge with only 7,000 crack cavalry.

The battle that ensued when Erhchu Jung's small force moved down towards the plain was remarkable. Ko Jung's men were not an unarmed rabble: they were professional soldiers who had been fighting in Hopei for years, moving across the countryside like a great swarm of locusts, leaving famine in their wake.[41] Giving his men ropes with which to tie up an enemy he expected to defeat easily, Ko Jung formed an arc-shaped line of battle which stretched from Yeh northwards for several tens of *li*. Erhchu Jung divided his small force into groups of several hundred men and had them stir up dust clouds and make as much noise as possible, thus concealing their small numbers. The horsemen were forbidden to use their

[39] *WS* 74, pp. 1648–9; 'Record', ch. 1. According to *Chou shu* 14, pp. 221–2, Kao Huan urged Jung to take the throne; but this is hardly a reliable source on such a matter.

[40] Ko, a former officer in the Huai-shuo garrison, was one of the leaders of the new rising of the frontiersmen in 526 (*WS* 74, pp. 1645–6; *Liang shu* 56, p. 833; *TCTC* 151–2). On prince Yüan of Kuang-yang see ch. 2 of the 'Record' with n. 100.

[41] *CMYS* 45.8.3.

swords, being issued with a weapon referred to as *shen-pang* ('miraculous cudgel') to be held beside the horse. The reason why the troopers were not allowed their swords was because cutting off heads would lose the impetus of the charge. The attack, delivered in and around the pass of Fu-k'ou, was a complete success (perhaps the first recorded instance of the shock power of massed heavy cavalry using lances to concentrate the full weight of a charging horse and horseman on a target), and Erhchu Jung completed the victory by striking at the enemy's rear. Ko Jung was captured on the field of battle, and the rest of his force collapsed and surrendered: an army of several hundred thousand had been shattered in a single morning. Erhchu Jung showed political sagacity by allowing the defeated men to settle where they chose outside a radius of 100 *li*, while keeping the ablest of them to swell his own forces.[42]

This battle indicates why Erhchu Jung was able to make himself the supreme warlord of north China: he was a soldier who knew how to use heavy cavalry as a shock force, and a frontiersman able to win the allegiance of many other able commanders of the non-Han races, including a high proportion of those who were to make the military and political history of China in the decades that followed. He was, however, much less capable as the ruler of all of north China, and as the commander of huge government armies.

The problems were brought home to the Erhchu by two immediate challenges to their power at the end of 528. The one that seemed more dangerous was the recrudescence of rebellion in Hopei; but early in 529, while Erhchu Jung and his close associate Yüan T'ien-mu were preoccupied with that threat, another was closing on the capital.

A small Liang expeditionary force had taken the town of Liang-kuo and was threatening Jung-yang before the main Wei armies, now Erhchu-led, could engage them. The former Ko Jung men who had swollen their vanquisher's strength to an alleged 300,000 were once again outfought by an enemy force of 7,000. The Liang commander Ch'en Ch'ing-chih combined tactical caution with strategic daring, avoiding

[42] *WS* 74, pp. 1649–50.

battle where his men would be exposed to the onslaught of the northern cavalry while moving boldly to seize Hu-lao, thus forcing the Erhchu to abandon the capital, taking their client emperor with them.

Ch'en Ch'ing-chih entered Loyang in triumph to install another member of the Wei royal house in the vacant palace. Yüan Hao, prince of Pei-hai, had fled to Chien-k'ang from the Erhchu advance the previous year and been appointed king of Wei as a Liang vassal: he can hardly have expected actually to take the Loyang throne. Nor can he have expected to weather the inevitable Erhchu counter-attack on the fortresses east of Loyang; but Ch'en Ch'ing-chih won another brilliant series of victories and forced all the Erhchu forces back north of the Yellow River.

Had the Liang emperor Wu-ti exploited these amazing successes by sending adequate reinforcements the course of Chinese history might have been quite different. But instead Erhchu Jung was able to regroup his forces and recover the initiative. Against his reorganized armies, now claimed to be a million strong, what chance had a few thousand men, however brave? Less than two months after entering Loyang, Ch'en Ch'ing-chih and Yüan Hao had to abandon it; and in the flight Yüan Hao was captured and killed, as were nearly all the southern soldiers.

The interlude of Yüan Hao's rule had done Loyang little good. The southern troops treated the city's civilians badly; and although the aristocrats and high officials who stayed in the capital during the southern occupation enjoyed impressing Ch'en Ch'ing-chih with their cultural superiority—or so at least Yang Hsüan-chih would have us believe—no lasting benefits were won for the city.[43]

Erhchu Jung was in a much stronger position on his return to the capital than he had been when he entered with his 10,000 in 528. His armies were far larger, and he now controlled most of Hopei and Shantung and was recovering much of Honan from the failed Liang invasion. In the first half

---

[43] On the Liang invasion, Ch'en Ch'ing-chih, and Yüan Hao's short rule see *WS* 21/1, pp. 564–6; *Liang shu* 32, pp. 461–3; *TCTC* 153, pp. 4758–66; and ch. 1 of the 'Record'. Ch'en's verbal encounters with Loyang society are recounted in ch. 2 of the 'Record'.

of 530 he extended his rule to the Wei valley, which had been fought over for years by various rebel groups of which the last and strongest were the forces of Moch'i Ch'ou-nu and Hsiao Pao-yin, that unlikely alliance of Hsienpei garrison soldier and southern prince. Erhchu Jung's armies under his kinsman Erhchu T'ien-kuang and the tough frontier soldier Hopa Yüeh did what Hsiao Pao-yin himself when a Wei commander and other officers sent out from Loyang as Loyang's soldiers had failed to do: they smashed the rebels and sent their leaders back to die in Loyang as Ko Jung and Hsing Kao had the previous year.[44]

The rebel leaders who had ended Loyang's control of the provinces were paraded in triumph through her streets; but these were not Loyang's victories. Nor does it seem likely that many of Loyang's inhabitants rejoiced in the ever more extravagant titles, honours, and gifts—the income of tens of thousands of households, tens of thousands of bolts of brocade, 300 palace women, and so on—that the client emperor piled on Erhchu Jung and his associates, who did not hide their contempt for the court and the capital. Chuang-ti was finding his master more and more intolerable; and even after the Ho-yin massacre the genealogical pride of the Han-Chinese aristocrats could not stomach the Erhchu demand that all the provincial governorships south of the Yellow River should go to northerners. Once Chuang-ti began to act towards Erhchu Jung as emperor towards subject, a clash seemed inevitable. Erhchu Jung told his closest ally Yüan T'ien-mu that his ambitions were for nothing less than the conquest of the whole of China, and that if the courtiers continued to show him insolence he would march those 'greedy and corrupt court nobles' out of the city and force them to fight tigers barehanded in the midst of his army.[45]

What actually happened filled the whole city with the noise of celebration. In the ninth month of 530 Chuang-ti, who showed the spirit of a real emperor, lured Erhchu Jung and Yüan T'ien-mu to make one of their rare appearances at court

---

[44] On this expedition see *WS* 74, p. 1653; 75, pp. 1673–6; 80, pp. 1872–5; *Chou shu* 14, pp. 222–4; *TCTC* 154, pp. 4771 ff.
[45] *WS* 10, pp. 263–5; 74, pp. 1652–4.

with the false report that an heir to the throne had been born. When they arrived they were killed, Chuang-ti dispatching Jung with his own sword.[46] The surviving Erhchu fled the city.

This was the finest hour of Loyang's later history for Yang Hsüan-chih, who served Chuang-ti in person and appears from his narrative of the killings and their aftermath to have been an eyewitness of this stirring though futile episode. The death of Erhchu Jung deprived the Erhchu of their natural leader, and led to an internecine struggle for supremacy that ended in their almost complete destruction within three years. But it was not to be the Wei dynasty that benefited from the ensuing chaos when the military coalition that Erhchu Jung had created broke into warring factions which were to struggle for north China for generations. Among the consequences was to be the abandonment of Loyang. Chuang-ti's deed may have warmed many a loyalist's heart; but the price that had to be paid for it, not only by him, was a heavy one.

The sad truth was that once the Erhchu had recovered from the initial shock of the killing of their chief, Loyang and Chuang-ti had little but courage with which to resist them. The Erhchu controlled the outskirts of the city, and were soon at the foot of the city walls sobbing and demanding their chief's body for burial. In vain did Chuang-ti bring out the contents of his storehouses to hire 10,000 men to fight the Hu. Though they gave battle for three days, they had no success against adversaries so much more experienced. Only an enterprising fire attack on the vital floating bridge on the Yellow River postponed the city's doom, by forcing the Erhchu to withdraw to the north of the river after massacring many of the common people who were not protected by the capital's walls. Although Chuang-ti managed to find between 18,000 and 30,000 troops to hold a bridgehead over the river, he could mobilize little effective support in the provinces, which were still almost entirely under Erhchu control. Once an exceptionally low water enabled the Hu armies to ford the river there was nothing to prevent them from murdering, looting, and raping in a capital that in their view deserved everything they

---

[46] See the accounts in chs. 1 and 4 of the 'Record' and in *TCTC* 154, pp. 4782–3, based largely on *WS* 19/3, pp. 511–12; see also *WS* 10, pp. 265–6; 74, pp. 1654–5.

did to it. A malicious couplet that circulated in Loyang afterwards had it that the last outrage was not unwelcome to the nuns of the city's grandest convent, the Yao-kuang; but for the emperor there was nothing in store but a journey to the Erhchu headquarters at Chin-yang and death by strangulation.[47]

Three months after Chuang-ti's death a new client emperor, Yüan Yeh, prince of Ch'ang-kuang, was brought to Loyang but forced to abdicate before he could be installed in the palace.[48] He commanded little respect; and once his patron Erhchu Chao was obliged to return north to deal with a rising in Shansi, Loyang's new master, Erhchu Shih-lung, compelled him to abdicate in the second month of 531, forcing him to kill himself the following year.[49] Erhchu Shih-lung's candidate was Yüan Kung, prince of Kuang-ling, a strong-minded man who had withdrawn from public life eight years earlier during Yüan Yi's dictatorship and maintained a show of dumbness ever since, even when threatened by armed men. Only when enthroned did he speak in public again, to the general astonishment.[50] He was a cousin of Chuang-ti's and he showed something of his spirit, refusing to act as a mere puppet.[51] The result was that Erhchu Shih-lung abandoned the pretence of running his area of China through the throne, deciding everything from his own home. He was said to kill at a whim and to be extremely corrupt; but it was also admitted that under his rule trade flourished and banditry was suppressed.[52]

This rule did not last long. Erhchu disunity was rapidly exploited by several of Erhchu Jung's former lieutenants, most notably Kao Huan, who had induced the foolish Erhchu Chao to put him in charge of over 100,000 former garrison men who had been moved to Shansi after Ko Jung's defeat. These diehard enemies of the Erhchu had rebelled against their hated Ch'i Hu masters so often that half their original numbers had

[47] On Chuang-ti's unsuccessful defence of Loyang see ch. 1 of the 'Record'. The pillage is mentioned in *WS* 75, p. 1662.

[48] See chs. 1 and 2 of the 'Record', and *WS* 11, pp. 273 ff.

[49] The abdication is described in ch. 2 of the 'Record'.

[50] According to *WS* 11, p. 273, and 75, p. 1669, he spoke to envoys of Erhchu Shih-lung before he was chosen as emperor.

[51] 'Record', ch. 2.

[52] Ibid.; *WS* 75, p. 1669.

been killed. Kao Huan had also found allies among the big Chinese clans of Hopei with their own private armies, and he was emerging as the Erhchu's leading rival in the east even before he came out openly against them in the summer of 531. He terrified the former garrison members into joining the rising by producing a forged document alleging that they were to be assigned to the Ch'i Hu as dependants (*p'u-li*).[53] In the spring of 532 Kao Huan, now master of Yeh, faced a combined Erhchu force near the city and defeated it in a battle at Han-ling in which he made good use of both his non-Han and his Han troops (the latter including some that were up to Hsienpei standards, who saved the day for him).[54] Once the Erhchu had been defeated many other former associates rose against them; and the dictator of Loyang, Erhchu Shih-lung, was captured and killed by the forces of Hussu Ch'un, who realized after Han-ling that he had to break with the Erhchu if he was not to perish with them.[55]

In the fourth month of 532 Kao Huan entered Loyang as its new master, deposing two 'emperors' on the same day—prince Kung of Kuang-ling, Erhchu Shih-lung's creation, and his own puppet Yüan Lang, prince of An-ting, whom he had named emperor less than six months earlier and now discarded as unsuitable—and enthroning a third by the old P'ing-ch'eng rites in the eastern outskirts of the city.[56] The reign of Yüan Hsiu, prince of Kuang-p'ing,[57] is one on which Yang is largely silent, perhaps because in 534 this emperor (known in eastern sources as Ch'u-ti and in western ones as Hsiao-wu-ti) sided with Kao Huan's enemies and fled with them to the west. During his two years on the Loyang throne (532–4) the remaining Erhchu forces were destroyed, their last stronghold falling to Kao Huan in the first month of 533. While Kao was

---

[53] On Kao's manoeuvres see *TCTC* 154, pp. 4794–6; 155, pp. 4802–5, 4811–16 (based on *PCS*). His relationship with leading Han clans in Hopei and their private armies is well examined in Hamaguchi's study of the origins of Kao power in vol. 2 of his 1966 collection; on these private armies see also Tanigawa (1971), pp. 219–57.

[54] *PCS* 1, ppl 7–8; *TCTC* 155, pp. 4819–20.

[55] *WS* 75, p. 1670; 80, pp. 1773–4.

[56] On the deposing of prince Kung and the brief 'reign' of Kao Huan's client Yüan Lang see *WS* 11, pp. 278–80. Neither survived his abdication for long.

[57] *WS* 11, pp. 281–92; *PS* 5, pp. 170–4.

away on military campaigns or staying at his own headquarters at Chin-yang, his nominee on the Loyang throne was
coming increasingly under the influence of Hussu Ch'un,[58]
who in the struggle between the two main military cliques that
now dominated the Wei territories sided first with Hopa Yüeh
and then with Yüwen T'ai in the west against Kao Huan, the
master of Shansi and Hopei.

While yet another civil war was in preparation Ch'u-
ti/Hsiao-wu-ti resumed some filial religious building in
Loyang, raising a new high pagoda in the P'ing-teng
Monastery and a brick stūpa in the Ta-chüeh Monastery, both
originally houses belonging to his father.[59] Nothing suggests
that the scale of construction matched the reckless building of
Loyang's years of splendour. Nor can they have done much to
offset Loyang's sense of loss when in the second month of 534
the city's pride, the Yung-ning Pagoda, was destroyed by fire
despite the efforts of 1,000 soldiers to extinguish it. The whole
population came out to watch and weep; and in the general
emotion three monks rushed into the mighty blaze to immolate
themselves.[60] With hindsight this disaster was seen as heralding
the end of the city; and the image of flames and smoke
devouring this breath-taking red-lacquered tower hung with
gold that had been raised over the capital in its years of glory is
a spectacular symbol of the end of Loyang.

The city's end was to be sudden, but not as cataclysmic as
the Yung-ning fire seemed to portend. Loyang had ceased to
be the effective political centre of a north China which was
now being divided between the two great military cliques of
east and west. Kao Huan was much stronger in numbers than
his rivals, but in his absence on campaign he had lost control of
the court. His own nominee on the throne was clearly in
league with his enemies. No doubt Kao Huan would not have
hesitated to get rid of Yüan Hsiu had he been able to get hold
of him; but he was not able to do so. Hussu Ch'un, the military
master of Loyang, persuaded the emperor that it would be wise
to strengthen his personal guard and was now the dominant

---

[58] See n. 78 to ch. 1 of the 'Record'.
[59] Described in chs. 2 and 4 of the 'Record'.
[60] See the dramatic account in ch. 1 of the 'Record'.

influence on him. The emperor also killed Kao Ch'ien, a leading associate of Kao Huan's at court.[61]

By the summer of 534 the emperor, who had mobilized an army on the pretext of an invasion of the south, was ready for a trial of strength with Kao Huan. Kao wanted to move the capital to Yeh, which was firmly under his control, and had tried unsuccessfully to persuade the monarch that Loyang was no longer suitable after the devastation it had suffered: it had lost its imperial air, and was besides poor in land by comparison with Yeh. The emperor would have none of it, appealing to the traditions of *t'ai-ho*. Persuasion having failed, Kao Huan moved his troops to the north bank of the Yellow River, seized the boats on the Pai Kou canal, and diverted the tax grain intended for Loyang to Yeh. He told his armies that he was fighting not the throne but Hussu Ch'un.[62]

The emperor had reliable allies to his west and held the area south of the Yellow River as far east as Hu-lao; but lacked the courage to strike with his army, over 100,000 strong, at the smaller forces Kao Huan had first sent to the north bank. This failure alarmed his supporters; and Yüwen T'ai, the powerful warlord of the west, sent only a token force to his aid. What with his indecision and the divisions within his camp, morale on the emperor's side was falling; and when he decided to flee to the west instead of standing and fighting over half of his army disappeared in the night. In the seventh month Kao Huan entered Loyang virtually unopposed.[63]

He was not back to stay. He called the senior officials of the capital to the Yung-ning Monastery and berated them for failing to give the emperor better advice, killing some of their number to underline his point.[64] In the tenth month, after vain attempts to persuade Ch'u-ti/Hsiao-wu-ti to come back, he created his third emperor, the ten-year-old Yüan Shan-chien (later known as Hsiao-ching-ti). A few days later Kao put into effect his plan to transfer the capital to Yeh. After a court discussion the order to move was given.[65]

[61] *WS* 80, p. 1774; *PCS*, p. 9.
[62] *PCS* 2, pp. 14–16; *TCTC* 156, pp. 4844 ff.
[63] *PCS* 2, pp. 16–17; *Chou shu* 1, pp. 12–13; *TCTC* 156, pp. 4847–51.
[64] *PCS* 2, p. 16; *WS* 77, p. 1968.
[65] *WSa* 12, pp. 297–8; *PS* 5, p. 184; *PCS* 2, p. 18.

Within three days of the decree, 400,000 families—perhaps 2,000,000 people—had to leave their homes in and around the capital to move to Yeh as autumn turned to winter.[66] While they were on their way the original inhabitants of the Yeh area were forced 100 *li* west—which would have driven them into the Taihang mountains—to make way for the new arrivals.[67] Most of the capital's soldiery went east with Kao: fewer than 10,000 men had chosen to move west with the emperor Ch'u-ti/Hsiao-wu-ti. Kao Huan's misappropriated grain supplies were soon called upon: 1,300,000 *shih* of grain were allocated to the new arrivals to help tide them over.[68] In the second month of 535 100,000 conscript labourers were sent back to salvage the structural timbers of Loyang's palaces and take them to Yeh.[69] Of the city's monasteries and convents, 421 remained at the time of the move. All their inmates were compelled to join the exodus.[70]

The end of the Northern Wei city of Loyang was as arbitrary as its founding had been; and it was even more abrupt. When western troops under Tuku Hsin entered the city in 537 they found it largely depopulated and ruined, as was the surrounding countryside.[71] Perhaps the plan to rebuild the city's palaces, for which purpose 3,000 men were sent off into the hills to fetch timber, indicates that the western warlords were seriously considering moving their capital from Ch'ang-an back to Loyang. But before they returned Tuku Hsin was besieged by Eastern Wei forces in the city's Chin-yung Castle, in the course of which siege the eastern general Hou Ching burned down all but 20 or 30 per cent of the surviving government offices and private houses.[72] When the eastern forces recovered the castle in 538, Kao Huan had its walls pulled down, thus completing the work of destruction.[73] Northern Wei Loyang was now utterly finished. Loyang

---

[66] *PCS* 2, p. 18.
[67] *WSa* 12, p. 298; *PS* 5, p. 184.
[68] *Sui shu* 24, p. 675; *TCTC* 156, p. 4857.
[69] *TCTC* 157, p. 4864.
[70] 'Record', ch. 5, end, and Preface.
[71] *Chou shu* 38, p. 680.
[72] *TCTC* 158, p. 4893.
[73] *PCS* 2, p. 20.

prefecture had a registered population of 3,659 households and 15,572 individuals in the 540s; and the whole of Lo-chou, formerly the capital and the imperial domain together, ran to only 15,679 households and 66,521 people.[74]

---

[74] *WS* 106/2, p. 2547.

Chapter 6

What Sort of Capital was Loyang?

We have looked at the origins and political history of Northern
Wei Loyang, and considered how and why Yang Hsüan-chih
may have written his 'Record' of the city. All that remains to
be done before reading his memoir, which brings the lost
capital back to life for us far more successfully than any
secondary work could do, is to discuss the layout, organization, culture, and nature of this remarkable city and to assess
briefly its relationship with the rest of north China.[1]

As the previous chapters have shown, this was not a city that
just happened or that grew naturally. Neither the peasantry
who fed and clothed it, nor the markets that catered to many of
its needs, determined what or even whether Loyang was to be.
One man called it into being, and another abolished it.
Emperors, empresses, princes, high officials, and generals
made the decisions, and the rest of the population had to fit in
with them as best as they could.

[1] The following are the principal modern studies of the city. I am especially
indebted to (a), (e), and the last two titles in (f). (a) The commentaries by Chou Tsu-
mo (1956, repr. 1963) and Fan Hsiang-yung (1958) to their editions of the 'Record'
(on which see Appendix I), which are invaluable supplements to Yang's text. (b) Lao
Kan (1948), and Mori Shikazō (1952) both useful contributions in their time. (c)
Miyakawa Hisayuki (1956), pp. 510–24, a good short account within a larger study of
capital cities in the Six Dynasties period. (d) Hattori Katsuhiko (1965 and 1968),
popular accounts of the city as it was portrayed by Yang. Their value to the student
lies principally in their thematic arrangement of Yang's material. Unfortunately
Hattori does not mention the commentaries of Fan and Chou, although his choice of
citations from other texts to amplify Yang shows remarkable similarities with theirs.
(e) Ho Ping-ti (1966, a revised version of a 1965 Chinese article), a distinguished study
of the planning and layout of the city which remains extremely valuable. (f) Kuo Pao-
chün (1955); Yen Wen-ju (1955); Chung-kuo k'o-hsüeh-yüan k'ao-ku yen-chiu-so Loyang kung-tso-tui (1973/1); Su Pai (1978/2). Of these accounts and discussions of
ground surveys and archaeological finds, the 1973 article summarizes the available
evidence very well, which Su Pai amplifies, adding some observations on the pattern of
royal and other burials outside the city. For brevity the 1973 article will be cited below
simply as 1973/1.

The domination of the city by the court is also clear from its layout, which can be reconstructed in outline by a combination of Yang's detailed but unsystematic information with the evidence from other written sources and the findings of archaeologists. The city's grid pattern was determined by Kao-tsu's planners on his orders, and though some of the spaces in the grid were later to be used in ways rather different from the founder's intentions, most notably for the many monasteries and convents built after his death, the underlying pattern seems to have been followed to the end.

This was city planning on an unprecedented scale. Yang tells us that Greater Loyang covered an area measuring 15 *li* from north to south, and 20 *li* from east to west.[2] If we take the linear *li* as 300 *pu*, each of 6 *ch'ih*,[3] and take 29.6 centimetres as the length of a *ch'ih*,[4] these dimensions are equivalent to 7.992 × 10.650 kilometres, dimensions rather greater than those of Ch'ing Peking. Even allowing for a little exaggeration this is still a big city. Its population matched its size: 109,000 households according to Yang, our only informant, and this indicates at least half a million people, and probably 600,000 or more. This short-lived city was rivalled for size only by Rome, Constantinople, Han Ch'ang-an and Loyang, and Chien-k'ang in or before its own time, and by few others in the next thousand years. These other cities had grown over centuries, but Loyang was planned from scratch within a year or so, and most of it was built in a decade. Even in modern times it is hard to find so large a city being created so fast from virtually nothing. It is easy to overlook the sheer size of the city in Yang's anecdotal pages, but it was intended from the beginning to be enormous.

The city walls of Eastern Han Loyang, which had also been used by its Ts'ao-Wei and Chin successors, served in Northern Wei times to limit the inner city only. There were extensive suburbs on all sides of the inner city except the north, where the Mang hills restricted the area that could conveniently be built up. Yang divides his book into five chapters, one for the inner city and one for each of the four suburban zones, and this

---

[2] Figures given at the end of ch. 5 of the 'Record'.
[3] Wu Ch'eng-lo (1957), p. 117.
[4] Tseng Wu-hsiu (1964).

convenient division may be followed in looking at the city's layout.

It made sense to use the old city walls for the inner city. Even now long stretches of the northern, eastern and western sections still stand, rising in places to between 5 and 7 metres in height. The base of the northern wall is still 25–30 metres thick, while that of the eastern and western walls is between 14 and 20 metres in width. The southern walls has been submerged by the Lo river, which now runs some 2 kilometres north of the course it took when the Northern Wei city was built. These massive structures formed a roughly rectangular shape known in Chin times as the 'nine-six walls' as it measured about 9 Chin *li* from north to south and 6 from east to west. As the southern wall cannot now be traced and the line of the others, especially the northern one with its two projections, is not regular, exact measurements are difficult; roughly speaking, it was a rectangle of about 3.8×2.5 kilometres, or 9.5 square kilometres.[5]

A glance at the 1973 map of the city walls and roads shows that they were based on two inconsistent alignment systems. The first includes the northern part of the west wall, the middle stretch of the eastern wall and a road that comes in from the gate numbered VII (the Kuang-mo), turns west, then heads south, nearly reaching the present course of the Lo. This alignment is roughly vertical to the eastern section of the northern wall. The other alignment governs the other roads, the southern part of the western wall, and most of the northern stretch and the surviving part of the southern end of the eastern wall. The central palace compound and the Yung-ning Monastery's compound fit neatly into this second system. I take this second one to be that used by Kao-tsu's planners in laying out greater Loyang's grid of wards and roads.

The central area stretched from the foot of the Mang hills south to within 2 kilometres of the bank of the Lo river. Somewhat to the west of its central axis are the remains of a palace compound, a rectangular walled complex measuring 1,398 metres from north to south and 660 metres from east to west.[6] As the archaeological evidence so far published indicates

---

[5] 1973/1 (see n. 1, p. 103 above).
[6] Ibid.

that there was only one such compound, it may well be that Kao-tsu had his main palaces built where the Ts'ao-Wei and Chin palaces had once stood, just as the builders of Ts'ao-Wei Loyang had used the foundations of the Han palaces. Although the buildings themselves would long since have disappeared, the stamped-earth foundations for the main structures and the compounds' external wall would probably have been visible. If we are right in thinking that this compound was used by him, it occupied about one-tenth of the area of the inner city. To this can be added a further unknown area for the Hua-lin Park that lay behind it. As Yang and the antiquarian topographer Li Tao-yüan mention nothing in the northernmost section of the inner city apart from the Chin-yung Castle, which also served as a palace, the 'small Loyang wall that had been built by the [Ts'ao-] Wei,' this park, and a plot of land left vacant for the building of a palace for an heir apparent old enough to have his own establishment (one was never needed), it appears that about a quarter of the inner city was reserved for imperial use. The splendour of the palaces and of their parks and gardens is well described by Yang and Li.[7]

Much of the rest of inner Loyang was given over to government offices, of which the majority known to us were in the south-west and central-southern parts, and between the eastern wall of the palace and the city wall.[8] In this last area there was also a granary that, if the huge granary of Sui and T'ang Loyang is anything to go by,[9] would have covered dozens of hectares. Eight of the nine residential wards that Yang identifies in his account of the inner city are in its southern half, and their residents included high officials. The eunuch Liu T'eng had a huge mansion west of the palace, and it seems likely that many of the palace staff may have lived near their work. We are not told of barracks, but they are unlikely to have been absent.

The central area also contained some of the capital's most magnificent monasteries and convents, including the Yung-ning Monastery, famous for its towering pagoda, which was

---

[7] *SCC* 16, p. 3/74.

[8] 'Record', ch. 1; *SCC*, loc. cit.

[9] Ho-nan-sheng po-wu-kuan and Lo-yang-shih po-wu-kuan (1972). That granary compound measured about 600 × 700 metres, and contained hundreds of storage pits.

built in palatial style in a rectangular compound of about 300 × 200 metres, and the Yao-kuang Convent, just outside the palace and much used by its ladies. Part of one building in the southernmost section of the city has been excavated and yielded some handsomely shaped decorative tiles.[10]

The road system of the walled city was a grid. Three roads ran straight between opposite gates in the east and west walls, continuing out into the suburbs on either side. The northern-most intersected the palace compound, perhaps dividing its main buildings from the gardens behind. Immediately to the south of the palace compound was the broadest of the three, some 40 metres wide. The third traversed the southern section of inner Loyang. These were intersected by north–south roads, of which the widest ran from the main palace gate to the Hsüan-ming Gate in the southern wall and continued across the Eternal Bridge to the wards and hostels for foreigners south of the Lo. This was the Bronze Ostrich Street, so called because the Ts'ao-Wei emperor Ming-ti had lined it with brazen ostriches and other beasts, and water courses ran on either side of it. Other roads led to the Chin-yang and K'ai-yang gates in the southern wall. Whether a fourth road—the one that is not parallel with the other three in the 1973 map—ran to the P'ing-ch'ang Gate is not established; Yang has no references to such a road. Apart from the value of these roads as arteries of communication, they also served with the city walls and their gates as reference lines in locating places in the city, as is apparent from Yang's book.[11]

Inner Loyang had a cunningly designed system of water channels, including some underground stone conduits, which drew water in at three points to the north and west, letting it out through the lower, south-eastern section of the wall. This system gave the imperial gardens and parks ponds and lakes to moderate the fires of summer, and was linked with other water-courses running round the walls on the outside. Water for consumption came from wells.[12]

The walled city was thus primarily used for palaces and

[10] Chung-kuo k'o-hsüeh-yüan k'ao-ku-yen-chiu-so Lo-yang kung-tso-tui (1973/2).
[11] 'Record', ch. 1; *SCC* 16, p. 3/75; 1973/1; Su Pai (1978/2).
[12] 'Record', ch. 1; *SCC* 16, pp. 3/68 ff.

government buildings, secondarily for residential wards, monasteries, and nunneries. There is no indication of any markets or shops in it: the site of one of the Chin city's markets, the Gold Market, was swallowed up by the Northern Wei palace system. Nor do we know of any other economic activity in it.

The layout of the outer city is harder to establish, as less information is given by Yang and other writers, and less evidence has been found by the archaeologist, than for the inner city. Yang's dimensions of 15 × 20 *li* seem to offer an outline, but when we compare them with the map that can be drawn from surviving remains they appear to be exaggerated by some 10 to 15 per cent. The city's western limit, for example, the channel that carried some of the waters of the Ku river south from the Chang-fen Bridge, can still be traced some 3.3 kilometres west of the inner wall, or about 400 metres less than Yang's '7 *li*' (at 532.5 metres to the *li*) would lead us to expect;[13] and a similar small apparent discrepancy can be found between Yang's '4 *li*' from the southern wall to the bridge over the Lo and the distance that can be calculated from the 1978 map. But these differences are not great, and could be explained by either a wrong estimate of the length of the Northern Wei *li*, or else by the use of Eastern Han, Ts'ao-Wei, or Chin measurements in calculating the city's plan.

The eastern limit of the city was an outer wall (*kuo*) 7 or 8 *li* from the inner wall and, presumably parallel to it. The northern boundary, only 2 *li* north of the inner city, lay along the lower slopes of the Mang hills, and the southern outer wall, of which a part of the foundations of the westernmost end can be seen, ran by or near the bank of the Lo, some 4 *li* or 2 kilometres south of the city wall. Across the river's only bridge was the foreign quarter, which evidently did not fit into the 20–15 *li* pattern. Like the inner city, outer Loyang was also organized on the grid principle, with walled wards as the basic unit.

The suburbs differed in character. The eastern one was mainly residential, and most of the Han-Chinese officials whose homes are located by Yang lived in the eastern suburb. One of its wards the Chien-yang, housed '2,000 households of

---

[13] 'Record', ch. 4; Su Pai (1978/2), map.

gentry and commoners', who between them supported ten monasteries and nunneries. The office of the Loyang county magistrate, who controlled the eastern half of the city, was in the Sui-min ward, and this area also included the Tax Ground, where the provinces' tribute grain could be brought by water up the Yang Canal from the Lo river, and from where it was perhaps transferred to the granaries inside the wall. The eastern suburb's Little Market was so called by comparison with the Great Market in the west. The only trade that Yang mentions in connection with it is butchery: the Liu brothers laid down their knives and became monks when a pig they were about to slaughter found the words to beg for its life. Next to the market was a commercial ward, presumably inhabited by market traders. Although this suburb did contain a few extensive mansions belonging to members of the royal house, and although some of its houses and gardens excited Yang's admiration, especially the artificial landscape garden of Chang Lun with its mountains, forests, and torrents, the general impression is of prosperity rather than of princely splendour.[14] There was at least one school in this quarter, where Confucian texts were taught to the sons of top Chinese families.[15]

The southern suburb[16] was divided by the Lo river, the northern part being the grander. Immediately south of the city wall was one of Loyang's biggest monasteries, and in Yang's view the finest: the Ching-ming. Its grounds were 500 paces (888 metres) square—three-quarters the size of the palace compound—and here was intalled the most advanced grain-processing machinery of the day: edge-runner and rotary mills, grain-pounders, and bolters, all powered by water. A couple of hundred years later such equipment (discussed in Appendix III) was quite commonplace, but at this time it was extremely rare, and it was probably a source of great profit for the monastery, like the state-run battery of water-mills installed on the Thousand Gold Dyke in the north-west of the city. There were other large Buddhist institutions in this part of the southern suburb, including the two luxurious monasteries

[14] 'Record', ch. 2.
[15] 'Record', ch. 3, near end.
[16] 'Record', ch. 3.

built by the dowager Hu and her sister for the benefit of their late father. The Ming-t'ang (Bright Hall) a building symbolizing cosmic and human order which Confucian interests could not get built until twenty-five or thirty years after the move of the capital, was a poor relation by contrast, as was the Imperial Academy. That could not be said of the literally palatial home of the richest of all the royal princes, prince Yung of Kao-yang, who had 6,000 slaves (many, no doubt, on his estates elsewhere) and 500 women in his harem, and lived in extraordinary luxury. Some at least of the capital's soldiers lived in this part of the southern suburb, as is shown by Yang's eerie story about the Tiger Guard who when back in the capital from the southern front visited the family of a comrade, only to find that they were all, as tends to happen in Chinese anecdotes, ghosts. Despite its princely palaces, the great monasteries, and the Confucian sites, the southern suburb was not thought much of by Loyang's snobs: as a boy Hsün Tzu-wen was teased for living in it.

One reason given for looking down on it was because of its ghetto for foreigners on the wrong side of the Eternal Bridge which crossed the Lo on pontoons. Between the Lo and the Yi rivers were four hostels for visitors and new immigrants from the four quarters, and four wards for permanent residents, of whom there were over 10,000 families, 3,000 of which lived in the southerners' Kuei-cheng ward. No doubt the siting of the ghetto indicated a certain suspicion of foreigners, but they were encouraged. Commerce with the west, for example, extended as far as the Roman empire. 'Foreign traders and merchants came hurrying in through the passes every day. This could indeed be called exhausting all the regions of the earth.' The many foreign merchants, not only from the west, sold their imported wares in the Four Directions Market. As it was also known as the Eternal Bridge Market is must have been at the southern end of the bridge. There was also a street market in the southerners' ward selling mainly the aquatic delicacies which were thought alien by the mutton-eating gentlemen of Loyang.[17] It was not only foreigners who kept south of the river: a rogue white elephant which had broken

[17] Mentioned in ch. 2 of the 'Record'.

out of the Imperial Stables was sent there, as was a Persian lion. Aliens were only allowed to move north of the river as a special favour. Those who did included some of the most aristocratic southern refugees, and many Buddhist monks.

The western suburb[18] accommodated some 3,000 of these religious immigrants in the Yung-ming Monastery built for them by Shih-tsung/Hsüan-wu-ti between 500 and 515; and another monastery in this suburb, the Fa-yün, that was founded by a monk from Udyāna and built in the western style must have sheltered many other western clerics. But these were but a small part of the population of the western suburb, which, at least until the Ho-yin massacre, was predominantly secular. Nearly all its identified houses belonged to either members of the royal family and its relations through marriage, or else to traders. Its westernmost part was a belt of slightly elevated land[19] 2 *li* wide running the full 15 *li* from the Mang hills south to the bank of the Lo that was known officially as the Longevity Hills and popularly as the Princes' Quarter. But even this area, which at nearly some 8 square kilometres was three-quarters the size of inner Loyang and much bigger than many other great cities in history, did not suffice for the Wei princes, whose palaces were to be found in other parts of the western suburb.

The great wealth of the royal princes and the size of their households has already been remarked upon, and there can be no doubt that these establishments, whose masters vied with each other and with the big spenders of Chin Loyang in conspicuous consumption, provided a huge demand for consumers goods and services. It thus made sense for Loyang's Great Market and main commercial district to be in the middle of this princely suburb.

The size and arrangement of the market and its associated residential wards is not made clear by Yang, and conflicting interpretations of his brief remarks on the subject can be made: these are discussed below in Appendix II. In my view the market was probably distinct from the wards in which the tradespeople lived. The wards were divided by trades. The

[18] 'Record', ch. 4.
[19] See Su Pai (1978/2), map.

inhabitants of the T'ung-shang (Circulation of Trade) and Ta-huo (Distribution of Goods) wards 'made their living as craftsmen, butchers, and traders. Their wealth ran into hundreds of millions.' The richest of these traders was the remarkable commodity dealer Liu Pao.

He had a station in all the leading centres of the provinces and prefectures, and kept ten horses in each of them. He [observed] the movement of prices of salt, grain, and other market prices every-where; he traded wherever boat or cart could go or foot could tread. Thus the goods from the whole area within the seas were assembled in his establishments.

Yang tells us that he built and lived like a prince. But men of his time and class believed that merchants had a low place and should keep to it. They had been allowed to make some advances in P'ing-ch'eng's later years, which had prompted the very rich Han-Chinese official Han Hsien-tsung to ask when the new capital was founded that merchants, en-tertainers, and the like be strictly segregated from the well-born lest they contaminate their betters,[20] and in 515 or shortly after the prince of Kao-yang persuaded the dowager Hu to restrict the wearing of fine clothes by slaves to those belonging to the noble.[21] This order was not effective for long, any more than was a similar one issued between 518 and 520.[22] Splendid though Liu Pao's household may well have been, are we really to believe Yang when he tells us he rivalled a prince?

Two of the other wards in the commercial quarter were reserved for instrumentalists and singers. Another pair of wards were mainly for brewers, and a third pair were for coffin-sellers and undertakers, who promoted their more expensive lines by arranging for a young man of good family—a Po-ling Ts'ui, no less—to return from the dead with dire warnings about how the underworld treated those who were buried in cheap wood. All we are told about the residents of the Fu-ts'ai (Great Wealth) and Chin-ssu (Golden stall) wards is that they were rich. Perhaps they were moneylenders or proto-bankers:

[20] *WS* 48, p. 1341.
[21] *WS* 21/1, p. 556.
[22] 'Record', ch. 4.

no doubt princely extravagance sometimes outran even princely resources.

It is striking that the known activities of Loyang's three commercial districts were the provision of consumer goods and services and commodity dealing. Of these only the last may have had some significance, however small, in the national economy by encouraging tendencies towards the creation of a nationwide market in agricultural products.

Were there, as Yang's silence suggests, no place of entertainment in this quarter? Was it not possible to go out on the town, as it was to be in the Sung capitals 500 years and more later, with their restaurants, fast-food stalls, bars, theatres, brothels, inns, and other such enterprises? There must at the least have been inns for travellers. Otherwise it may be that Loyang's life was not sufficiently commercialized and that the very rich had their luxury at home, hiring from the market such singers, dancers, cooks, concubines, and other entertainers as they wanted but did not own already.

The suburb about which there is least to be said is the northern one.[23] This was the smallest, being squeezed between the inner city and the Mang hills. Much of it was deliberately kept uninhabited as a military review ground or planted to lucerne grass; no doubt the security of the palace-dominated northern part of the inner city explains why valuable land was so employed. Few of the members of Loyang society lived there except in the capital's first years. Later some of it became known as the potters' quarter, and it was here that the capital's earthenware goods, including its countless millions of roof-tiles were made. Yang mocks them with a nasty little rhyme: let us here name at random a few of them whose handiwork has survived to our time: the craftsmen Fan Seng-te and Tai Lien; the throwers Li Yü and Ch'ing Lang; the tile-trimmers Min Lung-sheng and Li Tz'u; the polishers Han Chang-sheng and Chang Lang-jen.[24] Without the labours of them and their fellows there would have been no Loyang.

---

[23] 'Record', ch. 5. Nearly all this chapter is devoted to an account of a journey through central Asia to Udyāna and Gandhāra from 518 onwards.

[24] Chung-kuo k'o-hsüeh-yüan k'ao-ku yen-chiu-so Lo-yang kung-tso-tui (1973/2).

THE CONTROL OF THE CITY

The city had no autonomy. As in P'ing-ch'eng, the population was required to live in walled and heavily policed wards, which kept the people fragmented, segregated, and controlled. These wards were characteristic of north-Chinese capital cities,[25] and the walled or fenced compound with a controlled gate is a common feature in some parts of Peking. Yang tells us that there were a total of 220 wards (*li*) in greater Loyang, each a 300-pace (532.8-metre) square, and that the wards included everything except the temples of the soil, palaces, and government offices.[26] The building of their walls in 501 was mentioned in chapter 3 above. We may doubt whether the grid was entirely uniform: the ward systems in the Sui and T'ang capitals at Ch'ang-an and Loyang were not, and there are indications that this city was not either.[27] But even if ward sizes varied somewhat, the principle seems to have been generally applied. Each ward had four gates, and was controlled by two ward-heads, four constables, and eight gate-men, who may be regarded as part of Loyang's security force.[28] The ratio of these policemen to ordinary inhabitants—one for each thirty-five families, or about six for each 1,000 people—is several times that of contemporary Britain, and rather higher than that of London and other large cities. The ward security system was backed up by the large armies stationed in and around the capital, which could be used to arrest more dangerous criminals.

The system did not work very well in Loyang's first years. According to a revealing memorial submitted between 511 and 515 by Chen Shen, who as prefect of Ho-nan had responsibility for running the capital, robbery and murder were rampant, and the intended segregation of wards, each containing up to 500 or 1,000 households, had given place to overcrowding and

[25] On the development of the walled ward in Chinese cities see Sogabe Shizuo (1964).
[26] See the end of ch. 5 of the 'Record'.
[27] See Appendix II on the wards around the Great Market; and the Ching-ming monastery in the southern suburb could not have fitted into a ward as its compound had walls 500 paces long. It is noticeable that Su Pai's sketch-map, which superimposes a regular grid on the modern landscape, often fails to coincide with obvious traces of ancient walls or roads.
[28] 'Record', ch. 5, end.

chaos now that so many people had come flocking to the capital from throughout the realm. The petty officials running the wards were too dim and feeble to investigate crimes effectively. Wards housed aristocrats, high officials, the powerful, and the well-connected; and these households' overweening slaves and dependants harboured criminals. There was also the problem of provincial toughs forming gangs and raiding the markets. It was hardly surprising that the low-ranking ward-heads were unable to cope, and even turned a blind eye to robbers or sheltered them.

To cope with this anarchic situation Chen proposed that capable and honest army officers of the rank of eighth-grade general downwards be granted concurrent appointments in the metropolitan police force. The most senior should be made *liu pu wei* (perhaps meaning that they were each to be put in charge of policing a district of the capital); below them should be *ching-t'u wei* (possibly in charge of a block of wards delimited by intersecting imperial highways).

His proposals were adopted in part. Although security jobs were neither rated as highly as he had asked nor given exclusively to soldiers, they were upgraded. Another suggestion of his, that the Forest of Wings guard army should patrol the wards and streets of the capital and supervise crime investigations, was carried out. The result of these measures was that 'the capital was clean and quiet'.[29] The only known serious public disturbances occurred in 519, when the guardians of order themselves, the Forest of Wings guardsmen, rioted.[30] There were anecdotes suggesting that the county magistrates and prefects of greater Loyang were willing to strike down the powerful when they offended the dignity of the state and did make efforts to track down criminals.[31]

The government's control over the capital, exercised through the prefect of Ho-nan and his two subordinate county magistrates, extended also to its economic life. Commerce was regulated through strict supervision of the market-place. In

---

[29] *WS* 68, pp. 1514–15. *TCTC* 147, pp. 4600–1, places this memorial with the events of 511.

[30] See ch. 4 above.

[31] e.g. *WS* 77, pp. 1689–90.

addition, some leading officials used their power to cream off for themselves much of the markets' wealth, corruptly or otherwise.[32] Merchants, tradesmen, and entertainers were restricted to certain wards, and there are signs that they had not yet lost all traces of the semi-servitude to the state that had been theirs before the *t'ai-ho* reforms. The pious butchers Liu mentioned above were dependants of the Office of Temples and Sacrifices; and a memorial of 515 or after refers to 'hereditary households of artisans and merchants'.[33] This reminds us that what Yang and other gentlemen objected to in the wealth of Liu Pao and others was its presumption, not that they really rivalled princes.

It is likely that the state carried on some manufacturing in the city. At P'ing-ch'eng the palace compound had contained many workshops. The Northern Wei's successor regimes also ran their own manufacturing enterprises. The Northern Ch'i office of the *T'ai-fu* had a number of workshops, principally concerned with weaving special silks, dyeing, iron-founding, and pottery-making; while the Chou had departments in charge of weaving and dyeing, iron-founding, and making arms. The only one of these activities that can definitely be located in a capital is some weaving in Yeh.[34] It may thus well be that in or near Loyang's palace compound were some specialist workshops producing, say, fine silks and arms.

The state's political control of Loyang's Buddhism will be discussed shortly; suffice it to say here that it was more effective in preventing religious risings than in preventing the unbounded growth of monasteries and nunneries. Whether or not we believe the hostile observation in 518 that they occupied a third of the city's land,[35] Yang's statement that their number rose to 1,376 before the city was abandoned seems too precise to be a rhetorical exaggeration.[36]

---

[32] As did the eunuchs Liu T'eng (*WS* 94, p. 2028) and the rich Han official Li Ch'ung, a passionate and avaricious trader who accumulated a vast fortune in the markets of Yeh and Loyang (*WS* 66, p. 1473). Stories about his meanness are told in chs. 3 and 4 of the 'Record'. See also Han Kuo-p'an (1962), pp. 184–5.

[33] Cited in Han Kuo-p'an (1962), pp. 183–4.

[34] Han Kuo-p'an (1962), pp. 169–71; T'ang Chang-ju (1959), pp. 45–51.

[35] *WS* 114, p. 3045.

[36] 'Record', ch. 5, end.

THE POPULATION OF THE CITY

Loyang's 109,000 households may have represented a population of 600,000 or more, at five individuals to the household, and making extra allowance for the huge palace complex, the size of both princes' and officials' establishments, and the many thousands of inmates of the monasteries and nunneries who would not have been included in population figures as household members.

We can only guess at the proportions made up by various social groups in this number. The largest category was probably household staff—in the palaces, the princely mansions, the homes of officials, army officers, and merchants, and in the grander monasteries and nunneries. The royal establishment was presumably much larger than that of any of the princes, and if the largest of these had 500 female entertainers, its total staff must have been numbered by the thousand. So the royal palaces must have had thousands or even tens of thousands of people living and working in them; and the total staffs of all the princes in the capital must have run to many tens of thousands before the slaughter of 528.

We do not know how many graded officials there were in Loyang. If we allow the same ratio of metropolitan to provincial officials as in T'ang times, when it was 2,621:16,185,[37] we might estimate that something of the order of 1,100 graded officials were stationed in Loyang, and though the great majority of them would have had homes outside the capital, they must also have kept establishments there that, although not princely, were of some size. When one official, Kao Tzu-ju, had to justify his failure to leave the capital immediately it was invaded by Ch'en Ch'ing-chih's southern forces he explained that he had a household of 100 to look after there.[38] Some of the senior palace staff, especially the top eunuchs, had large households of their own, as would the capital's soldiers. A considerable proportion of all these domestics would have been slaves.

Even before 528 the religious population of Loyang must have been considerable. Yang mentions two monasteries with

[37] *TT* 19, p. 108.
[38] *WS* 77, p. 1713.

more than 1,000 rooms, one of which had 3,000 monks, of another that filled more than one ward, and another still that numbered its novices by the thousand.[39] There were many other large monasteries and nunneries among the city's 1,367 Buddhist institutions; their total population cannot have been less than 20,000, and may have been double that figure. It was probably at its highest in the years after the Ho-yin massacre, when the many princely mansions turned into monasteries may have included some of the members of their households.

Another large component in Loyang's population was the army. The first settlers in the new capital had been the soldiers of the southern expedition. By 495 there had been 150,000 of them, and the next year the number seems to have been even higher. We do not know how many of them lived in the capital and how many in the domain; but we have Yang's anecdote about a ghostly military family living on the banks of the Lo river in the southern suburb. We saw that in the early 500s many, if not most, of them were farming outside the capital in the imperial domain, having been required to bring their families down from the north, and were compulsorily registered as residents of Loyang. Over the years there may well have been a tendency for soldiers from the domain to drift into the city, leaving their lands to be worked by others. A very vague indication of the number of non-Hans, most of whom would have belonged to military families, in Loyang when the southern army occupied the city in 529 is that the southerners, who were some 10,000 strong, were said to have been outnumbered ten times over by the 'Ch'iang and Yi' (a generic literary term for various non-Han peoples).[40] Taken as a literal statement about the number of soliders in the capital this is inplausible. Loyang's armies had suffered heavy losses during the previous years, and the survivors were at the time fighting north and south of the Yellow River. The next year, after a measure of peace had been restored, the emperor Chuang-ti was hard pressed to raise 10,000 men immediately (perhaps from the city itself) and 30,000 soon afterwards (perhaps from

[39] These were the Ching-ming (ch. 2), the Yung-ming and Jung-chüeh (ch. 4), and the Ch'in T'ai-shang-chün (ch. 2).

[40] *Liang shu* 32, p. 463.

the domain) for Loyang's defence against the avengers of Erhchu Jung.[41] But although there cannot have been 100,000 soldiers in the city in 529, the number may be a rough guide to the number of soldiers' dependants in the capital.

Merchants, tradespeople, and entertainers, including the many foreign traders south of the river, must have numbered many thousands: there were ten wards of them in the western suburb, at least one in the eastern, and at least one in the southern one. There must also have been an army of minor government servants, such as the granary workers who filled a ward of their own, and the non-graded staff of the great central government offices.

Although graded officials and royal princes and other aristocratic northerners did not directly make much difference to the city's population, we have already noted the importance of their households in swelling its size. Here Kao-tsu's policy of compelling many northerners, including, apparently, the royal princes, to make their permanent homes in the capital profoundly affected its character, and was sufficient in itself to make Northern Wei Loyang different from its Han, Ts'ao-Wei, and Chin predecessors.

THE DOMAIN, THE FEEDING OF THE CAPITAL, AND ITS PLACE IN THE NATIONAL ECONOMY

The immediate environment of the city was the imperial domain. This was probably bounded by the Yellow River to the north, extending about 50 kilometres from the capital in other directions.[42] We do not know much about the domain, except that it was here that many of the forced immigrants from P'ing-ch'eng and its domain were settled. Some of these were soldiers; others would have been dependants of the city's leading monasteries. The Mang hills between Loyang and Meng-chin to the north-west were the principal burial grounds

---

[41] 'Record', ch. 1.

[42] On the development of the concept of the domain (*chi-nei*) in China and early Japan see Sogabe Shizuo (1964). He discusses the domains of the Northern Wei and its successors on pp. 372 ff., and makes the convincing suggestion that Loyang's domain corresponded with the province of Lo-chou set up by the Eastern Wei after the move to Yeh. On Lo-chou and its subordinate *chün* and *hsien* see *WS* 106/2, pp. 2547-9.

for the royal family and the Hsienpei aristocracy.[43] There is no information on how the original inhabitants of the domain were treated. Were they driven out, as were those of the Yeh area in 534? It seems likely that some of the 400,000 households in the capital and the domain in that year were indigenous. No doubt by then they were nearly all dependants of the immigrants.

No doubt too the countryside around Loyang provided the capital with much more food than had the famine-ridden domain in Tai. The *chün-t'ien* rules granted the owners of slaves and draught animals about as much land as they could use, and in addition all holders of office were given a special allocation of at least 100 *mu*. The former provision would have been of enormous benefit to the richer Hsienpei, required as they were to settle here; and the latter would have provided a local source of legitimate income for Han officials whose own estates were in the provinces.[44] We may expect that Loyang's richer monasteries and nunneries had dependants of their own in the domain, some wholly servile and some half-free, as in P'ing-ch'eng days; and some of the serfs and slaves on princely estates may have passed to the monasteries into which their masters' town houses were converted after the Ho-yin killings.

A good proportion of those who worked the land in the domain were probably slaves, and this proportion may well have been higher than for north China as a whole as the royal princes had so many slaves. There was a saying in late Northern Wei times that implies that field slavery was normal: 'If you want to know about farming, ask a male slave; if you

---

[43] On these tombs see the general account in Su Pai (1978/2). On particular tombs see Kuo Chien-pang (1966); Lo-yang po-wo-kuan (1973 and 1974); Lo-yang po-wu-kuan and Huang Ming-lan (1978). Many inscriptions from them are collected in *Han Wei Nan-pei-ch'ao mu-chih chi shih*, ed. Chao Wan-li.

[44] Under the *chün-t'ien* rules office-holders from the rank of county magistrate to provincial governor were granted the use of from 600 to 1,500 *mu* of land; but it is not clear from the bare outline of the regulations that survives (most conveniently available in *WS* 110, pp. 2853–5, with critical notes on p. 2868) whether central government officials received proportionate allocations. According to a work compiled in the late 570s, the *Kuan-tung feng-su chuan*, of which a relevant fragment is preserved in *TT* 2, p. 15, the Wei *ling* allocated one *ch'ing* (100 *mu*) of public land to all office-holders, irrespective of rank, for 'fodder'; this evidently refers to land round the capital. (On the *chün-t'ien* system see the references in n. 41 to ch. 2 above; on the *Kuan-tung feng-su chuan* see Ikeda On (1963), pp. 143 ff.; and Nishimura Genyū (1968), pp. 283 ff., where this fragment is analysed carefully.)

want to know about weaving, ask a female one.'[45] The *Ch'i min yao shu*, that remarkable late Northern Wei handbook of estate management, mentions both hired hands and slaves, and even uses slaves as a measure of value. Three-cart-loads of rape-turnip (*man-ching*) leaves sold at pickling time would buy a male slave, and twenty loads of the same plant's roots a female one.[46] Given that field slavery was so important a feature of Northern Wei agriculture (though not, perhaps, the predominant one) it is likely that many of the thousands of slaves belonging to the richest princes were put to work on the extensive estates in the domain to which big slave-owners were entitled, and there would have been many smaller holdings of officials and soldiers in the capital worked by slaves, tenants, or others.

The large and rich population of Loyang would have made market-gardening (of the sort recommended in *Ch'i min yao shu* to those who had land near towns) profitable. Loyang would also have needed the mutton and dairy products that its inhabitants, Han and Hsienpei alike, consumed as stamples, as is shown by several of Yang's anecdotes.

After the move to Yeh, where a domain had been created around the new capital by expelling the original inhabitants, there was a lively trade in ex-officio land allocations. Land-grabbers expropriated free peasants, turning them into hired labourers or dependants. The powerful took up the full allocations to which their slaves and oxen entitled them, even though small peasants had to do without.[47] All this shows that land round Yeh must have been well worth having, and there is no reason to think that this did not also apply to Loyang's domain. Land in the domain was not taxed until 526, and even then the rates were low: 5 sheng per *mu* on normal land, and twice that on 'borrowed' (hired) public land.[48] As the standard yield of millet was around 2 *shih* to the *mu*,[49] these rates were equivalent to only $2\frac{1}{2}$ or 5 per cent.

[45] *WS* 65, p. 1445.

[46] *CMYS* 18.5.2 and 3. (In both cases it was the product of 10 *mu* of land.)

[47] See the *Kuan-tung feng-su chuan* fragments and modern studies cited in n. 44, p. 120 above.

[48] *WS* 110, p. 2861.

[49] *CMYS* 52.3.1.

There is a good silent indication that the domain played a very big part in feeding the capital in the absence from historical records of reports of famine in Loyang in its later years, even when in 528 or 529 the capital's official granaries were empty.[50]

What would have made domain land so desirable would have been the sale of food to the capital. The city itself can have produced only a tiny proportion of what it ate. Its wards only contained 573 square metres for each household, less than half that allowed under the *chün-t'ien* rules for the house and vegetable patch of a family of three free adults or five slaves.[51] Yang does not give us the impression that the city's land was devoted to agriculture: the fruit from the capital's many fine orchards, like the fish from the Yi and Lo rivers which was more expensive than beef, was of gastronomic, not economic, significance. No doubt many kept chickens or pigs, or grew some vegetables. There was even one Hsienpei official, Liu Jen-chih, who when in Loyang experimented with the ancient *ou-t'ien* (also read *ch'ü-t'ien*) method of growing extremely heavy crops of millet in small shallow pits to which much labour and manure were devoted.[52] But Liu was regarded by conventional opinion as a notorious miser who kept his dependants in wretched conditions,[53] so that his ultra-intensive millet cultivation may be seen as an eccentricity that few others would have copied.

It is hard to assess how great an economic burden Loyang was on the rest of the country outside the domain. After the *t'ai-ho* reforms tax levels were not high, though the levies—2 *shih* of millet and a bolt of silk or hemp cloth—were raised on the married couple, not on that rather elastic unit, the household. If the couple received their full land entitlement and were only charged the legal amount, this may have been only 2 or 3 per cent of their gross income; and even if this estimate is doubled or tripled to allow for lower land allocations and higher actual tax demands, it would not be

---

[50] *WS* 110, p. 2861.
[51] 1.6 *mu*, or 1,201 square metres. See references in n. 44, p. 120 above.
[52] *CMYS* 3.19.12.
[53] *PS* 10, pp. 733–4; *WSa* 81, pp. 1794–5.

crippling except in an agrarian economy much more precarious than the Northern Wei one appears generally to have
been,[54] or when several years' taxes were levied at once.[55] We
saw in chapter 5 above how lackadaisical the Loyang authorities were about other sources of revenue. Such a casual
approach can be explained by the Wei rulers' old preference
for rewarding officials and generals with grants of land and
dependants, by their policy of trying to support the huge
armies on the northern and southern frontiers with dependent
agricultural colonies (or else simply neglecting the distant
soldiery), and by the size of the tax-paying population. In the
absence of good contemporary figures this may be roughly
estimated from some general indications and from the much
more detailed figures compiled by the Eastern Wei regime
between 543 and 550.[56] We are told that up to *cheng-kuang*
(520–5), the dynasty's golden years, its population (*hu k'ou*)
was twice[57] or even more than double that of *t'ai-k'ang* (280–
9), which was recorded as 2,459,800 households and
16,163,863 individuals.[58] This implies at least 5,000,000
households and 32,000,000 people. The catastrophic upheavals from 525 onwards are said to have wiped out the great
majority of these. This doubtless is true of the decline in the
numbers under the government's control, but the actual loss of
life, though appalling, is unlikely to have been as bad as that. A
more realistic figure for the Northern Wei population on the
eve of the split between east and west is 3,375,368 households,
a loss of a third. We may estimate that this meant some
20,000,000 people.

This large population consisted mainly of peasants. As the
Ch'i min yao shu and many modern studies of that extraordinary
book shows, they produced yields that were very good indeed

---

[54] For good short surveys of Northern Wei taxation policies see Li Chien-nung (1963
repr.), pp. 153–71, and Uchida Gimpu (1969). An earlier study is Yoshida Torao
(1943).
[55] As from 525 onwards—*WS* 110, pp. 2860–1.
[56] These figures are in *WS* 106. On the Northern Wei population, see Uchida Gimpu
(1975), pp. 185–211, which includes convenient tables of recorded and estimated
totals for the Northern Wei and its successors, as well as of all the *WS* 106 figures.
[57] *WS* 106/1, p. 2455.
[58] *TT* 7, p. 40.

by any pre-modern standards, surpassing Han dynasty levels of output and approaching the limits of what could be achieved in dry agriculture without the benefit of modern science-based techniques.[59] Despite the shortcomings of north China's transport and market networks, this highly productive agriculture produced a huge surplus when not too badly disrupted by war and the demands of war. That is why the domain was able to provide much of Loyang's food, and why the rest of the country was able to bear the burden of Loyang's other supplies. When approaching earlier Chinese history from the twentieth century it is easy to assume that the modern problems of an overcrowded rural population struggling to avoid starvation always applied. P'ing-ch'eng was plagued by famine because it was in an area that was only marginally agricultural; but the main farming regions of north China seem generally to have been prosperous in the late Northern Wei period. In Loyang's best decades the court had more tax cloth than it knew what to do with. Even in the chaotic year of 529 the taxes continued to pour in: at Jung-yang the southern invaders captured oxen, horses, grain, and silk in incalculable quantities, and at K'ao-ch'eng, also to the east of Loyang, they took 7,800 tax-grain carts.[60] In 534 Kao Huan could divert taxes from Hopei intended for Loyang to Yeh to provide a reserve from which he could issue the new settlers with 1,300,000 *shih*.[61]

An indication of the backwardness of the trading economy, by contrast with the high level of agricultural output, was the inadequacy of the currency system.[62] Even in the main cities there was not enough money. The first Northern Wei minting had to wait until 495, when the authorities cast a new *wu-chu* coin and permitted private mintings provided they were up to the standard of the government issue. The state, however,

---

[59] The best modern editions of *CMYS* is the *CMYS chin shih*, edited by Shih Sheng-han; the annotated Japanese translation by Nishiyama and Kumashiro (1969) is also valuable. Among studies of it may be singled out Shih Sheng-han (1957 and 1962); Wan Kuo-ting (1956); Li Ch'ang-nien (1959); Amano Motonosuke (1954). An excellent survey of recent work is Kumashiro Yukio (1971).

[60] *Liang shu* 32, pp. 461–2.

[61] See ch. 5 above.

[62] On Northern Wei currency see *WS* 77, pp. 1711–12; 110, pp. 2863–8; *TCTC* 148, pp. 4630–1; 153, p. 4767.

failed to maintain the quality of its own coins, so that the cash fell to less than two-fifths of its authorized weight. Much of the country north of the Yellow River continued to use cloth (sometimes town into small strips for small change), grain, or other commodities as media of exchange. Even in Loyang we find gold and horses used as forms of transferable wealth.[63] Values in the *Ch'i min yao shu* of different kinds of farm products are given most often in cash or plain silk, sometimes in grain or, as we have seen, in slaves. The interlude of comparative prosperity Loyang enjoyed around the year 531 may very well be connected with the issue of new, heavy, government coins in 529–30. The more general failure of the government to encourage the growth of the national market through providing enough cash was not unique to the Northern Wei: it is reflected in burials from throughout the centuries of the Ts'ao-Wei, Chin, and Northern and Southern Dynasties, which generally contain far fewer coins than Han tombs. Of the coins that are found, a high proportion are of Han date. This suggests the 'old coins' still circulating in some parts of the Northern Wei territory were Han ones. Silver coins from Persia and elsewhere in the west were also used to some extent.[64] Set against the indications of a flourishing agriculture, the impression we have of trade in north China is that, despite the efforts of the commodity-dealer Liu Pao and his like, it fell far short of its potential development and was crippled by lack of state support. Loyang itself was not essentially an economic centre. It generated a certain amount of trade simply because a lot of people, among them many very rich ones, were there; but its economy was essentially based on the control of rural estates in the domain by its leading inhabitants, and the state's appropriation through the tax system of a fairly small part of the output of a flourishing agriculture. P'ing-ch'eng was compared earlier to a huge villa in the centre of a gigantic *latifundium*; and, in an even bigger and more sophisticated way, this was true of Loyang. There is an economic sense in which Northern Wei Loyang, for all its enormous size and prosperity, never was a

---

[63] See the story of K'ou Tsu-jen in ch. 4 of the 'Record'.
[64] On Sassanian silver coins found in China see Hsia Nai (1974); for an anecdote about a Northern Wei prince scattering silver coins see *PCS* 31, p. 415.

city at all. And yet heavy though the burden of Loyang was on the peasants and cattle-rearers of the domain, it did not weigh too heavily on the rest of the country. What the city, and particularly the court, had to answer for to the people of Hopei and elsewhere was not so much the taxes it took as the political incompetence that unleashed such catastrophic wars and upheavals on them. In the end it perished through its folly rather than its greed.

LOYANG AS AN ADMINISTRATIVE CENTRE

Of the court factions at Loyang after the death of Kao-tsu enough has been told in the two previous chapters to make unnecessary any further comment on their failure, severally and collectively, to use the state's resources for the good of the state or the people. This failure can only be attributed to Loyang inasmuch as it was far from the northern frontier, making neglect easier, and it was not a necessary consequence of the move of the capital.

While it is possible to make fairly reliable reconstructions of the powers of the various departments of central government and of their changing relationships during Loyang's decades as capital—the subject is one that appealed to the profoundly bureaucratic inclinations of later historians and encyclopedists—it is hard to get very clear impressions of Loyang's administration of the provinces. In the years immediately before the move from P'ing-ch'eng a very thorough reorganization of local government had been ordered that was intended to bring effective state control right down to the level of the village. Regular assessments of officials' performance had also been instituted. But Kao-tsu had entrusted the running of this system to the leaders of the most powerful and long-established lineages, often allowing them to serve in their native districts. After his death central control over provincial officials weakened rapidly. Assessments became infrequent and had virtually stopped by the time Loyang was abandoned; and for several years before that the court had lost the power effectively to choose officials in areas under such powerful warlords as the Erhchu, even when those warlords were nominally loyal. Thus it was that, after the northern-garrison mutinies and their suppression by armies not Loyang's, large

areas of the countryside were under the actual control of local strongmen, some of whom had private armies.

In brief, once the initial effort of creating the new capital was over, Loyang seems to have played a less and less positive role in the provinces, particularly once the city's rulers abandoned any serious attempt at conquering the south from 516 onwards. The court's loss of interest in military adventures would have reduced demands for labour service in the provinces, and must certainly have been popular with the many Hsienpei military families settled in the capital and the domain. But with the joys of metropolitan living went a deterioration in the fighting qualities of the capital's armies, so that when Loyang needed to reassert its power in the north and the west from 525 onwards it failed utterly. Loyang's rulers had only themselves to blame.

It would be tedious to discuss at length the formal structure of the machinery of government in the capital. During Loyang's decades the effective centre of administrative power passed from the Chancellery (*Shang-shu sheng*), the department in charge of the various executive organs, to the Secretariat (*Chung-shu sheng*) and the Palace Bureau (*Men-hsia sheng*), and from these offices to the persons of the assistant secretaries (*she-jen*) who had their own office inside the palace and were in attendance on the monarch (or the dowager Hu).[65] The holders of this office were not necessarily the scions of great families so admired by Kao-tsu, but could be comparatively humbly born clerks who, like Hsü Ho and Cheng Yen, rose on their wits and could be easily got rid of if necessary. The dowager's first spell of power also saw palace eunuchs seize much ground from the regular bureaucracy. With the absence of a strong and effective emperor the command of the capital's armies became increasingly important. The tendency for the highest-graded and most distinguished posts to become empty honours was well established even before the Erhchu took this to the point of absurdity. And while the capital's soldiers were

---

[65] For an outline of the Northern Wei government structure in relation to others of the Wei, Chin and Northern and Southern Dynasties, see T'ao Hsi-sheng (1973), vol. 3. On the Secretariat, see the thorough monograph by Cheng Ch'in-jen, 1965. *T'ung tien* is an invaluable guide through the maze.

playing the political role of a Praetorian Guard, they were losing their ability to defend the city from external enemies.

Loyang's growing ineffectiveness as a centre for national civil and military administration cannot be blamed on its location or on the formal structure of government, except that a strong and clear-sighted ruler was needed to hold together a system whose inherent divisions and stresses were to be so visible from 525 onwards. Such a ruler was not to be had after Kao-tsu's death.

LOYANG AS A CULTURAL AND RELIGIOUS CAPITAL

We have seen how the attraction of Loyang's past was an important, perhaps even decisive, factor in Kao-tsu's decision to make it his capital; and this historical aura evidently fascinated Yang Hsüan-chih and others of his class. Loyang's own legend undoubtedly added something to the legitimacy of the Wei rulers in the eyes of the Han-Chinese aristocracy, and helped to perpetuate that legitimacy after the real power had gone. Loyang's heritage also made it much easier for the great Han-Chinese families to see the Wei emperors as authentically embodying Chinese, rather than barbarian, traditions of kingship. It was psychologically essential for their own sense of worth, that they were serving a state in the true succession of Chinese monarchy, that they should accept the clear determination of the ruling house since the time of the dowager Feng and Kao-tsu to be regarded as the heirs of the Han, Ts'ao-Wei, and Chin monarchies. Hence the immense significance to Yang and those who thought like him of the futile assertions of royal dignity by two of the client emperors of the city's last years.

Thus the palace's centrality and dominance in the capital was not just topographical. Yet such was the awe with which Yang saw it, even in his memory, that he did not describe the palace itself, only its parks and gardens. One wonders whether this was a conscious decision. At the same time he had the high-born official's contempt for many of the palace personnel.

Behind the loudly professed loyalism of the Han-Chinese aristocracy lurked other attitudes. They felt a lack of self-confidence because while they were serving a dynasty that until recently had made no secret of its barbarian origins and had

functioned as both a Hsienpei as well as a Han-Chinese monarchy, a rival Han-Chinese court in Chien-k'ang was constantly reminding them that their cultural and political legitimacy was not universally accepted throughout the civilized world as they understood it. The racial hatred of the Han aristocrats for their barbarian overlords was generally buried deep. In the previous century Ts'ui Hao had been executed together with his extended family for presuming on his good standing with the royal house to write history offensive to Hsienpei racial sensibilities, and some other leading Han clans had suffered similar fates.[66] This warning was heeded for several decades. When in 515 P'ei Chih remarked that long-established families such as his (which had been classed in the highest category by Kao-tsu) should outrank others, be they Chinese (*Hua*) or barbarian (*Yi*), his indiscretion led to the forced suicide of himself and his associates under pressure from the Hsienpei soldier Yü Chung.[67] Only four years later a similar expression of Han aristocratic arrogance by Chang Chung-yü prompted the military riot to which we referred in chapter 4. The taboo on discussing racial questions, as far as the Hsienpei were concerned, in Han writings of the period gives extra venom to the treatment of such groups as the Chieh or Ch'i Hu after the Erhchu had been defeated.

The attitudes to their southern rivals of Loyang's courtiers and officials were logically contradictory but psychologically complementary. On the one hand they tried to humiliate southern refugees, generals, or diplomats who came to their capital, maintaining that the southern taste for tea and fish was effete and barbaric when compared with the eating of mutton and swilling of treated milk in the northern capital. They also poured scorn on southern accents, missed no chance to point to non-Han influences in southern culture, and tended to regard as newfangled any ways in which the south had developed Ts'ao-Wei and Western Chin traditions, whereas the north prided itself on preserving faithfully the culture of the past. On the other hand, Loyang longed to have its cultural and

---

[66] On the death of Ts'ui Hao and its significance see Ishida Yoshiyuki (1967 and 1968), and Chou Yi-liang (1963), pp. 117 ff.

[67] *WS* 71, p. 1570.

political pretensions accepted by the south, and in its actions it sometimes acknowledged southern superiority.[68] Kao-tsu had made no bones about using southern gentlemen as advisers in the planning of the new capital and in reforming the Wei state's institutions. Yang Hsüan-chih purrs with pride as he reports the admiration for Loyang's culture expressed by the southern general Ch'en Ch'ing-chih, or the good impression supposedly made by northern diplomats and refugees in Chien-k'ang.

Loyang's rather self-conscious secular literary culture, in which Yang took such pride, is best understood as the product of the long years of disorder in the north since the fall of a previous Loyang in 316. Since the disastrous end of the lively and at times decadent cultural life of that doomed city, the powerful Han families had maintained in their rural seats traditions of conservative learning as a mark of identity and superiority, not as a means of self-expression. We find Loyang writers being praised not so much for what they wrote as for the speed and facility with which they got ornate prose on paper. The secular literature of Loyang seems, from the surviving examples, to have been derivative and of no great merit.[69] Its best-known example, Li Tao-yüan's *Shui ching chu* (Commentary on the Classic of Rivers), is a display of antiquarian topographical erudition which as literature is completely dead and can be read only in small doses as a work of historical reference. The most impressive work that has come down to us from the Northern Wei, the estate-holder's handbook *Ch'i min yao shu*, is a wholly admirable piece of plain and practical prose that tests written traditions against the experience of its own day, but there is nothing to connect it with Loyang. There was a revival of Confucian education at Loyang, both in such government institutions as the Imperial Academy and through private teaching by specialists in a

---

[68] On these attitudes see Yang's anecdotes about encounters with southerners in chs. 2 and 3 of the 'Record'. For north/south comparisons of a few decades later see Teng Ssu-yü's 1968 translation of the *Yen shih chia hsün*, a source drawn on in Moriya Mitsuo's excellent 1948 study of northern and southern customs in the Six Dynasties period.

[69] As can be seen from a perusal of the Northern Wei section of the *Ch'üan shang-ku San-tai Ch'in Han San-kuo Liu-ch'ao wen*.

particular text, but not enough is known of its content to permit a reliable assessment, beyond making the generalization that the most Loyang did for the Confucian tradition was to transmit it.[70] Even the palace library was so poorly stocked that Sun Hui-wei had to make great efforts to provide it with a set of standard texts. The Ming-t'ang took decades to build.[71] An apparent exception to this lack of distinction was the compiling of a new legal code in 504, in which, as Ch'en Yin-k'o has pointed out, the unsystematized development of law under the Southern Dynasties was disciplined by the precision of Han legal thinking as preserved in the north. This code, later known as the *Hou Wei lü*, was to be the foundation of Northern Ch'i, Sui, and T'ang codes, and thus in the direct line of development of Chinese law.[72] An area in which Loyang's distinction is still to be seen and admired was in calligraphy: the strong-boned elegance of Northern Wei tomb-inscriptions from the Mang hills is a model of classical restraint. But although Loyang did not see much of a flowering of Confucian or any other kind of Han culture, it had its share of officials honest and learned enough to be set against their colleagues who were neither; and there were always at least one or two willing to risk their lives by remonstrating with a difficult sovereign, dowager, or dictator.

There was much more vigour to Loyang's Buddhism.[73] The

[70] On Loyang's Confucian culture see, in addition to the 'Record', the evidence to be found in pp. 287–405 of Liu Ju-lin (1940). On Sun Hui-wei's efforts see *WS* 84, pp. 1852–4.

[71] It was apparently started between 508 and 511, but to judge from memorials in or around 520 (*WS* 41, pp. 933–4; 72, pp. 1613–14) and in 532 (*PCSa* 36, pp. 476–8; *PS* 43, pp. 1589–91) it was either never finished then or else not kept in decent condition. Yang ('Record', ch. 3) dates its building to between 520 and 525.

[72] On this code see Ch'en Yin-k'o (1963 repr.), pp. 109–12 and Ch'eng Shu-te (1963 repr.), pp. 339 and 352 ff. Matsunaga Masao (1970–1), shows that outside this code some concessions were still made to the traditional legal systems of the tribal peoples of the north.

[73] The fundamental works on Buddhism of this period remain T'ang Yung-t'ung's 1938 history (1963 repr.), especially chapters 14, 15, 19, and 20, and Tsukamoto Zenryū (1942). The 1970 set of essays on Northern Wei Buddhism edited by Ochō Enichi is of great value. Briefer introductions to the subject can be found in Kenneth Ch'en's 1964 history, and in Kamata Shigeo's 1977 article. On the material side of Loyang's religion Hattori Katsuhiko's 1965 and 1968 volumes should be consulted. On Lungmen and its inscriptions, see Mizuno Seiichi and Nagahiro Toshio (1941). The remarks on Loyang's Buddhism that follow are largely derived from these works and from Yang's pages.

material splendour of the city's bigger monasteries and
nunneries cannot escape the reader of Yang's 'Record'. They
included some of the city's finest buildings, including what
must surely have been its most spectacular, the Yung-ning
Pagoda. In their number and their magnificence they distinguished Loyang from any other city in China before it. The
great Buddhist festivals, especially the celebration of the
Śākyamuni's birthday in the fourth month, when 1,000 statues
assembled from throughout the capital in the enormous Ching-
ming Monastery south of the city wall were wheeled under
their jewelled canopies up the capital's main highway to have
flowers strewn on them by the emperor from above the palace
gates. Huge crowds of the faithful, also holding flowers, heard
Indian music and saw amazing performances by all sorts of
entertainers amid a fog of incense. Other spectacular shows
were laid on when the statues were taken from other monasteries and convents to the Ching-ming before the main
procession: that of the Ch'ang-ch'iu Monastery was accompanied by sword swallowers, fire-belchers, flagpole-
climbers, and rope-walkers and led by 'lion' and other beasts
who may have been the ancestors of the dancing lions of
modern Chinese celebrations, and these displays, which drew
such crowds that people were often trampled to death, were
matched by those of the Chao-yi Convent.[74]

These and other such occasions as the great maigre-feasts in
the Ching-lo Convent to which women only were admitted at
which 'songs curled round the roof-beams as dancing sleeves
slowly turned' to the accompaniment of silken strings and
pipes, or the later performances there in which the amazing
acts including flying through the air and displays of magic,[75]
helped to give Loyang's inhabitants a sense of community and
identity, and must have meant much more to nearly all of
them than dry Confucian traditions.

Loyang's Buddhism was not just for the rich and powerful.
Ordinary people in the city clubbed together to found small
monasteries, hold religious meetings, or carve stone images in

---

[74] On these processions see under the Ching-ming Monastery in ch. 3 of the 'Record'
and the Ch'ang-ch'iu Monastery and Ching-lo Convent in ch. 1.

[75] 'Record', ch. 1.

the cliff temples at Lungmen, and in their homes they kept gilded statuettes of various Buddhas. Their religion was, it seems, a fairly simple devotional one that emphasized virtuous conduct, as can be seen from the very popular and obviously apocryphal *T'i-wei Po-li ching* which combined Buddhist ideas with Chinese folk religion,[76] and encouraged rather than discouraged family sentiment, as is shown by many of the dedicatory inscriptions at Lungmen which showed that the intention of carving images was often to further the interests of dead parents, forebears, and other relatives, of the reigning monarch, or of the whole human race. The popular religious societies which had the images carved left inscriptions listing tens or hundreds of subscribers; their leaders might be officials, monks, nuns, or others; and contributions ranged from a hundred to several thousand cash. These figures can be contrasted with the 200,000 and 400,000 cash given by the high officials Li Ch'ung and Li Kuang to found a monastery in Loyang.[77] When the names of the contributors to the cost of images at Lungmen are listed they include many recognizably plebeian ones. The religious societies also held meetings at which members of the clergy might preach and ate vegetarian maigre-feasts together.

Religious enthusiasm was all-pervasive in the city, and the country's rulers took the lead. Kao-tsu's devotion to Chinese traditions did not prevent him from being a keen student of the difficult *Satyasiddhi śāstra* (*Ch'eng-shih lun*), an important text of the Mādhyamika school that since its translation by Kūmarajīva had been most influential in south China.[78] He was also devoted to *dhyāna* meditation. His successors generally encouraged other approaches to the religion, patronizing, for example, the simultaneous and rival translations of the *Daśabhūmika-sūtra śāstra* (*Shih-ti ching lun*) by Bodhiruci and Ratnamati, each kept under armed guard in a different hall of the palace, between 508 and 511.[79] They gave material evidence of their devotion in the great royal monasteries and

[76] Discussed in Tsukamoto (1942), pp. 295–353. On this and other popular scriptures of the period see also the article by Maki in the Ōchō volume.

[77] See under the Cheng-shih Monastery in ch. 2 of the 'Record'.

[78] *WS* 114, pp. 3039–40. See also Ōchō (1970), pp. 27 ff.

[79] T'ang Yung-t'ung (1963 repr.), pp. 848–50.

nunneries as well as in the cave temples at Lungmen and Kunghsien. The court took no effective measures to restrict the building of monasteries and convents during the reign of Shih-tsung/Hsüan-wu-ti and the two periods of domination by the dowager Hu, as is shown by the extraordinary number of Buddhist establishments in the capital.

This is not the place for a thorough account of Buddhist thought during Loyang's years as capital; some brief comments derived from those who have studied this huge subject properly must suffice.[80] The Loyang period was, it appears, one in which many important new influences from the West changed Chinese Buddhistm, and saw the early development of several schools that were to flourish later. Kao-tsu's interest in Mādhyamika thought gave way soon after his death to other approaches to Buddhism, largely under the stimulus of the arrival in the city of monks from central Asia and India by the thousand. Perhaps the most influential among these, in his own lifetime at least, was the great translator Bodhiruci who came to Loyang from his native India in 508 and was installed by imperial command with several hundred other monks in the Yung-ning Monastery. His translation team produced Chinese versions of 39 works, including the *Laṅkāvatāra sūtra*, *Lotus sūtra*, *Diamond sūtra*, and many writings by Vasubandhu and Asaṅga, the brothers who were the principal founders of the new Yogācārin school of Indian Buddhism in the fourth century. Among these the *Shih-ti ching-lun* (or *Ti-lun*) aroused great immediate interest, as was shown by the unusual circumstances in which it was competitively translated and the rivalry between the factions of each of the main translators, named for the parts of the city where their leaders were based, Ratnamati in the north and Bodhiruci in the south. The *Avataṁsaka sūtra* (*Hua-yen ching*), a knotty and demanding text from which the *Shih-ti ching* was drawn, was also studied in Loyang, notably by T'an-mo-tsui. The later followers of the *Ti-lun* factions were to be drawn into the Hua-yen school that flourished in the T'ang, a school in whose early growth the Northern Wei capital played an important part.

---

[80] I draw on the works of T'ang, Tsukamoto, Ch'en, and Kamata listed in n. 73, p. 131 above.

Another type of T'ang Buddhism that can be traced to Northern Wei Loyang was the Pure Land, with its reliance on a Buddha, be it Maitreya or Amitābha, to ensure one's rebirth in his paradise. The growth of this sort of faith was reflected in the imagery of Lungmen during Loyang's last two decades as Northern Wei capital; and it was after meeting Bodhiruci in Loyang that the monk T'an-luan, whose previous search had taken him from his native northern Shansi to the study of Taoist magic with a Maoshan teacher south of the Yangtse, abandoned all other approaches in favour of the single-minded recitation of the name of Amitābha and contemplation of him.

Yet another school that flourished in Loyang was the Ch'an. Meditation had been a part of Buddhism in China long before. The great complex of cave-temples at Yünkang had included many cells for eremites, and in Loyang's first years Kao-tsu had ordered the building of the Shao-lin Monastery in the hills south of the city for the Dhyāna master Fo-t'o, who gathered hundreds of followers there. The same monastery was to accommodate Bodhidharma, the monk from south India or Persia later to become a figure of legend as the first patriarch of the Ch'an tradition and on whom Yang gives us the only surviving information by someone who knew him. It was in Loyang, or the Shao-lin just outside it, that he passed on his teachings to the second patriarch, Hui-k'o, and taught him the *Laṅkāvatāra sūtra*, 'a work of quite exceptional spiritual profundity' in Conze's words.[81] The story of Bodhidharma gazing at a wall for nine years is unfortunately not to be literally believed; his teaching was rather that the mind should be as steady and undisturbed as a wall.

The insatiable demand for sūtras and for new Buddhist thinking was one of the motives behind the combined diplomatic and religious expedition sent by the dowager Hu to Gandhāra and Udyāna in 518, that brought back 170 sūtras and śāstras; the story of this heroic journey makes up the main part of Yang's fifth chapter. And the liveliness of the competition between rival schools can be glimpsed in Yang's anecdote about the monk Hui-ning who returned from the

[81] 1962, p. 251.

dead to report on how such rivals as the loquacious T'an-mo-tsui, a popular preacher on the *Parinirvāṇa* and *Avataṁsaka* sūtras, had been punished by king Yama's black-clad henchmen, as had other monks who had devoted themselves to having scriptures copied, statues made, or monasteries built, instead of confining themselves to meditation and the learning and recitation of scriptures by heart.[82] The story shows something of the passionate enthusiasm with which religion was embraced, and indicates the rising prestige of devotional and contemplative Buddhism in Loyang's last years at the expense of more intellectual approaches. Such was the power of the clergy by then that even Erhchu Shih-lung, who had ordered that they be taxed to help fill his war-chest and forbidden any protests on pain of death, relented when warned by the senior monk Hui-kuang that such a tax would be the end of his state.[83] The effects of Indian and central-Asian influences were not limited to religion. Scripture, painting, and monastery architecture were directly affected, and Loyang's music was enriched by Indian styles. It is likely that other areas, from medicine to mathematics, also benefitted from contact with the West.

Of Taoism in Loyang there is not much to be said. We have noted Yang Hsüan-chih's inclination towards a certain literary Taoism, but in general it was overshadowed by Buddhism in Loyang's decades, though not uprooted. In 520 the Taoist Ch'iang Pin was invited to take part in a palace disputation with T'an-mo-tsui on the relative antiquity of Lao Tzu and Buddha, and only Bodhiruci's pleas with the emperor Hsiao-ming-ti saved Ch'iang Pin from paying with his life for being judged the loser.[84]

The fundamental weakness of Northern Wei Loyang was that it was not really necessary. If anarchy were to be avoided,

[82] 'Record', ch. 2.
[83] *HKSC* 27, p. 5a.
[84] T'ang Yung-t'ung (1963), p. 536.

there had to be a state, and the state needed a capital, but it did not have to be on the banks of the Lo river; and even if it was there, Loyang was far bigger than was needed for effective administration. This size was not explained by any significant contribution it made to the national economy. Yet this enormous city that sprang up so fast could be built and fed without overstraining national resources. Loyang's early abandonment as capital was not inevitable; but the absence of any practical reasons for its continued existence once the political will to maintain it had gone made it fatally dependent on its rulers. And they, as we have seen, were incapable of preventing the rise of a dictator who had no time for the city, which could not survive for three days after his decision to evacuate it.

The contrast with the southern capital at Chien-k'ang is instructive.[85] Chien-k'ang was at the centre of a region of excellent natural waterways that had become increasingly commercialized for centuries. At its height its population was put at 280,000 families, over two and a half times as many as Loyang's. Yet none of the successive regimes that had made Chien-k'ang their capital since the early fourth century had been as strong as the Northern Wei in its prime. Misgovernment was at least as bad in the southern court as the northern, and about half a century was as long as any dynasty managed to last. The devastation inflicted on the city by Hou Ching in 549 was far worse than anything Loyang suffered before 534. And despite all this Chien-k'ang continued, whereas Loyang came and went. The explanation is, I believe, that while Loyang was essentially an extension of the palace, Chien-k'ang was a great trading entrepot in its own right with a thriving economic life. Curiously enough it was as a trading city that an earlier Loyang had flourished when it was only a minor political centre between 1,000 and 500 years earlier; and since then two other essentially political Loyangs had disappeared with the dynasties that had ruled them.

---

[85] On Chien-k'ang and the commercialization of the south see Okazaki Fumio (1967 repr.), ch. 3; Miyakawa Hisayuki (1956), pp. 524–36; Kawakatsu Yoshio (1971); and Han Kuo-p'an (1963), ch. 4.

Kao Huan's abandonment of Loyang did not, however, end its appeal to rulers of north China. The capital of the Eastern Wei and then the Northern Ch'i regime at Yeh was Loyang transplanted, even to the extent of having its palaces built with the timbers of Loyang's. The site itself continued to exercise its spell. In 579 the Northern Chou emperor Hsüan-ti, heir to the north China his father had conquered, and besotted with his own imagined divinity, visited the ruins; and later that year he announced that as the land between the Yellow and Lo rivers was cosmically suited to being a capital, Loyang was to be rebuilt. Forty thousand soldiers were mobilized to construct palaces at Loyang on a scale far greater than that of the Han and Wei palaces. One of the first acts of the son who succeeded him after his sudden death in 580 was to stop this unnecessary expense and effort.[86]

A quarter of a century later the building of a new Loyang began again when the Sui emperor Yang-ti set a conscript labour force of 2,000,000 to work on a site a few kilometres to the west of the ruins of the Northern Wei capital.[87] That Loyang, in one form or other, has survived to the present day. The Northern Wei capital is now mostly farmland.

[86] *Chou shu* 7, pp. 117, 118, 125; 8, p. 131.
[87] Su Pai (1978/3).

Part II

A translation of
'Record of the Monasteries of Loyang'
(*Lo-yang ch'ieh-lan chi*)

by Yang Hsüan-chih

Preface

The sayings of the Three Emperors and Five Kings of high antiquity and the words of the Nine Traditions and Hundred Schools of thought[1] coexist in the domains of men; their principles unify everything beyond the heavens. Of the fundamental teachings of the One Vehicle and Two Kinds of Truth, like the doctrines of the Three Insights and Six Faculties,[2] the West has full details, while the East has no record. After [Emperor Hsiao-ming of the Han (AD 58–76)] dreamed of a man crowned with the sun and shining like the full moon, figures with long eyebrows adorned the palace gates, and a Buddha with jet-black hair was painted in the Emperor's tomb.[3]

More recently there has been a rush to spread the influence of Buddhism. In the *yung-chia* years [307–13] of the Chin dynasty there were only forty-two temples, but after the August Wei came to power and established its capital by Mount Sung and the River Lo Buddhist faith and teaching both flourished. Aristocrats and high officials parted with their horses and elephants as if they were kicking off their sandals; commoners and great families gave their wealth with the ease of leaving footprints. As a result monasteries and pagodas were packed closely together. Men competed in drawing the heavenly beauty of the Buddha, and in copying the image he left in the mountains. Monastery spires were as high as the

---

[1] Chinese traditions.
[2] Buddhist doctrines.
[3] The legend that China's conversion to Buddhism began with Emperor Hsiao-ming's dream was established long before the sixth century.

Spirit Mound,[4] and the preaching halls were as grand as the O-p'ang Palace.[5] It was, indeed, more than just

> Woods clothed in silk and embroidery,
> Plaster covered with red and purple.[6]

When the many troubles of the years *yung-hsi* [532–4] caused the transfer of the imperial capital to Yeh the monks and nuns of the temples moved there as well.[7]

In *ting-mao*, the fifth year of *wu-ting* [547], my official duties brought me back to Loyang. The city walls had collapsed, palaces and houses were in ruins; Buddhist and Taoist temples were in ashes; and shrines and pagodas were mere heaps of rubble. Walls were covered with artemisia, and streets were full of thorns. The beasts of the field had made their holes in the overgrown palace steps, and the mountain birds had nested in the courtyard trees. Wandering herdsmen loitered in the highways, and farmers had planted millet between the cere-monial towers before the palace. At last I knew that the ruins of the Yin capital were not the only ones to evoke sorrow when covered with ears of wheat,[8] and I felt the grief that 'Heavy hangs the millet' conveys about the decline of the Chou.[9]

There had been over a thousand temples inside and outside the city wall, but now all were empty and the sound of their bells was never heard; so I compiled this record in case all this might be lost to prosperity. There were so many temples that I could not describe them all. This account in five chapters is confined to the big monasteries, except where strange and miraculous events or popular stories merit the inclusion of the medium-sized and smaller ones. I begin with those inside the city wall and go on to those outside, listing them by city gates

[4] On this symbol of Chinese kingship see ch. 3 below.

[5] The great palace complex begun by Ch'in Shih-huang-ti west of modern Sian in 212 BC which was a byword for magnificence. Popularly pronounced 'A-fang'.

[6] From Chang Heng (78–139), 'Prose-poem on the Western Capital' (*Wen hsüan* 2, p. 34), describing the splendid aristocratic mansions of Han Ch'ang-an.

[7] On these turbulent years see ch. 5 of Part I.

[8] The former Yin minister Wei Tzu is said to have written a poem called 'Ears of wheat' on passing the ruins of the Yin capital after the fall of the dynasty. (*Shih chi* 38, p. 1621.)

[9] A poem in the *Book of Songs* (M65) said to express the grief of a Chou nobleman at seeing the ruins of Chou palaces and temples.

to give an idea of the distances. As I have no talent for writing there are many omissions; may gentlemen of later generations fill in my gaps.

In the 17th year of *t'ai-ho* [493] the Emperor Kao-tsu moved the capital to Loyang, ordering the Lord Chancellor Mu Liang to build the palaces and houses.[10] The gates in the city wall were known by the names of the [Ts'ao] Wei and Chin dynasties.

In the eastern wall of the city there were three gates.

The northernmost of these was called the Chien-ch'un [Establishing Spring] Gate. During the Han it had been called the Shang-tung [First East] Gate. This is the gate in Juan Chi's poem 'As I walked out of the Shang-tung Gate'.[11] Chien-ch'un was the [Ts'ao] Wei and Chin name, which Kao-tsu followed.

To the south of this was the Tung-yang [Eastern Glory] Gate, which had been called Chung-tung [Middle East] Gate in the Han. Tung-yang was the Wei and Chin name that Kao-tsu followed without altering.

The next to the south was the Ch'ing-yang [Green Glory] Gate, which had been called Wang-ching [Looking at the Capital] Gate in Han times. In the Wei and Chin it was known as the Ch'ing-ming [Clear Brightness] Gate. Kao-tsu changed the name to Ch'ing-yang Gate.

In the southern wall of the city there were four gates.

The easternmost was the K'ai-yang Gate. Long ago, when Emperor Kuang-wu of the Han moved the capital to Loyang,[12] this gate had just been finished but had not yet been named. One night a column suddenly appeared on the watchtower of the gate. Later word came from K'ai-yang county in the prefecture of Lang-yeh that a column had flown away from the southern gate of the town wall. Envoys came to inspect it, and it was indeed the same one. This name, still used during the Wei and Chin dynasties, was continued by Kao-tsu.

The next gate to the west was the P'ing-ch'ang Gate, called

---

[10] On the move see ch. 3 of Part I. On Mu Liang, or Ch'iumuling Liang (*c.* 450–502), a non-Han northern aristocrat, see *WS* 27, pp. 667–71; Yao Wei-yuan (1962), pp. 25–6; and Tsukamoto (1942), pp. 430–3.

[11] For this poem by Juan Chi (210–63) see *Wen hsüan* 23, p. 490.

[12] In AD 25.

in Han times the P'ing Gate. Kao-tsu kept the Wei and Chin name of P'ing-ch'ang Gate.

Next again to the west was the Hsüan-yang Gate [Gate of Glory Proclaimed] which had been called Hsiao-yüan [Little Park] Gate in the Han. Hsüan-yang was the Wei and Chin name that Kao-tsu followed.

West again was the Chin-yang [North of the Ford] Gate, known in the Han dynasty as the Chin Gate. In the Wei and Chin it was called Chin-yang, which Kao-tsu did not change.

There were four gates in the western wall.

The southermost was the Hsi-ming Gate [Gate of Western Brightness]. The Wei and Chin kept its Han name of Kuang-yang Gate [Gate of Extensive Brightness], which was changed to Hsi-ming by Kao-tsu.

To the north of this was the Hsi-yang Gate [Gate of Western Glory], known as Yung Gate in the Han dynasty and Hsi-ming Gate in the Wei and Chin. Kao-tsu changed its name to Hsi-yang.

Next to the north came the Ch'ang-ho Gate, which was called Shang-hsi [First West] Gate in the Han, when the 'copper astronomical instruments to equalize the seven governors'[13] stood on it. The Wei and Chin called it Ch'ang-ho Gate, which Kao-tsu followed without change.

North again came the Ch'eng-ming Gate [Gate of Accepted Brightness]. This was created by Kao-tsu at the end of the main road which ran from west to east in front of the Chin-yung Castle.[14] When Kao-tsu lived in the Chin-yung Castle just after the move of the capital, before the palace had been built, he often went to the Wang-nan Temple west of the city wall to hear the monks discussing doctrine. This was why he had the gate made. Before it was given a name people called it the New Gate. In those days princes and ministers would meet His Majesty at this gate. Kao-tsu said to the Chief Censor Li Piao,[15] 'One of Ts'ao Chih's poems refers to "an audience with

---

[13] On the instruments *hsüan-chi* and *yü-heng* see Needham (1954–), 3, pp. 334 ff. The 'seven governors' were the sun, moon, and five planets.

[14] This walled stronghold, built between 227 and 237, has been identified with the three walled compounds found by modern archaeologisrs protruding from the north-western corner of the city wal. (*K'ao-ku*, 1973, 4, pp. 207 ff.)

[15] One of Kao-tsu's most influential and trusted assistants in the sinification of the Wei state, he died in 501. (*WS* 62, pp. 1381–98.)

the Emperor in the Ch'eng-ming Pavilion'',[16] so this gate should be called Ch'eng-ming.' Thus it got its name.

There were two gates in the northern wall.

The western one was the Ta-hsia [Great Hsia] Gate. In the Han it was called the Hsia Gate, and in the Wei and Chin it was called the Ta-hsia Gate. Emperor Hsüan-wu built a three-storeyed tower there that was 200 feet high. All the other gate-towers of Loyang were two-storeyed and 100 feet high: only the structure of the Ta-hsia gate-tower reached into the clouds.

The eastern gate, called the Kuang-mo [North Wind] Gate, was known as the Ku Gate in the Han and the Kuang-mo Gate under the Wei and Chin, which Kao-tsu followed. From the Kuang-mo Gate west to the Ta-hsia Gate a succession of palace buildings backed on the city wall.

Each gate had three passageways, or what is called the 'nine chariot-widths'.[17]

---

[16] *Wen hsüan* 24, p. 516. According to Fan the Ch'eng-ming Pavilion of that time was nowhere near the north-west corner of the city.

[17] According to the account of Chin Loyang by Lu Chi cited in *TPYL* 195, p. 941, the walled central lane of the gates and main roads were reserved for the Emperor and high officials. 'Nine chariot widths' is the canonical prescription for the main north–south roads of a capital in the *K'ao-kung chi* of the *Chou li*.

Chapter 1

Inside the City Wall

The YUNG-NING [Eternal Peace] MONASTERY[1] was founded by the Empress Dowager Ling, the Lady Hu,[2] in the first year of *hsi-p'ing* [516]. It lay to the west of the imperial highway 1 *li* south of the Ch'ang-ho Gate in front of the palace.[3]

To its east were the Headquarters of the Grand Marshal and to its west the Yung-k'ang [Eternal Calm] ward. To the south it fronted with the Department of Monasteries [the 'Department of Explaining the Mysteries']^4 and its neighbour to the north was the Censorate. To the east of the imperial highway leading from the Ch'ang-ho Gate were the Headquarters of the Left Guard,[5] south of which was the High Premier's Office. South again was the Imperial Academy[6] whose hall contained a picture of Confucius flanked by Yen Yüan asking about goodness and Tzu-lu inquiring about government.[7] Next south was the Office of the imperial Clan,[8] followed by the Imperial Ancestral Temple, the Headquarters of the Household Brigade, and the Yi-kuan [Cap and Gown] ward. To the right of the imperial highway were the

---

[1] An earlier monastery of this name had been built in the old capital P'ing-ch'eng in 467 with a 300-foot high pagoda in seven storeys (*WS* 114, p. 3037). The site of the Loyang Yung-ning Monastery has been partially excavated since 1962; it was enclosed by a rectangular wall totalling 1,040 metres in length. (*K'ao-ku* 1973, 4, pp. 204–6.)

[2] Ling was the posthumous title of this remarkable woman, on whom see chs. 4 and 5 of Part I.

[3] Not to be confused with the gate of the same name in the city wall.

[4] This department of government to keep the Buddhist church under state control seems to have been a Northern Wei innovation. (See Tsukamoto (1942), pp. 139–64, for a full treatment.)

[5] With the Right Guard responsible for palace security.

[6] Refounded in 520. It had only thirty-six students in 521 and seventy-two between 532 and 534. (Lü Ssu-mien (1948), pp. 1343–4; *WS* 9, p. 229.)

[7] See *Analects* 12.1 and 13.1.

[8] In charge of imperial genealogies.

Headquarters of the Right Guard, then, going south, the Headquarters of the Grand Marshal, the Construction Department, the Bureau of Official Grading ['of the Nine Grades'],[9] the Altar of the People, then the Ling-yin [Icy Shade] ward where ice was stored in the Chin dynasty.

In the Yung-ning Monastery was a nine-storeyed pagoda built with a wooden frame that rose 900 feet high. Its golden pole rose another 100 feet so that its total height was 1,000 feet.[10] You could see it even at a distance of 100 *li* from the capital. When the foundations, which went down to the underworld, were being dug thirty gold statues were found. The Empress Dowager regarded them as proof of the sincerity of her faith—this was why the scale of the building was so excessive. On top of the pole was a golden precious vase with a capacity of 25 bushels under which were eleven golden dishes for collecting the dew hung all around with golden bells. The pole was supported by four iron chains running to the corners of the pagoda, and on them were more golden bells the size of bushel pots. The pagoda was nine-storeyed, and bells hung from all the corners, making a total of 120.[11] In each of the four sides of the pagoda were three doors and six windows, all lacquered red. On the leaves of the doors were five rows of golden studs,[12] a total of 5,400 studs, and in addition golden rings mounted in holders. It was a triumph of building, a masterpiece of construction, and one could not conceivably describe the excellence of the sacred objects within it. The decorated pillars and the golden ring-holders were breathtaking. When the bells chimed in harmony deep in a windy night they could be heard over 10 *li* away.

[9] Ho Ping-ti (1966), p. 96, guesses that this may have been an office in charge of civil appointments.

[10] At 296 metres this would have rivalled the Eiffel Tower. Other witnesses allow it 490 feet (145 metres) from golden vase to ground (*SCC* 16, pp. 3–75) or 400 feet (118 metres) for the pagoda, possibly excluding the finial (*WS* 114, p. 3043), still a very high building reflecting the skill of its architect Kuo An-hsing (*WSa* 91, p. 1972) and builder Ch'imu Huai-wen (*HKSC* 33, pp. 2b–3a). What now remains is a roughly square base, the lower part of stamped earth roughly 101 × 98 metres and standing 2.1 metres high; the next layer a smaller stamped-earth platform about 50 metres square and 3.6 metres higher; and the top part an adobe brick platform about 10 metres square and some 2.2 metres higher still, in which are sockets for the wooden foundation posts. (*K'ao-ku*, 1973, 4, loc. cit.)

[11] In some other accounts 130.

[12] In some accounts golden bells.

North of the pagoda was a Buddha Hall modelled on the T'ai-chi [Supreme Ultimate] Hall of the palace.[13] In it were an 18-foot-high gold statue, ten man-sized gold statues, three statues studded with pearls, five statues woven from gold thread, and two jade statues. They were all of brilliant and unmatched workmanship. The monk's cells, the towers and the pavilions made up over 1,000 rooms; their carved beams, painted walls, and delicately decorated doors and windows could scarcely be put into words. Junipers, cypresses, firs, and cedars spread over the eaves while bamboo clumps and fragrant herbs grew around the steps. This was why Ch'ang Ching[14] wrote for a stone tablet.

> Of the precious halls on Mount Sumeru,[15]
> Of the pure palaces in the Tuṣita heavens.[16]
> None can compare with this.

All the sutras and pictures that foreign countries had presented were stored in this monastery, and the walls round its courtyard were roofed with tiles supported on beams like palace walls. There was a gate in each of the four walls, and the southern was surmounted by triple gate-towers with three roadways beneath them. They rose 200 feet from the ground and were just like the present Tuan Gate[17] with cloud motifs, paintings of saints and miraculous creatures, and splendid decorations. Four powerful demigods and four lions adorned with gold, silver, pearls, and jade supported the gates with a dazzling magnificence never known before. The east and west gates were only different in that their gate-towers were double. Above the north gate, which had only a single carriageway, there was no building, making it like a 'crow head' gate. Bluish locust trees were planted outside all four gates, which were connected by green waters. Travellers in the capital would shelter under the trees which stopped the dust-clouds from the

[13] The main ceremonial building in the palace. The presumed remains of the hall have been located north of the base of the pagoda.

[14] Ch'ang Ching (d. 550) was evidently admired by Yang, who mentions him four times in his book, as a frugal and upright scholar-official. His long official career covering some fifty years was spent mainly as a legal and ritual specialist. (*WSa* 82, pp. 1800–8, after *PS* 42.)

[15] The central mountain of every universe in Buddhist cosmology.

[16] Where all Buddhas are reborn before appearing on earth.

[17] The main southern gate of the palace compound.

road without the help of rain and where fresh breezes blew cool air that did not come from fans.

The Assistant Secretary Ch'ang Ching was ordered by the Emperor to compose a commemorative inscription for the monastery. Ch'ang Ching, courtesy name Yung-ch'ang, a Ho-nei man, was a scholar of wide learning who was famous throughout the country. In the nineteenth year of *t'ai-ho* [495] the Emperor Kao-tsu appointed him Professor of Laws in recognition of his ability, and he was often consulted on difficult criminal cases. In the first year of *cheng-shih* [504] he was commanded to revise the laws and regulations and put them into a permanent and universal form. He was instructed to edit and compile them together with the Assistant Chief Censor Kao Seng-yü,[18] the Captain of the Forest of Wings Guard Wang Yüan-kuei, the Chancellery Department Head Tsu Ying,[19] the Supernumerary Aide Li Yen-chih,[20] and others. The Emperor also commanded Prince Hsieh of P'eng-ch'eng,[21] the Grand Tutor, and Liu Fang,[22] the Governor of Ch'ing-chou, to participate in the discussions. In rectifying the ordinances Ch'ang Ching considered the laws of antiquity and his own time, and his well-ordered results were published as the present twenty volumes of *Statutes*.[23] He and Liu Fang also worked out the names for the palaces, halls, gates, pavilions, streets, and wards of Loyang. When Ch'ang Ching was promoted to go to Ch'ang-an as its mayor, his contemporaries compared him to P'an Yüeh.[24] Later he served successively as Assistant Secretary, Gentleman in Waiting, Keeper of the

[18] 475–522. A member of the aristocratic Kao clan from Po-hai (*WS* 48, pp. 1090–91.)

[19] A learned official whose family had held office for five generations. (*WSa* 82, pp. 1798–1800, after *PS* 47.)

[20] A member of the Li clan of Ti-tao, Lung-hsi, with a very high opinion of his own scholarship who died in 533. (*WSa* 82, pp. 1797–8, after *PS* 100.)

[21] A younger brother of Kao-tsu closely associated with his sinification policies, including the move to Loyang. He was killed in the palace in 508. (*WS* 21/2, pp. 571–84.)

22 452–513. A captured southerner who became a respected court scholar at P'ing-ch'eng and later at Loyang. (*WS* 55, pp. 1219–33; *Yen-shih chia-hsün* 8, p. 15.)

[23] This code, combining the Han traditions of jurisprudence as preserved in the north-west and developed in the south, was the basis of Northern Ch'i, Sui, and T'ang codes. (Ch'en Yin-k'o (1963), pp. 109–12; Ch'eng Shu-te (1963), p. 339.)

[24] 247–300. This famous and beautiful writer also held that post.

Palace Archives, Governor of Yu-chou, and Honorary Senior Minister. Men were proud to be his students. Although in close attendance on the Emperor when in the capital and a high official when in the provinces, his house was frugally furnished and his way of life like a farmer's except that he had classics and history books by the cartload or bookcase-full. His collected works were published in several hundreds of volumes with a preface by the Senior Palace Counsellor Feng Wei-po.[25]

When the decoration of the pagoda had been finished Emperor Ming-ti and the Empress Dowager climbed it together.[26] They gazed down at the palace as if into the palms of their hands, and the whole of the capital seemed no bigger than a courtyard. As it overlooked the palace climbing it was forbidden.

I once climbed it with Hu Hsiao-shih, the prefect of Ho-nan, and it was absolutely true that one could look down on clouds and rain.

In those days there was a monk from the West called Bodhidharma, a Persian who had come to the central lands from remote and desolate parts. When he saw the golden discs reflecting the sunlight beyond the clouds and heard the bells in the wind sending their chimes up to the sky he chanted a eulogy and sighed with admiration for what was indeed a divine construction. 'In my 150 years,' he said, 'I have been everywhere and travelled in many countries, but a temple of this beauty cannot be found anywhere else in the continent of Jambudvīpa and all the lands of the Buddha.' He held his hands together and chanted '*namaḥ*' for several days on end.[27]

In the second year of *hsiao-ch'ang* [526] there was a hurricane which blew down houses and uprooted trees, bringing down the golden vase on the pole above the pagoda; it fell over 10 feet into the ground. Artisans were instructed to cast a new one.

In the first year of *chien-yi* [528] Erhchu Jung, Prince of T'ai-yüan, assembled his troops in this monastery.

---

[25] A scholarly aristocrat who was killed in a rising in 527 or 528. (*WS* 32, pp. 766–7.)
[26] In 517 (*WS* 67, pp. 1495–6).
[27] One of the few contemporary accounts of the legendary founding patriarch of Ch'an Buddhism in China. On his life see T'ang Yung-t'ung (1963), pp. 779–91 and Yanagida Seizan in Ōchō (ed.) (1971), pp. 135–41.

Erhchu Jung, courtesy name T'ien-pao, was from North Hsiu-jung.[28] His family were hereditary ruling chiefs of the first rank[29] and Dukes of Po-ling-chün. He had over 8,000 [families of] tribesmen, several tens of thousands of horses, and wealth to match a heavenly treasury. In the second month of the first year of *wu-t'ai* [528] the Emperor [Hsiao-ming-ti] died leaving no son.[30] Chao, the heir to the Prince of Lin-t'ao,[31] was put on the throne at the age of three *sui* to continue the Great Enterprise, because of the Empress Dowager's lust for control of the government. 'When the Emperor died at eighteen,' said Erhchu Jung to Yüan T'ien-mu,[32] the Governor of Ping-chou, 'the gentry and commoners of the land were still calling him their child sovereign. How can there be any hope of peace now that a baby who cannot yet speak has been put on the imperial throne? My family has benefited from the grace of the dynasty for generations so I cannot sit idly by and watch whether or not this leads to disaster. I shall take 5,000 iron-clad horsemen to mourn at the burial mound and ask the ministers in attendance the cause of His Majesty's decease. What do you say to this?'

'Your family, illustrious lord,' said Yüan T'ien-mu, 'has controlled Ping and Ssu[33] for generations. You are a man of outstanding valour and among your tribesmen you have 10,000 bowmen. If you succeed in deposing one ruler and installing another then our age will see another Yi Yin or Huo Kuang.'[34]

Erhchu Jung and Yüan T'ien-mu then swore brotherhood. As T'ien-mu was the older Jung honoured him as the elder brother; and T'ien-mu bowed to Jung as the leader of the alliance. In secret discussions they were undecided as to which of the princely descendants of earlier monarchs should rule, so

[28] In Shuohsien, Shansi. On Erhchu Jung see chs. 4 and 5 of Part I.

[29] On the Northern Wei feudal system of hereditary chieftainship see Chou Yi-liang (1963), pp. 177–98.

[30] There were rumours that he had been poisoned on the Dowager Hu's orders.

[31] A great-grandson of Kao-tsu.

[32] A very distant member of the royal clan who had impressed Erhchu Jung as a natural soldier during the suppression of the northern-garrison mutinies (*WSa* 14, pp. 355–6).

[33] In northern Shansi south of P'ing-ch'eng (Tat'ung).

[34] Who both dealt firmly with errant Emperors to save a dynasty.

they had statues cast of them all at Chin-yang.[35] None was successful except that of Tzu-yu, Prince of Ch'ang-lo,[36] which came out as a wonderfully majestic statue, perfect in both likeness and lustre. His mind now set on Tzu-yu, Erhchu Jung sent his slave Wang Feng into Loyang to secure his consent to the throne. When Tzu-yu assented they split a 'rendezvous tally'.[37] Erhchu Jung's armies, clad in mourning-white, raised their banners and headed south.

When the Empress Dowager heard that Jung had risen she summoned the princes and nobles for consultation. None of those who came to the council was prepared to speak out as the royal family was embittered at the way the Hu clan enjoyed all her favour. Only the Gentleman in Waiting Hsü Ho[38] spoke. 'Erhchu Jung', he said, 'is a petty barbarian from Ma-yi, a man of mediocre talents who has turned his arms against the palace without "measuring his virtue and weighing up his strength". He is like a mantis trying to stop a cart-wheel at the end of its track or a man who piles up brushwood and waits on it for it to burn him. Now with our palace guards and our military and civil officers we are able to fight, so we should simply hold the Yellow River Bridge[39] and observe his intentions. His unsupported army 1,000 *li* from its base will be exhausted and weary, so if we meet his tired troops with our fresh ones his defeat is inevitable.'

The Empress Dowager, agreeing with Hsü Ho, sent the Commanding Officer Li Shen-kuei[40] with Cheng Chi-ming and others at the head of 5,000 men to guard the Yellow River Bridge. On the eleventh day of the fourth month Erhchu Jung passed through Ho-nei and went straight to the post-station at Kao-t'ou. Tzu-yu, the Prince of Ch'ang-lo, crossed the Yellow

[35] This method of divination had long been used by the T'opa and other frontier peoples, as by potential Wei Empresses and by Erhchu Jung himself, whose four failures at it dissuaded him from seizing the Wei throne. (*WS* 74, p. 1648.) What was unusual here was that it was done by proxy.

[36] Later known as Chuang-ti (d. 532).

[37] Committing Jung to act within a set time.

[38] A humbly born official who was a trusted adviser to the Dowager Hu in her last spell of personal rule. He escaped to south China before Jung could catch him. (*WS* 93, pp. 2007–9.)

[39] A pontoon bridge near modern Menghsien.

[40] A trusted official and allegedly a lover of the Dowager's. (*WS* 66, p. 1475.)

River at Lei-p'o and went to Erhchu Jung's camp. When Li Shen-kuei, Cheng Chi-ming and the others realized that the Prince of Ch'ang-lo had left Loyang they opened the gates at the Yellow River Bridge and submitted.

On the twelfth Erhchu Jung encamped north of the Mang Hills in the countryside of Ho-yin.[41] On the thirteenth he summoned all the officials to come and pay homage to the Emperor, then slaughtered every one of them. Over 2,000 people died, from princes, nobles, and ministers to the court officials.[42]

On the fourteenth the Emperor entered Loyang, granting an amnesty to the world and changing the title of the year to the first year of *chien-yi* ['justice established']. He was now [the Emperor later known as] Chuang-ti. After the recent heavy fighting in which all the leading personalities had been exterminated those who had fled were still too frightened to come out of hiding: when Chuang-ti entered the T'ai-chi [Great Ultimate] Hall in the palace to dispense benevolent government the Chevalier in Attendance, Shan Wei,[43] was the only man to pay homage at the southern ceremonial gates of the palace. Erhchu Jung was appointed Senior General Controlling Domestic and Foreign Military Affairs, Commissioner for the Northern Circuit, Military Commander of ten *chou*, Commander of the Imperial Bodyguard and Prince of T'ai-yüan.[44] Yüan T'ien-mu was created Imperial Assistant, Grand Marshal, Hereditary Governor of Ping-chou, and Prince of Shang-tang. Countless others were elevated to be dukes, ministers, governors, and prefects. Loyang was confused and unsettled, riven by deadly hatreds and conflicting loyalties. Noble and powerful families had fled from their homes, while poor and humble folk had run away carrying their children on their backs. On the twentieth a decree awarded honours to those who had been so recklessly slaughtered. Those of the third grade and above were [posthumously] made honorary senior ministers; those of the fifth grade and over

---

[41] The plain between the Mang Hills north of the capital and the Yellow River.

[42] In various texts of *LYCLC* and other sources figures of 1,300 and 3,00 are also given.

[43] A non-Han northerner. (*WSa* 81, pp. 1792–4.)

[44] A formidable and unprecedented array of titles.

were made ministers or deputy ministers; men of the seventh grade and higher were appointed provincial governors; and commoners were created prefects and garrison captains. This induced a somewhat calmer situation. The Emperor took the daughter of Erhchu Jung as his Empress, promoting Jung to be a Pillar of State General[45] and Controller of the Chancellery with his other appointments as before. Yüan T'ien-mu was promoted to be a senior general with his other offices unchanged.

When Yüan Hao, Prince of Pei-hai, re-entered Loyang in the fifth month of the second year of *yung-an* [529][46] he too mustered his troops in this monastery.

Yüan Hao, the paternal first cousin of Emperor Chuang-ti, was garrisoning Chi prefecture at the end of *hsiao-ch'ang* [528]. When he heard of Erhchu Jung's entry into Loyang he fled to the court of Hsiao Yen.[47] When Yüan Hao entered Loyang [in 529] Chuang-ti had left for a northern tour, so he put himself on the throne, changed the title of the year to the first year of *chien-wu*, and sent Chuang-ti a letter that read:

As the Great Way is in eclipse the empire is not being run for the general good. Disaster and blessing do not follow each other in the proper order, and the able are no longer consulted. We would have preferred, like the Five Emperors,[48] not to have resorted to armed force. Indeed, we regard the state as mere chaff and the throne as a trifle. We do not lust for royal honours or long for the world's wealth.

When Erhchu Jung entered Loyang last year he was a loyal supporter of Your Majesty, but he ended up as a traitor against Wei, turning his mutinous sword upon Your Majesty's kin and slaughtering your officials. Few of the Yüan clan, young or old, survive. He has decided either to seize power for himself, as did Ch'en Heng in Ch'i, or else to carve up the country like the six leading clans of Chin.[49] As

---

[45] A post specially invented for him.

[46] On this invasion by a small Liang force under Ch'en Ch'ing-chih see ch. 5 of Part I.

[47] Better known to history as the Liang Emperor Wu-ti (r. 502–49).

[48] Of mythical antiquity, who each abdicated to a suitable successor.

[49] Famous usurpations of the fifth century BC.

the empire is still in turmoil he could not yet usurp the throne; this was why you and he were, for the time being, ruler and subject, and why he has falsely paid you homage and put you in power, killing your brothers and leaving you isolated on the throne. He was building up his strength and biding his time: how long would he remain a loyal subject?

Our hearts went cold at the thought, so we fled south of the Yangtse, pleading in tears at the Liang court and vowing to avenge this humiliation. Like the wind we went to Chien-yeh,[50] and like lightning came back to the Three Rivers.[51] We intended to punish the Erhchu and free you from your shackles. We sympathize with your profound anger at the fate of your own flesh and blood, and will release the common people from their agony.

We expected you to clap your hands and meet us with shining eyes, coming in person that we might discuss your sorrows and join in punishing that murderous Chieh. Unexpectedly when we entered Ch'eng-hao you had crossed to the north bank. Although you were not a free agent and were forced to cross by that murderer[52] we wondered if you had changed your ideas, laid down your sword and grown suspicious of us. At this news we sighed long and beat our breast in sorrow.

Why should this be? We two are close cousins, leaves from the same branch. We stand or fall together. Even if they have disputes at home, cousins should resist external oppression, particularly we two whose friendship is so close. When it comes to help in trouble, there is nobody like a cousin.

How can you justify abandoning your own family and going over to our enemy when the traces of Erhchu Jung's disloyalty were strewn around unburied? His plot against the Wei state is as obvious to a fool as to a wise man. You must understand that in nurturing illusions about inevitable disaster you have entrusted your fate to a wolf, and placed your body in a tiger's mouth. If you abandon your family and help a rebel your own cousins must take up arms against you. Whatever people and land you capture will really belong to Jung; the cities and towns you take will not remain yours. You are endangering the ancestral country only to strengthen an enemy. You may rejoice in the intentions of a rebel like Wang Mang,[53] hoping to

---

[50] The southern capital, modern Nanking.

[51] Lo, Yi, and Yellow.

[52] According to *WS* 77, p. 1715, Chuang-ti made a free choice and fled north unaccompanied.

[53] Who ended the Western Han dynasty and enthroned himself in AD 9.

benefit from others' strife as did Pien Chuang.[54] Any wise gentleman would be ashamed to do this.

The propserity or collapse of the dynasty depends on us two. If, with heaven's favour, we pledge ourselves to this just cause, the ancestral sacrifices of the august Wei can continue for ever. But if Heaven is not tired of chaos and the Hu and Chieh barbarians are not exterminated they will go on shrieking like owls and eating each other like wolves as they feed off the lands north of the Yellow River. This will be success for Erhchu Jung and disaster for you. Why do all this for a stranger? Please consider carefully the thoughts I have expressed in this letter. You can act in accordance with both justice and your own interest to protect your wealth and honour. To follow him would be ill considered. Even if you are loyal to him he will destroy you. Choose the propitious course; do not give yourself grounds for later regret.

This letter was composed for him by the Gentleman in Waiting Tsu Ying. At the time the Emperor was at the town of Ch'ang-tzu[55] where the Princes of T'ai-yüan and Shang-tang [Erhchu Jung and Yüan T'ien-mu] came to his rescue. In the sixth month the Emperor beseiged and unsuccessfully stormed Ho-nei,[56] which was held for Yüan Hao by its prefect Yüan T'ao-t'ang, the General of Chariots and Cavalry Tsungcheng Chen-sun, and others. In the scorching heat of high summer officers and men were exhausted. The Prince of T'ai-yüan, Erhchu Jung, wanted to send the emperor to Chin-yang[57] and wait till autumn before raising the forces of righteousness again. Unable to make up his mind the Emperor ordered Liu Chu[58] to consult the milfoil oracle. Liu Chu said that they were bound to win, so they put everything into an attack at dawn the next day and took the city as predicted. Yüan T'ao-t'ang and Tsungcheng Chen-sun were beheaded as an example to the army. When Yüan Hao heard of the fall of Ho-nei he led his officers in person to garrison the Yellow River Bridge and sent

---

[54] Who, in a story, when faced with two tigers let them fight to the death then dispatched the weakened survivor.

[55] In south-east Shansi.

[56] Which controlled the northern approach to the Yellow River Bridge.

[57] The Erhchu headquarters (modern T'aiyuan).

[58] Pedlar, bandit, and market-place fortune-teller before rising to high office as Erhchu Jung's personal soothsayer. Later rebelled against the Erhchu and was executed in 531. (*WS* 91, ppl. 1958–60.)

the Imperial Assistant Yüan Yen-ming, Prince of An-feng, to hold Hsia-shih.[59]

In the seventh month the Emperor reached Ho-yang and faced Yüan Hao across the Yellow River. The Prince of T'ai-yüan ordered the General of Chariots and Cavalry Erhchu Chao[60] to take his troops across the river, and he defeated Yüan Yen-ming at Hsia-shih. When Yüan Hao heard of Yüan Yen-ming's defeat he fled. All the 5,000 youngsters from the Yangtse and the Huai he brought with him took off their armour and wept as they clasped hands and took leave of each other. Yüan Hao tried to escape with a few dozen horse to the southern ruler Hsiao Yen, but the villagers of Ch'ang-she[61] cut off his head and sent it to the capital. On the twentieth the Emperor returned to Loyang. He elevated the Prince of T'ai-yüan to be Pillar of Heaven General and the Prince of Shang-tang to be Great Steward. They both kept their old offices as before.

In the third year of *yung-an* [530] the rebel Erhchu Chao imprisoned the Emperor Chuang-ti in this temple.

At this time the Prince of T'ai-yüan had been arrogant because of his high position; his great glory had made him reckless in his ambitions. He gave or took away on a whim, granting or withholding his consent at will. 'I would rather die like the Duke of Kao-kuei-hsiang,'[62] said the Emperor angrily to his attendants, 'than live like Emperor Hsien-ti of the Han.'[63]

On the twenty-fifth day of the ninth month he sent a false message that an heir to the throne had been born, at which Erhchu Jung and Yüan T'ien-mu came to the court. Chuang-

[59] Where the Yellow River could sometimes be forded.

[60] Also called T'umor. A brave and ferocious nephew of Erhchu Jung who was briefly the clan leader after his uncle's death until Erhchu power dissolved into facional strife. After defeat by Kao Huan he hanged himself in 533. (*WS* 75, pp. 1661–5; *Chou shu* 1, p. 10; *Liang shu* 32, p. 463.)

[61] In Linying hsien, central Honan.

[62] One of the last rulers of the Ts'ao-Wei line, he fought to the death against Ssuma Chao's usurpation in AD 260.

[63] Who abdicated in 220 after many years as a puppet.

ti stabbed Jung with his own hand in the Kuang-ming Hall [Enlightenment Hall], and T'ien-mu was killed by Lu Hsien, a soldier lying in wait. Erhchu Jung's eldest son, a tribal leader, was also killed by concealed soldiers, as were Erhchu Yang-tu, a General of Chariots and Cavalry in Erhchu Jung's forces, and nineteen others as they entered the Tung-hua [Eastern Glory] Gate of the palace.

Only the Junior Deputy Head of the Chancellery Erhchu Shih-lung[64] happened to stay at home, and as soon as he heard of Jung's death he assembled Jung's retainers, burned down the Hsi-yang Gate and fled to the Yellow River Bridge. On the first of the tenth month Erhchu Shih-lung and Jung's widow, the Princess of Pei-hsiang, went to the Feng-wang Monastery [Monastery of Prince Feng] on Mount Mang to perform rites for the happiness of Erhchu Jung. He sent Erhchu Hou-t'ao-fa and Erhchu Na-lü-kuei-teng with 1,000 Hu cavalry dressed in mourning white to the city wall to demand the Prince of T'ai-yüan's corpse for burial. After climbing to the top of the Ta-hsia Gate to look at them the Emperor sent his Master of Writing, Niu Fa-sheng, to say to Na-lü-kuei-teng, 'The Prince of T'ai-yüan did not live up to his former achievements and he secretly plotted rebellion. The royal law is impartial, and he has met with the due penalty. Only Jung himself has been found guilty; no questions will be asked about anyone else. Why do you not submit? You may keep your offices and titles as before.'

'I came with the Prince of T'ai-yüan to pay homage to Your Majesty,' he replied, 'so I could not possibly suddenly abandon my duty. Your subject intends to go back to Chin-yang, but I will not go empty-handed. I want the body of the Prince of T'ai-yüan for burial even if it costs me my life.' As he spoke he was so uncontrollably distressed that he wept copiously. The distraught sobbing of the Hu host shook the capital, and the Emperor himself was moved to sorrow at the sound of it. He sent Chu Yüan-lung,[65] the Imperial Assistant, to give Erhchu

---

[64] 500–32. A relatively civilized Erhchu who organized the clan's initial response to the death of Jung in 530 and who held Loyang for most of the next two years till he was killed by the troops of Hussu Ch'un (*WS* 75, pp. 1668–71.)

[65] Also known as Chu Jui. Probably chosen because he had been a trusted agent of Jung's in the palace before switching loyalties. (*WS* 80, pp. 1769–70.)

Shih-lung an iron scroll promising that his life would be safe and his offices unchanged.[66] 'The achievements of the Prince of T'ai-yüan,' said Erhchu Shih-lung to Chu Yüan-lung, 'reach from earth to heaven. He saved the people and served the country with a true heart. The gods know this, but [the Prince of] Ch'ang-lo broke their covenant and unjustly killed a good and loyal man, so what trust can I put today in mere written words? I will avenge the Prince of T'ai-yüan and I shall never submit.'

When Chu Yüan-lung heard Erhchu Shih-lung refer to the Emperor as [the Prince of] Ch'ang-lo he knew that he was no longer loyal, which he reported to the Emperor. The Emperor brought out the contents of his storehouses and had them placed outside the gates in the west wall of the city to recruit men willing to die to punish Erhchu Shih-lung. Although 10,000 enlisted in a single day and fought Na-lü-kuei-teng they were unable to improve the terrible situation. Kuei-teng frequently entered the fray, killing with great ease, and as the men of the capital were untrained their power did not match the courage they all showed. Three days of incessant fighting did not dispel the spirit of the mobile attackers.

The Emperor then recruited more men to cut the Yellow River Bridge. Li Miao, a man from Han-chung, commanded a flotilla and sent fire [boats] down the stream to burn the bridge.[67] On seeing that the bridge had been burnt Shih-lung massacred many of the common people and headed north into the T'ai-hang mountains. The Emperor sent the Imperial Assistant Yüan Tzu-kung and the Gentleman in Waiting Yang K'uan to garrison Ho-nei with 30,000 horse and foot.[68]

When Erhchu Shih-lung reached Kao-tu he enthroned Yüan Yeh, Prince of Ch'ang-kuang and prefect of T'ai-yüan, as monarch.[69] The title of the year was changed to the first year of *chien-ming* ['establishing brightness']. Eight members of the Erhchu clan created themselves princes. The Prince of Ch'ang-

---

[66] Such scrolls, also in gold, generally promised future immunity from execution.

[67] A well-born defector from the south whose bold move was unsupported: he died in the fighting. (*WS* 71, pp. 1594–7.)

[68] For more on this episode see ch. 2 below.

[69] A remote and undistinguished member of the royal clan who was to be deposed six months later and made to kill himself in 532. (See ch. 2 below and *WS* 11, pp. 273 ff.)

kuang made his capital at Chin-yang and sent Erhchu Chao, the Prince of Ying-ch'uan, to lead an expedition against the metropolis.

After defeating Yüan Tzu-kung's army Erhchu Chao forded the river at Lei Bank and captured the Emperor in the Shih-ch'ien [Modelled on Heaven] Hall of the palace. The Emperor had thought that as the Yellow River was in spate Erhchu Chao would be unable to make a rapid crossing, never imagining that he could ford it without boats. That day the water was too shallow to reach the horses' bellies; hence the disaster. This was unprecedented in written record. I, Yang Hsüan-chih, am of this opinion: when in the old days Emperor Kuang-wu of the Han received the mandate of heaven a bridge of ice formed over the Hu-t'o River;[70] and when [Liu Pei] the Emperor Chao-lieh [of Shu] arose, his horse Ti-lu leapt out of a muddy stream.[71] They were both right with heaven and blessed by the gods: this was why they were able to save the world and protect the common people. But if the august divinity had any perception he should have seen how evil was this Erhchu Chao, with his hornet's eyes, jackal's voice, and conduct as unspeakable as the owl[72] or the *p'o-ching*,[73] who instead of holding back his troops slaughtered his monarch and his family. Yet to aid his treason the divinity made the Meng ford come only up to the knees. If this is any test the saying in the *Changes* that heaven smites the wicked and the spirits bless the humble is meaningless.

At this time Chao encamped in the Chancellery. He had an Emperor's gongs and drums set up [for himself], placed a water-clock in the courtyard, and packed imperial consorts and concubines behind the curtains [of his bed]. The Emperor was chained up in one of the Yung-ning Monastery's gate-towers, and as it was now the twelfth month he asked Erhchu Chao for a head-cloth. Chao refused, then sent the Emperor as a prisoner to Chin-yang, where he was garrotted in the Triple-Storeyed Pagoda. Just before he died the Emperor prayed to

---

[70] Enabling him to escape from his enemies in AD 24.

[71] When carrying Liu Pei away from pursuers the horse made a thirty-foot leap out of a muddy stream to save them both.

[72] Still regarded as an evil bird.

[73] A creature like a wolf or leopard but smaller that devours its mother after birth.

the Buddha not to be a king again. He also wrote a poem in five-word lines:

> With power gone my road of life is short,
> Yet in distress the path to death seems long.
> Full of regrets I left Loyang behind;
> Sadly I enter now the land of ghosts.
> After I am shut inside the tomb,
> No more will that dark court see light.
> A bird sings pensively among green pines;
> Amid white poplars mourns the wind.
> Long have I heard it said that death is bitter:
> I never thought to bring it on myself.

In the winter of the year of *t'ai-ch'ang* [532] his body was placed in the coffin and taken to the capital. At his burial in the Ching Ling [Quiet Tumulus] his poem was sung by those who bore his coffin. Everyone in the court and the countryside who heard it were deeply grieved; when the common people saw the coffin they all covered their faces to hide their tears. In the second month of the third year of *yung-hsi* [534] the pagoda was burned down. The Emperor[74] climbed the Ling-yün [Cloud-touching] Tower to look at the blaze. He sent Yüan Pao-chü, Prince of Nan-yang,[75] and Changsun Chih,[76] the Controller of the Secretariat, with a thousand men of the Forest of Wings Guard to fight the fire. Everyone was so saddened that they went away in tears. The fire started in the eighth storey at dawn when the sky was dark with thunder clouds and sleet and snow were falling. All the people, clerical and lay, came out to watch the blaze, shaking the city with their sobs. Three monks killed themselves by rushing into the blaze. The fire lasted three months before going out; it went into the ground to look for the foundation piles, and smoke came out for a whole year.

In the fifth month of the same year someone came from Tung-lai with the news that a dazzling bright pagoda looking

---

[74] Yüan Hsiu, Prince of P'ing-yang (510–34). He was a grandson of Kao-tsu put on the throne by Kao Huan in 532. In 534 he fled west, only to be poisoned. In the east he was later known as Ch'u-ti.

[75] A drunken roué who succeeded Yüan Hsiu as puppet Wei emperor in the west.

[76] A northern aristocrat who also fled west later that year.

just as if it were new had appeared in the sea, where it had been seen by all the inhabitants of the coast before a mist arose to conceal it.[77] In the seventh month the Prince of P'ing-yang fled to Ch'ang-an under compulsion from Hussu Ch'un.[78] In the tenth month the capital was transferred to Yeh.

The CHIEN-CHUNG MONASTERY was founded in the first year of *p'u-t'ai* [531] by Erhchu Shih-lung, the Head of the Chancellery and Prince of Lo-p'ing. It was originally the residence of the eunuch and Lord Chancellor Liu T'eng.[79]

It was built on a sumptuous scale with beams and ridge poles far beyond regulation size. Its passages and verandas filled and overfilled a whole ward; its hall rivalled the palace's Hsüan-kuang Hall [Hall of Glory Proclaimed], and its gates the palace's Ch'ien-ming Gate [Gate of Heavenly Brightness]. None of the princes had anything to match its spacious magnificence.

It was in the Yen-nien [Years Prolonged] ward to the north of the imperial highway that ran to the Hsi-yang Gate.

To the east of Liu T'eng's residence was the Livestock Office.[80] East of this was first the Imperial Stables Section and then the Military Stores Section which had once been the mansion of the [Ts'ao] Wei Premier, Ssuma Chao,[81] Prince Wen. East again was the Ch'ang-ho Gate of the palace.

South of the imperial highway inside the Hsi-yang Gate was

[77] As Tung-lai was very near Po-hai, where the dictator Kao Huan was enfeoffed and claimed ancestry, this story was evidently a propaganda device of his.

[78] It is unlikely that Yüan Hsiu's flight was coerced. Hussu Ch'un, a frontier soldier of Kaoch'e/Ch'ihle (i.e. Turkic) descent, controlled Loyang from 532 till 534 and was then one of the leaders of the Western Wei regime until his death in 537. (*WS* 80, pp. 1772–5; *PS* 49, pp. 1785–7.)

[79] Who grew extremely rich and powerful in the service first of the Dowager Hu then, after joining in the 520 coup against her, of the dictator Yüan Yi till his death in 523 (*WS* 94, pp. 2027–8).

[80] As this controlled millions of state-owned animals its head could make a fortune, as Liu T'eng and others did.

[81] Dictator in last years of Ts'ao-Wei rule (255–65).

the Yung-k'ang [Eternal Calm] ward in which was the house of the Commanding General Yüan Yi.[82]

When an old well was being re-dug a stone inscription was found that said this was the house of the Han Great Marshal Hsün Yü. When during the *cheng-kuang* period [520–5] Yüan Yi held all power, keeping the Empress Dowager immured in the depths of the palace, Liu T'eng was the chief plotter. Yüan Yi was the son of Yüan Chi, Prince of Chiang-yang, and was married to the younger sister of the Empress Dowager. At the beginning of *hsi-p'ing* [516–18] the royal princes shared power as the Emperor Ming-ti was so young. The Empress Dowager appointed Yüan Yi Imperial Assistant, Commanding General, and Commander of the Imperial Bodyguard. Although she put all her trust in him by giving him the command of all the palace guard armies, she was immured in the women's quarters of the palace for six years in return. 'I have reared a tiger to attack me,' she wept, 'and nourished a baby snake into a viper.'

In the second year of *hsiao-ch'ang* [526] the Dowager, after resuming control of the government, had Yüan Yi and his associates executed, and confiscated Liu T'eng's land and house. On the day of Yüan Yi's execution Liu T'eng was already dead, but when the Dowager thought back on Liu T'eng's crimes she had his tomb opened and his corpse mutilated so that his spirit would have nowhere to return. She gave his house to Yüan Yung, Prince of Kao-yang.[83] Erhchu Jung, Prince of T'ai-yüan, stayed here after Yüan Yung's death until he was executed.

In the first year of *chien-ming* [530] the Head of the Chancellery, Erhchu Shih-lung, Prince of Lo-p'ing, turned his mansion into a monastery in order to obtain blessing for Erhchu Jung. With its vermilion gates and yellow pavilions it was a place fit for immortals. The front hall became a Buddha

---

[82] Whose personal name is sometimes incorrectly given as Ch'a. (On his career see, in addition to what is written below, *WS* 16, pp. 403–8; his tomb inscription in Chao Wan-li, 1956, 3, pl. 78; and the reports of his tomb's excavation in *Wen wu*, 1974, 12, pp. 53–60.)

[83] A son of Hsien-wen-ti who survived the various upheavals in Loyang till he died at Ho-yin. (*WS* 21/1, pp. 552–7.) On his style of living see ch. 3 below.

hall and the rear building a preaching room. The whole place was filled with golden flowers and precious canopies. There was a Cool Breeze Lodge where Liu T'eng used to avoid the heat of summer: it was always cool and free of flies throughout the summer, surrounded by very ancient trees.

The CH'ANG-CH'IU [Comptroller] MONASTERY was founded by Liu T'eng. It was so called because Liu T'eng had once been Comptroller of the Empress's Household. It was 1 *li* north of the imperial highway inside the Hsi-yang Gate.

This monastery, also in the Yen-nien ward, was where the Gold Market of the Chin capital Chung-ch'ao had been. North of the monastery was the Meng-ssü Pool that was full of water in summer but dry in winter.

Inside the monastery was a three-storeyed pagoda the gleam of whose golden urn and sacred pole could be seen throughout the city. There was also a statue of a six-tusked elephant bearing Śākyamuni Buddha on its back through the void.[84] The ornaments and Buddha statue were made entirely of gold and jewels, and its unique workmanship would beggar description . On the fourth of the fourth month it used to be taken out in procession[85] with lions and gryphons leading the way before it. Sword-swallowers and fire-belchers pranced on one side of the procession; there were men who climbed flagpoles, rope-walkers and every kind of amazing trick. Their skill was greater and their clothes stranger than anywhere else in the capital, and wherever the statue rested spectators would pack round in a solid crowd in which people were often trampled to death.[86]

---

[84] To his earthly mother's womb.

[85] Processions of statues in honour of the Buddha's birthday came to China from Central Asia, and were an annual event in P'ing-ch'eng before the move. Although all *LYCLC* texts give this date, it was on the seventh day of the fourth month that the capital's other statues were taken to the Ching-ming Monastery ready for the next day's procession.

[86] Many of the acts had central-Asian connections. An acrobatic troupe had been established by the dynasty's founder in 403. (*WS* 109, p. 2828.)

The YAO-KUANG [Precious Light] CONVENT, founded by Shih-tsung, the Emperor Hsüan-wu, was inside the Ch'ang-ho Gate of the city wall to the north of the imperial highway. Two *li* to the east of it was the Ch'ien-ch'iu [Thousand Autumns] Gate [of the palace].

Inside the Ch'ien-ch'iu Gate of the palace and north of the highway was the Hsi-yu Park [Park of the Westward Journey]. Inside the park was the Ling-yün [Cloud-touching] Tower which had been built by the Emperor Wen-ti of the [Ts'ao] Wei. Beside the Tower was the Octagonal Well, and to the north of this Emperor Kao-tsu built the Liang-feng [Cool Breeze] Pavilion. If one climbed this one could see right up the Lo River. Below the Ling-yün Tower was the Ch'ü-ch'ih [Curving Pond] of the Pi hai [Jade-green Lake]. East of the tower was the Hsüan-tz'u [Mercy Proclaimed] Pavilion which was 100 feet high. East of the pavilion was the Ling-chih [Magic Fungus] Fishing Tower, built on wooden piles which raised it over 200 feet above the water. Breezes were born from its doors and windows while clouds rose from its beams and rafters; its red columns and carved beams had immortals painted on them. The Fishing Tower was borne on the back of a carved stone whale that seemed to be leaping up from the ground or flying down from the sky. To the south of the Fishing Tower was the Hsüan-kuang Hall [Hall of Glory Proclaimed]; to the east was the Chia-fu Hall [Hall of Great Blessing]; to its west was the Chiu-lung [Nine Dragon] Hall in front of which was a pool filled by water coming from the mouths of nine dragons. All four of these halls were connected by 'flying passageways' to the Ling-chih Fishing Tower where the Emperor stayed in the dog-days of summer to avoid the heat.

The Yao-kuang Convent had a five-storeyed pagoda 500 feet high on top of which 'immortals' hands' touched the void and bells hung down above the clouds. The excellence of the workmanship matched that of the Yung-ning Monastery. There were over 500 preaching rooms and nuns' cells. Carved patterns spread from one wall to the next, and the rooms were connected by doors and windows. One could not describe the wealth of rare trees and fragrant plants: 'ox-sinew' and 'dog-bone' trees, 'chicken-heads' [water lilies], and 'ducks-feet' [mallows] were all there. This was where the Junior Consorts

and Imperial Concubines from the Scented Apartments studied the Way, with the Beauties of the Side Court among them.[87] There were also maidens of famous families who in their love for this place of enlightenment cut off their hair and left their parents to worship in this nunnery. Abandoning their jewelled finery they put on religious habits, placed their faith in the Eightfold Path, and came back to belief in the One Vehicle.

When in the third year of *yung-an* [530] Erhchu Chao entered Loyang and allowed his troops to loot, some dozens of Hu horsemen from Hsiu-jung entered the nunnery and committed rape. This gave rise to some jeering and the saying went round the capital, 'When the women of the capital were desperately braiding their hair,[88] the nuns of Yao-kuang Convent were grabbing husbands.'

North of the Yao-kuang Convent was the Ch'eng-ming Gate and the Chin-yung Castle that had been built by the [Ts'ao] Wei. During the *yung-k'ang* years [300–1] of the Chin dynasty the Emperor Hui-ti was imprisoned inside this wall. East was the Small Loyang Wall built during *yung-chia* [307–13].[89] In the north-east corner of the [Chin-yung] Castle was the Hundred-Foot Tower of the Emperor Wen-ti of the [Ts'ao] Wei.[90] It still looked as it had when new despite its age. Inside the castle Kao-tsu built the Kuang-chi Hall [Hall of the Brilliant Ultimate], after which he named the gate in the Chin-yung Castle the Kuang-chi Gate. He also built multi-storeyed buildings and flying passageways that soared all around the wall and looked like clouds when seen from the ground.

[87] These designations are bureaucratic ranks in descending order. Empresses also frequented this convent, and one, Dowager Hu's rival Kao, was virtually imprisoned here from 515 until her sudden death in 518.

[88] Presumably to disguise their sex as men wore a pair of braided topknots. (Some texts read 'men for 'women', but this makes no sense here.)

[89] This fortress was combined with the Chin-yung, but it has not yet been identified on the ground.

[90] Reigned 220–6.

The CHING-LO [Great Happiness] CONVENT was founded by the Grand Instructor Yüan I, Prince Wen-hsien of Ch'ing-ho.[91]

Yüan I was a son of the Emperor Hsiao-wen [Kao-tsu] and younger brother of the Emperor Hsüan-wu [Shih-tsung]. The convent was south of the Ch'ang-ho [Palace] Gate and east of the imperial highway. The Yung-ning Monastery was directly opposite to the west of the highway. To the west of the convent was the High Premier's Office, east of it was the mansion of the Senior General Kao Chao,[92] and to the north it bounded the Yi-ching [Well of Justice] ward. Outside the north gate of this ward was a copse of trees under whose foliage was a sweet-water well with a stone tank and an iron pitcher. This provided water and shade for passers-by, and many people rested here.

In the nunnery there was a Buddha-hall in which was kept a carriage for a Buddha-statue. The carving in this hall was the finest of the age. Lodges and porticoes surrounded it on all sides and rooms led from one to another. Delicate branches brushed against the doors, and blossom covered the court-yards. At the six maigre-feasts[93] there were always women musicians. Songs curled round the roof-beams as dancing sleeves slowly turned. Clear sounded the silken strings and the pipes, and enchanting were their harmonies. As this was a nunnery men were not allowed in, but those who could go to see it felt that they were in paradise. When Prince Wen-hsien died the restrictions in the nunnery were somewhat eased and ordinary people were no longer prevented from coming and going.

Later Yüan Yüeh, Prince of Ju-nan,[94] the younger brother of Prince Wen-hsien, restored the convent. He summoned all

[91] See the laudatory account of the life and character of this comparatively literate prince, killed by Yüan Yi in 520 for opposing his coup, in ch. 4 below.

[92] A Korean who as maternal uncle to Shih-tsung/Hsüan-wu-ti was all-powerful and hated during his nephew's reign and fell immediately after it ended in 515. (See ch. 3 of Part I.)

[93] These great vegetarian banquets were held six times a month. (See Gernet (1956), pp. 249 ff., and Tsukamoto (1942), pp. 302–4, 315, 317.)

[94] A thoroughly unpleasant man: a savage wife-beater and inventor of sadistic punishments for robbers, he was willing to serve Yüan Yi who had killed his brother. He later twice offered himself as a puppet emperor before being killed in 532. (WSa 22, p. 593, and WS 11, p. 286.)

kinds of musicians and entertainers to display their talents there. Strange animals and outlandish beasts danced and clapped in the halls and courtyards. There was flying through the air and other illusions such as had never been seen before; the practitioners of many strange arts assembled here, including those who skinned asses then threw them down wells, or planted jujubes or melons that were ready for eating in a moment. The gentlemen and ladies who saw it were dazed and astonished. As a result of the frequent heavy fighting in the capital from *chien-yi* [528] onwards these performances lapsed.

The CHAO-YI CONVENT was founded by the eunuchs. It was 1 *li* inside the Tung-yang Gate south of the imperial highway. North of the highway inside this gate were the Imperial Granary Section and the Husking Section. To the south-east was the Chih-su [Grain Control] ward where the officials and employees of the granaries lived.

When the Empress Dowager was in power the eunuchs were very much in her favour and their households grew extremely wealthy, thus occasioning Hsiao Hsin's remark, 'All the tall covered carriages are for the eunuch's "widows", and any foreign horse with tinkling jade pendants is bound to belong to one of their adopted sons.'

Hsiao Hsin, a Yang-p'ing man, was a lover of literature but not famous until the favour and splendour enjoyed by the eunuchs prompted this saying that made his name and won him an appointment as Assistant Chief Censor.

The convent had one Buddha statue and two of bodhisattvas. The perfection of their modelling was unrivalled throughout the capital. On the seventh of the fourth month these statues were always taken to the Ching-ming Monastery, whose own three statues were brought out to welcome them. The splendid music and entertainments rivalled those of Liu T'eng's monastery. In front of the hall was a wine tree[95] and a flour tree.[96]

[95] Perhaps a tree whose fruit fermented quickly.
[96] A breadfruit tree?

The Chao-yi Convent also had a pond that the scholars of the metropolis called the Ti Spring. I, Hsüan-chih, would add that according to Tu Yü's commentary on the *Spring and Autumn Annals* the Ti Spring was to the south-west of the Imperial Granary of the Chin dynasty which was, I believe, inside the Chien-ch'un Gate; it is therefore my opinion that this is obviously not the Ti Spring as it is to the south-west of the modern Imperial Granary inside the Tung-yang gate.

Later the recluse Chao Yi[97] said that this was the pool belonging to the house of the Chin dynasty Imperial Assistant Shih Ch'ung. South of the pool had been Green Pearl's Pavilion. This woke the scholars up, and those who passed by thought they saw Green Pearl.[98]

South-west of the pool was the YÜAN-HUI MONASTERY [Monastery of Vows Assembled] founded when the Deputy Secretary Wang Yi gave his house. In front of the Buddha-hall grew a mulberry tree which went straight up for 5 feet, at which height the branches and twigs thrust themselves out horizontally all round, creating a dense foliage that looked like the feathered cover of a carriage. Another 5 feet up it did this again, and this happened five times altogether. Each section had its own different type of bark and leaves; the clerics and lay people of the capital called it the Magic Mulberry Tree. Spectators came in crowds, and very many of them made donations to the monastery. The Emperor was displeased to hear of it as he felt it disturbed the masses, so he ordered the Gentleman in Waiting Yüan Chi to have it cut down. It was a dark and misty day, and blood flowed to the ground from wherever the axe struck. All those who saw it wept for sorrow.

South of the convent lay the Yi-shou [Helping Longevity] ward in which was the house of Tuan Hui, the magistrate of Pao-hsin county.

[97] For his incredible story see ch. 2 below.
[98] Shih Ch'ung, famous for his wealth, cruelty and extravagance, was executed in 300 for refusing to give Green Pearl, his favourite concubine, to the dictator Sun Hsiu. She killed herself by leaping from this pavilion.

In this house the sound of a bell was often heard coming from underground and a light of many colours regularly shone in the main hall. This astonished Tuan Hui. When he had the place where the light shone excavated they found a gold statue some 3 feet high with two bodhisattvas. It was inscribed at the base 'Made for the Imperial Assistant and Head of the Secretariat Hsün Hsü on the fifteenth of the fifth month in the second year of *t'ai-shih* [266] in the Chin.' It was generally agreed that this must have been the house of Hsün Hsü. Tuan Hui consequently gave his house to become the KUANG-MING [Shining Light] MONASTERY. When some robbers later tried to steal the statue the image [of Buddha] and the bodhisattvas all cried 'thieves', at which the robbers collapsed in terror, to be caught by the monks who heard the statues' shouts.

The HU T'UNG [Abbess Hu's] CONVENT was founded by a cousin of the Empress Dowager's father who became a nun and lived in this convent. It was over 1 *li* south of the Yung-ning Monastery and had a five-storeyed pagoda topped by a tall golden pole and enclosed by nuns' cells whose doors and windows faced each other. The red doors and white walls made a most beautiful sight. The nuns of this convent, famous throughout the capital for their spiritual quality, were fine preachers who put great skill into explaining the Truth and used to go into the palace to talk about the dharma to the Empress Dowager. The nuns were kept in unparalleled luxury.

The HSIU-FAN [Cultivating Calm] MONASTERY lay to the north of the imperial highway inside the Ch'ing-yang Gate. The SUNG-MING [Lofty Enlightenment] MONASTERY was to the west of it. With its carved walls, high roofs, and matched buildings joined one to the next this too was a famous monastery. The Hsiu-fan Monastery had a

vajra[99] where pigeons and other birds never perched. Bodhidharma said that this was the true image of a *vajra*.

North of the monastery was the Yung-ho [Eternal Peace] ward in which had been the house of the Han dynasty Grand Commander Tung Cho.[100] In the north and south of the ward were ponds that had been dug by Tung Cho and still held water, never going dry in summer or winter. The ward contained the houses of the Grand Instructor and Controller of the Chancellery Changsun Chih, the Junior Deputy Head of the Chancellery Kuo Tso,[101] the Minister of Establishments Hsing Luan,[102] the Chief Justice Yüan Hung-ch'ao, the Security Minister Hsü Po-t'ao, and the Governor of Liang-chou, Wei Ch'eng-hsing.

All these residences had lofty gateways and splendid buildings with elegant and spacious lodges and studios. Catalpa and locust trees shaded the roads, on either side of which grew *t'ung* trees and poplars. This was known as a grand ward. Digging here often yielded gold, jade, and precious trinkets: cinnabar and several hundred thousand copper cash with an inscription saying that they all belonged to the Grand Commander Tung Cho were dug up in Hsing Luan's house. Later Tung Cho came by night to demand them from Hsing Luan, who refused to give them up. A year later he dropped dead.

The CHING-LIN [Great Orchard] MONASTERY was inside the K'ai-yang Gate, to the east of the imperial highway. Preaching halls towered one behind the other, joined to other buildings by cloisters. Red railings gleamed in the sun as the

---

[99] The diamond sceptre that symbolized the power to destroy evil; it is still a feature of the decoration of Tibetan monasteries.

[100] Who destroyed Loyang when he abandoned it in AD 190.

[101] A northern Chinese aristocrat who was a leading arbiter of the lineage and character of candidates for office, and a strict assessor of their performance when appointed, he was killed in 516. (*WS* 64, pp. 1421–7.)

[102] Probably the Hsing Luan (written with a similar character) mentioned as holding this post in 520 in *KHMC* 1, p. 7b, and *HKSC* 30, p. 3a, not the Hsing Luan (464–514) of *WS* 65, pp. 1437–8.

breezes blew through decorated roof-beams. It was indeed a handsome place.

To the west of the monastery was a garden rich with exotic fruit-trees where was unbroken song from the birds in spring and the cicadas in autumn. In the garden was a meditation building containing Jetavana cells[103] which although tiny were exquisitely built. The stillness of the meditation room, the remote calm of the cells, the splendid trees framing the windows and the fragrant azaleas around the steps gave the feeling of being in a mountain valley rather than a city. Monks practised stillness on rope seats, eating the wind and submitting to the Way as they sat cross-legged and counted their breaths. There was a stone inscription in the writing of Lu Pai-t'ou, styled Ching-yü,[104] a professor of the Imperial Academy and a man of Fan-yang. A lover of quiet, he used to wander among hills and gardens. He had mastered the Six Classics and understood the hundred schools of thought. Early in *p'u-t'ai* [531–2] he was created professor of the Imperial Academy, and even when living within its vermilion gates he occupied himself with writing commentaries. His commentary on the *Chou Changes* was circulated.

Inside the Chien-ch'un Gate and south of the imperial highway were the Royal Parks Section, the Farming Section,[105] and the Sacrificial Fields Section. South of the Sacrificial Fields Section was the Office of the Minister of Agriculture.[106] North of the imperial highway was some empty ground where it had been intended to build a palace for the heir apparent.[107] In Chin days, when Loyang was Chung-ch'ao, this was where the Imperial Granary was situated. South of this was the Ti Spring whose waters meandered through three wards. This was the Ti Spring mentioned in the *Spring and Autumn Annals* as the place where Wangtzu Hu and Hu Yen of Chin made a covenant.[108] The water was still so

---

[103] Monastic cells, named after the park in which Śākyamuni was given a cell.

[104] Biographical note in *PS* 30, pp. 1098–9.

[105] Possibly in charge of the *chün-t'ien* system of land allocation.

[106] Whose responsibilities included the three sections mentioned above.

[107] From Kao-tsu's death to the fall of Loyang in 534 there was never an heir apparent old enough to need his own palace.

[108] In 631 BC the representatives of the Chou king and several north Chinese states formed a covenant here.

clear and bright that one could distinguish the fishes and turtles hidden in the depths. Kao-tsu situated the office of the prefect of Ho-nan[109] north of the spring. This was where the Pu-kuang ward of the Chin city of Chung-ch'ao had been.

West of the spring was the Hua-lin [Forest] Park. As the spring rose east of the park Kao-tsu called it the Ts'ang-lung Lake [Lake of the Azure Dragon]. Inside the Hua-lin Park was a large lake that had been the Pool of the Heavenly Deep in Han times. The Chiu-hua Tower [Tower of Nine Glories] of the [Ts'ao] Wei Emperor Wen-ti still stood in the middle of the pool. On this tower Kao-tsu built the Ch'ing-liang Hall [Hall of Coolness]. Emperor Shih-tsung had a P'eng-lai [Fairy] Mountain constructed in the lake with an Immortals' Lodge on it. There was also a Fishing Tower Hall by the lake that could be reached across a rainbow bridge that soared through the air. On the day of the purificatory ceremony in the third month and on the day ssu-ch'en in the last month of autumn the Emperor would board a dragon-boat or a bird-prowed boat to enjoy himself on the lake.

West of the lake was the Ice Storehouse from which ice was taken to give to the officials in the sixth month. South-west of the pool was the Ching-yang [Sunlight] Hall. East of the hill was the Hsi-ho Ridge surmounted by the Wen-feng [Warm Breeze] Chamber. West of the Hill was the Heng-o Peak with the Han-lu [Cold Dew] Pavilion on top of it. These buildings were connected by 'flying passages' that climbed the mountains and strode across the valleys. North of the hill was the Hsüan-wu [Northern God] Pool, and south of it was the Ch'ing-shu [Cool Summer] Hall; east of this hall was the Lin-chien Shelter [Shelter Overlooking the Ravine] and west of it the Lin-wei Terrace [Terrace Overlooking the Precipice].

South of the Ching-yang Hill was the Orchard of One Hundred Fruits. The various kinds of fruit-trees were planted in separate stands, and in each of these was a pavilion. There were Immortals' Jujubes 5 inches long. If one removed both ends the stone was as fine as a needle; they ripened at the time of Frost Descending[110] and were delicious. According to

[109] The official in charge of the local administration of the capital.
[110] Late October and early November.

popular tradition they came from the K'un-lun Mountains,[111] and one name for them was Queen Mother of the West Jujubes. Then there were Immortals' Peaches, red right through, that also ripened with the touch of heavy frost; they came from the K'un-lun Mountains, and were sometimes called Queen Mother Peaches.

South of the crab-apple copse was a stone tablet inscribed 'Thatched Cottage Tablet' that had been put up by Emperor Ming-ti of the [Ts'ao] Wei. Kao-tsu built the Miao-tz'u [Thatched Cottage] Lodge to the north of this tablet. In the middle year of *yung-an* [529] when the Emperor Chuang-ti was practising mounted archery in the Hua-lin Park the officials all came and read the tablet and thought that the character *miao* was wrong. Li T'ung-kuei, a professor of the Imperial Academy, said, 'Ming-ti of the Wei, a man of great talent, long known as one of the Three Patriarchs [of poetry], was aided by Wang Ts'an and Liu Chen. As we don't know what he originally meant we can't say that it is a mistake.' I, Hsüan-chih, was then a Court Guest[112] and this was my explanation: 'They covered the lodge with artemisia; that was why they called it "thatched". There is no mistake.' Everyone expressed admiration and said that I got back to the original meaning.[113]

East of the crab-apple copse was the Tu [Capital] Lodge and the Liu-shang [Floating Goblet] Pool. East of the Lodge was the Fu-sang Sea.

All these pools were connected by underground stone conduits running from the Ku River in the west to the Yang Canal in the east, also joining up with the Ti Spring. Even when the demon of drought was afflicting the city the Ku River would flow into the pools and prevent them from drying up; and in times of flood the Yang Canal drained them so that they did not overflow.[114] Strange and exotic scaly, shell-covered, feathered, and furry creatures sported in their waves just as if they were natural.

---

[111] Probably the mountains of northern Ch'inghai.

[112] After Teng Ssu-yü (1968), p. 151 n. 2. This was a first step on the official ladder for young gentlemen.

[113] An explanation of this trivial misunderstanding would not be worth the space.

[114] This system of conduits dated back to the Later Han: see *SCC* 16, p. 3/73.

Chapter 2

East of the City Wall

The MING-HSÜAN [Great Brightness] CONVENT was founded by Yüan Hsieh, Prince of Wu-hsüan of P'eng-ch'eng. It lay outside the Chien-ch'un Gate to the south of the Stone Bridge.

The Ku River winds around the city walls until it flows eastward outside the Chien-ch'un Gate and joins the Yang Canal at the Stone Bridge.[1] The bridge had four columns,[2] and on one south of the river was the inscription 'Built by the High Artificer Ma Hsien in the fourth year of *yang-chia* [AD 135] in the Han'. In the third year of *hsiao-ch'ang* [527] in our dynasty floods from a torrential downpour destroyed the bridge, burying the southern columns. The two columns north of the road still stand. In my view the statements in Liu Teng-chih's *Mountains and Rivers Yesterday and Today* and Tai Yen-chih's *The Western Expedition* that this bridge was built in the first year of *t'ai-k'ang* [280] during the Chin are completely wrong. As I see it they were both born south of the Yangtse and had never travelled in the central lands until they passed briefly through them while campaigning,[3] which meant that they did not see most of the antiquities with their own eyes and so fabricated accounts on the basis of what they heard on their travels. They have been deceiving later students for too long.

There was a three-storeyed pagoda that had not been decorated. East of the convent had been the Ever-Full Granary of Chin times. Kao-tsu made it the Tax Ground where tribute and grain taxes from the whole world were stored.

---

[1] The waters of the Ku River encircled Loyang, the main stream going round the north then the east wall, while the Yang Canal drawn from it went round the west and south walls before rejoining it outside the eastern wall just south of the Stone Bridge.

[2] *SCC* 16, p. 3/73, indicates that they were commemorative, not structural.

[3] Probably during the southern occupation of Loyang from 416 to 420. Their books do not survive. The Eastern Stone Bridge (see below) *was* built in 280.

176

The LUNG-HUA [Dragon Glory] MONASTERY was founded by the Forest of Wings Guards and the Tiger Guards of the Night Guard. It lay outside the Chien-ch'un Gate to the south of the Yang Canal. South of it was the Tax Ground.

North of the Yang Canal was the Chien-yang [Establishing the Positive] ward in which was an earthen terrace 30 feet high topped by two monastic cells. Chao Yi said that this terrace had been the flag tower of Chung-ch'ao. There had been a two-storeyed building on this terrace in which hung the drum that was beaten to close the market.

There was [in the monastery] a bell that when struck could be heard 50 *li* away. For this reason the Empress Dowager had it moved into the palace and placed in front of the Ning-hsien Hall [Hall of Leisure Achieved] where the monks who recited the Inner Scriptures[4] struck it to mark time. Early in *hsiao-ch'ang* [525] Hsiao Tsung, Prince of Yü-chang and a son of Hsiao Yen, came to submit,[5] and he found the sound of this bell so remalrkable that he wrote three poems 'On hearing the bell' which were circulated.

Hsiao Tsung, whose style was Shih-ch'ien, was the posthumous son of Hsiao Pao-chüan, the Confused Monarch of the bogus Ch'i dynasty, under whose debauched rule the people of Wu suffered. Hsiao Yen, the Governor of Yung-chou, enthroned Hsiao Pao-jung, Prince of Nan-k'ang, and marched his troops against Mo-ling.[6] When this had succeeded he killed Hsiao Pao-jung and took the throne for himself. He favoured Wu Ching-hui, a beauty of Hsiao Pao-chüan's who was already one month pregnant with Hsiao Tsung, and on

---

[4] The Buddhist scriptures.

[5] To simplify a complicated story, Hsiao Tsung was almost certainly the posthumous son of the so-called 'Confused Monarch', the last Ch'i ruler in the south. He was born to a concubine of the 'Confused Monarch' after she was taken into the harem of Hsiao Yen, who seized the throne as the first Emperor of the Liang dynasty in 502. Although treated by Hsiao Yen as a favourite son, Hsiao Tsung had a compulsive interest in his presumed real father and defected to Wei in 525. He died in 530. (See also *WS* 59, pp. 1325–6; *Liang shu* 55, pp. 823–45; *Nan shih* 53, pp. 1315–18.)

[6] i.e. Chien-k'ang (Nanking), the southern capital.

Tsung's birth took him for his own son. Tsung's childhood name was Yüan-chüeh and he was created Prince of Yü-chang. Tsung was very like the Confused Monarch in his looks and movements, so his mother told him [about his father] and warned him to look after himself. He came to our sage portals, changed his given name to Tsan and his style to Shih-wu, and only then did he wear three years' mourning for his father Hsiao Pao-chüan. Ming-ti appointed him Grand Marshal and created him Prince of Tan-yang.

In *yung-an* [528] he married Chü-li, the Princess of Shou-yang, who was a younger sister of the Emperor Chuang-ti. The princess was very beautiful, and Tsung treated her with great respect, always calling himself 'your servant' when speaking to her. He was later appointed Governor of Ch'i-chou and allowed a Personal Headquarters. When the capital fell[7] he abandoned his province and fled north. Erhchu Shih-lung, who was dictator at the time, had the princess brought back to Loyang. When he tried to force her she reviled him with the words, 'How dare you insult the wife of a heavenly prince, you barbarian dog? I would die by the sword rather than be sullied by a mutinous barbarian.' In his fury Erhchu Shih-lung strangled her.

The YING-LO [Necklace] MONASTERY was outside the Chien-ch'un Gate and north of the imperial highway in what was called the Chien-yang [Establishing the Positive] ward. This had been the Pai-she [White Altar] ground in Chung-ch'ao times where Tung Wei-nien lived. The following ten monasteries and convents were in the ward: the YING-LO, the TZ'U-SHAN, the HUI-HO, the T'UNG-CHÜEH, the HUI-HSÜAN, the TSUNG-SHENG, the WEI-CH'ANG, the HSI-P'ING, the CH'UNG-CHEN, and the YIN-KUO. All 2,000 and more households of gentry and commoners who lived in the ward faithfully honoured the Three Jewels,[8] and the people provided food and money for the monks and nuns.

[7] To Erhchu Chao and Erhchu Shih-lung in 530.
[8] The Buddha, the Dharma, and the Saṅgha.

The TSUNG-SHENG [Honouring the Sage] MONASTERY had a 38-foot-high statue, singularly majestic and complete with all the image and goodness of the Buddha, on which gentry and commoners gazed wide-eyed. Whenever this statue was brought out it emptied the market-places as its blazing lustre shone beyond the confines of the world. The marvellous entertainers and musicians of all sorts there were second only to Liu T'eng's,[9] and many men and women came to the monastery to watch.

Hui-ning, a monk of the CH'UNG-CHEN [Honouring the Truth] MONASTERY came back to life after being dead for seven days. Having been examined by King Yama[10] he was set free because a mistake had been made over his name. He gave this account of his experiences:

When I went over, five other monks were examined with me. One said that he was Chih-sheng from the Pao-ming Monastery. Because of his asceticism and sitting in meditation he was allowed to ascend to paradise.

Another monk, Tao-p'ing of the Po-jo [Prajñā] Monastery, also went up to paradise for reciting the forty rolls of the *Parinirvāṇa sūtra*. A monk calling himself T'an-mo-tsui from the Jung-chüeh Monastery preached on the *Parinirvāṇa* and *Avataṁsaka* sutras and usually had a following of a thousand. 'Preachers of the sutras', said King Yama, 'have minds full of them and me' and in their arrogance they insult other beings. This is the worst form of coarseness among monks. Now you must try to devote yourself to sitting in meditation and reciting sutras and be done with preaching.' 'Throughout my career,' replied T'an-mo-tsui, 'my only love has been preaching and

---

[9] i.e. the Chang-ch'iu Monastery (see ch. 1).
[10] King of the Underworld and judge of the dead.

I have never been able to recite by heart.'[11] King Yama ordered him to be handed over to the authorities, and ten black-clad men escorted him to the north-west gate, where all the houses were black. It did not seem to be a good place.

Another monk said he was Tao-hung from the Ch'an-lin Monastery. He claimed that he had converted four generations to becoming alms-givers, copying out the entire Canon,[12] and making ten golden statues of the Buddha. To this King Yama said, 'The monk must control his mind and follow the way, devoting himself to meditation and chanting scriptures. He should not concern himself with worldly affairs or be involved in action. To have sutras copied and statues made he must obtain wealth from others, and the getting of wealth is the beginning of avarice. Thus the Three Poisons[13] are not eradicated and they cause vexation.' He too was handed over to the officials and taken thrigh the black gate with T'an-mo-tsui.

Yet another monk, calling himself Pao-ming of the Ling-chüeh Monastery, said that before becoming a monk he had been prefect of Lung-hsi and built the Ling-chüeh Monastery. When it was completed he had given up his office to enter the Way, and although he had never practised meditation or chanting he had never defaulted in his worship. 'When you were a prefect,' said King Yama, 'you twisted justice and bent the law. You robbed the people of their wealth to build that monastery. It was not your efforts that built it, so don't talk about it.' He too was handed over to the officials and taken through the black gate by the black-clad runners.[14]

When the Empress Dowager heard of this she sent the Gentleman in Waiting Hsü Ho to make inquiries on the basis of Hui-ning's statement at the Pao-ming and other monasteries. There was a Pao-ming Monastery east of the city wall, a Po-jo inside the city, and a Jung-chüeh, a Ch'an-lin and a Ling-chüeh to the west of the city. On asking about Chih-sheng, Tao-p'in, T'an-mo-tsui, Tao-hung, and Pao-ming he

[11] On T'an-mo-tsui and his monastery see also ch. 4 below. In *HKSC* 30, pp. 1b–3b, he is classified as a 'defender of the dharma', perhaps for his success in a disputation with the Taoist Chiang Pin held before the Emperor in 520. The size of the Jung-chüeh Monastery indicates the esteem in which Loyang's rulers held him: Hui-ning evidently did not share their view. According to *HKSC* T'an-mo-tsui did in fact both meditate and recite.

[12] Even then the rolls of the Buddhist canon in China were numbered by the thousand.

[13] Greed, anger, and stupidity.

[14] This whole story appears to be propaganda for the Dhyāna sect, though its criticism of some of the abuses of religion in Loyang seems convincing.

found that they had all in fact existed. He proposed that as people receive punishment or blessing after death 100 monks who sat in meditation should be invited to come to the inner palace and be supported there. A decree was issued forbidding begging at the roadwide while holding sutras and statues. Copying sutras and making statues with one's private wealth was permitted.

Hui-ning retired to the Pai-lu Mountain to live as a hermit and cultivate the way, and the monks of the capital all practised meditation and chanting, taking no more interest in preaching the scriptures.

Over 1 *li* outside the Chien-ch'un Gate was the Eastern Stone Bridge that ran from north to south and had been built in the first year of *t'ai-k'ang* [280] during the Chin. South of the bridge had been the Horse Market of [Ts'ao] Wei times where Hsi K'ang was executed.[15]

North of the bridge and west of the highway was the Chien-yang ward. East of the highway was the Sui-min ward [Ward of the People Calmed] which contained the house of Liu Hsüan-ming of Ho-chien. During *shen-kuei* [518–19] he opposed the imperial will with frank remonstrations and was beheaded for it. When he was decapitated his eyes stayed open and his body walked a hundred paces. People said at the time that he had been unjustly killed. Liu Hsüan-ming was famous from his youth and thoroughly versed in the classics and histories. His execution was the result of his dangerous action.[16]

The WEI-CH'ANG CONVENT was founded by the eunuch Li Tz'u-shou, Governor of Ying-chou.[17] It was in the southeast corner of the ward. This had been the Horse Market in Chung-ch'ao times where Hsi K'ang was executed.

The convent was next to the Eastern Stone Bridge. This

---

[15] Poet, musician, alchemist, metallurgist, and free spirit. Executed on false charges in 262.

[16] According to *WS* (9, p. 229, and 59, p. 1292) he was plotting treason.

[17] He made fortunes both in this post and as Livestock Minister. (*WS* 94, p. 2026.)

bridge, which ran north-south,[18] was the Bridge South of the Market of Chin times that was built in the first year of *t'ai-k'ang*. Liu Teng-chih and the other writer saw this inscription, which made them think that the [other] stone bridge had been built in the first year of *t'ai-k'ang*.

On the road south of the Stone Bridge was the CHING-HSING [Great Flourishing] CONVENT which had been founded collectively by the eunuchs. It had a golden statue on a carriage that stood 30 feet high and was covered with a precious canopy from which hung pearls and golden bells on all four sides; flying devas, musicians, and dancers gazed down on the statue from beyond the clouds. The excellence of its craftsmanship beggared description. On the day the statues were brought out in procession 100 Forest of Wings guardsmen were ordered to carry it, and musicians and performers were also sent by royal command.

A little over a *li* to the east of the Chien-yang ward was the Sui-min ward in which was situated the Loyang county offices[19] that overlooked the canal. Outside its gates was the memorial to the integrity of Yang Chi, magistrate of Loyang county.[20] East of the Sui-min ward was the Ch'ung-yi ward [Ward of Justice Honoured] which contained the house of Tu Tzu-hsiu, a man of Ching-chao. It was set in spacious ground and its gates opened on the imperial highway.

There was at that time one Chao Yi, a recluse who claimed that he was a survivor of the time of the Chin Emperor Wu-ti [265–90] and made a record of many events of the Chin dynasty. On seeing Tu Tzu-hsiu's house when he came to the capital in early *cheng-kuang* [520–5] he said with a sigh, 'This was the T'ai-k'ang Monastery in Chung-ch'ao times.' Not believing him, people asked him about the origin of the

[18] Across the Yang Canal.

[19] The local government for the eastern part of the capital.

[20] An honest official who remained poor, he held this post during the years 516–18. Yang Hsüan-chih would doubtless have expected his contemporary readers to remember that he was executed by Kao Huan in 533. (*WS* 77, pp. 1706–7.)

monastery. Chao Yi said that it was founded after the conquest of Wu by the Dragon-Prancing General Wang Chün[21] and had originally contained a three-storeyed pagoda. 'That is where it used to be,' he said, pointing into Tu Tzu-hsiu's garden. When Tu Tzu-hsiu had the place dug up to check on this, he found several hundred thousand bricks and a stone inscription reading, 'On the eighth day *hsin-ssu*, in the ninth month, a month beginning on the day *shen-hsü*, in the year *yi-ssu*, the sixth of *t'ai-k'ang*,[22] [285] in the Chin this was respectfully built by Wang Chün, Marquis of Hsiang-yang and honorary senior minister.' The garden was then rich in fruit and vegetables and thick with trees. Chao Yi was now believed and called a sage.

Tu Tzu-hsiu gave his mansion to become the LING-YING [Miraculous Response] MONASTERY, and the bricks that were found were rebuilt into a three-storeyed pagoda.

The curious used to follow Chao Yi around and ask him how the Chin capital compared with the modern one. 'In Chin times', Chao Yi would reply, 'the population was smaller but the houses of the princes and nobles were much like those of today.' 'In the 200 years and more since *yung-chia* [307–13],' he would also say, 'sixteen monarchs have founded states and proclaimed themselves kings. I have visited all their capitals and seen what happened with my own eyes. On examining their historical records after their fall I always find that they give false accounts, putting the blame on others and taking the credit for themselves. Although Fu Sheng liked brave men and was a drunkard he was kind and not a killer. Look at his statutes of government and you will find no cruelty in them. But if you examine the histories you will find all the evil in the world is blamed on him.[23] Fu Chien, who presented himself as a good ruler, seized the throne from his monarch then had lying accounts of his "wrongdoings" written.[24] All official

---

[21] Conqueror of Wu in 280.

[22] A date that never occurred.

[23] Fu Sheng, who ruled north-west China from 355 to 357 as the third (Former) Ch'in Emperor had a bloody career (see *Chin shu* 112) that makes this judgement surprising.

[24] Cousin, killer, and successor of Fu Sheng, he unified north China and came close to overunning the south before his defeat on the Fei River in 383 led to the disintegration of his empire and, two years later, his own death. (See *Chin shu* 103–4; Rogers (1968); Wang Chung-lo (1961), pp. 177–87.)

historians are like this. Everyone believes it right to honour the distant and despise what is near. It is very curious that people these days can be stupid when alive and wise after death.' When asked what he meant he went on to say, 'A man who was humdrum in his lifetime has only to die for his memorial inscription and epitaph to say that "his great virtue reached from the earth to the bounds of the heavens and he had every talent with which man can be gifted." If he was a ruler "he could be compared to Yao and Shun",[25] and if a minister "he was the equal of Yi Yin[26] and Kao Yao.[27] If he was a provincial administrator, "swimming tigers admired his cleaning up of abuses",[28] and if a law officer he "buried the wheels of his chariot to show his uprightness".[29] One might say that a brigand when alive becomes a sage after his death. Such flattery harms the right, and this flowery language destroys the truth.' These remarks made the writers of the day feel ashamed.

The Colonel of Foot Li Ch'eng asked when the brick pagoda in front of the Headquarters of the Grand Marshal that looked very old in its construction but had never collapsed had been built. 'It was built by the soldiers,' said Chao Yi, 'in the twelfth year of *yi-hsi* [416] in the Chin during Liu Yü's expedition against Yao Hung.'[30] When the Prince of Ju-nan heard this he was so astonished that he adopted Chao Yi as his honorary father and asked him what should be eaten and drunk to obtain long life. 'I have never had time,' replied Chao Yi, '"to nourish my life", and my longevity is quite natural. Kuo P'u[31] found out for me by divination through milfoil that I would live to 500, so I have only just passed the halfway mark.' The Emperor gave him a foot-drawn carriage in which to travel around the market places and wards [of the city]. He recalled

[25] Sage Emperors of mythical antiquity.
[26] The minister who helped the Shang founder overthrow the last Hsia king.
[27] Shun's minister.
[28] Liu K'un was so good an administrator that the tigers took their cubs and left his prefectur. (*HHS* 79/1, p. 2550.)
[29] Chang Kang buried the wheels of his cart and refused to take office under a bad superior. (*HHS* 56, p. 1817.)
[30] The expedition mentioned in n. 3 above, in which Yao Hung, the last ruler of the Later Ch'in dynasty was captured and killed in 417.
[31] (*c.* 276–324) polymath and soothsayer.

many old anecdotes about the places to which he went. Three years later he disappeared and nobody knew where he went.

East of the Ch'ung-yi ward was the stone-built Seven Li Bridge where in Chung-ch'ao times Tu Yu[32] rested on his way to Ching-chou. One *li* east of the bridge was the gate of the outer wall of the city. As it had three roads through it people used to call it the Triple Gate; 'I'll escort you to the other side of the Triple Gate' was often said at partings as this was where the gentlement of the capital saw off people when they departed or greeted them on their return.

The CHUANG-YEN [Glory] MONASTERY was 1 *li* outside the Tung-yang Gate and north of the imperial highway in what was known as the Tung-an [Eastern Peace] ward. To its north was the Tax-Grain Ground. In the ward were the homes of the Assistant Imperial Charioteer Ssuma Yüeh,[33] Tao Hsüan, the Governor of Chi-chou, Li Chen-nu,[34] the Governor of Yu-chou, and Kungsun Hsiang, the Governor of Yü-chou.

The CH'IN T'AI-SHANG-CHÜN [Grand Duchess of Ch'in] MONASTERY was founded by the Empress Dowager Hu, whose formal title was Ch'ung-shun [Respectful and Obedient] and who ruled the empire with the rites of a mother. She gave her father the title of Grand Duke of Ch'in and her mother that of Grand Duchess of Ch'in.[35] She built this monastery to win blessings for her late mother—hence the name.

---

[32] Now best known for his excellent commentary on the *Tso chuan*, he left Loyang for a military command at Ching-chou in 278.

[33] There is some confusion between texts of *LYCLC* and parallel passages in other works as to which of the Ssuma family is here meant. The post mentioned was reserved for the sons-in-law of Emperors.

[34] This name is probably wrong: he died in 477. (*WS* 46, pp. 1039–42.)

[35] These unprecedented posthumous titles shocked contemporary opinion. (*WS* 94, p. 2027.)

It was 2 *li* outside the Tung-yang Gate and north of the imperial highway in what was called the Hui-wen ward which contained the houses of the Grand Protector Ts'ui Kuang,[36] the Grand Instructor Li Yen-shih, the Governor of Chi-chou Li Shao,[37] and the Privy Secretary Cheng Tao-chao.[38] Sumptuous halls rose where huge gateways opened on cavernous depths. 'The Hui-wen ward,' said Chao Yi, 'used to be the Mao-tao ward of Chin times. Li Yen-shih's house was the house of Liu Shan the Shu monarch,[39] and east of it was Harmony Mansion in which the Wu ruler Sun Hao lived.[40] Li Shao's house was that of the Chin Lord Chancellor Chang Hua.'

The monastery contained a five-storeyed pagoda whose spire reached up into the clouds. Its high gateway faced the street, and the magnificent decorations of its statues rivalled the Yung-ning Monastery. Rooms for chanting and meditation surrounded it in a double enclosure, and its steps were thickly covered with flowering trees and sweet-smelling plants. There were always monks famous for their great virtue preaching on all the scriptures, as well as novices by the thousand receiving instruction.

The Grand Instructor Li Yen-shih was the maternal uncle of Chuang-ti. During *yung-an* [528–30] he was appointed governor of Ch'ing-chou.[41] When he came to take his leave the Emperor said to him, 'People who carry bricks in their bosoms are always said to be ungovernable. You will have to devote your mind to carrying out the mission with which the court has entrusted you.' 'I am nearing the grave,' Li Yen-shih replied, 'and my breath cannot outlast the morning dew. Every little longer that I spend among men brings me closer to the tomb, and I have long been begging to retire. But now that Your Majesty has extended this favour to your aged uncle I am

---

[36] (451–523). A captured southern gentleman raised to high office from poverty by Kao-tsu. In his old age he remonstrated with the Dowager Hu when her breaches of etiquette went too far. (*WS* 67, pp. 1487–1500.)

[37] First cousin of Li Yen-shih. (*WS* 39, pp. 886–7.)

[38] A defender of Confucian culture. (*WS* 56, pp. 1240–2.)

[39] Who lived in Loyang from his capture in 223 till his death in 271. (*SKC* 33, pp. 893–903.)

[40] From his capture in 280 till his death three years later. (*SKC* 48, pp. 1162–83.)

[41] Central Shantung.

taking up this office despite my advancing years and going 10,000 *li* to learn my job. I shall not dare to fail your illustrious decree.'

The Gentleman in Waiting Yang K'uan[42] who was at the emperor's side did not understand what 'carry bricks in their bosoms' meant, so he discreetly asked the Assistant Secretary Wen Tzu-sheng.[43] 'I have heard,' replied Wen Tzu-sheng, 'that when His Majesty's respected elder brother, the Prince of P'eng-ch'eng,[44] was made governor of Ch'ing-chou he asked what the people were like. A retainer who was going to Ch'ing-chou with him said, "Ch'i[45] people are shallow. They go in for empty argument and high-flown talk, and all they care about is profit and fame. When a prefect first enters his territory they hide bricks in their bosoms and kowtow to him to make their intentions seem good. But when he is replaced and goes home they throw the bricks at him." That is why the rhyme in the capital goes.

> No prisoners in the jails,
> No Ch'ing-chou men in your house.
> Then even if family is on hard times
> You need have no worries.

This is where the saying "holding bricks in the bosom" comes from.'

Hsün Chi of Ying-ch'uan was a famous gentleman of untrammelled nature whose lofty perception and refined understanding distinguished him from his contemporaries.[46] Assessing the gentlemen of Ch'i, he said to Ts'ui Shu-jen[47] of

---

[42] A Hua-yin man who sided with the west when Wei split and died in 561. (*Chou shu* 22, pp. 111–13.)

[43] Regarded as one of the leading writers of the age. His official career began in 516 and ended when he was killed in 547 on suspicion of involvement with Hsün Chi in a plot to overthrow the dictator Kao Ch'eng and restore power to the Eastern Wei Emperor. (*WSa* 85, pp. 1874–7. See also ch. 1 of Part I.)

[44] Shao, son of Prince Hsieh, killed at Ho-yin in 528. (*WS* 21/2, p. 584.)

[45] Ch'ing-chou in particular and the Shantung area more generally. On the political overtones see p. 7 of Part I above.

[46] As he was executed in 547 for his part in the loyalist plot, Yang's praise of him, like his remarks quoted here, are heavy with innuendo. (On Hsün see *KHMC* 7, pp. 1a–7a, and *PS* 83, p. 2786.)

[47] Notorious for his corruption, for which he was forced to kill himself between 539 and 542. (*WS* 69, p. 1527.)

Ch'ing-ho, 'Ch'i people make a clever show of being benevolent and just, but in their hearts they are vulgar and mean. They are as light as hairs or feathers and as sharp as awls and knives. They chase after empty fame and make their names by toadying. In their scramble to get at the place of power they shoulder each other aside, and they take an enormous delight in the pursuit of glory and profit. They are the most notorious worshippers of power in the world.' He always referred to the men of Ch'i as the power-worshipping gentlemen. Some officials from Lin-tzu[48] who were in the capital were all ashamed when they heard about 'bricks in the bosom' and 'worshipping power' except for Ts'ui Hsiao-chung[49] who did not accept these strictures. When asked why, he said, 'The ways of Lin-tzu were improved by T'ai Kung,[50] and from the Confucian scholars of Chi-hsia academy came rites and morality.[51] Even though it may be in decline Ch'i is still a model to the world. Hsün Chi is no Hsü Shao or Kuo T'ai;[52] he can't recognize a sage. His filthy words can put nobody to shame.'

The CHENG-SHIH MONASTERY was founded by the officials in the first year of *cheng-shih* [504]—hence the name— outside the Tung-yang Gate and south of the imperial highway in what was known as the Ching-yi ward [Ward of Justice Respected]. In this ward was the Department of Mountains and Marshes.

With the purity of its buildings this monastery was more beautiful than the Ching-lin. Tall trees faced the windows of the monks' cells; bluish pines and green tamarisks linked their branches and intertwined their shadows. There were many

---

[48] The capital of Ch'ing-chou, in antiquity the capital of Ch'i.

[49] Who had 'no talent but his beauty'. (*WS* 57, p. 1274.)

[50] Lü Shang, trusted adviser to King Wen of Chou and first ruler of Ch'i.

[51] The academy flourished in the fourth and third centuries BC, and its members had a much wide range of interests than Confucian 'rites and morality'.

[52] Two second-century bureaucratic talent-spotters. (*HHS* 68, pp. 2225–7 and 2234.)

bitter-orange trees that produced inedible fruit.[53] It had a stone name-tablet with an inscription on the back saying that the Imperial Assistant Ts'ui Kuang had donated 400,000 cash and Li Ch'ung, Marquis of|Ch'en-liu,[54]| 200,000; the others had paid graded contributions of which the smallest was not less than 5,000 cash. This inscription had been carved later.

South of the Ching-yi ward was the Chao-te [Illustrious Virtues] ward in which were the houses of the Deputy Head of the Chancellery Yu Chao,[55] the Chief Censor Li Piao, the Minister for the Army Ts'ui Hsiu,[56] the Governor of Yu-chou, Ch'ang Ching, and the Minister of Agriculture Chang Lun.[57] Of these Li Piao and Ch'ang Ching were Confucian scholars who lived frugally in simple houses; Chang Lun was the most extravagant. In the splendour of his house, the exquisitely rare things he wore and amused himself with, and the number of horses and carriages that were always coming and going he outdid a monarch; none of the princes could rival the beauty of his gardens with their trees, hills, and ponds. He had a Ching-yang Mountain constructed that looked quite natural; there was range upon range of towering crags, while deep chasms and cavernous gullies led into each other. Tall forests of giant trees blotted out the sun and moon; mists drifted in the wind through the hanging creepers and dangling vines. Rough stone paths would seem to be impassable and yet allow a way through; the beds of torrents would twist around and then run straight. A lover of mountains and the wilds could wander there till he forgot to return.

Chiang Chih of T'ien-shui, a man of wild and extravagant nature who wore hempen clothes and shoes made from dolichos fibre, had the disposition of a recluse.[58] He fell in love

---

[53] *Poncirus trifoliata*, whose bitter fruit is normally only used in medicines.

[54] 455–525. His official career was long and active, and he suppressed banditry and uprisings until the mutinies in the northern garrisons. He also made a huge fortune in the markets at Loyang and elsewhere. (*WS* 66, pp. 1465–77.) See chs. 3 and 4 below for anecdotes about his meanness.

[55] Died in 520 respected for his integrity and scholarship. (*WS* 55, pp. 1215–18.)

[56] Father of the corrupt Ts'ui Shu-jen, and himself draconian in provincial postings, he died in 523. (*WS* 69, pp. 152–7.)

[57] Died in 528 or thereabouts. (*WS* 24, pp. 617–19.)

[58] It is evident from the prose-poem that follows that he had Taoist inclinations. Wei Shou maintained that his poetry was generally found vulgar. (*WS* 79, p. 1755.)

with Chang Lun's mountain when he saw it and could not but write the 'Prose-Poem on the Pavilion and the Mountain', which was widely circulated. This is how it went:

Those who tend to the heavy
Like the simple purity of the ancients.
A pure and simple body
Is a bridge leading to nature.
The gentleman above the river
And the clerk below the pillar[59]
Awoke to inaction and were enlightened.
Their ambition was to trust in nature,
Their wealth was mountains and waters.
They saw no honour in the hat of office,
Sinking or swimming as they felt;
Their lives were placid and dull.
Now Mr. Chang, the Director of Agriculture,
Is following in their footsteps.
His great capacity illuminates the externals;
Casually he penetrates to the truth.
The green pine cannot match his integrity
Nor is white jade as precious as he.
His heart, set on Nothing, only perches on Being.
His feelings penetrate the old to reach the present.
He does not give himself over to debauchery
Nor does he go in for extravagant display.
He pitches his tent between action and stillness,
Not forgetting mountains and waters.
A pavilion rises betwixt hill and valley,
Letting the eye reach the thoughts of the mind.
He advances without noise or pomp,
And in retirement he does not let himself go.
Now he splits rocks and makes the springs flow,
Raises leaning crags before his eaves,
Soaring level with the clouds
And joined by winding balconies.
They send down mists from the Milky Way
And receive the distant clouds of the Eastern Ocean.
The delicate peaks seem eternal,
Poised to crash for a thousand years.
The sheer ridges and overhanging cliffs
Are precipitously steep.

[59] i.e. Chuang Tzu and Lao Tzu.

The spring waters flow as majestically as ocean waves;
Many are the dangers in the lofty mountains.
Within fifty feet are a hundred crags,
And in ten paces one turns a thousand times.
I know that Mount Wu[60] has not its equal—
P'eng-lai perhaps, though I have never seen it.
The mist-shrouded flowers and dewy plants
Lean, as if about to fall;
Frosty trunks and wind-swept branches
Stand, some upright and some drooping.
Jade leaves and golden stalks
Cover the steps and the level ground.
The beauty that dazzles the eye,
The scents that tingle in the nostril,
Are luxuriant as the green of spring
Yet as pure as the whitest snow.
Some say that the very groundwork of the Divine,
The essence of the Negative and Positive,
Were born here unknown to heaven and earth;
So how can men or spirits find their names?
Many and varied are the birds
Whose colours mingle blue and yellow,
Green heads and purple cheeks,
Turquoise mingled with fragrance.
White storks, born in remote counties,
Redfoot birds from distant places,
Gather here from far and wide
To soar above the waters and trees.
They no longer remember spring in the desert
And forget about autumn in Kao-yang.
If he had not brought them here,
How could these migratory birds have forgotten their way?
This could not be done by the low and vulgar—
It is so strange and marvellous.
All who come here write songs about it;
No visitor fails to compose a prose-poem.
Some go where the winds blow free,
Or climb to places amid the clouds.
Chrysanthemum ridges and plum-blossom hills
Are awakened by autumn and spring.
Immortals come from afar to enjoy this garden
Known so well to the gentlemen of the court:

[60] By the Yangtse gorges.

Eager to shed their official robes and pendants,
They wait at the mountain's foot.
Master Ying swims among the fish in these jade-pure waters,
Wang Ch'iao tethers his stork to the pine branches.[61]
They find the magic Fang-chang island no comparison
When singing the praises of this amazing place.
Had Juan Chi[62] heard of it he would have been moved;
If Hsi K'ang had known, it would have shaken his soul.
If only they could rise from the grave
To get drunk once by this mountain gate.
Then there are the young nobles and princes
Who, modest and withdrawing,
Turn their thoughts to hills and rivers,
And follow each other here in their carriages.
They fall in love with the angles of the peaks,
And climb the creased and wrinkled rocks.
Because this garden is a field of wisdom and goodness,
This mountain could be planted here.
Richly grow the flowers and trees,
Nurturing mists and breezes.
One of these pines could avert old age,
Half a rock might prolong one's years.
If you do not lie back beside them,
Or wander among them in spring and summer,
Your skeleton will rot in vain,
And your heart will have nothing to remember.

The P'ING-TENG [Equality] MONASTERY was founded
when Yüan Huai, the Martial and Majestic Prince of Kuang-
p'ing,[63] gave his house. It was 2 *li* outside the Ch'ing-yang
Gate and lay to the north of the imperial highway in what was
called the Hsiao-ching [Filial Respect] ward. Its halls were
mighty and handsome, the grounds were full of spreading
trees, and its terraces and walkways were the finest of the age.

[61] Two Taoist immortals. Ying rode up to heaven on a fish, and Wang Ch'iao flew
off on the back of a stork after thirty years as a recluse.
[62] 210–63. Taoist, musician, drinker, poet, and nihilist.
[63] A son of Kao-tsu who died in 517 at the age of twenty-nine. (Fan, p. 109 n. 1.) On
his suburban house see ch. 4 below.

Outside the monastery gates was a gold statue 28 feet high. This majestic image had the divine property of showing when disasters were going to hit the country.

In the twelfth month of the third year of *hsiao-ch'ang* [527] the statue's face had a sorrowful expression. Tears streamed from both its eyes and its whole body was wet. People called this 'Buddha sweating'. The gentlemen and ladies of the capital flocked from ward and market to look at it. When a monk wiped the tears away with clean silk floss it became soaked through in a moment, and when he used some more that too was soaked immediately. This went on for three days before it stopped.[64] In the fourth month of the following year Erhchu Jung entered Loyang and slaughtered the officials, strewing the ground with corpses.

In the third month of the second year of *yung-an* [529] the statue sweated again; the gentry and commoners of the capital all went to look at it once more. In the fifth month the Prince of Pei-hai [Yüan Hao] entered Loyang and the Emperor Chuang-ti went north. In the seventh month the Prince of Pei-hai suffered a great defeat and all the young men from the Yangtse and Huai valleys he had brought with him were captured: not one returned home.

In the seventh month of the third year of *yung-an* [530] the statue wept again as before. As every manifestation of its divine powers caused such fear in court circles and everywhere else nobody was allowed to look at it. In the twelfth month Erhchu Chao entered Loyang and captured the Emperor Chuang-ti, who later died at Chin-yang. The palaces in the capital were empty and there was no monarch for a hundred days. Loyang was garrisoned by Erhchu Shih-lung, the Head of the Chancellery, Governor of the Metropolitan province, and Prince of Lo-p'ing. Merchants were able to travel in all directions and there was no brigandage.

In the second year of *chien-ming* [531] the Prince of Ch'ang-kuang came to the capital from Chin-yang, but when he arrived at the outer wall of the city Erhchu Shih-lung forced

[64] Atmospheric condensation might be a more prosaic explanation of this phenomenon.

him to abdicate in favour of Prince Kung of Kuang-ling[65] as he belonged only to a distant branch of the royal family and had no reputation for administration. Yüan Kung, a paternal cousin of Chuang-ti, had been a Gentleman in Waiting during *cheng-kuang* [520–5], and when he saw that under Yüan Yi's dictatorship power was in the hands of yes-men he pretended to be struck dumb and stayed out of politics. In *yung-an* [528–30] he retired to the mountains of Shang-lo[66] only to be arrested and sent back to the capital by Ch'üan Ch'i, the Governor of the province.[67] Suspecting that Yüan Kung's dumbness was feigned, Chuang-ti sent some men to rob him of his clothes at night and draw their swords as if to kill him, but Kung only opened his mouth and pointed at his tongue without saying a word. Chuang-ti now believed that his affliction was real and allowed him to go back to his residence. Yüan Kung often stayed at the Lung-hua Monastery,[68] and it was there that Erhchu Shih-lung and others deposed the Prince of Ch'ang-kuang and put Kung on the throne. The abdication edict read:

The Emperor has consulted with Prince Kung of Kuang-ling. Since our August Wei has owned the world successive sages have developed and defended it; while the foundation has been strengthened the realm has been extended. We have overcome the myriad lands, spreading our glory to the four seas, so that our way is fuller than that of all other princes and our divine influence is all-embracing.

On the decease of the Filial Emperor Ming-ti men and gods alike were left without a monarch. The Pillar of State General and Lord High Minister, Prince Jung of T'ai-yüan, who although serving as a minister in the provinces, was greatly concerned about the possible collapse of the Royal House; wherefore did he advance Tzu-yu, Prince of Ch'ang-lo, to continue the interrupted cause in the hope that the empire would grow mightier each day and the dynasty would enjoy seven centuries of blessings.

But the world was not yet at peace; times were still turbulent. Men looked about them anxiously, facing each other with implacable hostility. Then one action by the High Minister pacified the world.

---

[65] Also known as Ch'ien-fei-ti or Chieh-min-ti, he was deposed the next year by Kao Huan. (*WS* 11, pp. 273–8.)

[66] In Shanghsien, eastern Shensi.

[67] A post held by virtual hereditary right by his family. (*Chou shu* 44, pp. 785–7.)

[68] Which he or his brother founded—see ch. 3 below.

Meanwhile Tzu-yu, unmindful of the ancestral heritage, hated and avoided those who had distinguished themselves by their virtue, gathered about him irresponsible gallants, and surrounded himself with flatterers. He was as cruel as King Chou of Yin who cut men's hearts out, and the agony of it was like having teeth pulled. Indeed, things were even worse than when the golden tablet appeared to make its accusation[69] or the giant birds were moved by the goodness [of the mistreated minister].[70] From then on the hopes of the empire were suddenly turned away from him.

Realizing that the throne cannot be left empty for long and that the divine office cannot have no lord, I decided to follow the general will by assuming temporary rule over the common people. Now that the armies have moved south and are on the banks of the Yellow River, facing the capital, I am filled with regret. I in my unworthiness am but a distant member of the imperial clan, and thus quite unfit to hope for the sympathy of heaven above and be entrusted with the aspirations of the people below.

Your Majesty's virtue, however, glorifies our ancestors, and your fame will last for ever. In the past our destiny was a troubled one and the world went through hard times. For many years you have kept your feelings to yourself in silence, but now heaven is mindful of your radiant virtue and the people love you as their ruler. The true succession is yours, and all sing your praises. Now that you are acting in response to their wishes I respectfully present you with the imperial seal and shall return to my private residence. Your Majesty should reverently carry out the royal mission, holding power with sincerity at the centre. Do not rest even when you want to do so, and be careful every day. Obey this.

Kung declined with the following statement:

The heavenly mandate is a very serious matter, and the imperial power is no trifle. As I am lacking in the divine power needed to achieve harmony between Heaven, Earth and Man, and my merits have not saved the world, my name cannot be entered on the list of Emperors and I am unworthy of being chosen by the masses. Despite my ignorance I know that I lack foresight, so I dare not accept the great mandate even if it is handed down to me. I beg that your edict be withdrawn in order to satisfy my humble loyalty.

[69] At the killing of the minister Kuanlung Feng by the tyrannical King Chieh of Hsia.

[70] When Yang Chen, who had poisoned himself in protest against the men in power in AD 124, was reburied birds 10 feet high came to weep and wail at his coffin according to *HHS* 54, pp. 1767-8.

To this the Prince of Ch'ang-kuang replied:

Your Majesty's virtue fits you for the imperial roll and all the officials support you; wherefore are you worthy to hold power at the centre, ascending gloriously the imperial throne. If you spare trouble by not declining, men and gods alike will feel the greatest happiness.

After declining the throne three times Kung finally accepted it, changing the title of the year to *p'u-t'ai*. The Gentleman in Waiting Hsing Tzu-ts'ai[71] drafted an amnesty in which he included the charge that Chuang-ti had murdered the Prince of T'ai-yüan, but the Prince of Kuang-ling said, 'For the Emperor of the *yung-an* period to dispatch with his own hand an over-powerful subject showed no lack of virtue; but because heaven had not yet ended the troubles he was killed by one of his own ministers.' Then he called to his attendants, 'Bring us a writing brush: we shall write it ourselves.' Speaking directly to the Palace Bureau he said, 'Despite our paltry virtues a happy fate has elevated us, and we wish to celebrate this with the millions. Let there be a general amnesty in accordance with normal usage.' At his first words after eight years' silence all gentry and commoner within the seas proclaimed that he was a sage monarch. He enfeoffed the Prince of Ch'ing-ling as Prince of Tung-hai and created Erhchu Shih-lung an honorary senior minister, Head of Chancellery, and Prince of Lo-p'ing, in addition to the offices he already held. The Prince of T'ai-yüan was [posthumously] created Minister of State and Prince of Chin, and was granted the Nine Awards.[72] A temple for him was erected on the Shou-yang peak of the Mang ridge where the Duke of Chou's temple had been in remote antiquity. Erhchu Shih-lung built it because he wanted to put the achievements of the Prince of T'ai-yüan on a par with those of the Duke of Chou. After it was completed it was destroyed by fire. One column went on burning for three days without going out until a thunderbolt shattered it in a thunderstorm three days later; the stone base of the column and the tiles of the temple all fell in fragments to the bottom of the mountain.

[71] See ch. 3 below.
[72] Originally given by the throne to outstanding ministers, they included the right to paint one's gates red, a carriage and horses, imperial Tiger Guards, and other signal honours.

When the officials were ordered to recommend that the Prince of T'ai-yüan receive sacrifices together with former Emperors, the inspector Liu Chi-ming[73] dissented. When asked why by Erhchu Shih-lung he said, 'Would he receive sacrifices with the Emperor Shih-tsung to whom he did no service? Is it to be with the Filial Emperor Ming-ti whose mother[74] he killed with his own hand? Would it be with Chuang-ti by whom he was killed for treason? Taking all this into consideration there is no Emperor with whom he could receive sacrifices.' 'Death on you,' exclaimed Erhchu Shih-lung in fury. 'My humble office requires me to express my opinion,' Liu Chi-ming replied, 'and what I said was quite in order. If my words offended your sage mind imprisonment or execution must be my fate.' All the other advisers sighed with admiration at the way Liu Chi-ming stood up to so powerful a man; and despite Shih-lung's angry words Liu Chi-ming came to no harm in the end.

Previously, when Erhchu Shih-lung mutinied and went north,[75] the Emperor Chuang-ti had sent the General to pacify the East Shih Wu-lung and the General to Subdue the North Yang Wen-yi to lead jointly a force of 3,000 men to hold the T'ai-hang range.[76] The Imperial Assistant Yüan Tzu-kung was garrisoning Ho-nei. When Erhchu Chao turned his horse's head to the south Shih Wu-lung, Yang Wen-yi and the rest of them surrendered with all their men to Erhchu Chao, after which Yüan Tzu-kung's forces saw how things were going and disintegrated. Erhchu Chao followed up his victory by pursuing the defeated troops straight to the capital, where his men reached the ceremonial entrance to the palace and shot their arrows into the royal apartments. When rewards for meritorious service were being considered Shih Wu-lung and Yang Wen-yi were each [put forward for] a fief of 1,000 households, but the Prince of Kuang-ling said, 'Wu-lung and Wen-yi served Your Highness but not their country,' and refused the awards. He was then regarded as a man of stern integrity.

---

[73] Also known from *WS* 108/4, p. 2809, as a stickler for correct Confucian ritual.
[74] The Dowager Hu.
[75] In late 530, after the death of Erhchu Jung.
[76] And thus prevent the Erhchu from moving south from their Chin-yang base.

Erhchu Chung-yüan, Prince of P'eng-ch'eng and a cousin of Erhchu Shih-lung,[77] submitted a memorial when commanding the garrison at Hua-t'ai[78] in which he asked permission to appoint his lieutenant Yi Yüan as Governor of Western Yen-chou, which he had in fact already done. The Prince of Kuang-ling replied, 'Why send all this way to ask permission if you can fill the post locally?'

Whenever Erhchu Shih-lung attended a palace banquet the emperor would observe that the Prince of T'ai-yüan had deserved to die for the crime of taking credit due to heaven. Erhchu Shih-lung was so scared by this that he never went to court again. He seized state power for himself and became ever more evil. He controlled the Censorate and the Chancellery from his chair and ruled the country from his home.[79] Everything, whether important or trivial, had to be referred to his residence before it could be carried out. Meanwhile the Son of Heaven sat on his throne with folded hands and had nothing to do with it all.

When the Prince of P'ing-yang ascended the throne in the first year of *yung-an* [532] he erected a five-storeyed pagoda in this monastery.

The Prince of P'ing-yang was a younger son of the Martial and Majestic Prince [of Kuang-p'ing]. He ordered the Deputy Secretary Wei Shou and some others to compose a stone inscription for the pagoda, which was completed on the fifth day of the second month of the second year of *yung-hsi* [533], when the Emperor led the officials to a monastic grand assembly [*pañca-pariṣad*] there.[80] All that day a stone statue outside the monastery gates moved for no reason, bowing its head and raising it again. The Emperor went and worshipped it himself, so astonished was he at this phenomenon. The

[77] During the Erhchu dominance he was the virtually independent warlord controlling the rich areas of Yen and Hsü (east Honan and Shantung) until driven out by Kao Huan in 532. (*WS* 75, pp. 1666–7.)

[78] A strategically vital triple-walled city controlling a crossing of the Yellow River (*SCC* 5, p. 1/83) near its junction with several other important waterways that Erhchu Chung-yuan made his headquarters in 532.

[79] His dictatorship was effectively limited to the Loyang area by his rival Erhchu warlords.

[80] Something is missing here as some of what follows refers to the year after. The monastic grand assembly has been compared with the great quinquennial assembly reported by Fa-hsien in Khalcha.

Assistant Secretary Lu Ching-hsüan[81] said, 'In remote antiquity stones stood up and altars moved; Your Majesty need not be alarmed.' The Emperor then returned to the palace. In the seventh month[82] the Emperor was forced by the Imperial Assistant Hussu Ch'un to flee to Ch'ang-an, and at the end of the tenth month the capital was moved to Yeh.

The CHING-NING MONASTERY [Monastery of Illustrious Peace] was founded by the Grand Protector and High Premier Yang Ch'un.[83] It lay 3 *li* outside the Ch'ing-yang Gate to the south of the imperial highway in what was known as the Chingning [Illustrious Peace] ward.

When Kao-tsu moved the capital to Loyang Yang Ch'un was the first to live in this ward. Later he divided off part of his home to be a monastery and named it after the ward. It was beautifully built and decorated; its pillars were covered with openwork silk and the door-curtains were studded with pearls. Yang Ch'un's younger brother Yang Shun was a Governor of Chi-chou, and Shun's younger brother Chin was Lord Chancellor. They were all generous and cultured men who honoured justice and made light of wealth. Four generations lived together, including uncles, great-uncles, and great-great-uncles: nobody else in the court or the ascendancy could match the propriety of their domestic life. In *p'u-t'ai* [531–3] they were slaughtered by Erhchu Shih-lung, after which their house was given to become the Chien-chung Monastery.

Three *li* outside the Ch'ing-yang Gate to the north of the imperial highway was the Hsiao-yi [Filial Piety] ward in the

---

[81] Personal name Pien. The younger brother of the Lu Pai-t'ou mentioned in ch. 1, he later played an important part in the creation of institutions for the Chou regime. (*Chou shu* 24; *PS* 30, pp. 1099–1104.)

[82] Of 534.

[83] 455–531. His long career at court and in provincial posting was marred by several indictments for corruption. Despite what is said below, it was the display rather than the accumulation of wealth he avoided. Yang's praise of the family may be due in part to their support for Chuang-ti against the Erhchu. (See biographies in *WS* 58.)

north-west corner of which was the grave-mound of Su Ch'in.[84] Beside this tomb was the Pao-ming Monastery.

The monks often saw Su Ch'in going in and out of the tomb with a ceremonial retinue of chariots and horses, just like a modern chief minister.

East of the Hsiao-yi ward was the Little Market of Loyang, and to the north was the house of Chang Ching-jen, the General of Chariots and Cavalry. Chang Ching-jen was a man from Shan-yin in Kuei-chi. Early in *cheng-kuang* [520–5][85] he came over with Hsiao Pao-yin.[86] He was appointed Commander of the Forest of Wings Guard and given a house south of the city wall in the Kuei-cheng [Returning to Orthodoxy] ward, also known as the Wu Quarter because many of the southerners who came over lived there. It was near the Yi and Lo rivers to let them feel more at home. There were over 3,000 households in the ward and they had set up their own street market selling mainly aquatic delicacies. People called it the Fish and Turtle Market. Chang Ching-jen found living here so humiliating that he moved to the Hsiao-yi ward. As the court wanted at the time to welcome men from distant parts it treated southerners with great generosity. Men who had tucked up their skirts to cross the Yangtse were given very high positions. Chang Ching-jen enjoyed fame and high office although he performed no service.[87]

In the second year of *yung-an* [529] Hsiao Yen sent the Head Clerk Ch'en Ch'ing-chih to escort the Prince of Pei-hai when he usurped the imperial throne in Loyang.[88] Ch'en Ch'ing-chih then became Imperial Assistant. Chang Ching-jen, who had known Ch'en Ch'ing-chih in the south, prepared a banquet for him and invited him home. The Deputy Minister

[84] The Loyang man who enjoyed a legendary career as a roving political adviser till his failure and death in 320 BC.

[85] This date is wrong as Hsiao Pao-yin came to Wei in 501.

[86] Son of a Ch'i Emperor who came north when the dynasty fell and served Wei as a soldier till rebelling in the west in 527. In 530 he was captured and made to kill himself. (*WS* 59, pp. 1313–24.)

[87] Evidently northern resentment.

[88] 485–539. A career officer in the Liang service who rose from humble origins to hold high military and civil posts. His capture of Loyang in 529 with only 7,000 men to put Yüan Hao, Prince of Pei-hai, on the throne was a brilliant adventure only foiled by overwhelming numbers against him. (*Liang shu* 32, pp. 459–64.)

of Agriculture Hsiao Piao and the Junior Assistant Head of the Chancellery Chang Sung, both southerners, were also there; the Counsellor Yang Yüan-shen and the Palace Councellor Wang Hsüan were the only gentlemen from the northern plains present. When he was drunk Ch'en Ch'ing-chih said to Hsiao Piao and Chang Sung, 'The Wei dynasty is flourishing but it is still referred to as a barbarian one. The true succession should be south of the Yangtse, and the imperial jade seal of the Ch'in dynasty is now in the Liang court.'

'South of the Yangtse,' replied Yang Yüan-shen solemnly, 'they enjoy a temporary peace in their remote corner. Much of your land is wet; it is cursed with malaria and crawling with insects. Frogs and toads share a single hole while men live in the same flocks with birds. You are the gentlemen of the cropped hair, and none of you have long heads. You tattoo the puny bodies with which you are endowed. Floating on the Three Rivers or rowing on the Five Lakes you are untouched by the Rites and the Music and cannot be reformed by official statutes. Although some Ch'in survivors and Han convicts provided an admixture of Han speech, the awkward languages of Min and Ch'u are beyond improvement. You may have a monarchy but your rulers are overweening and your masses unruly. This was why Liu Shao murdered his father[89] and Liu Hsiu-lung later committed incest with his mother.[90] Such breaches of human propriety make you no better than birds or beasts. On top of this the Princess of Shan-yin used to ask for bought men as husbands, ignoring the jeers in her domestic debauchery.[91] You, sirs, are still soaked in these old ways and have not yet absorbed civilization. You are like the people of Yang-ti who are so used to goitres that they do not find them ugly.[92]

[89] Liu Shao killed his father, the Sung Emperor Wen-ti, in 453 and was himself killed soon afterwards.

[90] Brother and killer of Liu Shao, he ruled the south from 453–64 as the Sung Emperor later known as Wu-ti. The accusation of incest is also found in the lurid *Wei shu* account of Sung (97, p. 2144); the *Sung shu* biography of his mother refers to her lovers and bad reputation but names no names (*Sung shu* 41).

[91] Liu Hsiu-lung's daughter, who resenting the unfairness of Emperors being allowed women by the thousand was allowed by her brother when on the throne thirty male concubines (*Sung shu* 7).

[92] Presumably because of a local iodine deficiency. Yang-ti is in Yühsien, central Honan.

'Our Wei dynasty has received the mandate of heaven, founding a stable government by Moung Sung and the Lo River. The Five Mountains are our peaks and the Four Seas are our home. Our laws to reform the people are comparable to the achievements of the Five Emperors. Our flourishing court ritual, music, constitution, and edicts excel those of the hundred kings. If you fishes and turtles come to pay homage at our court out of admiration for our justice, drinking from our pools and eating our rice and millet, how can you be so arrogant?'

When Ch'en Ch'ing-chih and the others heard this elegant and cultured speech from Yang Yüan-shen they rushed about in all directions keeping their mouths shut and pouring with sweat. A few days later Ch'en Ch'ing-chih fell ill with acute heart pains. When he asked people to cure him Yang Yüan-shen said that he could do it, so Ch'en Ch'ing-chih asked him to come. Yang Yüan-shen filled his mouth with water and spurted it over Ch'en Ch'ing-chih. 'Wu devils,' he said, 'live in Chien-k'ang. You wear your hats too small and your clothes too short. You call yourselves "a-nung" and each other "a-pang". Your staple foods are the seeds of tares and grasses; you drink tea, sip at water-lily soup, and suck at crab spawn. In your hands you hold cardamoms and you chew betel in your mouths. When you find yourselves in the central lands you long for your home country and scamper back to Tan-yang[93] as fast as you can go. As for your humbly born devils, you catch fish and turtles with your nets from islands in rivers when your hair is still long. You nibble at water-chestnut and lotus-root, pick "chicken-head" plants,[94] and regard frog broth and oyster stew as great delicacies. In your hempen coats and grass sandals you ride facing backwards on water-buffaloes. On the Yüan, Hsiang, Yangtse, and Han rivers you wield the oar as you float along with the current or row upstream; you gape like fishes as you swim. You whirl white grasscloth in your dances, scattering the waves as you sing your ballads. Clear off as fast as you can—go back to your Yang province.'

'You have humilitated me deeply, Mr. Yang,' said Ch'en

---

[93] Probably the Chien-k'ang (Nanking) area is meant here.
[94] *Euryale ferox*: an aquatic plant yielding edible fruit and pith.

Ch'ing-chih, burying his head on his pillow; and from then on southerners did not dare to ask for diagnoses.

When the Prince of Pei-hai was executed Ch'en Ch'ing-chih scurried back to Hsiao Yen, who appointed him Governor of the Metropolitan province. Ch'en Ch'ing-chih gave far more responsible jobs to northerners than had been given before, which made Chu Yi[95] so indignant that he asked why. 'Ever since Chin and Sung times,' Ch'en Ch'ing-chih replied, 'Loyang has been called a desolate region, and here we say that everyone north of the Yangtse is a barbarian; but on my recent visit to Loyang I found out that families of capped and gowned scholars live on the northern plains, where proper ceremonial and protocol flourish. I cannot find words to describe the magnificent personages I saw. In the language of the old saying, the imperial capital was majestic, a model for the four quarters.[96] How could I fail to honour northerners? Men who have climbed Mount T'ai think little of mere hills, and those who have been on the Yangtse or the open sea despise the Hsiang and Yüan.' From then on Ch'en Ch'ing-chih adopted the Wei style of feathered canopies, insignia, and dress. Gentlemen and commoner alike south of the Yangtse competed in imitating him; wide-skirted gowns and broad belts were worn even in Mo-ling [Chien-k'ang].

Yang Yüan-shen was a man of Hung-nung and a descendant in the sixth generation of Yang Ch'iao, Governor of Chi province during the Chin dynasty. His great-grandfather Yang T'ai came in through the passes with Emperor Wu-ti of the Sung and was prefect of Shang-lo for seven years.[97] He turned away from that bogus regime and came over to our court. Emperor Ming-yüan[98] conferred on him the marquisate of Lin-chin and appointed him prefect of Kuang-wu and Ch'en. He was also made Governor of Liang-chou and given the posthumous title of Marquis Lieh. His grandfather Yang Fu

[95] Like Ch'en a career official of quite humble origin who was virtually running the machinery of the Liang state by then. He died in 549. (*Liang shu* 38, pp. 537–40; *Nan shu* 62, pp. 1514–19.)

[96] As the Shang capital was described in the last poem of the *Shih ching*.

[97] As Shang-lo was near his ancestral Hung-nung it is not surprising that Yang Ch'iao chose to stay when Liu Yü withdrew from the north in 520.

[98] Reigned 409–23.

was a classical expert and a professor; his father Yang Tz'u found happiness in valleys and hills, and did not serve the mighty. His father's younger brother Yang Hsü was prefect of Ho-nan and of Shu. His family had been famous for generations for its learning and conduct, and its reputation stood high in province and ward alike.

Yang Yüan-shen had a pure and lofty spirit. His behaviour was superior from childhood, and he did not allow convention to prevent him from acting as he felt inclined. He took pleasure in mountains and rivers, loving to wander among forests and marshes. He was widely read and a brilliant talker, unbeatable at the impromptu capping of lines of poetry. He was a student of Lao Tzu and Chuang Tzu and an able expositor of the hidden principles.[99] So fond was he of liquor that he could drink gallons of it without discomposure. He used to sigh with regret that he had not been a contemporary of Juan Chi's. As he did not want to hold office he was made a Counsellor without Portfolio; he would often stay away from court on a pretext of sickness. He never showed his respect to the powerful or bothered with condolences or congratulations for his relations and acquaintances. As he made friends sparingly he was unknown to the world at large. Sometimes admirers of his principles would send their cards in at his gate but he would pretend to be sick and stay in lofty idleness. In addition, his thinking was profound and he was good at interpreting dreams. When in *hsiao-ch'ang* [525–7] Yüan Yüan, Prince of Kuang-yang, had just been made an honorary senior minister and was mustering 100,000 troops to march north against Ko Jung,[100] he dreamed that he was wearing the *kun* robes[101] and leaning on a locust tree. Imagining that this was a good omen he asked Yang Yüan-sheng about it. 'It means that you will become one of the senior ministers,' said Yang Yüan-shen.

[99] Of Taoism.

[100] Yüan Yüan had first been sent to deal with northern-garrison mutinies in 523, but despite his perceptive analysis of the grievances of the northern officers his suggestions for winning them back to loyalty were ignored. In 526 he was sent back north to deal with the former garrison men under Hsienyü Hsiu-li and others. (Biography, under the T'ang substitute-name Shen, in *PS* 16, pp. 616–21; *WSa* 18, pp. 429–34.) Ko Jung was an officer in the Huai-shuo Garrison who became the main rebel leader in Hopei from 526 till his defeat by Erhchu Jung in 528.

[101] A privilege of the Three Senior Ministers.

Yüan Yüan was delighted, but Yang Yüan-sheng told people after returning home that the Prince of Kuang-yang was going to die. 'Locust-tree 槐 is a ghost 鬼 standing beside a tree 木. He will only become a senior minister after his death.' The Prince of Kuang-yang was indeed killed by Ko Jung[102] and posthumously made High Premier just as Yang Yüan-shen had predicted.

Early in *chien-yi* [528] Hsüeh Ling-po, the prefect of Yang-cheng, fled east from his prefecture when he heard that the Prince of T'ai-yuan had executed the officials and put Chuang-ti on the throne. He asked Yüan-shen about a dream in which he had shot a wild goose. ' "The minister holds a lamb;" "the counsellors holds a wild goose" ',[103] said Yüan-shen. 'You will be made a counsellor.' Hsüeh Ling-po was suddenly made a Remonstrating Counsellor.

Hsü Ch'ao of Ching-chao dreamed that he was imprisoned for sheep stealing and asked Yang Yüan-shen about it. 'You will be made magistrate of Ch'eng-yang,' said Yüan-shen. He was later created Marquis of Ch'eng-yang for his distinguished services. Although magistrate is not quite the same as marquis I would say the modern magistrate has 100 *li* to rule just like a marquis in antiquity, and argue that this too was a brilliant achievement.

His contemporaries compared him to Chou Hsüan.[104] When Erhchu Chao entered Loyang he resigned his office and wandered in the Shang-lo hills with Wang T'eng-chou, the recluse of Hua-yin.

East of the Hsiao-yi ward and north of the market was the Chih-huo [Commercial] ward in which lived Liu Hu and his four brothers, dependants of the Office of Temples and

---

[102] In 526.

[103] Quoting the *Chou li* (18, p. 762, and 30, p. 845) on what officials should hold in their hands on various occasions.

[104] An interpreter of dreams in the Three Kingdoms period. (*SKC* 29, pp. 810–11.)

Sacrifices, who were butchers by trade.[105] One day in *yung-an* [528–30] a pig that Liu Hu was slaughtering cried out, begging for its life. When the neighbours heard they all thought that the Hu brothers must be fighting, and when they came to look they saw that it was a pig. Liu Hu consequently donated their house to become the KUEI-CHÜEH [Returning to Enlightenment] MONASTERY, in which all the brothers became monks.[106] In the first year of *p'u-t'ai* [531] a golden statue in this monastery grew hairs all over its eyebrows and scalp. The Senior Assistant Head of the Chancellery Wei Chi-ching[107] said to someone, 'When it happened to Chang T'ien-hsi his country was wiped out.[108] This time it is also a bad omen.' The next year the Prince of Kuang-ling was deposed and died.

[105] They probably were allowed to work most of the time as retail butchers on their own account but also required to deal with sacrificial animals for the Office of Temples and Sacrifices. Although a decree of 531 raised their status to *min*, they were previously *tsa-hu*, hereditary semi-slaves.

[106] Back in 518 Yüan Ch'eng, Prince of Jen-ch'eng, had singled out in a general attack on the excessive growth of monasteries in Loyang those that were 'filling the city and spilling over into butchers' stalls', so that 'the stench of meat' lingered round statues and pagodas. (*WS* 114, p. 3045.)

[107] Cousin of the historian Wei Shou and famous as a writer. (*PS* 56, p. 2043.)

[108] Who ruled a small independent state in Liang-chou (Kansu) until it was overrun in AD 376.

Chapter 3

South of the City Wall

The CHING-MING MONASTERY was founded by the Emperor Hsüan-wu during *ching-ming* [500–3]—hence the name. It lay 1 *li* outside the Hsüan-yang Gate to the east of the imperial highway. The monastery extended for 500 paces from east to west and from north to south. It faced the Shao-shih hill of Mount Sung, and behind it was the wall of the imperial city. The shade of its dark trees and the patterns of its green waters made it a refreshing and beautiful place and there were over 1,000 rooms in its towering buildings. The windows and gutters of many-storeyed halls and structures joined and faced each other; dark terraces and purple pavilions were connected by flying passages. No matter what the season outside, it was never freezing or torrid in here; beyond the eaves of the buildings were only hills and lakes. Pine, bamboo, orchid, and iris overhung the steps, holding the wind and gathering the dew as they spread their fragrance.

During *cheng-kuang* [520–5] the Empress Dowager built a seven-storeyed pagoda here which rose to a great height; this was why Hsing Tzu-ts'ai said in the inscription he wrote for it:

One looks down and hears the thunder
While shooting stars flash past.

The splendour of the monastery's ornamentation rivalled the Yung-ning; its golden pole and precious bells gleamed beyond the clouds.

There were three pools in the monastery where reeds, rushes, water-chestnuts, and lotuses grew. Yellow turtles and purple fish could be seen among the waterweeds; black ducks and white geese dived and swam in the green waters. There were edge-runner mills, rotary mills, pounders, and bolters all powered by water.[1] This was regarded as the finest of all the monasteries.

[1] On this remarkable equipment see Appendix III.

In those days the Great Blessing was very popular. On the seventh day of the fourth month all the statues in the capital were brought to this monastery. According to the Department of Sacrifices of the Chancellery they numbered over 1,000. On the eighth the statues were taken in through the Hsüan-yang Gate to the front of the Ch'ang-ho Palace where the Emperor scattered flowers on them.[2] The gold and the flowers dazzled in the sun, and the jewelled canopies floated like clouds; there were forests of banners and a fog of incense, and the Buddhist music of India shook heaven and earth. All kinds of entertainers and trick riders performed shoulder to shoulder. Virtuous hosts of famous monks came, carrying their staves; there were crowds of the Buddhist faithful, holding flowers; horsemen and carriages were packed beside each other in an endless mass. When a monk from the West saw all this he would proclaim that this was indeed a land of the Buddha.

In *yung-hsi* [532–4] Hsing Tzu-ts'ai,[3] the President of the Imperial Academy, composed an inscription for the monastery.

Hsing Tzu-ts'ai, a man of Ho-chien, was endowed with intelligence and culture. He would think deeply behind his study curtain and was thoroughly versed in things ancient and modern. Among literary giants Hsü Shao or Kuo T'ai could not have matched his elegant style or wide learning. This was why capped-and-gowned gentlemen flocked to his gate while lovers of the Way filled his house. All who entered his halls felt as if they had passed through Confucius' gate; those who earned his praise regarded it as most valuable. He was very famous in his day and his reputation spread both far and near. At the end of *cheng-kuang* [520–5] he/put aside his commoner's short robe to serve as a Mourner for Shih-tsung and Court Guest, later being promoted to Deputy Secretary and Gentleman in Waiting.

---

[2] As his ancestors had done in P'ing-ch'eng (*WS* 114, p. 3032), in the Indian and central-Asian manner.

[3] Regarded as one of the great writers of the Eastern Wei and Northern Ch'i period, he is given a chapter to himself in *Pei Ch'i shu* (36). Little needs to be added to Yang's eulogy. He was against excessive spending on the great monasteries; he so neglected his wife for his books that her dog barked at him when he went to her room; and he thought life too short to allow one to collate texts carefully.

Hsing Tzu-ts'ai's learning was wide and all-embracing; there was no aspect of state organization with which he did not concern himself. When disturbances shook the imperial house education in the palace came to an end, but later he was made President of the Imperial Academy, planning and supervising the teaching in the higher schools. He rewarded the diligent and punished the lazy, devoting his full attention to encouraging and guiding the students, who strove to master the elegant arts; the spirit of the schools of Confucius flourished once more. At the end of *yung-hsi* [532–4] he offered his resignation on the grounds of his mother's old age, but the Emperor refused to accept it. Hsing Tzu-ts'ai made his respectful pleas with such extreme sincerity that the tears poured from his eyes. The Emperor then gave his permission, appointing him a Distinguished Gentleman so that he could return home to look after his family, and giving him five serving men. He was to attend court once a year to offer his advice. The farewell banquet he was given by the princes and nobles was like the send-off the court gave the two Shus.[4]

After the imperial residence was moved to Yeh there was a spate of civil litigation; old regulations and new decrees existed side by side and in conflict with each other. The law officers did not know how to deal with cases, so that mountains of files accumulated. Hsing Tzu-ts'ai and the Chevalier in Attendance Wen Tzu-sheng then compiled on imperial command the *New Ordinances of Lin-chih* in fifteen rolls.[5] With these government offices were able to settle difficult cases, while the provinces and prefectures used them to establish order. During the years *wu-ting* [543–50] he was appointed a Senior General of Galloping Cavalry and Governor of Western Yen province. The officials and the people were contented under his uncorrupt and peaceful rule. Later he was promoted to be Head of

[4] Shu Kang and his nephew Shou, who retired from the Western Han court before disaster could strike them, were given a magnificent send-off by the gentlemen of the capital.

[5] According to Ch'eng Shu-te, 1963, pp. 397–8, there were two codes named after the Lin-chih Hall in Yeh, one issued in 541 and one, much more thoroughly revised, in 550. Hsing was involved in preparing the latter code, but the former must be meant here as Wen Tzu-sheng died in 547. Ch'en Yin-k'o (1963, pp. 111–12) shows that the great Han-Chinese clans succeeded in introducing Confucian principles of jurisprudence into Eastern Wei and Northern Ch'i codes.

the Secretariat. At that time the war horses were in the suburbs and the court was very busy, so all state protocol and court ceremony was decided by Hsing Tzu-ts'ai. The poems, prose-poems, mandates, policy papers, memorials, inscriptions, eulogies, comments, and records he composed ran to 500 rolls and were all circulated. Neighbouring states respected him: court and countryside alike marvelled at him.

The TA-T'UNG [Great Unity] MONASTERY was to the west of the Ching-ming Monastery in what was known as the Li-min [Profit the People] ward. South of it was the house of the assistant to the Senior Ministers Kao Hsien-lüeh.

On several nights he saw a red glow moving around in front of his hall; and after digging over 10 feet deep below the place where the glow was seen he found 100 pounds of gold inscribed: 'The family gold of Su Ch'in. May the finder perform good deeds on my behalf.' Kao Hsien-lüeh then built the CHAO-FU MONASTERY. People said that this had been the site of Su Ch'in's house. When Yüan Yi, who was in power at the time, heard that gold had been found he demanded some from Kao Hsien-lüeh and was given 20 pounds of it.

In my view performing good deeds did not necessarily refer to building a monastery as there was no Buddhism in Su Ch'in's time. It must have been some kind of inscription praising Su Ch'in's fame and achievements.

To the east were the two CH'IN T'AI-SHANG-KUNG [Grand Duke of Ch'in] MONASTERIES which were 1 *li* south of the Ching-ming Monastery. The western one was founded by the Empress Dowager and the eastern by the Imperial Aunt.[6] They were both built to bring blessings for

---

[6] Perhaps the sister of the Dowager Hu married to Yüan Yi.

their father—hence the name—and were known to the public as the Two Daughters' Monasteries.

Both of their gates were on the Lo River, shaded by the leaves of spreading trees. Each had a five-storeyed pagoda 500 feet high which was as splendidly painted in white and colours as that of the Ching-ming Monastery. On the six days of maigre-feasts each month there was always a palace eunuch present to supervise the proceedings. The monks were clothed and housed better than those of any other monastery.

East of the monasteries was the Ling-t'ai [Spirit Mound], and although in ruins its base was still over 50 feet high. It had been built by the Emperor Kuang-wu of the Han.[7] East of the Spirit Mound was the [site of the] Pi-yung [Royal College] built by Emperor Wu of the [Ts'ao] Wei, to the south-west of which a Ming-t'ang [Bright Hall] was built during *cheng-kuang* [520–5] of our era which was round above and square beneath with four doors and eight windows.[8] The Prince of Ju-nan built a brick pagoda on the Spirit Mound.

At the beginning of *hsiao-ch'ang* [525–6], when fiendish rebels were attacking in all directions, capturing provinces and prefectures, the court held a muster north of the Bright Hall. All who volunteered for active service were appointed Field Generals, Under Generals, and Supplementary Generals. The armoured and helmeted soldiers were then known as the Bright Hall Force.

In those days there was a Tiger Guard called Lo Tzu-yüan, who said he was a Loyang man, and was stationed at P'eng-ch'eng[9] during the years *hsiao-ch'ang* [525–7]. When P'an Yüan-pao, another soldier from his camp, went back to the capital on leave Lo Tzu-yüan gave him a letter to take to his family. 'My home is by the Lo river south of the Spirit Mound,' he said, 'and if you go there the members of my family will

---

[7] The remains are still to be seen. (Chung-kuo k'o-hsüeh-yüan K'ao-ku yen-chiu-so Lo-yang kung-tso-tui, 1978, and pls. I and II.) The building symbolized the monarch enjoying popular support.

[8] The pursuit of an ideal form for the Ming-t'ang, a building intended to do no less than harmonize the universe, was the great Snark-hunt of Confucianists at this time. It was also very hard to get the material and forced labour needed to build it. One was started in *yung-p'ing* (508–11); and this one was in a bad state in 532 (*PCS* 36, pp. 476–8.)

[9] Modern Hsüchou, north Kiangsu. The pivot of the south-eastern frontier.

come out to see you.' P'an Yüan-pao went south of the Spirit Mound as he had been told, but there was nobody there he could ask. He was standing around on the point of going when an old man suddenly appeared, asking him where he had come from and why he was waiting around. When P'an Yüan-pao told him the whole story, the old man said, 'He is my son.'

He took the letter and led Yüan-pao inside, where he saw spacious and magnificent pavilions and other handsome buildings. When they had sat down a slave-girl was told to bring some liquor. A moment later the girl went past with a dead baby in her arms, which greatly disconcerted Yüan-pao at first. Then the liquor came; it was deep red, very delicious, and served with fine foods from land and sea. When they had finished drinking he took his leave. The old man saw him out and sent him on his way with great courtesy, observing, 'How sad it is that we shall never meet again.'

When the old man went back indoors the gate and the lane vanished: all P'an Yüan-pao could see was a high bank facing green waves of the river rolling to the east, and a recently drowned boy of about fourteen with blood pouring from his nose. Only then did he realize that the liquor he had drunk was this boy's blood. On his return to P'eng-ch'eng he found that Lo Tzu-yüan had disappeared; and although he had served with Lo for three years he had never before realized that he was the Spirit of the Lo River.

The PAO-TE [Virtue Rewarded] MONASTERY was founded by Kao-tsu, the Emperor Hsiao-wen, to obtain blessings for the Dowager Empress Feng.[10] It was 3 *li* outside the K'ang-yang Gate.

East of the imperial highway outside the K'ai-yang Gate had stood the Imperial Academy of Han times. Here there used to be twenty-five tablets carved on both sides with the

[10] 441–90. After taking power through a palace coup in 466 she played a great part in the sinification of the Wei state and had an unhealthy profound influence on Kao-tsu, whose mother she may have been, from his childhood onwards. (See ch. 2 of Part I.)

classics in three kinds of script. The *Spring and Autumn Annals* and the *Book of History* were written by the Han Commander of the Right Guard Ts'ai Yung[11] in the curly, tadpole, and clerkly scripts. There were still eighteen of these tablets, albeit in a ruined state. There were also forty-eight tablets carved on both sides with the *Chou Changes*, the *Book of History*, the *Kung Yang Commentary*, and the *Record of Rites* in the clerkly script.[12] Another tablet bearing *In Praise of Study* also stood in front of the academy. Four of the six tablets of the *Model Essays* of Emperor Wen-ti of the [Ts'ao] Wei stood in the seventeenth year of *t'ai-ho* [493]. Kao-tsu called this area the Ch'üan-hsüeh [Encouragement to Study] ward. In the fourth year of *wu-ting* [546] the Senior General [Kao Ch'eng] moved the Stone Classics to Yeh.[13]

Inside this ward were the TA-CHÜEH [Great Enlightenment], SAN-PAO [Three Treasures], and NING-YÜAN [Pacifying the Distant] MONASTERIES. They were surrounded by orchards where grew such precious fruits as Ta-ku pears which weighed 6 pounds and would turn to liquid if they fell from the tree and hit the ground, and Ch'eng-kuang apples. The CH'ENG-KUANG MONASTERY also had many fruit trees, and its apples were the best in the capital.

To the east of the Ch'üan-hsüeh ward was the Yen-hsien [Receiving Sages] ward in which was the CHENG-CHÜEH [True Enlightenment] CONVENT which had been founded by Wang Su, the Head of the Chancellery.

---

[11] 133–92. A great calligrapher.

[12] Fan shows that Yang seems to have confused two different sets of classics carved on stone in Eastern Han times.

[13] Half of the tablets that still survived were lost when they fell into the Yellow River in a landslip. (*Sui shu ching-chi chih*, p. 37.) Kao Ch'eng (521–49), elder son of Kao Huan, succeeded his father in 547 as the dictator behind the Eastern Wei throne and was assassinated by a kitchen slave two years later.

Wang Su, courtesy name Kung-yi, was a Lang-yeh man and the son of Wang Huan, the Governor of Yung-chou for the bogus Ch'i regime. His learning was extensive and he was a brilliant writer. He was Deputy Privy Secretary in Ch'i until he turned his back on those rebels and came over to our side in the eighteenth year of *t'ai-ho* [494].[14] This was just when Kao-tsu was reconstructing Loyang and making many reforms. As Wang Su was so well versed in things ancient he was of the greatest help;[15] Kao-tsu had the highest opinion of him and would address him as 'Master Wang'. It was in Wang Su's honour that the ward was called the Receiving Sages ward.

In his days south of the Yangtse Wang Su had married a daughter of the Hsieh clan,[16] and when he came to the capital he married a princess. Later the Lady Hsieh became a nun and came to join Wang Su. When she found that he had married the princess[17] the Lady Hsieh wrote some lines to him:

> Once I was a silkworm on a tray,
> Now, a thread stretched upon the loom,
> I follow the reed, remembering
> The time we were entangled.

The princess replied to her on Wang Su's behalf thus:

> The needle must always be threaded with yarn;
> In its eye must ever be silk.
> When it has thread it sews a new seam:
> It never can patch up the past.

Wang Su, moved to regret by the Lady Hsieh's beauty, built the Cheng-chüeh Convent as a place for her to live.

Mindful of his father's unjust death Wang Su wanted revenge as had Wu Tzu-hsü on the State of Ch'u.[18] As he wore

---

[14] Wang Su (464–501) fled from the south when his family rose in an unsuccessful rebellion, coming north at just the right time for Kao-tsu, who admired his 'elegant accent' and treated him as a trusted adviser from the first. He was a hawkish advocate of war against the south and died in the frontier fortress of Shou-ch'un. (*TCTC* 138, pp. 4327–8; *WS* 63, pp. 1407–12; *Nan Ch'i shu* 57, pp. 994–8.)

[15] Most notably in revising the grading of official posts for the new system introduced in 499 and 500.

[16] One of the most aristocratic in the south.

[17] Inserted by Fan from the version of this story in *T'ai-p'ing kuang-chi*.

[18] After the King of Ch'u had killed his father in 522 BC Wu Tzu-hsü worked tirelessly for the overthrow of his native Ch'u by its neighbour Wu.

mourning for the rest of his life and never listened to music, he was called Tzu-hsü by his contemporaries.

When he first came to our country he did not eat or drink such things as mutton[19] or yoghourt-drink,[20] feeding himself on carp broth and drinking tea. When the gentlemen of the capital saw that he could down a gallon of it at a sitting they nicknamed him the Bottomless Cup. Several years later when at a palace banquet with Kao-tsu he consumed a great deal of mutton and yoghourt. Kao-tsu was astonished. 'Of the foods of China,' he asked, 'how does mutton compare with boiled fish or tea with yoghourt?' 'Mutton is the finest product of the land, and fish the best of the watery tribe. They are both delicacies in their different ways. As far as flavour goes there is a great gap between them. Mutton is like a big country the size of Ch'i or Lu and fish are like such small states as Chu and Chü.[21] Tea is way off the mark and is the very slave of yoghourt.' Roaring with laughter, Kao-tsu raised his wine-cup and said, 'Three threes across, two twos down. I'll give a golden goblet to anyone who can work that one out.' Li Piao, the Chief Censor, said:

> 'The crone selling wine pours from vat to bottle;
> The butcher chopping meat gets the weight just right.'

Chen Ch'en,[22] the Senior Chancellery Assistant, replied:

> 'When southerners swim they call it skill;
> When the dancing-girl tosses her sleeve it floats in the air.'

'At last I see that the word is 習 [practice],' said Prince Hsieh of P'eng-ch'eng. Kao-tsu gave the golden goblet to Li Piao.

---

[19] Much more important in the north-Chinese diet then than now. *Ch'i min yao shu* devotes much more space to sheep and goats than to pigs, an indication of their comparative economic significance at the time.

[20] A tentative translation of *lo-chiang*. See *CMYS* 57 for detailed instructions on the preparation of various kinds of *lo* from the milk of sheep, goat, or cows: fresh *lo* was made much as the *urum* of the Mongols. (Lattimore (1941), pp. 205–6). This is another feature of Northern Wei tastes striking by modern Chinese standards, as is the contempt for tea.

[21] Two large and two small states in Spring and Autumn times, all in Shantung.

[22] d. 525. A member of a leading family whose main contribution to Loyang was a memorial he submitted as Metropolitan Prefect which led to better security in the capital. (*WS* 68, pp. 1509–17. See also ch. 6 of Part I.)

The court admired Li Piao for his intelligence and Chen Ch'en for matching his couplet so quickly.

'You do not really esteem the big countries of Ch'i and Lu,' said the Prince of P'eng-ch'eng to Wang Su, 'as you prefer the small states of Chu and Chü.' 'One cannot help liking the best things of one's home,' replied Wang Su. 'If you come to see me tomorrow,' said the prince, 'I shall give you Chu and Chü food with "the slave of yoghourt".' This was why tea was often known as 'the slave of yoghourt'.

The Palace Counsellor Liu Kao made a practice of drinking only tea out of admiration for Wang Su's style, so the Prince of P'eng-ch'eng said to him, 'Instead of the eight princely foods, sir, you like a drowned slave. You could rightly be compared to the man by the sea who followed the foul smell[23] or the woman who practised frowning.'[24] The Prince of P'eng-cheng also teased a southern slave in his household in this way. From then on everyone was shamed out of drinking the tea provided at banquets given by the court and the nobility except the refugees from the other side of the Yangtse who had come from afar to submit; they still liked it. Later, when Hsiao Cheng-te, Marquis of Hsi-feng and a son of Hsiao Yen,[25] came over to our side Yüan Yi was going to give him some tea. 'How often have you been drowned?' Yüan Yi asked. Hsiao Cheng-te, failing to get the point, replied amid the sniggers of Yüan Yi and all the other guests, 'Although born in a land of rivers I have never had the troubles of the Marquis of Yang.'[26]

The LUNG-HUA [Dragon Glory] MONASTERY was founded by the Prince of Kuang-ling[27] and the CHUI-SHENG

[23] Of a man driven from his home because nobody could bear his stench.

[24] The ugly woman who imitated the great beauty Hsi Shih's frown, thus looking worse than ever.

[25] Hsiao Yen's adopted son who fled to Wei to escape the consequences of his various crimes in 522. He lived up to his reputation in the north by killing a child before returning south to be forgiven and continue his robberies and murders. He was executed in 549. (*Liang shu* 55, pp. 828–9.)

[26] Who drowned himself in antiquity.

[27] Probably Kao-tsu's brother Yü, something of a Hsienpei traditionalist, is meant. He was fatally wounded by the husband of a mistress. (*WS* 21/1, pp. 545–51.)

[Emulating the Sages] MONASTERY was founded by the Prince of Pei-hai.[28] They both lay to the east of the Pao-te Monastery. The Buddha statues and the monks' cells were as good as those of the Ch'in T'ai-shang-kung monasteries. All the monasteries in the capital grow various kinds of fruit, but none of them could compete with the flourishing orchards of these three.

Four *li* outside the Hsüan-yang Gate a floating bridge crossed the Lo river.[29] It was called the Eternal Bridge.

In *shen-kuei* [518–20] Ch'ang Ching wrote an *Ode to the North Bank of the Lo.*

Mighty the great river,
Deep, deep the clear Lo.
It was led from the Bear's Ear Mountains,
Made to run in a great valley.
It receives the Ku and swallows the Yi,
Flows through Chou[30] and the waters Po.[31]
Nearby it joins the ancestral Yellow River;
Far away it pays homage to the Sea God.
Only the Lo was chosen by the oracle bone;[32]
Rightly is it called the Centre of the Earth.[33]
It corresponds to the Chang and Liu constellations,
And lies between Mount Sung and the Yellow River.
It is hot and cold in moderation,
Sun and moon shine clear.
The illustrious seat of the royal house,
The cultural harmonizer of the whole of China.
It faces the heights of Shao-shih,
And has its back to the T'ai-hang range.
The pass of Chih[34] is its eastern region,

---

[28] Probably Yuan Hsiang, another brother of Kao-tsu, who was one of the officials in charge of building Loyang. During the first years of Shih-tsung's reign he was a tyrannical and corrupt regent until dislodged by the coup of 504. (*WS* 21/1, pp. 559–64; *TCTC* 145, pp. 4538–9.) His son Yüan Hao could also be meant.

[29] Built soon after the move of the capital. (*WS* 79, pp. 1754–5.)

[30] i.e. Ch'eng-chou founded by the Duke of Chou to the west of the Northern Wei city.

[31] Probably referring to the early Shang city whose extensive remains have been found at Erhlit'ou, Yenshih county, just across the Lo River from Northern Wei Loyang.

[32] When the Duke of Chou divined to find a site for an eastern headquarters for Chou power. ('Lo Kao' in the *Shang shu*.)

[33] In the 'Shao kao' of the *Shang shu*.

[34] An archaic name for Hu-lao or Ch'eng-kao.

The Hsiao heights are its western limit.
This is a place surrounded by natural barriers,
Yet also a centre of communications.
He who relies on virtue is protected here,
But those who lose the Way perish.
As the precedents of history show,
As one can see from the classical books,
Some rulers have abdicated, some been overthrown,
Some have been solid and some elegant.
With Chou's decline there was a ninefold split;
At the end of the Han the empire broke into three.
The [Ts'ao] Wei was feeble in its evening,
The Chin dynasty vanished at dusk.
Then heaven and earth shone with brightness,
The propitious signs appeared, the mandate was given:
The dynasty was founded mightily,
Its divine glory unmatched.
The Wei's authority came from heaven;
It holds power by divine writ.
The imperial seal went to the successful.
And the mandate was given with the dragon chart.
It gave thought to standardizing the script and wheel-guages,
Always embracing stability.
Spreading its illustrious traces,
Releasing a flood of excellent example,
It succeeded to our robes of office,
And brought to order the centre of power.
Here land and water meet,
And the roads of Chou and Cheng cross;
Therefore we erect an inscription on the north bank of the Lo,
To tell all this to the Central regions.

On the northern and southern banks of the river there were winged columns 200 feet high on top of which were statues of phoenixes which looked as if they were about to soar up into the sky.

South of the Eternal Bridge, north of the Round Mound[35] and between the Yi and the Lo rivers were the four hostels and the four wards for foreigners. The hostels were east of the imperial highway and were called Chin-ling, Yen-jan, Fu-sang and Yen-tzu. To the west of the highway were the four

[35] Where the imperial sacrifices to heaven were made.

foreigners' wards: the Kuei-cheng [Returning to Truth], Kuei-te [Returning to Virtue], Mu-hua [Admiring Civilization], and Mu-yi [Admiring Justice].

The men of Wu who came over to our country were put in the Chin-ling Hostel, and after they had been there for three years they were given houses in the Kuei-cheng ward. Early in *ching-ming* [500–3] Hsiao Pao-yin, Prince of Chien-an under the bogus Ch'i, submitted to us. He was ennobled as Lord of Kuei-chi and a house was built for him in the Kuei-cheng ward. Later he was elevated to be Prince of Ch'i and given the Princess of Nan-yang in marriage. As Hsiao Pao-yin felt humiliated at being classified among the foreigners he got the princess to petition the Emperor Shih-tsung asking to be allowed to move into the city. Shih-tsung agreed and gave him a house in the Yung-an ward. In the fourth year of *cheng-kuang* [524] Hsiao Cheng-te, Marquis of Hsi-feng, submitted to us, and he too was put in the Chin-ling Hostel until a house was built for him in the Kuei-cheng ward. Hsiao Cheng-te later gave this house to become the KUEI-CHENG MONASTERY

When barbarians from the north came over to us they were put in the Yen-jan Hostel[36] for three years and then given houses in the Kuei-te ward.

In the first year of *cheng-kuang* [520] the Juju [Joujan][37] ruler Yüchiulü Anakuei came to pay homage at court.[38] The responsible authorities did not know where to rank him until the Assistant Secretary Ch'ang Ching suggested, 'When the Ch'anyü[39] came to pay homage in *hsien-ning* [275–80] the Chin

---

[36] Named after the mountains in the western Mongolian People's Republic (now called Hangay) where in AD 89 and 429 Eastern Han and Northern Wei armies had inflicted catastrophic defeats on the Hsiungnu and Joujan respectively.

[37] The Joujan (abusively called Juju 'wriggly worms' by their Chinese neighbours) had controlled the northern steppe since the late fourth century, since when they and the Northern Wei had struggled for control of the northern frontier, both sides launching massive expeditions against each other. (See *Jou-jan tzu-liao chi-lu*; Kollautz and Miyakawa (1970); Uchida Gimpu (1975), pp. 273–421.)

[38] Also known as Anakuei, the Joujan *k'o-han* (Khan) from 520 to 552. He was restored to his throne with Wei aid after fleeing to Loyang when deposed in a coup; and he exploited Wei divisions after 523 to extend his control south. He died during the wars in which the rising power of the T'uchüeh (Turks) destroyed the Joujan state.

[39] The Hsiungnu ruler, possibly Tuyung who submitted to Chin in 279, or else Liu Yüan.

put him below princes, dukes, and men of special distinction in precedence. Anakuei should come between enfeoffed princes and honorary senior ministers.' The court accepted his suggestion. Anakuei was lodged in the Yen-jan Hostel and later given a house in the Kuei-te ward.

When the chieftains of the northern barbarians sent their sons to be attendants at court they would always arrive in autumn and leave in spring so as to avoid the Chinese hot season; because of this they were popularly known as the 'wild-goose subjects'.[40]

The eastern barbarians[41] who came to submit were put in the Fu-sang Hostel and [later] given houses in the Mu-hua ward.

Western barbarians who came over were put in the Yen-tzu Hostel and given houses in the Mu-yi ward. From the Ts'ung-ling [Pamir] mountains westwards to Ta Ch'in [the Roman Orient][42] 100 countries and 1,000 cities all gladly attached themselves to us; foreign traders and merchants came hurrying in through the passes every day. This could indeed be called exhausting all the regions of heaven and earth.

The number of those who made their homes there because they enjoyed the atmosphere of China was beyond counting; there were over 10,000 families of those who had come over to our way of life. The gates and lanes were neatly arranged and the entrances packed tight together. Dark locust-trees gave shade and green willows hung down over the courtyards. As all the rare goods of the world were concentrated there another market, the Four Directions Market, was founded south of the Lo River. It was popularly called the Eternal Bridge Market. Much fish from the Lo and Yi rivers were sold there, and whenever gentlemen or commoners wanted some fish-mince, they always went there for it. The fish was delicious, and there was a saying in the capital that

> Lo carp and Yi bream
> Are finer than beef or mutton.

[40] Such frontier chiefs as the Erhchu, who were essentially feudal vassals of the Emperor, are meant.
[41] Koreans from Koryŏ and various peoples of Manchuria.
[42] On Ta Ch'in see ch. 4 below.

South of the Eternal Bridge were the Pai-hsiang [White Elephant] and Shih-tzu [Lion] Quarters.

A white elephant was presented by the King of Gandhāra in the second year of *yung-p'ing* [509].[43] It carried on its back a multicoloured screen and a howdah made of the seven precious things that could hold several [dozen] people: it was a truly remarkable creature. The elephant was kept at first in the Imperial Stables, but it once escaped, smashing buildings and knocking down walls. It uprooted all the trees and demolished all the walls it came across, making the common people flee pell-mell in terror. The Empress Dowager then had the elephant moved to this quarter.

The lion was presented by the King of Po-ssu [Persia].[44] It was captured by the rebel Moch'i Ch'ou-nu[45] and kept by his bandit gang. Only when Moch'i Ch'ou-nu was defeated at the end of *yung-an* [528–30] did it finally reach the capital. 'I have heard,' said the Emperor Chuang-ti to the Imperial Assistant Li Yü,[46] 'that a tiger will submit to a lion on sight. I would like to test this.' He ordered the nearest mountainous prefectures and counties to capture tigers and send them. Kung county and Shan-yang sent two tigers and a leopard. The Emperor watched the spectacle in the Hua-lin Park. When the tigers and the leopard saw the lion they shut their eyes, not daring to look up. The Emperor then sent for a very tame blind bear that was kept in the park to see what it would do. When the foresters led it to within smelling distance of the lion it leapt in terror and fled, dragging its chains behind it. The emperor roared with laughter. When the Prince of Kuang-ling came to the throne in the first year of *p'u-t'ai* [531] he issued an edict that said, 'To hold birds and beasts in captivity is to go against their nature. They should be sent back to the hills and forests.'

[43] On Gandhāra see ch. 5 below. The same elephant is presumably referred to in *WS* 8, p. 207, as coming from 'the Ephthalites and Po-chih' (or 'the Ephthalite [vassal state] Po-chih').

[44] King Kavādh (r. 488–531), an Ephthalite client. His country was under Ephthalite and Roman pressure externally, and internally in the middle of the Mazdakite troubles. Persian missions came to Loyang in 517, 518, 521, and 522. (*WS* 9.)

[45] A tribal soldier in the Kao-p'ing (Kuyuan, Ninghsia) garrison who joined the 524 mutiny and came to control much of the Kuan-Lung area of Shensi and eastern Kansu until defeated by Erhchu T'ien-kuang in 530. (*TCTC* 150–4.)

[46] His brother-in-law, executed in 534 or 535. (*WSa* 83/2, p. 1837.)

He ordered that the lion should be sent back to its own country. The men who were taking the lion reckoned that it would be impossible to get it to Persia so they killed the animal on the way and came back. The authorities prosecuted them for disobeying an imperial decree, but the Prince of Kuang-ling said, 'How can men be punished for the sake of a lion?' and pardoned them.

The P'U-T'I [Bodhi] MONASTERY was founded by fore-igners from the West. It was in the Mu-yi ward.

When the monk Ta-to[47] was excavating a gravemound for bricks he found a man inside whom he presented to the throne. The Empress Dowager and Emperor Ming-ti were then staying in the Tu Lodge in the Hua-lin Park. Thinking that he must be some kind of supernatural freak they asked the Gentleman in Waiting Hsü Ho if that sort of thing had happened in antiquity. 'When the former Wei excavated some tombs,' Hsü Ho replied, 'they found a family slave of Huo Kuang's son-in-law Fan Ming-yu[48] who gave an account of the rise and fall of the Han dynasty which corresponded to the history books. This is nothing to be surprised at.' The Dowager then told Hsü Ho to ask him what he was called, how long he had been dead, and what he had eaten and drunk. 'Your subject's surname is Ts'ui,' the dead man replied, 'personal name Han and courtesy name Tzu-hung. I'm from An-p'ing in Po-ling. My father's personal name is Shang, my mother's surname Wei, and my home is west of the city in the Fu-ts'ai [Great Wealth] ward. I was fourteen when I died and am now twenty-six; I was twelve years underground. It was like lying in a drunken stupor, and I ate nothing. Sometimes I would wander around and come across food, but it was all too much like a dream for me to be able to tell what it was.'

The Empress Dowager then sent the clerk of the Palace Bureau Chang Hsiu-chün to look up Ts'ui Han's parents in the

---

[47] He has not been identified, but the name looks Indian.
[48] Fan Yu-ming in some versions of the story; he lived in the first century BC.

Fu-ts'ai ward. He actually found a Ts'ui Shang married to a woman surnamed Wei. 'Has a son of yours died?' Chang Hsiu-chün asked Ts'ui Shang. 'Our son Han died when he was fourteen,' Ts'ui Shang replied. 'Someone has found him,' said Chang Hsiu-chün. 'He has come back to life. He is now in the Hua-lin Park, and our Mistress has sent me to make inquiries about him.' Ts'ui Shang, shaken and frightened, said, 'I never had that son. I was lying.' When Chang Hsiu-chün had returned and given a full report, the Empress Dowager told him to take Ts'ui Han back to his home. As soon as Ts'ui Shang heard that Han was there he lit a fire in front of the gate and grasped a knife; his wife Wei held a peach branch.[49] 'You're not to come here,' said Ts'ui Shang, 'I'm not your father and you're not my son. Clear off at once if you don't want to bring us trouble.' Ts'ui Han went away, and from then onwards he wandered around the capital, often spending nights under monastery gateways. The Prince of Ju-nan gave him a suit of yellow clothing. Ts'ui Han was afraid of the sun and never dared look at it; he also feared water, fire, and sharp blades. He used to pace around the streets until he was exhausted and then stop; he never strolled slowly. Everyone said he was a ghost. North of the Great Loyang Market was the Feng-chung ward, many of whose residents sold funerary accessories and coffins. 'Make coffins of cypress,' said Ts'ui Han, 'and don't line them with mulberry wood.'[50] When asked why he replied, 'When I was underground I saw the ghost-raising soldiers. One ghost pleaded to be spared as his coffin was of cypress, but the officer in charge of the soldiers said, "Although your coffin is of cypress it's lined with mulberry wood, so you can't be spared." ' When this remark of his spread throughout the capital the price of cypress soared, giving rise to the suspicion that Ts'ui Han had been bribed to make it by the undertakers.

---

[49] From remote antiquity to the present a wood held to avert evil.
[50] Doubtless plentiful and therefore cheap.

The PRINCE OF KAO-YANG'S MONASTERY was originally the house of Yüan Yung, Prince of Kao-yang. It was 3 *li* outside the Chin-yang Gate to the west of the imperial highway. After Yung was murdered by Erhchu Jung his house was given to become a monastery.

In *cheng-kuang* [520–5], when Yüan Yung was Prime Minister, he was given a troup of musicians who played under a feathered canopy and 100 Tiger Guards with wooden swords.[51] As he was the most honoured of the Emperor's subjects his wealth embraced mountains and seas and his mansion was on a par with the imperial palace. White walls and vermilion columns led one after another into the distance; soaring eaves with up-curved ends spread far in all directions. His slaves numbered 6,000 and his concubines 500.[52] Enormous pearls shone like the sun and silken-gauze clothing floated in the breeze. No prince since Han and Chin times was his equal in extravagance. When he went out he rode on the imperial highway with horsemen shouting to clear the way and a whole procession of insignia; gongs and trumpets rang out while flutes weaved their melancholy notes. When at home he had girls singing and dancing to the sound of the lute and the pan-pipes; silk-stringed and wind instruments played by turns all day and all night. His bamboo groves and fishponds were the equal of those in the imperial gardens; fragrant herbs seemed to be piled in heaps and precious trees gave an unbroken shade.

Yung fed very richly, spending tens of thousands of cash on a single meal, and a vast spread of delicacies from land and sea would be set before him. Li Ch'ung, Marquis of Ch'en-liu, once said, 'What the Prince of Kao-yang has at a single meal would last me for a thousand days.' Li Ch'ung, Head of the Chancellery and an honorary senior minister, had 1,000 slaves and was one of the richest men in the world. He was also an extreme miser. His clothes were poor and his food coarse; he only ate cooked and pickled scallion. His retainer Li Yüan-yu once said, 'My Lord Li has eighteen dishes at every meal.'

---

[51] Exceptional honours.
[52] Nobody else in Northern Wei times is known to have had so many slaves. They would have entitled him to enormous land-holdings.

When asked how this could be he said, 'Two "scallions" make eighteen.'[53] Everyone roared with laughter at what was later generally regarded as a dig at Li Ch'ung.

When Yung died all his concubines were ordered into nunneries but some of them got married. The beauty Hsü Yüeh-hua was a wonderful harpist; when she played and sang *The Bright Consort Goes out through the Passes* all who heard her would be visibly moved. In *yung-an* [528–30] she became a secondary wife of the Grand General Yüan Shih-k'ang whose house was near the Ch'ing-yang Gate. As the plaintive sounds of Hsü Yüeh-hua singing to her harp rose to the clouds crowds of passers-by would stop and listen. 'The prince had two great beauties,' she said once to Yüan Shih-k'ang. 'One was called Hsiu-jung and the other Yen-tzu. Hsiu-jung could sing the *Song of Green Waters* and Yen-tzu was wonderful in the *Phoenix Dance*. They were the best beloved of the harem, the favourites among all his concubines.'

North of the Prince of Kao-yang's house was the Chung-kan ward.

Hsün Tzu-wen of Ying-ch'uan lived in this ward. As a child he was brilliant and his character was exceptional: when he was twelve neither Huang Wan[54] nor K'ung Jung[55] could have excelled him. When P'an Ch'ung-ho of Kuang-tsung was lecturing on Mr. Fu's *Spring and Autumn Annals* commentary[56] in the Chao-yi ward to the east of the city wall, Hsün Tzu-wen tucked up his clothes to take him as his teacher. Li Ts'ai of Chao-chün asked Tzu-wen, 'Where do you live, Master Hsün?' Tzu-wen replied that he lived in the Chung-kan ward. 'Why do you live south of the city?' asked Li Ts'ai, teasing him because it was south of the city that the foreigners' hostels and wards were found. 'The south of the capital is an excellent district,' said Tzu-wen, 'so why are you surprised that I live there? For rivers the Yi and the Lo flow between towering cliffs, and if we are to speak of antiquities there is the Spirit

[53] Both 'nine' and 'scallion' are pronounced *chiu.*

[54] (141–92) He made his name at six by neatly describing a partial solar eclipse: 'what is left is like the new moon.' (*HHS* 61, pp. 2039–41.)

[55] (153–208) Also a child prodigy. (*HHS* 70, pp. 2261–80; *SKC* 12, pp. 370–72.)

[56] The standard interpretation of the text under the Northern Dynasties.

Mound and the Stone Classics. Of beautiful monasteries we
have the Pao-te and the Ching-ming; and among the richest
and noblest men of the age we have the Princes of Kao-yang
and Kuang-p'ing. The customs of the four quarters of the globe
and of countless countries and cities are represented here.' Li
Ts'ai was unable to answer, and P'an Ch'ung-ho remarked,
'How true it is that "the gentlemen of Ju and Ying are as sharp
as awls, while those of Yen and Chao are as blunt as
hammers." '[57] The whole class laughed.

The CH'UNG-HSÜ [Honouring Emptiness] MONASTERY
to the west of the city[58] was the Chuo-lung Yüan [Dragon
Washing] Park of the Han dynasty.

In the ninth year of *yen-hsi* [166] the Emperor Huan-ti
worshipped Lao Tzu in the Dragon Washing Park, setting up a
canopied throne and using the music of the Sacrifice to
Heaven; this was where it happened.

This land was given to the people soon after Kao-tsu moved
the capital to Loyang, but because many of those who settled
here saw demons and monsters everyone went away. Later the
monastery was founded here.

[57] Adapted from a fourth-century *bon mot* (Fan, p. 182) to attack Li Ts'ai's native Chao
and avoid insulting the old Wei capital in Tai.
[58] Both the location of this monastery west of the city and its mention in this chapter
have been questioned by commentators.

Chapter 4

West of the City Wall

The CH'UNG-CHÜEH [Sudden Enlightenment] MON-
ASTERY was founded when the Grand Instructor Yüan I,
Prince of Ch'ing-ho, gave his house. It was 1 *li* outside the
Hsi-ming Gate to the north of the imperial highway.

Yüan I was the most famous of all the princes of the blood.
When Shih-tsung died in the fourth year of *yen-ch'ang* [515] he
left an edict instructing him, Prince Yung of Kao-yang and
Prince Huai of Kuang-p'ing to help and protect the [Emperor]
Hsiao-ming. As the Emperor was only just five the Empress
Dowager ruled on his behalf, and she often consulted Yüan I
on matters great and small because of his great integrity and
his uprightness. Thus it was that during *hsi-p'ing* and *shen-kuei*
[516–20] he was more powerful than the monarch, and the
splendour of his mansion outstripped that of the Prince of Kao-
yang. In the north-west corner of the grounds was a tower
higher than the Ling-yün Tower which overlooked the court
and from which you could see all of the capital. It was just as
the ancient poem said:

> In the north-west is a tower
> Soaring as high as the drifting clouds.[1]

Below the tower were the Ju-lin Pavilion [Pavilion of the
Scholars] and the Yen-pin Hall [Hall for Entertaining Guests]
which resembled the Ch'ing-shu Hall. The artificial mountain
and the fishing pool were the finest of the age; the jagged peaks
seemed to thrust through the windows while curved ponds
encircled the hall. The trees rang with birdsong, and the steps
were covered in clumps of flowers and herbs. Yüan I enjoyed
keeping retainers and appreciated literary ability; men of
talent converged there from all over the country. He also

---

[1] The opening couplet of the fifth of the *Nineteen Ancient Poems*.

selected his subordinates and assistants from among outstanding men.

On fine, clear mornings he would hurry to the southern terraces where rare delicacies were served, and fragrant wine filled the goblets of his noble guests to the sound of lute and pipe. This would have made the Prince of Liang ashamed of his excursions in his Rabbit Park, or the Prince of Ch'en-ssu blush for his banquets in his Bronze Sparrow Terrace.[2]

When Yüan Yi seized power early in *cheng-kuang* [520] and confined the Empress Dowager to the Back Palace he had Yüan I killed in the Palace Bureau. On coming back to power in the first year of *hsiao-ch'ang* [525] the Dowager posthumously created Yüan I Grand Tutor to the Heir Apparent, Senior General, Domestic and Foreign Military Commander and Holder of the Golden Axe. She gave Yüan I a funeral ceremony with a chariot with bells, nine pennants, a yellow canopy, a yak-tail banner, a funeral carriage, two bands of musicians in feather-canopied carriages, 100 Tiger Guards and two groups of keeners.[3] It was modelled on that of the Chin dynasty Prince Fu of An-p'ing.[4] His posthumous title was Wen-hsien, and his portrait was painted for the Chien-shih [Foundation] Palace. She also elevated Han Tzu-hsi, Chief Asistant in the principate of Ch'ing-ho, to be a Gentleman in Waiting:[5] for a minister in a principate to be made a palace official had never happened before in recent times.

A five-storeyed pagoda in the style of the one in the Yao-kuang Convent was built to obtain blessings for Yüan I.

The HSÜAN-CHUNG MONASTERY [Monastery of Loyalty Proclaimed] was founded by the Imperial Assistant

---

[2] These two conspicuously extravagant parks were created for two princes of the Han dynasty, one from the earlier and the other from the later part of that dynasty.

[3] Exceptional honours.

[4] Given a magnificent funeral after his death at the age of ninety-two in 272.

[5] Han Tzu-hsi, who refused to hold office after his master's execution, demanded vengeance for him after the Dowager's return to power. He later rose to high rank and died around 540. (*WS* 60, pp. 1334–7.)

and Governor of Ssu province, Prince Hui of Ch'eng-yang.[6] It was 1 *li* outside the Hsi-yang Gate, south of the imperial highway.

When the Prince of Pei-hai [Yüan Hao] entered Loyang and the Emperor Chuang-ti went north in *yung-an* [528–30] all the other princes wavered in their loyalty except Hui, who alone accompanied the Emperor to Ch'ang-tzu-ch'eng. When the great army was held up at the Yellow River[7] and the issue was yet to be decided, Hui vowed that if the royal troops entered Loyang he would turn his mansion into a monastery.

At the end of *yung-an* [530] the Emperor Chuang-ti, worried that he had not got a plan to kill Erhchu Jung that would succeed, asked Hui to work one out for him. 'If you announce the birth of an heir,' said Hui, 'Jung will have to come to court; he can then be killed.' 'The Empress is not yet in her tenth month,' the Emperor replied, 'she is only at the beginning of her ninth. Will this work?' 'Some women,' said Hui, 'give birth after a longer pregnancy and some after a shorter one. There would be nothing odd about it.' The Emperor accepted his advice and announced the birth of an heir, sending Hui to the residence of the Prince of T'ai-yüan with the news that a crown prince had been born. Erhchu Jung and Yüan T'ien-mu, Prince of Shang-tang, were gambling at the time. Hui pulled off Jung's hat and whirled around in a dance of joy. As he was normally a man of great composure who never wore his emotions on his face the sight of him whirling round the hall shouting for happiness convinced Jung, who went to the palace with Yüan T'ien-mu.

When he learnt of Erhchu Jung's arrival the Emperor went pale without realizing it. The Assistant Secretary Wen Tzu-sheng said, 'You have gone pale, Your Majesty.' The Emperor at once sent for wine, drank it, then went ahead with the plan.

After the executions of Erhchu Jung and Yüan T'ien-mu, Hui was appointed Grand Tutor and Minister of War in

[6] A great-grandson of Shih-tsu/T'ai-wu-ti (r. 424–51). After Chuang-ti's death he played a leading part in the Dowager's second period of personal rule. (*WS* 19/3, pp. 510–12.)

[7] i.e. the armies of Erhchu Jung and Yüan T'ien-mu which were held up north of the Yellow River for a while.

addition to all his previous titles. He was also given a special responsibility for organizing the palace guard.

When Erhchu Chao captured Emperor Chuang-ti, Hui took refuge with K'ou Tsu-jen,[8] a former county magistrate of Loyang. K'ou Tsu-jen came from a family of provincial governors who had served under Hui as officers, and it was because of these past favours that Hui took refuge with him. 'As rumour has it,' said K'ou Tsu-jen to his sons and younger brothers, 'Erhchu Chao is so eager to have the Prince of Ch'eng-yang that he has offered a marquisate of ·1,000 households to anyone who captures him. Today we make our fortunes.' He then cut off Hui's head and sent it to Erhchu Chao.

Hui had given K'ou Tsu-jen 100 pounds of gold and fifty horses when he took refuge in his house; K'ou Tsu-jen had acted out of greed for Hui's wealth. He divided the gold and the horses equally among his relatives. How true it is that, 'the common man gets into no trouble, but he who carries a jade disc in his clothes asks for trouble.' Erhchu Chao did not reward K'ou Tsu-jen when he received Hui's head; Hui came to Chao in a dream and said, 'There are 200 pounds of gold and 100 horses of mine in K'ou Tsu-jen's home. You may have them all.'

When he woke up Erhchu Chao reflected that the dream might be true, as although the Prince of Ch'eng-yang had held high office and had never had a reputation for integrity or poverty, no gold or silver had been found when his house was plundered. So he had K'ou Tsu-jen brought to him at dawn and demanded the gold and the horses. K'ou, supposing that someone had informed against him, thought it wisest to admit that he had actually taken 100 pounds of gold and fifty horses. Chao, suspecting him of trying to conceal the rest, demanded what he had been told of in the dream. K'ou Tsu-jen handed over the 30 pounds of gold and thirty horses that were all he had in his various houses but could not meet the demand in full. Erhchu Chao was so angry that he arrested K'ou Tsu-jen, hung him by the head from a tall tree with a boulder

---

[8] Also called K'ou Mi. (*WS* 42, p. 948.)

suspended from his feet, and had him flogged to death. This was generally felt to be no more than he deserved.

What I, Hsüan-chih, have to say is, 'The house that honours goodness has good fortune to spare, but the family that accumulates evil attracts every misfortune.' K'ou Tsu-jen turned on his benefactor, killing him out of greed for his property; so Hui exaggerated the quantity of gold and horses in the dream and used Erhchu Chao to kill K'ou Tsu-jen in revenge. He made K'ou Tsu-jen suffer a cruel beating and undergo the greatest misery. Not even the flogging of T'ien Fen by the Marquis of Wei-ch'i[9] or the Ch'in monarch's stabbing of Yao Ch'ang[10] were better examples [of posthumous revenge].

To the east of the Hsüan-chung Monastery was the WANG TIEN-YÜ [Imperial Food Taster Wang] MONASTERY founded by the eunuch Wang T'ao-t'ang.[11] This monastery he founded was the only religious establishment endowed by a eunuch that was not a nunnery. Everyone acclaimed it as majestic.

There was a three-storeyed pagoda at the gate even more finely built than the one in the Chao-yi Convent. It was indeed the best of all the temples founded by the eunuchs. On the six maigre-feasts of each month there was drumming, songs, and dancing at the monastery.

[9] Shortly after executing his rival Tou Ying, Marquis of Wei-ch'i, in 131 BC, T'ien Fen died, tormented in his dreams by Tou Ying and another of his victims. (*Shih chi* 107.)

[10] Fu Chien, the last ruler of the Ch'in state, refused to abdicate to Yao Ch'ang, who had him strangled in AD 385. In 393 Yao, now Emperor, died (from a growth in the groin where a diabolical spear had struck him in a dream) deliriously calling himself Fu Chien's subject. (*Shih-liu kuo ch'un-ch'iu chi-pu* 38, p. 298, and 50, p. 386.)

[11] He rose to high office before his death in the Ho-yin massacre in 528. (*WS* 94, p. 2031.)

The PAI-MA [White Horse] MONASTERY, founded by Emperor Ming-ti of the Han dynasty,[12] was where Buddhism first came to China. It was south of the imperial highway 3 *li* outside the Hsi-yang Gate.[13]

Emperor Ming-ti saw in a dream a golden man standing 10 feet 6 inches high with the light of the sun and moon behind his head. This foreign god was called Buddha, and the Emperor sent to the West to look for him. There sutras and statues were found. The monastery was given its name after the white horse that carried the sutras back.[14] When Ming-ti died a Jetavana was built on his tumulus, and from then on ordinary people sometimes built stupas on their tombs.

The box for sutras is preserved in the monastery to the present day. Incense is regularly burned to them, and the box sometimes shines brighter than the light of the sky. Clerics and lay people alike worshipped it as if it were the true Buddha himself.

The pomegranates[15] and grape-vines planted in front of the pagoda were different from those found anywhere else, so luxuriant was their foliage and enormous their fruits. The pomegranates weighed 7 pounds, and the extraordinarily delicious grapes, bigger than jujubes, were the best in the capital. The Emperor sent for them when they were ripe and sometimes gave them to his palace women, who in turn sent them to their families as rare delicacies. The recipients did not eat them all themselves, and so they would pass through several households. 'One sweet pomegranate from the White Horse,' the saying in the capital went, 'is worth an ox.'

There was a monk called Pao-kung whose origin was unknown. Although he looked repulsive he had clairvoyant powers and could see past, present, and future. His sayings were too cryptic to be understood until after the event, then they proved to be right. When the Empress Dowager Hu heard of him she asked him about current affairs. 'When you give

[12] Reigned AD 58–75.

[13] A monastery of this name still stood on the site in 1965.

[14] Although Buddhist shrines were established in Loyang by Ming-ti's reign, the legend of the dream and the mission to fetch scriptures only makes its recorded appearance some centuries later.

[15] Following Chou's emendation.

millet to the chicken,' said Pao-kung, 'you call "chu chu".'
Nobody was able to unravel this until the Empress Dowager
was killed by Erhchu Jung in the first year of *chien-yi* [528].[16]

Chao Fa-ho, a Loyang man, asked whether he would ever
be ennobled. 'A big bamboo arrow that needs no feathers; an
eastern room hastily built,' was Pao-kung's reply. Chao Fa-ho
did not understand it. Ten days later his father died. The 'big
bamboo arrow' was the mourner's staff and the 'eastern room'
the mourner's hut.

Pao-kung composed twelve hour-songs which contained all
he had to say.

The PAO-KUANG [Precious Light] MONASTERY was
outside the Hsi-yang Gate and north of the imperial highway.
It contained a three-storeyed pagoda on a stone base which
seemed very old from the way it looked and was built. It was
painted and carved . . .[17]

The recluse Chao Yi sighed when he saw it and said, 'The
Stone Pagoda Monastery of the Chin dynasty has now become
the Precious Light Monastery.' When asked why he said this
he replied, 'The forty-two[18] temples of the Chin were all
destroyed except this one. That was the bath-house,' he said,
pointing to a place in the garden. 'There should be a well five
paces in front of it.' When the monks dug there they found a
building and a well. Although the well had been blocked up its
brick top was as good as new. There were still several dozen
flagstones below the bath-house. The garden was level and
spacious, and all who saw its luxuriant fruit and vegetables
sighed with admiration.

There was a pool in the garden, called the Hsien Pool,[19]
whose banks were covered with reeds. The pool itself grew

---

[16] '*Chu chu*' has been a standard call to chickens in China from Han times to the present
day; it is also '*erh chu*' (two '*chu*') a play on the surname Erhchu.

[17] This sentence appears to be incomplete.

[18] This is emended from the thirty-two of all *LYCLC* editions to match the figure in the
Preface and in *WS* 114, p. 3029.

[19] Named after the place where the sun bathed.

water-chestnuts and lotuses, and was surrounded with green pines and emerald bamboo. On fine mornings the gentlemen of the capital would ask for bath leave and invite their friends to make a trip to this temple with them. Their carriages would pack in crossboard to crossboard, and their feathered canopies made a continuous shade. Sometimes they amused themselves by drinking wine among the trees and streams, writing poems about the flowers, breaking off lotus roots, and floating gourds.

At the end of *p'u-t'ai* [532] Erhchu T'ien-kuang, governor of Yung province and Prince of Lung-hsi,[20] assembled horse and foot in this monastery. All the gates of the monastery collapsed for no cause, to Erhchu T'ien-kuang's horror. The same year he was executed in the eastern market, after being defeated in battle.

The FA-YÜN [Dharma Clouds] MONASTERY was founded by the foreign monk T'an-mo-lo from the country of Wu-ch'ang [Udyāna][21] in the West. It directly adjoined the Pao-kuang Monastery on its west.

T'an-mo-lo was a brilliant man who had studied [the teachings of] Śakyamuni exhaustively and learnt the Wei tongue and the clerkly script when he came to China. He understood everything he ever heard or read. All people—cleric and lay, high and low—flocked to him in admiration. He had built a Jetavana of magnificent craftsmanship.

The Buddha halls and the monks' cells were all decorated in the foreign style with dazzling reds and whites and gleaming gold and jade. There was a picture of the True Image which looked like the Buddha when he appeared in the Deer Park;[22] its divine radiance was that of the Diamond One between the

---

[20] 496–532. The Erhchu warlord in the north-west until his campaign against Kao Huan in 532, after the failure of which he was brought back to Loyang for execution. (*WS* 75, pp. 1673–7.)

[21] On Udyāna (Swat) see ch. 5 below; the monastery was perhaps financed from that country.

[22] To preach his first sermon and win his first converts.

two trees.[23] Within the monastery flowers and fruit-trees grew in profusion, fragrant herbs intertwined, and handsome trees shaded the courtyard. All the monks of the capital who loved the foreign dharma came to learn of it from T'an-mo-lo. The austerity of his monastic discipline was beyond praise. His secret and miraculous spells were unique in the world of Jambudvīpa: he could make a dead tree grow new twigs and leaves, and turn a human being into a donkey or a horse, to the astonishment and terror of all who saw it. All the crematory relics and teeth of the Buddha, sutras, and pictures that were presented to us by the West were kept in this temple.

North of this monastery was the house of the Imperial Assistant and Head of the Chancellery Prince Yü of Lin-huai.[24] He was well versed in classical books and gifted with a discriminating intelligence. His manners were exquisite and his bearing a joy to behold. When all the princes assembled in the capital on the morning of New Year's Day he would stroll along the palace corridors with a gold cicada gleaming on his head, jade tinkling at his waist, and his tablet of office in his hands. All who saw him would forget their weariness and sigh with admiration. He was both a lover of forests and streams and a convivial man. When the flowers and trees were brightly coloured like brocade in the spring breezes he would eat his morning meal in the southern pavilion and banquet in the back garden at night with crowds of officials and aristocrats. Instruments of silk and *wu-t'ung* wood played while the goblets were passed around. Lyrics and prose-poems went hand in hand, and brilliant conversation was made up on the spur of the moment. Everyone grasped the mysterious and put narrow vulgarity out of their minds; all who went to Yü's house said it was like becoming an immortal. Chang P'ei, a Man of Exalted Talent from Ching province, once wrote a poem in five-word lines which contained this outstanding couplet:

> In different woods the flowers share their colours;
> In other trees the bird-song is the same.

[23] Under which he attained nirvāna.

[24] One of the most thoroughly assimilated into aristocratic Han-Chinese culture of the royal clan. He fled to the Liang court after the Ho-yin massacre, returned to Loyang, and was beaten to death by Erhchu Chao's men in 530. (*WSa* 18, pp. 419–22.)

Yü rewarded him with some brocade in a dragon design. Others were given red silks and purple damasks. One man, P'ei Tzu-ming of Ho-tung, was told to drink a picul of wine as a punishment for writing feeble versus; he drank four-fifths of it before collapsing in a drunken stupor.[25] His contemporaries compared him to Shan T'ao.[26]

When Yü was killed by the soldiers of Erhchu Chao after they entered the capital he was mourned by court and commoners alike.

South of the imperial highway and 4 *li* outside the Hsi-yang Gate was the Great Loyang Market. It was surrounded by eight wards,[27] and to the south of it was the Princess Tower[28] which had been built by Senior General Liang Chi of the Han dynasty.[29] It still stood 50 feet high. During *ching-ming* [500–4] the monk Tao-heng built the LING-HSIEN [Divine Immortal] MONASTERY on top of it. To the west of the tower was the Ho-yang county seat,[30] and to the east the house of the Imperial Assistant Hou Kang.[31] To the north-east of the market was an artificial hill and a fishpond that had both also been constructed for Liang Chi. This is the place to which the [*Later*] *Han History* refers when it says 'they piled up earth to build mountains with nine slopes and a perimeter of 10 *li* which looked like the two Hsiao peaks.'[32]

[25] According to Wu Ch'eng-lo's figures, a Northern Wei picul would have been nearly 40 litres: this cannot be literally meant.

[26] 205–83. He performed a comparable feat in front of the Chin ruler Wu-ti. (However, the Chin picul was only a little over half the Northern Wei one.)

[27] On the interpretation of this passage see Appendix III.

[28] Originally built as the P'ing-lo Mound in AD 62 to receive some exotic animals from the West; renamed when a Han princess was buried beside it.

[29] The text appears to be corrupt here: Liang Chi's artificial hill stood north-east of the market and he had no connection with the Princess Tower.

[30] Ho-yang county was north of the Yellow River: this is probably a copyist's error for Ho-nan county, the local authority controlling the area of Great Loyang west of the inner city.

[31] A favourite of Shih-tsung's who was later an associate of Yüan Yi's, falling soon after he was ousted. (*WS* 93, pp. 2004–6.)

[32] *HHS* 34, p. 1182.

East of the market were the T'ung-shang [Circulation of Trade] and Ta-huo [Distribution of Goods] wards in which all the people made their livings as craftsmen, butchers, or traders. Their wealth ran into hundreds of millions.

Liu Pao's was the richest household [in the quarter]. He had a station in all the leading centres of the provinces and prefectures and kept ten[33] horses in each of them. He [observed] the movement of the prices of salt, grain, and other commodities everywhere;[34] he traded wherever boat or cart could go or foot could tread. Thus the goods from the whole area within the seas were assembled in his establishments. His property was comparable to a copper-bearing mountain, his wealth to a cave of gold. The scale on which his house was built exceeded the proper limits, and its pavilions and towers soared up through the clouds. His carriages, horses, clothes, and ornaments were like those of a prince.[35]

South of the market were the Tiao-yin [Melody] and Yüeh-lü [Musical Pitch] wards in which lived instrumentalists and singers. The world's most famous musicians came from here.

One of these was T'ien Seng-ch'ao, a virtuoso of the *chia* pipe[36] who could play the *Song of the Warrior* and the *Lament of Hsiang Yü*.[37] Ts'ui Yen-po,[38] the General to Conquer the West, was a great admirer of his.

When Kao-p'ing fell at the end of *cheng-kuang* [524][39] harsh officials abounded. When the rebel leader Moch'i Ch'ou-nu played havoc in the area of Ching and Ch'i[40] the court was so

[33] Following *Yüan Ho-nan chih* 3, p. 158: all editions of *LYCLC* read 'one horse'.

[34] The text at this vital spot does not make sense as it stands: 'the prices of salt, grain, and other market goods moved up and down together everywhere'. That would have been impossible in the conditions of the time. I take it that Liu used his horses to keep him informed of the movement of prices, thus enabling him to buy and sell to his best advantage.

[35] Despite sumptuary regulations controlling commoners' display.

[36] A curved wooden pipe of west-Asian origin.

[37] Doubtless celebrating the last hours of the unsuccessful rival of the founder of the Han dynasty.

[38] A defector from the south in Kao-tsu's time who served the Wei as a soldier. His last campaign, mentioned below, is described more fully in his *WS* biography (73, pp. 1636–9).

[39] To its own soldiers. Kao-p'ing (Kuyüan, Ninghsia) was the main Wei frontier fortress in the north-west; Moch'i Ch'ou-nu was its most successful rebel commander.

[40] The area south of Kao-p'ing, previously under the rival rebels of Moche T'ien-sheng, which Moch'i Ch'ou-nu attacked in 525.

worried it could not eat at the right time. Ts'ui Yen-po was ordered to muster 50,000 horse and foot with which to subdue him. He set out with his host from the Chang-fang Bridge—the Hsi-yang Pavilion of the Han dynasty—which lay to the west of Loyang. The ministers and high officials gave them a banquet as they left, and the road was lined with carriages and horsemen. Ts'ui Yen-po, wearing a tall hat and a long sword, went before them in martial splendour, while T'ien Seng-ch'ao followed playing the *Flute Song of the Warrior*, the sound of which turned cowards into heroes, and made swordsmen long for action.

Ts'ui was a man of outstanding courage and military ability who won great fame early in life. He toiled for his country for more than thirty years; no city could withstand his assault, nor line of battle hold firm against him. That was why the court gave him so warm a send-off. Whenever he was about to join battle he ordered T'ien Seng-ch'ao to play the *Song of the Warrior*, arousing the armoured soldiers to a high pitch of excitement. When Ts'ui Yen-po rode against the enemy's line of battle he dominated the field. He was the bravest man in the whole army, and his reputation overawed the soldiers. For two years [524–5] he won a string of victories until Moch'i Ch'ou-nu recruited some first-rate archers to shoot T'ien Seng-ch'ao. After T'ien Seng-ch'ao was killed Ts'ui Yen-po grieved for him with a sorrow that in his subordinates' view was no less than Po Ya's grief at the death of Chung Tzu-ch'i.[41] Ts'ui Yen-po himself was later hit by a stray arrow and died in the ranks of his army, with the result that his force of 50,000 men immediately scattered and fled.[42]

To the west of the market were the Yen-ku [Prolonged Liquor] and Chih-shang [Ordered Goblet] wards, most of whose inhabitants made their living through brewing.

Liu Pai-to, a Ho-tung man, was an excellent brewer.[43] In

[41] When Chung Tzu-ch'i died, it was said, Po Ya smashed his *ch'in*, for there was now nobody would could understand the meaning of his music.

[42] The rebels feigned flight, lured Ts'ui's troops into abandoned stockades then struck back at them while they were looting, killing Ts'ui and over 10,000 other Wei troops. Evidently Ts'ui was more brave than competent as a commander.

[43] On brewing methods of the period see *CMYS* 64–7, and Shih Sheng-han, (1962), pp. 70–82. 'Pai-to' was used from Chin times onwards as a synonym for liquor; it may have been the name of a type of brew, and may also have been used as a brewer's nickname.

the sixth month, the most torrid time of summer, he would put his liquor in vats and stand them in the sun. Ten days of this would fix the flavour of the liquor. It was delicious; and anyone drunk on it would not wake up for a month. When members of the court and nobility went to the provinces or the border this was sent to them over distances of more than 1,000 *li*. Because it travelled so far it was called 'Crane Cup' and 'Donkey Rider'.

In *yung-hsi* [532–4] Mao Hung-pin,[44] the Governor of Nan-ch'ing province, took some of this wine with him when he went to his post. Some bandits he encountered on his journey were all captured after drinking themselves silly on it. Thus the wine was given a third name—'Brigand Catcher'. The swashbucklers of the day had a saying:

> No need to fear the sword or bow
> But Pai-to's hooch will lay you low.

North of the ward were the Tz'u-hsiao [Filial Piety] and Feng-chung [Last Rites] wards, where lived mainly coffinsellers and hirers of hearses.

There was a professional keener called Sun Yen whose wife had never taken her clothes off to go to bed in three years of marriage. Finding this odd he waited till she was asleep one night before discreetly undressing her. He found that she had hairs 3 feet long, like a fox's tail, and drove her out in horror. Before she went she cut off his hair with a sword. When the neighbours chased her she turned into a fox, so that they were unable to catch her. After this 130 men in the capital had their hair cut off. The foxes would turn themselves into attractively dressed women and walk along the road. Men who saw them went up to them with delight, and they all had their hair cut off. For a time all brightly dressed women were called fox-demons.[45] This lasted from the fourth month of the second year of *hsi-p'ing* [517] until autumn.

[44] A hereditary chieftain who assembled a loyalist private army in the troubled years from 524 onwards which controlled parts of central Shensi north of the Wei River, whither he returned from Southern Ch'ing province (Shantung) in 534. (*PS* 49, pp. 1808–10.)

[45] Can fox-spirit stories be aimed at women with more pubic hair than most? Perhaps some were driven by persecution to take this bizarre revenge. *WS* 112/1, p. 2923, attributes this outbreak to the rule of an Empress Dowager. Those caught were given 100 strokes of the cane.

There were also the Fu-ts'ai [Great Wealth] and Chin-ssu [Golden Stall] wards where the rich lived.

In these ten wards lived many craftsmen, merchants, and men of property. Families worth 1,000 pieces of gold were neighbours, and high buildings towered in rivalry. Their houses had double gateways and interconnecting covered walks that overlooked each other. Gold, silver, brocades, and embroidered silks were worn even by their slaves, and their bondsmen ate the finest delicacies. During *shen-kuei* [518–20] it was proposed to the throne that as artisans and merchants were usurping privileges to which they had no right, they should not be allowed to wear gold, silver, or embroidered silk. Although such a ban was issued it remained a dead letter.[46]

In the Fu-ts'ai [Great Wealth] ward was the K'AI-SHAN [Beginning of Benevolence] MONASTERY which had originally been the home of Wei Ying, a man of Ching-chao.

When Wei Ying died young his wife, a woman surnamed Liang, married again without observing the requirements of mourning. She continued to live in Wei Ying's house with her new husband, Hsiang Tzu-chi of Ho-nei. On learning that his widow had remarried Wei Ying came riding back with several retainers in broad daylight. He stopped in front of the courtyard and shouted, 'Ah-liang, have you forgotten me?' In his terror her new husband shot him with his bow. He instantly fell to the ground, turning into a figure of peachwood. His steed became a horse made of reeds, and his retainers men of rushes. Liang was so horrified by this that she gave the house to become a monastery.

There was a man of Nan-yang called Hou Ch'ing who had a bronze statue a little over a foot high and an ox he intended to sell to pay for the gilding of the statue; but he fell on hard times and had to put the ox to a different use. Two years later Hou Ch'ing's wife, who was surnamed Ma, dreamt that the statue said to her, 'You and your husband have begrudged me my gilt for too long, so I am going to take away your son Ch'ou-to to pay for it.' She woke up feeling most uneasy, and that morning

---

[46] Similar restrictions were promulgated in 515 at the suggestion of Prince Yung of Kao-yang, but were only enforced briefly. (*WS* 21/1, p. 566.)

the boy took ill and died. As Hou Ch'ing was fifty he cried so bitterly at losing his only son that even passers-by were moved. The day the boy died the statue covered itself with gilt, a light shone from it into the houses all around, and everyone within 1 *li* could smell incense. Lay, cleric, young, and old alike all came to see it. When the Senior Deputy Head of the Chancellery Yüan Shun[47] heard of all the strange things that had happened in the ward he changed its name from Great Wealth to Joker [Ch'i Hsieh] ward.

To the west of the Yen-ku ward and east of the Chang-fang Ditch was an area 2 *li* from east to west and 15 *li* from north to south. It was bounded in the south by the Lo river and in the north by the Mang hills. This whole district was called Shou-ch'iu [Longevity Hills] wards. As members of the royal family lived here it was popularly known as the Princes' Quarter.

   In those days all within the seas was peaceful, everywhere men followed their occupations, the records were all of good events and there were no natural disasters. The common people prospered and rich harvests brought joy to the masses. Widows and unmarried men did not know the taste of dogs' and pigs' food; orphans did not have to dress like oxen or horses. Princes and nobles of the imperial clan, princesses, and the Emperor's relations through marriage seized for themselves the wealth of mountains, seas, forests, and rivers. They competed in building gardens and mansions, boasting to each other of their achievements. They erected splendid gateways, sumptuous houses whose doors connected one with the next, flying passageways to catch the breezes, and high buildings shrouded with mist. Tall towers and fragrant terraces were built in every home, and each garden had flowering copses and

[47] Littérateur, snob, and outspoken critic of the Dowager Hu and others. He was killed at Ho-yin despite Erhchu Jung's warning to stay away. (*WS* 19/2, pp. 481–5.)

twisting pools. They were all verdant with peach in summer and with bamboo and cypress in winter.

The most magnificent of them all was Prince Shen of Ho-chien,[48] who rivalled the Prince of Kao-yang. He built a Wen-pai [Patterned Cypress] Hall, in imitation of the Hui-yin [Sweet Music] Hall of the palace, and a well of jade with a golden pail on a silk rope of many colours. He had 300 singing girls who were all ravishing beauties, and a concubine, Ch'ao-yün, who was a marvellous flautist; her repertoire included the *Song of the Round Fan* and the music of Lung-shang. When Shen was Governor of Ch'in province the Ch'iang people revolted and gave their allegiance elsewhere.[49] Having failed in several campaigns to subdue them he ordered Ch'ao-yün to disguise herself as a poor old flute-playing beggar-woman. The Ch'iang all wept when they heard her play. 'Why did you leave your homes,' she asked them one after the other, 'to become bandits in mountain valleys?' She then led them in to submit. 'An old woman and her flute', said the people of Ch'in, 'did better than strong lads on fast horses.'

When Shen was in Ch'in province his rule was a failure, but despite this he sent envoys as far west as Persia in search of fine horses. He got one 1,000-*li* horse called Chestnut Wind-chaser and over ten 700-*li* steeds to which he gave names, a silver trough, and trappings of pure gold.

The other princes could not match his great wealth. He once said 'Although he was a commoner, Shih Ch'ung of the Chin dressed in clothes made from the feathers on pheasants' heads and the fur of foxes' armpits. The eggs he ate were painted and his firewood was carved. So why shouldn't I, a heavenly prince of the Great Wei, be extravagant?'

He built a Welcoming the Breeze Pavilion in his garden, and above its windows he had placed dark copper cash in chains, jade phoenixes with bells in their mouths, and golden dragons spitting out precious ornaments. Under the eaves grew

[48] A grandson of Kao-tsu reputed to be outrageously corrupt. He died in 527. (*WSa* 20, p. 529.)

[49] The Ch'iang of western Shensi, central Kansu, and eastern Chinghai were militarily still powerful. In 524–7 Moche Nien-sheng and his father led Ch'iang risings in the west. (*TCTC*; Chou Yi-liang (1963), pp. 161–8; Yao Wei-yüan (1962), pp. 319–37.)

branches of white crab-apple and red plum that his singing girls could pick and eat as they sat upstairs.

Shen once set out all his valuable vessels for a banquet given for imperial clansmen: over 100 golden and silver bottles, with bowls, dishes on legs, plates and covers to complement them. In addition to these the wine vessels included dozens of crystal cups, bowls of agate and of glass,[50] and red jade goblets. They were all exquisitely made in ways not known in the central lands as they all came from the West. He also showed off his girl musicians and fine horses. He led the princes on a tour of his storehouses, full of brocade, felt goods, pearls, ice gauze, and mist silk; the quantities of embroidery, coloured silk, and all kinds of silk textile, patterned or plain,[51] as well as money were incalculable. 'I don't mind not having met Shih Ch'ung,' observed Shen to Prince Jung of Chang-wu,[52] 'but I do regret that he never saw me.' Prince Jung, a greedy and violent man whose ambitions knew no bounds, sighed for grief at the sight of all this and made himself ill without realizing it. He went back home to spend three days in bed without rising. When Prince Chi of Chiang-yang[53] came to visit him and asked, 'With your wealth you should compete with him, so why sigh with jealousy and get yourself into this state?' 'It used to be said', replied Jung, 'that the only man richer than me was the Prince of Kao-yang; I never imagined that the Prince of Ho-chien would get ahead of me.' Chi laughed and remarked, 'Do you want to be like Yüan Shu, who when he was in Huai-nan didn't know of Liu Pei's existence?'[54] Jung sprang up, called for wine, and made merry.

In those days the state was rich and its treasures and storehouses were filled to overflowing. Incalculable quantities of coins and silk were piled in the open under porticoes. The

---

[50] Then a great rarity in China, as it had been since Han times.

[51] The text lists the various textiles; which I am unable to translate individually.

[52] The father of Kao Huan's first puppet emperor Yüan Lang, killed by former northern garrison troops in 526. (*WS* 19/3, pp. 514–15.)

[53] Father of the dictator Yüan Yi, and for long the general commander of the northern frontier. (*WS* 16, pp. 400–3.)

[54] In 197 Yüan Shu, a great warlord, was indignant at being attacked by Liu Pei, of whom he had not even heard. Two years later Yüan died, defeated by Liu Pei. (*HHS* 75, pp. 2443–7.)

Empress Dowager therefore gave the officials all they wanted; all the officers of the court carried off as much as their strength allowed them.[55] Jung and Li Ch'ung, Marquis of Ch'en-liu, fell and broke their ankles when they tried to carry off more than they could manage. The Dowager decided to give them none, and they left empty-handed. The Imperial Assistant Ts'ui Kuang took only two bolts of silk, and when asked by the Empress Dowager why he had taken so little he replied, 'As your subject has only two hands he can only take two bolts, and even that is too much.' All the court and the nobility admired his integrity.

After the Ho-yin campaign the Yüan clan was exterminated and many of the princely and lordly mansions were turned into monasteries, so that in the Shou-ch'iu [Longevity Hills] wards temples stood packed close together and pagodas soared into the sky. On the eighth day of the fourth month many of the men and women of the capital used to go to the Ho-chien Monastery, and all of them would sigh with admiration when they saw its splendid porticoes, and reckon that even the immortals' houses on P'eng-lai could be no better. On going through to the garden at the back they saw twisting canals and lofty stone steps, red lotuses over the ponds, and green duckweed floating on the water, flying bridges leaping over pavilions and tall trees soaring up through clouds; they all sighed, for not even the Rabbit Park of the Prince of Liang could have been anything to compare with this.

The CHUI-HSIEN [Blessings for the Departed] MONASTERY in the Shou-ch'iu wards had been the house of the Imperial Assistant and Head of the Chancellery Prince Lüeh of Tung-p'ing.

Lüeh was born handsome and he matured early; he was widely read and untiring in his love of right conduct. During *shen-kuei* [518–20] he became a Gentleman in Waiting. When Yüan Yi held dictatorial power and treated the Premier [Yüan

---

[55] *TCTC* tells this story with the events of 519. (149, p. 4646.)

I, Prince of Ch'ing-ho] cruelly, Lüeh plotted secretly with his elder brother Prince Hsi of Chung-shan, the Governor of Hsiang province, to rise and hand him over to the Emperor for punishment. But their noble plans went astray and there was quarrel among the conspirators. All three of Lüeh's brothers were killed, while Lüeh alone escaped to the south of the Yangtse.[56]

Hsiao Yen had heard of Lüeh's fame, and when he saw how elegant and cultured Lüeh was, he treated him with the respect due to a man of importance. 'How many more are there like Your Highness in Loyang?' he asked Lüeh. 'When I lived in my own country,' replied Lüeh, 'I held office despite my inferior ability. As for the splendour of the imperial clan and the wealth of officials, one could compare them to a flight of phoenixes or a grove of fine trees. Officials like myself were, as Chao Tzu said,[57] no easier to count than the number of bushels in a cartload of grain.' Hsiao Yen roared with laughter. He enfeoffed Lüeh as Prince of Chung-shan with an income of 1,000 households and all a prince's mark of rank. Lüeh was also made prefect of Hsüan-ch'eng and given a pipe and drum band as well as 1,000 swordsmen. Lüeh's rule was strict and uncorrupt, and he had a great reputation for good government. For all their excessive pride the court and nobility south of the Yangtse were awed by Lüeh's deportment when they saw him come to court. He was promoted to be Martial General and Governor of Heng province.

In the first year of *hsiao-ch'ang* [525] Emperor Ming-ti pardoned Chiang Ko, a Wu man, and invited Lüeh to return to his country. Chiang Ko was a senior general of Hsiao Yen's.[58] 'We would sooner lose a Chiang Ko', said Hsiao Yen, 'than be without Your Highness.' 'My family has suffered a calamity,' replied Lüeh, 'and their bleached bones have not yet been gathered together. Allow me, I beg you, to return to

---

[56] On the rebellion of Prince Lüeh and his brothers against Yüan Yi at Yeh in 520 see also *WS* 19/3, pp. 503–7, and Yüan Hsi's tomb inscription in Chao Wan-li's corpus.

[57] When asked a similar question at the Ts'ao-Wei court, where he was representing the state of Wu on a diplomatic mission. (Commentary to *SKC* 47, pp. 1123–4.)

[58] In fact an exchange: Chiang Ko was a career official taken prisoner in the frontier city of P'eng-ch'eng who refused to show any deference to his Wei captors. (*Liang shu* 36, pp. 522–6.)

my own country that I may record who has survived and who has not.' He began to weep. Hsiao Yen had to let Lüeh go, albeit with a heavy heart, and gave him 5,000,000 copper cash, 200 pounds of gold, 500 pounds of silver, and innumerable brocades, embroideries, and other precious objects. He led the officials in person to see him off beside the Yangtse, and over 100 people presented Lüeh with poems in pentameters. He was treated everywhere with comparable respect.

As soon as Lüeh crossed the Huai River Emperor Ming-ti appointed him Imperial Assistant and Prince of Yi-yang with the revenue of 1,000 households. When Lüeh came back to our court, a rescript read:

In times of old Liu Ts'ang[59] was a lover of goodness who brought great benefits to Tung-p'ing, while Ts'ao Chih with his great literary gifts did much for his principality of Ch'en. Their fame and excellence brought glory to their imperial clans. The Imperial Assistant, Prince Lüeh of Yi-yang, has himself acted to protect the country, and his family's glorious achievements are long established. He has brought benefits at home and distinction abroad, and great too were his brothers. To do what was right they put aside their family, and they gave their lives for their country. Their loyalty shall be spoken of forever, never to be forgotten. Although he stayed for a while in Liang he has now returned to our court. He has determination and integrity, and he carries through to the end all he undertakes. His story shall grace the histories with the brightness of the sun and moon. Before Lüeh had reached our court we hastily gave him a title, enfeoffing him with Yi-yang. But this fief was on the frontier, and despite his pleas it was less than perfect to make him live in an unfamiliar place. He deserves a fief to match his excellence that will add lustre to past glory, so he is to be re-enfeoffed as Prince of Tung-p'ing with the same number of households as before.[60]

Lüeh was rapidly created Head of the Chancellery, Honorary Senior Minister, and President of the Imperial Academy, remaining Imperial Assistant as before. He was relaxed, elegant, and brilliantly endowed by heaven. When he left the south and returned north, he once more attained the heights. His speech and deportment were taken as models both at court and elsewhere. In the first year of *chien-yi* [528] he was

[59] A son of the founder of the Eastern Han regime.
[60] Behind the rhetoric lies the Dowager's enthusiasm for an old enemy of Yüan Yi.

killed at Ho-yin. He was created Grand Guardian and given
the posthumous title of Wen-chen. His mansion was given by
his heir, Ching-shih, to become this monastery.

The JUNG-CHÜEH [Brilliang̣ Enlightenment]
MONASTERY was founded by I, the Wen-hsien Prince of
Ch'ing-ho. It lay 1 *li* outside the Ch'ang-ho Gate to the south
of the imperial highway, and contained a five-storeyed pagoda
which was as high as the one in the Ch'ung-chüeh Monastery.
A whole ward was not sufficient to contain its Buddha-halls
and monastic cells.

The bhiksu T'an-mo-tsui was an expert in the study of
dhyāna.[61] He preached on the *Nirvāṇa* and *Avataṁsaka* sutras[62]
and had 1,000 disciples. When P'u-t'i-liu-chih [Bodhiruci],[63]
the foreign monk from India, saw him, he revered him, calling
him a bodhisattva.

Bodhiruci was famous in the West for his expositions of the
meaning of Buddhism, and the various foreigners called him an
arhat. He knew the Wei language and the clerkly script and
translated twenty-three sutras and śāstras[64] including the *Ten
Stage [Daśabhūmikā]*[65] and *Laṅkāvatāra* sutras.[66] His achievement was not even matched by the golden words in the stone
room[67] or the transmission of the True Teaching in the

[61] In ch. 2 he was accused of being opposed to dhyāna: perhaps Yang here uses the
term *ch'an-hsüeh* to stand for Buddhist learning in general.

[62] The *Avataṁsaka sūtra*, translated into Chinese early in the fifth century, taught that
the all-pervading principle of the universe is serenity of mind. (Conze (1951), p. 164.) On
the spread of its influence in the late Northern Wei period see T'ang Yung-t'ung (1963),
pp. 871–6.

The *Mahāparinirvāṇa/sūtra* was said to have been delivered by Śākyamuni on the eve of
his nirvāna.

[63] Probably the most important translator of Buddhist scripture to work in Northern
Loyang, where he arrived in 508. (*HKSC* 1, pp. 12b ff. See also ch. 6 of Part I.)

[64] According to the *Nei tien lu* (followed by *HKSC*, loc. cit.), thirty-nine.

[65] Bodhiruci and others translated Vasubandhu's commentary on this sutra, which
was already available in Chinese. It deals with the ten stages of bodhisattvahood, leading
to Buddha-hood.

[66] This important Yogācārin text had been translated in the south during the fifth
century: Bodhiruci and his colleagues did their version in 513.

[67] i.e. the *Scripture in Forty-two Sections* which the Han Emperor Ming-ti is said to have
kept in a stone room.

Thatched Hall Monastery.[68] When Bodhiruci read T'an-mo-tsui's *Essays on the Meaning of the Great Vehicle* he would snap his fingers and sigh with admiration and cry out how subtle and brilliant they were. He translated them into his foreign tongue and sent them to the West, where the monks often turned east to pay their respects to him and gave T'an-mo-tsui the title of 'Holy Man of the East'.

The TA-CHÜEH [Great Enlightenment] MONASTERY was founded when the mansion of Prince Huai of Kuang-p'ing was given for the purpose. It was about 1 *li* to the west of the Jung-chüeh Monastery. To the north it commanded a view of the Mang range; to the south it overlooked the bank of the Lo River; to the east the gate-towers of the palace could be seen, and to the west the flag-tower. It was magnificently situated on the spacious and open river bank. This was why Wen Tzu-sheng wrote in his inscription for the monastery:

> It faces water and is backed by hills,
> With the palace to the west and the market to the east.

Statues of the Seven Buddhas[69] had been erected in the pavilion where Prince Huai once lived. Its copses, pools, and flying verandas rivalled those of the Ching-ming. When the trees swayed in the spring breeze, orchids opened their purple petals; and at the touch of autumn frost on the grass, yellow chrysanthemums burst into flower. Famous monks of great virtue stayed here in peace to avoid worldly cares. In the years *yung-hsi* [532–4], when the Prince of P'ing-yang was on the throne, a brick pagoda of exquisite craftsmanship was built here. The Assistant Secretary Wen Tzu-sheng was ordered by the Emperor to compose an inscription for it.[70]

---

[68] The great translator Kumārajīva was installed with 800 Buddhist scholars in the monastery of this name in Ch'ang-an by the Later Ch'in monarch Yao Hsing in 401 to translate scriptures.

[69] Probably Śākyamuni and his six predecessors.

[70] See *Yi wen lei chü* 77, pp. 1312–13.

The YUNG-MING MONASTERY [Monastery of Eternal Radiance], which was to the east of the Ta-chüeh Monastery, was founded by the Emperor Hsüan-wu. In those days Loyang was full of Buddhist statues and scriptures and foreign monks congregated there like spokes coming to a hub; they came to this paradise with staves in their hands and scriptures on their backs. Shih-tsung [Hsüan-wu] built this monastery for them to stay in. The complex of cells and covered cloisters included more than 1,000 rooms. Graceful bamboo lined the courtyards, lofty pines brushed against the eaves, and rare and exotic flowers clustered round the steps. There were over 3,000 monks here from many countries.

The most distant part of the West is Ta Ch'in [the Roman East] which is at the western extreme of earth and sky. They plough, hoe, and spin; the common people live in sight of each other in the countryside; and their clothes, horses, and carts are much like those of China.[71]

In the south is the country of Ko-ying,[72] which is very far from the capital. Its customs are quite different from ours as it has never had any contact with China: even in the two Han dynasties and the [Ts'ao] Wei nobody ever got that far. But now for the first time the monk P'u-t'i-pa-t'o [Buddhabhadra] reached Loyang from there. He said of his journey: 'After travelling north for one month I reached Kou-chih.[73] Eleven more days to the north I came to Tien-sun.[74] From there I

[71] This description, like the slightly fuller one in *PS* 97, pp. 3227–8, shows a mixture of fact and fantasy comparable with that in the account of the land of the Taugast (i.e. T'opa) given in the seventh book of the *Historia* of the Byzantine historian Theophylactus Simocattes: there is a striking realization on both sides that the other civilization is somehow equivalent to their own.

[72] Generally located in southern India, though somewhere in Malaysia or Indonesia seems more likely. (See *TPYL* 790, p. 3501; Wheatley (1961), p. 23.)

[73] On the variety of Chinese renderings of this name and the reasons for regarding a location in the isthmian part of the Malay peninsula as probable, see Wheatley (1961), pp. 23–5.

[74] Also called Tun-sun in Chinese sources, and said to be 3,000 *li* south of Fu-nan. From the *Liang shu* account it evidently lay across the Malay peninsula (Wheatley (1961), pp. 15–21.)

headed north for forty days until I arrived in Fu-nan,[75] which with its area of 5,000 *li* is the biggest and most powerful of the countries of the southern barbarians. The people of Fu-nan are many and rich. Their country produces pearls, gold, jade, and crystal, and it abounds in betel-nuts. A further month's journey to the north brought me to Lin-yi, [Tsan-yi— Champa][76] and on leaving Lin-yi [Tsan-yi] I entered the country of Hsiao Yen.

After spending a year in Yang province Buddhabhadra came with Fa-jung, a monk of Yang province to the capital. When the monks of the capital asked him about the customs of the south Buddhabhadra said, 'The people of Ku-nu-tiao[77] drive horse-drawn four-wheeled chariots. The country of Ssu-tiao[78] produces asbestos, which they make from the bark of a tree that doesn't burn when you put it on a fire.[79] In all the countries of the south the people live in walled cities and most of these countries are rich in jewels. The people are honest, good, straightforward, and just. They are in contact with Ta Ch'in [the Roman Empire], An-hsi,[80] and Shen-tu [India]. It takes them 100 days sailing in many directions. As believers in the Buddhist faith they all treasure life and hate killing.'

West of this monastery was the Yi-nien [Satisfied with the Times] ward in which were the mansions of Prince Ching-hao

[75] The once-powerful Khmer state centred in southern Cambodia. By the time Yang wrote it had been conquered by Chen-la/Kambuja. (Pelliot (1903); Coedès (1948 and 1962); Briggs (1957).)

[76] The Campā of Sanskrit sources and Champa of later periods, founded in the late second century AD with its capital in what is now Quang Nam province, Vietnam. The first syllable of its Chinese name 林, generally read Lin, should probably be taken as a phonetic representation of something like 'Cham'. (See Yang Hsien-yi's discussion of Chinese names for Byzantium, in which he points out that a cognate character 拂 can be read *ts'an* (1950, p. 63).) On Lin-yi see the works of Coedès cited above; *Liang shu* 54; *Nan shih* 78; *TPYL* 786, pp. 3478–80. I have not seen R. Stein, *Le Lin-yi* (Peking, 1947).

[77] According to Pelliot this name represents Kanadvīpa, and it should be located in the Malayan peninsula or Indonesia.

[78] On the knotty question of the location of Ssu-tiao, see Laufer (1915); Ferrand (1916); and Fujita (1929). Somewhere in Indonesia seems likely.

[79] On the legends concerning 'fire-washed cloth', or asbestos, see Laufer (1915). The belief that it was a vegetable fibre was widely held in China.

[80] The term used in Han times for the Arsacid state of Parthia, which had barely outlasted its Chinese contemporary. Here it is probably used anachronistically for Sassanian Persia, called Po-ssu elsewhere in this text, instead of for the small state of An-hsi between the Pamirs, Sogdiana, and Persia which is listed in *PS* 97, p. 3227, and *Chou shu* 50, p. 919; and described in more detail as An-kuo in *SS* 83, p. 1849.

of Ch'en-liu and of Hu Yüan-chi, Imperial Assistant and Duke of An-ting.[81]

Ching-hao was the son of Tso, the Chuang Prince of Ch'en-liu and Governor of Ho province. His character was untrammelled and he showed great breadth of mind from childhood. He was a very sociable man who treated people with great hospitality. He was once particularly fond of mystery talk and the cause of the Taoists, but later he gave up half of his mansion and installed Buddhists there to chant several of the Mahāyāna scriptures. He invited to his banquets the four Masters of the Law of great virtue in the capital—Ch'ao, Kuang, Tan, and Jung[82]—as well as the foreign Tripitaka Master, Bodhiruci, and others. Men possessed of special skills came from all parts to visit him. There was a Meng Chung-hui of Wu-wei, a court guest whose father Pin had been prefect of Chin-ch'eng. Hui was a man of intelligence who had studied widely in Buddhism and thoroughly understood the Four Truths.[83] He often came to Ching-hao's mansion for discussions with the monks and was known by his contemporaries as Master Mysterious. Then he made a *chia-chu* statue of Buddha when he was on earth whose appearance was of a rare majesty.[84] He put it in Ching-hao's front hall on a Sumeru throne. In the second year of *yung-an* [529] this statue walked round its throne every night, and its footprints could be seen in the ground all around. Gentlemen and masses alike all came to look at it in their astonishment. Countless were those who were enlightened by it. In the autumn of the third year of *yung-hsi* [534] it suddenly took itself off; nobody knew where it had gone. That winter the capital was moved to Yeh. In the fifth year of *wu-ting* [547] when Meng Chung-hui was secretary to the commander of Lo province he made new inquiries about the statue but there was still no sign of it.

Seven *li* outside the Ch'ang-ho Gate was the Chang-fen Bridge.

[81] A half-brother of the Dowager Hu. (*WSa* 83/2, p. 1836.)

[82] Which four monks are here referred to in abbreviated form is not clear.

[83] The universality of suffering; the accumulation of suffering; the elimination of suffering; and the eightfold path thereto.

[84] From *HKSC* 35, pp. 17b–18a, it is clear that the *chia-chu* process involved the modelling of a body (possibly of clay) to which lacquered cloth was then applied.

When Loyang was the Chin capital Chung-ch'ao the Ku river once overflowed, flooding below the city walls and damaging many of the homes of the people. This stone bridge was built to control it: when the waters rose (*chang*) it divided (*fen*) them, diverting some into the Lo—hence the name Chang-fen Bridge. Another story has it that it was originally called the Chang Fang Bridge because Chang Fang's army camped here when the Prince of Ho-chien sent him from Ch'ang-an to attack the Prince of Ch'ang-sha.[85] I do not know which story is true. Nowadays the common people incorrectly call it Madame Chang's Bridge.

When the gentlemen of the capital welcomed or saw each other off they often did so here.

West of the Chang-fen Bridge was the Ch'ien-chin [Thousand Gold] Dyke, so called because it was reckoned that the water it provided gave a profit of 1,000 pieces of gold a day.[86] It was originally built by Ch'en Hsieh, the Metropolitan Water Controller.[87] A thousand men kept it in good repair throughout the year.

---

[85] During the internecine wars between the Chin princes (301–6) Chang Feng beseiged the Prince of Ch'ang-sha in Loyang, then roasted him to death after capturing him.

[86] It also prevented the waters of the Ku from flooding Loyang.

[87] In Ts'ao-Wei times. It was rebuilt in Western Chin times, during Liu Yü's occupation, and in Kao-tsu's reign. (*SCC* 16, pp. 3/68–9.) The profit may partly have come from the 'tens' of water-mills installed on it at Ts'ui Liang's suggestion. (*WS* 66, p. 1481.)

Chapter 5

North of the City Wall

The CH'AN-HSÜ [Contemplating Emptiness] MONASTERY lay outside the Ta-hsia Gate to the west of the imperial highway. In front of the monastery was the Yüeh-wu ch'ang [Military Review Ground]. It was here that the armoured troops drilled in the agricultural slack season at the end of the year and thousands of vehicles and tens of thousands of horsemen often gathered.

A member of the Forest of Wings Guard, Ma Seng-hsiang, was an expert at martial games.[1] He could throw a spear as high as a 100-foot tree. The Tiger Guardsman Chang Ch'e-chü[2] could throw a sword 1 *chang* higher than a tall building. The Emperor, who watched the games from a tower, would often order these two to compete.

The Martial Splendour Ground of Chin times was north-east of the Ta-hsia Gate. In modern times it was the Kuang-feng Park where lucerne grass[3] was grown.

The NING-HSÜAN MONASTERY was founded by the eunuch Chia Ts'an, the Governor of Chi province.[4] It was east of the imperial highway and 1 *li* outside the Kuang-mo Gate in what was known as the Yung-p'ing [Eternal Peace] ward.

---

[1] *Chiao-ti-hsi*, a term referring to various kinds of performance over the centuries, but here evidently meaning something like modern *wu-shu*.

[2] One of the Dowager Hu's personal guards. He was killed after an attempt to kill the dictator Yüan Yi. (*PS* 13, p. 504.)

[3] As a fodder crop. See *CMYS* 29 for a contemporary guide to cultivation.

[4] One of the Yüan Yi-Liu T'eng faction. The Dowager had him killed after her return to power in 525 when he was going to take up this provincial appointment. (*WS* 94, p. 2029.)

Note:[5] this is where the temple of the Great High Emperor of the Han used to be.[6] When the capital was first moved to Loyang Chia Ts'an lived here for a while, but when his mother died he gave the house to become a monastery. It was situated on high ground, overlooking the city wall and the palace gates. With its splendid buildings and colonnades, its groves of bamboo and cypress, it was indeed a place where one could purify one's conduct and rest one's mind. Innumerable verses in five-syllable lines were written by the princes and ministers who came to visit this monastery.

North-west of Loyang city wall had been the Shang-shang [Honouring the Shang] ward where the people of the [Shang-] Yin once lived.[7] Kao-tsu renamed it the Wen-yi [Listening to Righteousness] ward.

When the capital had been newly moved to Loyang many of the courtiers stayed there, but they were jeered at so much on account of it that they all finally moved away. Only the potters lived there, and it was from here that all the tiles used in the capital came. A song was sung about it that went:

> In the Shang-shang ward north-east of Loyang
> The pig-headed Yin folk used to be squatters.
> Now that everyone else has gone,
> Only the potters are left, the rotters.

Only the Champion General Kuo Wen-yüan sought relaxation there, and his halls, gardens, and groves were a match for those of a monarch. Lu Yüan-ch'ien of Lung-hsi, an enthusiast for alliteration, once said when he passed Kuo Wen-yüan's mansion and saw his splendid gateway, 'Whose house? Impressive indeed!' The slave-girl Ch'un-feng came out and said, 'Commander Kuo's quarters.' At this Li Yüan-ch'ien remarked, 'My! Mere maidservants all alliterate.' 'Refrain, I request, from slandering this slave,' retorted Ch'un-feng.

---

[5] A relic of the original layout of the book, with the main entries in large script and author's notes, written small in double columns, inserted in the text.

[6] The text seems corrupt here.

[7] When the eastern capital of the Chou was built on the Lo in the eleventh century BC, some of the inhabitants of the Shang-Yin capital were moved to another settlement nearby. (See 'To shih' and 'Shao kao' in Shang shu.)

In the Wen-yi ward was the house of Sung Yün, a Tun-huang man who went on a mission to the West with Hui-sheng.[8]

In the eleventh month of the first year of *shen-kuei* [518] which was in the winter, the Empress Dowager sent Hui-sheng, a monk of the Ch'ung-li Monastery, to fetch scriptures from the West. He obtained 170 scriptures, all marvellous classics of the Great Vehicle.

They set out from the capital and after travelling west for forty days they reached the Ch'ih Ling [Bare Range].[9] This is the western boundary of the country where the frontier defences of the Imperial Wei are situated. There is no vegetation on the Bare Range—hence the name. In these mountains birds and rodents live in the same holes, different species cohabiting: male birds mate with female rodents.

Twenty-three days west of the Bare Range they crossed the Rolling Sands, and reached the country of T'U-YÜ-HUN.[10] The journey was very cold; there were many blizzards in which all that could be seen was flying sand and pebbles. Only around the city of T'u-yü-hun itself was it a little warmer. The script and clothes here are the same as those of Wei, but their customs and government are generally modelled on those of the southerners.

Three thousand, five hundred *li* to the west of T'u-yü-hun they came to the city of SHAN-SHAN[11] which used to have its own king until it was swallowed up by T'u-yü-hun. The present master of the city was the second son of the T'u-yü-hun ruler, the hereditary West-Pacifying General who had 3,000 men with which to protect it from the Western Hu.[12]

[8] The account of Sung Yün and Hui-sheng's journey given in the pages that follow is a document of the first importance for the history of Central Asia at this time; only the briefest of notes on it are offered here in a book about Loyang.

[9] The Jih-yüeh shan of eastern Ch'inghai.

[10] Around Lake Kokonor.

[11] Charkhlik (Joch'iang) in southern Sinkiang.

[12] The Ephthalites and their vassals.

One thousand, six hundred, and forty *li* to the west of Shan-shan they came to the walled town of TSO-MO,[13] in which lived about 100 families. As no rain falls on the land here they breach the banks of the rivers in order to grow wheat. As they do not know the use of oxen they will the fields with hand-ploughs. None of the pictures of Buddhas and bodhisattvas in this town has Hu features. When the older inhabitants were asked about this they said that the pictures had been painted during Lü Kuang's expedition against the Hu.[14]

One thousand, two hundred, and seventy-five *li* west of the city of Tso-mo they reached MO-CH'ENG,[15] outside of which grow flowers and fruit like that of Loyang: the only difference is that the adobe buildings are flat-roofed.

Twenty-two *li* to the west of Mo-ch'eng they came to the walled town of HAN-MO,[16] 15 *li* to the south of which was a large monastery which had over 300 monks and a golden statue 1 *chang* 6 feet high. This is of such exceptional magnificence that it seems to glow. It always faces east and will never look towards the west. The elders of the place said that it had originally flown there from the south. The King of Yüt'ien [Khotan] had come to worship it in person and had tried to take it back with him; but one night on the journey it had suddenly disappeared and returned to the spot from which he had removed it. The king thereupon raised a stūpa, which he endowed with 400 households for its maintenance. If anyone who is ill covers the corresponding part of the statue with gold leaf he is mysteriously cured. Later generations erected thousands of statues 1 *chang* 6 feet high with stūpas beside it, and tens of thousands of coloured banners and parasols were hung on them. Most of the banners were from the country of Wei, on many of which was written in the clerkly script 'nineteenth year of *t'ai-ho* [495] 'second year of *ching-ming*' [501], or 'second year of *yen-ch'ang*' [513]; there was just one dated to the time of Yao Hsing [394–415].[17]

[13] At or near the site of Charchan (Ch'iehmo).
[14] In AD 383–4.
[15] Probably a town in the country of Han-mo.
[16] The identification of this name is problematical, but it must have been somewhere between modern Keriya (Yüt'ien) and Chira.
[17] Second ruler of the Later Ch'in in the north-west.

Another 878 *li* to the west[18] they came to the country of YÜ-
T'IEN [Khotan], whose king wore a golden crown like a
cockscomb with a piece of silk 2 feet long and 5 inches wide
hanging down behind as a decoration. His ceremonial insignia
included drums, trumpets, gongs, a bow and arrows, two
halberds, and four lances. He had only 100 swordsmen as his
attendants.

It is the custom in that country for women to wear trousers
and belted tunics and to gallop around on horses just as their
menfolk do. The dead are cremated, after which the bones are
buried and a stūpa raised over them. Those who are in
mourning cut off their hair and shave their faces as marks of
their grief. When their hair has grown four inches long again
they go back to normal living. The king alone is not cremated
when he dies; he is buried in a coffin far out in the wilds, and
temples and sacrifices are established in his memory.

Once a King of Khotan did not believe the Buddha's Law. A
Hu trader brought a monk called P'i-lu-chan [Vairocana] with
him, installed him under an apricot tree south of the city, and
went to the king to say apologetically, 'I have ventured to
install a foreign monk under an apricot tree south of the city
wall.' The infuriated monarch went to see Vairocana. 'The
Tathāgata,' Vairocana said to him, 'has sent me here to bid
your majesty build a stūpa shaped like an upturned bowl, in
order to ensure yourself eternal blessings.' 'If you let me see the
Buddha,' replied the king, 'I shall do as you tell me.'
Vairocana informed the Buddha by ringing a bell, and the
Buddha sent Lo-hou-lo [Rāhula] to him. Rāhula took the form
of a Buddha; the True Image appeared out of the void. The
king threw himself to the ground, and [later] founded a
monastery under the apricot tree and had a picture of Rāhula
painted. When Rāhula suddenly disappeared the king built
avihāra to enclose the picture. Now a tile-covered image
projects above the building; all who see it turn towards it. It
contains a shoe of a Pratyeka Buddha made neither of leather
nor of silk that has not decayed to the present day; nobody
knows of what it is made.

---

[18] The distance is too great: 278 *li* would be better.

In my opinion the territory of Khotan does not exceed 3,000 *li* from east to west.

On the 9th of the seventh month of the second year of *shen-kuei* [519] they entered the country of CHU-CHÜ-PO,[19] where the people live in the hills and the various fruits all grow in abundance. Their diet is bread of leavened wheat. They do not slaughter animals, eating meat only when the animals die naturally. Their way of life and their speech are similar to those of Khotan, and their script is like the Brahman one. The boundary of this country can be gone round in five days.

On the 8th of the eighth month they entered the territory of the country of HAN-P'AN-T'O,[20] and after travelling west for six days they climbed into the Ts'ung-ling Mountains.[21] Three more days' journey to the west brought them to the walled town of PO-YÜ,[22] and three further days to the Pu-k'o-yi mountains. This is an extremely cold place, deep in snow throughout the year.

There was a lake in the mountains in which lived an evil dragon. Once, when 300 merchants encamped for the night beside this lake, the dragon was so angry that it drowned them. On learning of this the King of Han-p'an-t'o abdicated in favour of his son and went to Wu-ch'ang [Udyāna] to learn Brahman spells. Having mastered all these arts within four years he resumed his throne, went to the pool, and cast a spell on the dragon. The dragon turned into a human being and apologized to the king for his wrongdoing. The king exiled him into the Ts'ung-ling Mountains, over 2,000 *li* from this pool. This king was the ancestor in the thirteenth generation of the present monarch.

From here westwards precipitous mountain tracks lead across precipices 1,000 *li* tall and overhanging cliffs rising 10,000 measures. This is indeed a natural obstacle that reaches to the sky. The Meng Gates and T'ai-hang Mountains are not

---

[19] Probably in the valleys of the Polung and Ulugh south of Karghalik (Yehch'eng) where Yül-arik and Kök-yār are to be found.

[20] The high Tāsh-kurgān valley of south-west Sinkiang.

[21] The Taghdumbash, Mariom, and Little Pamirs.

[22] Not firmly identified. The text in the following four paragraphs seems a little jumbled.

steep compared with them; the Hsiao Pass and Lung Hills seem level ground.[23]

From the moment they started into the Ts'ung-ling Mountains they climbed with every step they took until at the end of four days they reached the highest range. Although one only seems to be at a middling or low altitude here it is in fact half way up to the sky.

The capital of Han-p'an-t'o is among the mountain peaks. From the Ts'ung-ling westwards all rivers flow west, and people say that it is the centre of the world. The common folk breach the banks of rivers for water for agriculture. When they heard that in China the fields were not sown until it rained they laughed and said, 'How can heaven be on time?' East of the city was the Meng-chin River[24] which flowed to Sha-le (Kashgar). No vegetation grows on the high peaks of the Ts'ung-ling, and the weather is already cold by the eighth month. When the north winds drive the wild geese away flying snow covers 1,000 *li*.

In the middle of the ninth month they entered the country of PO-HO [Wakhan]. The mountains were steep, the valleys deep, and the paths as precipitous as ever. The place where the king lives is walled by mountains. All the clothes the common people wear are made of felt, and as their land is so cold they live in caves, where men and animals crowd in together when biting blizzards rage. On the southern borders of the country are great snow mountains that thaw in the morning and freeze again at night; they look like peaks of jade.

At the beginning of the tenth month they reached the country of YA-TA [the Ephthalites].[25] The land is fertile, and there are mountains and waters as far as the eye can see. The people do not live in towns, and government is carried out from travelling encampments. They live in houses of felt and go wherever there is water and grass, moving to cool places in summer and to warm ones in winter. They are illiterate, completely lacking in etiquette or culture. They do not know

---

[23] Describing the climb up to the Wakhjir Pass.

[24] Probably the Tāshkurghān.

[25] Whose power was centred in eastern Afghanistan and spread much more widely across central Asia.

how to calculate the changes of the seasons; their months do not vary in length and their years never contain an intercalary month—they simply regard twelve moons as one year. They receive tribute from many countries: as far south as Tieh-lo,[26] as far north as the Ch'ih-le,[27] from Yüt'ien [Khotan] in the east and from Po-ssu [Persia] in the west—over forty countries in all.

The king lives in a large felt pavilion 40 feet square which is surrounded by a wall of carpets. He wears brocade clothes and sits on a golden throne with four golden phoenixes as its feet. When he received the embassy of the Great Wei he bowed and knelt down twice to receive the edict; then he gave a banquet during which one man sang while the guests sang with him, whereupon the banquet was over. The travellers observed no other kinds of music.

In the country of Ya-ta the king's wives also wear brocade clothes which are over 8 feet long with a 3-foot train which servants carry for them. On their heads they wear a kind of horn 3 feet high decorated with jade and pearls of many colours. When the king's wives go out they ride in chariots, and indoors they sit on thrones made in the form of six-tusked white elephants and four lions, accompanied by the wives of the ministers. Horns also rise from their parasols, making them look like the canopies over Buddha-statues.

There are distinctions in clothing between noble and humble. They are the most powerful of the foreigners of the four quarters. They do not believe in the Buddha's Law; many of them worship other gods. They kill living things and drink their blood, and use the Seven Treasures as vessels. All countries offer tribute to them, and they are extremely prosperous.

In my opinion Ya-ta is over 20,000 *li* from our capital.

At the beginning of the eleventh month they entered PO-CHIH [Pashai][28] a country whose territory is so limited that it can be walked round in seven days. The people live in the mountains and are very poor; they are so barbarous that when

---

[26] Not identified.
[27] The Turkic tribes between Lake Baikal and the Aral Sea.
[28] In the Hindu Kush, somewhere between Zebak and Chitral. The texts all read Po-ssu.

they see their king they treat him without ceremony. He only has a few attendants with him when he goes out. There is a river in this country that used to be very shallow until a landslide blocked it and made it into two lakes in which lived an evil dragon that caused many disasters. In the summer there are often torrential downpours, and the place is deep in snow during the winter; travellers consequently often have a very hard time of it. The glare from the snow is so dazzling that one has to shut one's eyes and can see nothing. Sight is restored by sacrificing to the Dragon King.

In the middle of the eleventh month they entered the country of SHE-MI.[29] As this country merges with the Ts'ung-ling range, its land is stony and barren. Most of the people are poor, and its precipitous tracks are suitable only for men and horses. A direct route leads from Po-lu-lo[30] to Wu-ch'ang [Udyāna]. One has to cross iron-chain bridges across bottomless chasms; there is nothing to hold on to, and at any moment one may suddenly fall 10,000 fathoms. This is why travellers abandon their journeys at the sight of it.

At the beginning of the twelfth month they reached WU-CH'ANG [Udyāna],[31] which extends as far as the Ts'ung-ling mountains in the north and T'ien-chu [India proper] in the south. The climate is warm and the country several thousand *li* in extent. The people are as wealthy as those of the divine region of Lin-tzu, and the land is as fertile as the best soil at Hsien-yang. This was where Viśvantara gave his children away and the bodhisattva threw down his body. Although these were the customs of long ago this way of life still continues. The king of the country is most zealous; he regularly eats vegetarian food, and he worships the Buddha morning and night to the accompaniment of drums, conches, mandolins, harps, and pipes. He only attends to state business after midday. If a man is guilty of murder he is not executed but is exiled to an uninhabited mountain and allowed to eat and drink as best he can. If there is any doubt over a case the

[29] In Chitral, south of Po-chih.
[30] Probably Gilgit.
[31] In the valley of Swāt.

litigants are given a drug that makes it possible for the innocent to be distinguished from the guilty. Sentence is given on the spot according to the gravity of the offence.

The land is rich and beautiful; the people are prosperous. All the grains grow and many kinds of fruit ripen. At night the sound of bells seems to fill the whole world. There are many exotic flowers in both summer and winter; lay and cleric alike pick them to offer to the Buddha.

When the King received Sung Yün, the envoy of the Great Wei, he raised his hands to his head and bowed to accept the edict. On hearing that the Empress Dowager honoured the Buddha's Law he turned east, put his hands together, and prostrated himself as he paid his respects to her from afar. He sent someone who understood the Wei language to ask Sung Yün, 'Are you from where the sun rises?' 'To the east of my country', Sung Yün replied, 'is a great ocean from which the sun rises: it is indeed as His Majesty suggests.' The king then asked, 'Does your country produce sages?' Sung Yün explained about the excellence of the Duke of Chou, Confucius, Chuang Tzu, and Lao Tzu; he went on to tell him about the silver gate-houses and golden halls of Mount P'eng-lai and the immortals and sages who live there; he spoke about the soothsaying of Kuan Lu, Hua T'o's healing powers, and Tso Tz'u's magic. He gave systematic account of all such things. 'If it is as you say,' replied the king, 'then yours is indeed a land of the Buddha. I hope to be reborn there when this life of mine is ended.'

After his audience Sung Yün went with Hui-sheng out of the city to look for relics of the Tathāgata Buddha's teaching. East of the river was the place where the Buddha dried his clothes. Formerly, when the Tathāgata was preaching in Udyāna, a Dragon King (Nāgarāja) glared angrily and caused a great storm, so that the Buddha's *sanghāṭī* [double cloak] was soaked right through. When the rain stopped the Buddha sat on the east side of a boulder and dried his *kāsāya*. Although it happened so long ago the [imprint] is as bright as new. The seams are clearly visible [on the stone], and even the individual threads of the weave can be distinctly made out. When Sung Yün and Hui-sheng first looked at it, it was as if the garment had never been taken away; and if the marks had

been scraped they would have been clearer than ever. There are stūpas to mark the places where the Buddha sat and where he dried his clothes.

West of the river is the pool where the Dragon King lives, beside which is a monastery with over fifty monks. Whenever the Dragon King performs miraculous transformations the king sacrifices to him, flinging into the lake gold and jewellery which float out later for the monks to gather up. As all the food and clothing for this monastery are provided by the dragon, it is known as the Dragon King Monastery.

Eighty *li* north of the capital is the footprint of the Tathāgata in stone. This footprint in stone, which is enclosed in a stūpa, looks as if someone had trodden in mud. Its measurements canot be taken as it varies in size. There is now a monastery there with seventy monks. Twenty paces south of the stūpa is a sprig of willow he used to clean his teeth. It grew and is now a large tree known in the Hu tongue as *p'o-lou*.

North of the city is the T'o-lo Monastery which has very many Buddha statues. Its stūpa is lofty and the monks' cells are crowded closely together. The monastery is surrounded by 6,000 gilded statues. The great assembles that the king calls every year, when all the monks of the country gather together are held here. Sung Yün and Hui-sheng saw that the monks of this monastery observed the Discipline with great asceticism and were much impressed by their style of life; they gave two of their own slaves to be menials there.

After travelling for eight days to the south-east of the city they came to the place where the Tathāgata gave his body to feed the hungry tigress while he was practising asceticism. It was a high mountain, a precipitous peak jutting into the clouds where noble trees and magical fungus abounded amid captivating forests and streams and flowers whose colours dazzled the eye. Sung Yün and Hui-sheng gave some of their travelling expenses to have a stūpa built on the summit, and they engraved for it in the clerkly script an inscription recording the achievements and virtue of the Wei. On this mountain there is the Gathered Bones Monastery with more than 300 monks.

Over 100 *li* south of the capital is the place in the country of Mo-hsiu [Masūra] where the Tathāgata once took off his own

skin to make paper and broke off a bone to use as a writing implement. King Aśoka built a stūpa 10 *chang* high around it. Where the bone was broken the marrow flowed out and stained the stone. From the look of its glossy colour it is still as fatty as when the bone was newly split.

Five hundred *li* to the south-west of the city is the Shan-ch'ih [Dantaloka—Goodness Giving] Mountain[32] which has springs of sweet water and fruit as excellent as that mentioned in the scriptures. As the mountain valleys are warm, the plants and trees here stay green throughout the winter. When Sung Yün and Hui-sheng were there it was early spring, and warm winds were already blowing. What with the birds singing in the spring trees and the butterflies dancing through the flowers, Sung Yün was so overcome with homesickness as he gazed at the fragrant scenery of this distant land that his feelings went to his stomach and activated an old ulcer. The illness lingered on for months before Brahmin spells restored him to health.

To the south-east of the summit is the stone hut of the crown prince. It has one entrance and two rooms, and ten paces in front of it is a large square boulder on which the crown prince is supposed to have sat. King Aśoka raised a stūpa to commemorate this. One *li* south of the stūpa is the place where the crown prince had a thatched hut. Fifty feet down the mountain to the north-east was the place where the son and daughter of the crown prince tied [a rope] around a tree and refused to go; and the tree still stands where the Brahmin beat them with a stick till their blood flowed to the ground. There is now a spring at the spot where the blood fell. Three *li* west of the hut was where Śakra [Indra] changed himself into a lion and sat on the road to Mandi [or Madri]. The mark of the lion's tail and claws are still clearly visible on the rock. The cave of Adjuta and the place where the disciples fed his blind parents are also marked with stūpas.

On the mountain are the beds of the 500 arhats of antiquity and two lines of seats facing each other to the north and south. There is a huge monastery with 200 monks as well as one to the north of the spring from which the crown prince drank. Several donkeys carry grain regularly up the mountain; they come and

---

[32] Probably the hill Mekhasanda near Shāhbāz-ghari, east of Mardān.

go by themselves without anyone to drive them. They set out at dawn and arrive at noon, in time for the midday meal. They do this in obedience to Śiva, the guardian deity of the monastery.

There was once a novice at this monastery who often used to cover himself with ashes and enter into divine meditation. When the disciplinary monk pulled at him, his skin and bones came apart without him being aware of it; and the deity Śiva was there where the novice had covered himself in ash. The king of the country set up a temple to Śiva and made a picture of him which was cvered in gold leaf.

Over the mountains was the P'o-chien Monastery that had been built by yakṣas. It had eighty monks, and it was said that arhats and yakṣas came to feed them, do the sprinkling and sweeping, and fetch firewood for them so that no common monk would stay there. The Great Wei monk Tao-jung went there to worship then left, not daring to linger.

In the middle of the fourth month of the first year of *cheng-kuang* [520] they entered the country of KAN-T'O-LO [Gandhāra].[33] The terrain is like that of Udyāna. The country was originally called Ye-po-lo, but it was defeated by Ya-ta, who put their *Ch'in-chin*[34] on the throne; they had now ruled the country for two generations. They were cruel and violent men much given to slaughter, not believing in the Buddha's Law but sacrificing to spirits and demons. As the people of the country were all of Brahminic stock, honoured the Buddha's teachings, and loved to read the scriptures, they deeply resented having these kings thrust suddenly upon them. The present king, proud of his martial prowess, had been fighting continually for three years with Chi-pin [Kashmir] over territory. He had 700 war-elephants, each of which carried ten halberdiers and attacked the enemy with swords tied to its trunk. The king often stayed on the frontier for long periods without returning, thus exhausting both his army and his subjects and making the common people murmur with discontent.

When Sung Yün reached the royal military encampment and handed the king the imperial decree, the king was so rude

---

[33] Essentially the valley of the Kābul from Jālālābad to the Indus, possibly extending to the upper Jhelum valley.

[34] Probably the Turkish word *tegin*, 'prince'.

and discourteous as to receive it seated. Realizing that he was a barbarian too distant to be controlled, Sung Yün was unable to upbraid him and had to put up with his arrogance. The king sent a messenger to say to Sung Yün, 'Surely it has been most exhausting to come through so many countries on a journey beset with so many dangers.' To this Sung Yün replied, 'My Emperor, with his deep love for the Great Vehicle, wants scriptures from distant lands. Even though the journey has been dangerous I would not say that I was tired. But Your Majesty personally takes his armies to this remote frontier and keeps them here for years on end. Surely that is exhausting.' 'Your questions puts me to shame, sir,' the king replied. 'I am unable to subdue that tiny country.'

Sung Yün had earlier let it pass when the king read the imperial decree seated, thinking that as a barbarian the king could not be taken to task over etiquette; but now that they had exchanged visits and had something of a personal friendship he put the matter to him. 'There are high mountains and low hills,' he said, 'great rivers and little streams; and of the people on this earth some are mighty and others humble. The kings of the Ephthalites and Udyāna both bowed when they received the decree, so why should Your Majesty alone not do so?' 'If I saw the Wei King in person I would bow to him,' replied the King of Gandhāra, 'but what is wrong with reading a letter from him sitting down? When people get letters from their parents they read them sitting down, so of course it shows no discourtesy if I stay seated to read a letter from the Great Wei, which is like a father and mother to me.' Sung Yün was unable to cap this argument. Later Sung Yün was taken to a monastery which was very poorly provided for.

The King of Pa-t'i [Bactria] sent the King of Gandhāra a pair of lion cubs at this time and when Sung Yün saw the spirit and ferocity of these animals he realized that Chinese paintings had never captured their likeness.

After travelling west for another five days they came to the place where the Tathāgata gave his head away.[35] There is a stūpa and a monastery with twenty monks here. Another three days' journey west brought them to the great Hsin-t'ou [Indus]

[35] Taxila, west of Rāwalpindi.

River, on the west bank of which the Tathāgata had emerged
as a giant *makara* fish and fed the people with his flesh for
twelve years. Here a commemorative stūpa had been built,
and the rock still bears the pattern of fish scales.

Another thirteen days to the west brought them to the city of
FO-SHA-FU, whose straight walls stand in a fertile river
plain.[36] The people are many and prosperous and it luxuriates
in woods and streams. The land is rich, and the way of life
simple and good. There are old monasteries everywhere, both
inside and outside the city, in which live many famous and
holy monks of lofty and outstanding conduct. One *li* north of
the city is the White Elephant Palace, in which the very many
Buddha statues are all handsome and majestic stone ones
covered in gold leaf. They were a dazzling sight. In front of the
monasterty grows the tree to which the white elephant was
once tied; it was because of this that the monastery was
founded. The blossom and leaves are like those of the jujube-
tree, but the fruit only begins to ripen in late winter. The old
men of the city told them of the tradition that when this tree
perished the Buddha's Law would die with it. Inside the
temple is a picture of the crown prince and his wife asking the
brahmin for their son and daughter; all the Hu who see this
picture weep for sorrow.

After a further day's journey to the west they came to the
place where the Tathāgata plucked out his eyes to give them
away. There was also a stūpa-monastery in which was a stone
with a footstep of Kāśyapa Buddha.

Travelling west for another day they took a boat across a
deep river over 300 feet wide,[37] 60 *li* to the south-west of which
they reached the city of KAN-T'O-LO [Gandhāra].[38] Seven *li*
to the south-east of this is the Ch'üeh-li Stūpa.[39] (*The Life of
Tao-jung* says: '4 *li* east of the city.') Its origin can be traced
back to the Tathāgata's lifetime. Once when he and his
disciples were begging for food here he pointed east of the city
and said, 'Two hundred years after I enter nirvāṇa this
country will have a king called Chia-ni-se-chia [Kaniṣka] who

[36] Probably at the Shaikhan Dheri site near Chārsadda.
[37] The Kābul River.
[38] Peshāwar.
[39] At Shāh-ji-ki-Dheri, south-east of Peshāwar.

will build a stūpa here.' Two hundred years after the Buddha entered nirvāṇa there was indeed a king of this country called Kaniṣka. He went out on an excursion east of the city and saw four boys build a stūpa about 3 feet high out of cattle-dung and then disappear. (*The Life of Tao-jung* says, 'the boys recited a gāthā to the king in mid-air.') The king was so astounded at these boys that he had a stūpa built to cover their one, but the dung stūpa kept growing till it protruded above his and stood 400 feet high. The king then made his one over 300 feet taller. (*The Life of Tao-jung* says 390 feet.) They constructed the wooden structure of this building, and it was correctly balanced at the very first attempt. (*The Life of Tao-jung* says: 'It was thirty feet high.')[40] The steps and the pillars were made of veined stone, and the wooden superstructure was in thirteen storeys.' Above this was an iron column 300 feet high and thirteen golden dishes: the total height was 700 feet. (*The Life of Tao-jung* says: 'the iron column was 88 feet high and 80 *wei* around. There were fifteen golden dishes and the total height was 632 feet.') When the building of the main stūpa was finished the dung stūpa reverted to its original form and moved 300 feet south of the main one. Once a brahmin, not believing that it was made of dung, poked it to find out and made a hole in it. Although it was so old the dung had never decomposed, and no amount of scented plaster could ever fill it. It is now covered with a heavenly palace.

The Ch'üeh-li Stūpa had been burned down by lightning three times since its construction, and the kings have always rebuilt it as it was before. The old people say that when it is burned down by lightning for the seventh time the Buddha's Law will perish.

The Life of Tao-jung says:

When the king was building the stūpa and the wooden parts had all been completed, nobody was able to raise the iron column into position. The king built towers at all four corners which he had covered with gold, silver, and other precious things. Then he, his queen, and his sons all burned incense and scattered flowers from the tops of these towers, praying to the gods with all their hearts. After

---

[40] Presumably referring to the base of the building.

this it was raised into position first time with windlass and rope. The Hu said that the four Heavenly Kings must have helped as it would have been impossible to raise it by human strength alone.

All the Buddha statues in the stūpa are of gold or precious stone, and so many are their variations that one could never hope to name them all. When the morning sun began to rise their golden haloes shimmered; and, if a light breeze blew, precious bells chimed in harmony. This is far and away the finest stūpa in the West.

When it was first completed it was covered with a net of real pearls, but the king reflected that they were worth a great deal of gold. 'When I die,' he thought, 'they might be stolen; and besides, if the stūpa falls down there may be nobody willing to rebuild it.' So he had the net of pearls taken down, put in a brass cauldron, and buried 100 paces to the north-west of the stūpa. Above it he planted the tree known as the bodhi-tree [bodhidruma]; the dense foliage of its spreading branches blots out the sky. Under the tree are four seated statues [of the Buddha] each 15 feet high. The pearls are always guarded by four dragons, and disaster would inevitably befall anyone who even thought of stealing them. There is a stone inscription giving instructions that if this stūpa falls down in future good men are to dig up the pearls and rebuild it.

Fifty-feet south of the Ch'üeh-li Stūpa is a stone stūpa perfectly round in shape and 20 feet high. It has the divine power to predict good or bad fortune. If your future is good the bells on the stūpa will ring when you touch it with a finger; but if your destiny is bad they will not ring even if you shake the whole building. As Hui-sheng was in a distant country and afraid that he might not be lucky enough to return home, he bowed to the miraculous stūpa and begged it to give him a prophecy; then he touched it with a finger and the bell rang. This prophecy relieved his mind, and he did in fact return safely.

On the day Hui-sheng left Loyang the Empress Dowager had ordered that he be given 1,000 multi-coloured 100-foot streamers, 500 brocade incense bags, and 2,000 streamers from princes, nobles, and gentlemen. Hui-sheng had been distributing them liberally at all the Buddhist shrines from Khotan to

Gandhāra, and by now they had all gone except a 100-foot banner from the Empress Dowager which he was intending to offer at the Stūpa of the King of Shih-pi [Śibi]. Sung Yün gave two of his slaves to be menial workers in the stūpa for the rest of their lives. Hui-sheng then cut down on his travelling money and commissioned skilled artisans to make bronze models of the Ch'üeh-li and the four Śākyamuni stūpas.

Then they travelled north-west for seven days and crossed a big river, which brought them to the place where the King of Śibi saved the dove. Here stood another stūpa and another monastery. Once the King of Śibi's granary was burned down, and all the rice in it was scorched. This rice still exists; if you eat just one grain of it you will never get malaria. The people of that country take one every day when they need medicine.

The Life of Tao-jung says:

They went to the country of NA-CHIA-LO-AH [Nagarahāra]⁴¹ where there was the top of the Buddha's skull. It was a rounded 4-inch square in shape and coloured whitish-yellow.

Underneath it had so many finger-sized holes that it looked like a beehive. At the Ch'i-ho-lan [Khakkara] Monastery there are thirteen of the Buddha's cassocks; when measured their length varies. There is also a monastic staff of the Buddha's 17 feet long that is kept in a wooden tube and covered with gold leaf. Its weight is not constant; at its heaviest 100 men could not lift it and at its lightest one man can. In the city of Nagarahāra are a tooth and some hair of the Buddha that are both kept in jewelled boxes; offerings are made to them morning and evening. In the Chü-lo-lo-lu [Gopāla] cave they saw the image of the Buddha. When they took fifteen paces into the cave and looked westwards towards the entrance all the pictures were clearly visible, but when they looked at them from close to they could see nothing. When they felt with their hands there was nothing but a stone wall. It was only when they walked slowly backwards that they saw the pictures [again]. Such striking images are rare in all the world. In front of the cave is a square boulder on which are footprints of the Buddha, and 100 paces to the south-west of the cave is the place where he washed his clothes. One *li* north of this cave is the cave of Mu-lien [Maudgalyāyana], to the north of which is a mountain. Under this mountain is a stūpa 100 feet high which the seven Buddhas built with their own hands. It is said that when it collapses the Buddha's Law will perish with it. There were also seven

---

⁴¹ Centred on Jalālābād in eastern Afghanistan.

stūpas with a stone inscription to the south of them that was said to be in the Tathāgata's own writing. The Hu letters are still clear and can be read to this day.

Hui-sheng spent two years in Udyāna, but a detailed account of the various customs of the Western Hu cannot be given here. In the second month of the second year of *cheng-kuang* [521/2] he returned to the capital.

In my opinion *Hui-sheng's Travels* often fails to give a full account, so I have also quoted from the *Life of Tao-jung* and Sung Yün's family records to fill some of the gaps.

The capital measured 20 *li* from east to west and 15 *li* from north to south;[42] over 109,000 households lived in it. Apart from temples of the soil, palaces, and government offices, a 300-pace[43] square made up a ward, which had four gates. Each ward had two ward-heads, four constables, and eight gate-men. There were a total of 220 wards and 1,376 monasteries, of which 421 remained in Loyang when the capital was moved to Yeh-ch'eng in the first year of *t'ien-p'ing* [534].[44]

In the Northern Mang Hills were the Feng Wang [Prince Feng] and Ch'i Hsien-wu Wang [Prince Hsien-wu of Ch'i] Monasteries.[45] At the rocky passes to the east of the capital were the Yüan Ling-chün [Commanding General Yüan] and Liu Ch'ang-ch'iu [Comptroller Liu] Monasteries.[46] In the

---

[42] These dimensions (about 8 × 10.65 km, or 85 km²) refer to greater Loyang, not to the inner walled city which was about 6 × 9 *li* in size.

[43] About 533 metres.

[44] As Yang says in his Preface that *all* the monasteries and nunneries were moved to Yeh in 534 (when Loyang and its surrounding area were almost completely abandoned) it seems likely that 421 was the number of Buddhist temples remaining in Loyang on the eve of the move: they could not have been supported afterwards.

[45] The former was one of many built for Feng Hsi (d. 495), the brother of the formidable Empress Dowager Feng, who had seventy-two built around the country, where possible on high peaks; when reproached with the deaths thus caused, he remarked that 'posterity will see only the pagodas and will know nothing of the men and oxen.' (*WSa* 83/1, pp. 1818–20.) The latter must have been founded by or for Kao Huan, and can only have been known by his posthumous title after his death in 547.

[46] Named after the dictator Yüan Yi and the court eunuch Liu T'eng. They were perhaps near the Dowager Hu's cave temples (in the county of Kunghsien).

heights of Mount Sung were the Hsien-chü [Leisure],[47] Ch'i-ch'an [Meditation],[48] Sung-yang [South of Moung Sung],[49] and Tao-ch'ang [Bodhimanda—Enlightenment Terrace] Monasteries. On the summit was the Chung-t'ing [Central Peak] Monastery. In the passes to the south of the capital were the Shih-k'u [Stone Cave] and Ling-yen [Sacred Cliff] Monasteries.[50] By the Ch'an and Chien rivers to the west of the capital were the Pai Ma [White Horse] and Chao-le [Radiant Joy] Monasteries. All such monasteries as these were outside the city limits and consequently not included in the figures, so I have listed them here individually.

[47] The finest of all the monasteries in the hills, built for Shih-tsung. (*WSa* 90, pp. 1931–2.) The Dowager Hu's threat to retire here in 524 hastened the end of Yüan Yi's dictatorship. (*WS* 16, p. 405.)

[48] Thought by T'ang Yung-t'ung to be a Dhyāna establishment. (1963, p. 776.)

[49] Built for the Dhyāna master Sheng in 484. (Inscription in Fan, p. 352.)

[50] The impressive and well-known cave temples at the Yi-ch'üeh or Lungmen gorges 13 kilometres south of Loyang are covered in Mizuno and Nagahiro (1939) and Tsukamoto (1942); dealt with more briefly in Kenneth Ch'en (1964); and illustrated in the Lung-men Pao-kuan-so's album. The three main Northern Wei imperial temples were created between 500 and 523 at the cost of 802,366 work-days; in addition aristocrats, officials, clergy, nuns, and commoners had hundreds of other images carved in the cliffs of the Yi.

Appendix I

The Texts and Date of the *Lo-yang ch'ieh-lan chi*

The extant versions of the *Lo-yang ch'ieh-lan chi* are all apparently descended from the two Ming printed editions— the Ju-yin t'ang and *Ku-chin yi-shih* ones—which contain the only known texts of the work to have survived the millennium separating them from the time of the book's composition. Later editions are all based directly or indirectly on one or both of these. As they are defective some modern editors have also drawn on citations, paraphrases, or summaries of passages from the *LYCLC* found in works earlier than the two earliest editions. They have also used their imaginations. A summary of the various editions of the *LYCLC* can be found at the end of this appendix. The two best working editions of the *LYCLC* and those on which my translation is based are the modern ones of Fan Hsiang-yung and Chou Tsu-mo.

The evidently delapidated texts, the discrepant readings of the Ju-yin t'ang and *Ku-chin yi-shih* editions, and the frequent variations between them and the passages quoted or paraphrased from the *LYCLC* in other works of the Ming period and earlier all combine to suggest there is not one sentence in the book that can with certainty be taken as just what Yang Hsüan-chih wrote. The occasional abrupt change of subject in the middle of a train of thought or exposition, and a few pre-Ming quotations from the *LYCLC* not found in the surviving editions,[1] show that an indeterminable but probably small amount has been lost in transmission. The chapter that has most obviously suffered in transmission is the fifth, where the many foreign names from central and southern Asia have led copyists into manifest and manifold error and confusion.

But although the individual components of the book's fabric are faulty, the work as a whole is in reasonably good shape. There is no evidence of later accretions to the text such as those made to the contemporary *Ch'i min yao shu* over the centuries; and we have no grounds for believing that it has been thought worthy of systematic corruption by later generations.

---

[1] Four are collected on p. 355 of Fan's edition; but three of these may possibly have been wrongly attributed to the *LYCLC*.

273

One important structural loss has been the elimination of Yang's original divison of the book into a main text and notes. We know from the T'ang student of historiography Liu Chih-chi (661–721) that when Yang wrote the book he observed a distinction, not uncommon at the time, between his main text written in normal-sized writing and, interspersed within it, his own notes written in a smaller hand in double columns within the width of a single column of main text. This device, known as *tzu chu*, was used by a number of historians of the period writing in their private capacity to provide a mass of detail while leaving the main lines of their arguments uncluttered.[2] This method may have been borrowed from Buddhist writings of the period.[3]

During the 1,000 years between the book's composition and its earliest surviving editions the text and notes were run in together. Although some editors have followed the suggestion made by Ku Kuang-ch'i (1770–1839) that scholars should try to reconstruct the book's original format,[4] their efforts are only guesswork; it is not surprising that there is little agreement among them. The only place where a distinction between Yang's original main text and notes can be made with certainty is in the section on the Ning-hsüan Monastery in chapter 5. After a brief statement of who founded the monastery and where it was to be found, the word 'note' (*chu*) introduces a fuller account of the history and beauty of the site. This presumably was originally in small script: but where this particular note ended cannot be known: it may have been only a sentence long, or it may have included nearly all the rest of the chapter. The running together of Yang's main text and notes makes his structure less obvious to the eye, and gives the impression of excessive inconsequentiality that is not entirely justified. However, in making this version I have left the transmitted structure as it stands rather than impose any arbitrary new division of text and notes apart from that implied by the paragraphing of the translation.

Another change, perhaps of no great importance, has been the variation in the number of *chüan* into which the *LYCLC* was divided. Generally, as in all surviving texts, it has been in five *chüan*. Sometimes it is recorded in bibliographies and library catalogues as in one *chüan*—which may only mean that it was found as one volume. More surprising are the references in some Sung, Yuan, and Ming booklists to the *LYCLC* in three *chüan*, which would not suit the

---

[2] *Shih t'ung* 17, p. 1/85.

[3] Ch'en Yin-k'o, 'Tu *LYCLC* hou', reprinted on pp. 385–8 of his 1971 volume, and in abridged form on pp. 374–9 of Fan.

[4] *Ssu-shih-chai chi* 14, quoted on p. 364 of Fan.

present contents of the book, divided as they are in surviving texts into the areas within the city wall and to the east, south, west and north of it. This minor mystery cannot be solved on the evidence now available.[5]

The dates of the *LYCLC*'s composition can be established with reasonable confidence. We know from its Preface that its writing was prompted by a visit to the ruins of Loyang in the fifth year of *wu-ting* (547). The same Preface also refers to the 'August Wei' (Huang Wei), an expression that would have been reckless folly after the seizure of the Eastern Wei throne by Kao Yang in the fifth month of 550. Nothing in the book reveals any knowledge of events after the Ch'i accession; and there is no sure indication that Yang Hsüan-chih ever served the Ch'i regime.[6] The book cannot have been finished before the killing of Kao Yang's elder brother and deadly rival, the dictator Kao Ch'eng, in the seventh month of 549, as it included high priase for one man executed for an earlier, unsuccessful attempt on Kao Ch'eng's life and for another who died in prison on suspicion of being involved. (On these events see chapter 1 of Part I.) Such praise would probably have been fatal for its author during Kao Ch'eng's lifetime, but may well have been acceptable after his death. It therefore seems likely that the book was finished in late 549 or early 550.

THE PRINCIPAL EDITIONS OF THE LO-YANG CH'IEH-LAN CHI[7]

1. The *Ju-yin t'ang edition* is the earliest surviving edition of *LYCLC*, and has been dated by its appearance to the *chia-ching* (1522–66) or *lung-ch'ing* (1567–72) years; its plates would appear to have been cut in Soochow. The establishment 'Ju-yin t'ang' named in the edition's margins has been identified, tentatively but plausibly, by Chao Wan-li with the Ju-yin ts'ao-t'ang of Lu Pien of Ch'ang-chou, an amateur of Six Dynasties literature. This rare book has been reproduced several times in this century, notably in the Sung-fen shih edition of Tung K'ang in 1915, and in the third series of the Ssu-pu ts'ung-k'an with a preface written in 1936.

It is possible that the Ju-yin t'ang version is the *LYCLC*'s *editio princeps*. I know of no definite reference to any earlier printing of the

---

[5] See the entries from many lists gathered on pp. 358–60 of Fan.

[6] See ch. 1 of Part I.

[7] What follows is largely based on the information given by Chou Tsu-mo in the *hsü-li* (introduction) to his edition, by Fan Hsiang-yung in the *li-yen* (introduction) and the second appendix to his edition; on the article of Hatanaka Jōen; and on my examination of the various editions at Peking Library and elsewhere.

book, unless Chao Ch'i-mei's 'old edition' (see below) was not referring to this one. Unfortunately it offers a defective text. Black gaps are substituted for some missing characters; other passages are manifestly corrupt; and three pages from *chüan* 2 have been missing since late Ming times.

In this edition the first character of the surname Erhchu (which occurs with such baleful frequency) is written with the short character 尒.

2. The *Ku-chin yi-shih edition* of Wu Kuan, a beautifully printed book, generally dated to the *wan-li* period (1573–1620), is evidently *not* derived from the Ju-yin t'ang edition. Its readings are often different; it gives the long character for the first syllable of Erhchu; and its gaps for missing characters are in white. It is more corrupt than the Ju-yin t'ang, evidently being derived from an inferior manuscript tradition. The bibliophile Ch'ien Tseng (1629–1701) transcribes a postface to *LYCLC* by Chao Ch'i-mei in which Chao tells how he obtained a copy of the *Ku-chin yi-shih* edition in 1599, was appalled by its corrupt state, bought four manuscript copies of *LYCLC*, and with their help corrected 488 wrong characters and added 320 missing ones. In 1606 he was able to correct over fifty more characters with the help of another 'old edition'. This shows that 1599 is the latest possible date for the *Ku-chin yi-shih* edition. Whether the 'old edition' was the Ju-yin t'ang one or an even earlier one cannot be told. Unfortunately Chao Ch'i-mei's collated text was destroyed in the fire that burned down his library; the manuscripts he used do not seem to have survived either.[8]

3. The *Lü chün t'ing*, or *Chin-tai mi-shu edition* was cut for the great bibliophile, publisher, and patron of scholarship Mao Chin (1599–1659). 'Lü chün t'ing' was a name sometimes used by Mao for his publishing house; and the *Chin-tai mi-shu* was one of many series he edited. This edition is generally dated to the *ch'ung-chen* years (1628–44) and appears to be derived largely from the Ju-yin t'ang edition, differing in only about 110 readings.

4. The *Han-Wei ts'ung-shu* editions. Modern Chinese editors seem to be aware of the *LYCLC* included in the expanded reprint of this series produced by Wang Mo in or around 1791 as the *Tseng-ting Han-Wei ts'ung-shu*. Hatanaka observes that *LYCLC* was previously included in the second instalment of this famous series published in the *wan-li* years (1573–1620) by Ho Yün-chung as the *Kuang Han-Wei ts'ung-shu*, and that the 1791 *LYCLC* was an emended version of the *wan-li* edition, which in turn is evidently based on Wu Kuan's *Ku-chin yi-shih* edition.

---

[8] Ch'ien Tseng, *Tu shu min ch'iu chi*, cited on pp. 360–1 of Fan.

5. *Hsü Yü-ch'ing's edition* is undated, but believed by Fan to be of early Ch'ing date and to be derived from Wu Kuan's *Ku-chin yi-shih* version.

6. The *Chen-yi t'ang edition*, set in movable type with a preface written in 1811 by a Mr. Wu (Wu Chih-chung), is the earliest edition to combine the Ju-yin t'ang and *Ku-chin yi-shih* traditions. It also drew on the reading of an unknown manuscript version by one Ts'ao Yen in 1785.

7. The *Hsüeh-chin t'ao-yuan edition*, published by the Chao-k'uang ko of Chang Hai-p'eng, is apparently derived from the Ju-yin t'ang through the Lü chün t'ing's *Chin-tai mi-shu* edition.

8. The *LYCLC chi-cheng* of Wu Jo-chün (preface and postface both bearing dates in 1834) is the first surviving critical edition of *LYCLC*, and the first known attempt to reconstitute the original division between main text and notes.

Wu took the Ju-yin t'ang edition as basic, collating it with the earlier *Han-Wei ts'ung-shu* and the Lü chün t'ing editions and passages from the *T'ai-p'ing yü-lan*, *T'ai-p'ing kuang-chi*, *Fa-yüan chu-lin*, and other books.

The *chi-cheng* edition was recut and reprinted for the Hsi hua ch'an-yuan of Loyang (preface, 1876) and again for Li Pao-hsün postfaces, 1903).

9. The *LYCLC kou-shen* of T'ang Yen (preface dated to 1915) is an eclectic edition, with occasional readings of the editor's own invention, and a new arrangement of the text. It appeared in the *Lung-ch'i ching-she ts'ung-shu*.

SIX MODERN EDITIONS

10. The *Taishō Tripitaka edition*, included in the great Japanese Buddhist canon (*Taishō shinshū daizōkyō*), is based on the Ju-yin t'ang edition with some variant readings noted. This is only a sketchy critical edition and should not be treated as authoritative.

11. The *LYCLC chi-chu* of Chou Yen-nien, lithographed for the Wan-chieh chai (Shanghai, 1937), follows the layout of the *kou-shen* edition, and is annotated with the findings of many years' reading.

12. *LYCLC ho-chiao-pen* of Chang Tsung-hsiang, first published in 1930 simply as *Lo-yang ch'ieh-lan chi*, was reprinted under fuller title (Shanghai, 1955). Chang's text is compiled from the Ju-yin t'ang and other early editions, and includes a summary critical apparatus.

13. The *LYCLC chiao shih* of Chou Tsu-mo was first published in 1956; reference is to the Peking 1963 edition. An excellent working edition including a critical apparatus and commentary. Chou's choice of readings seems generally sound, and his comments to the point.

14. *LYCLC chiao chu* of Fan Hsiang-yung (Shanghai, 1958). The fullest critical apparatus and commentary of any edition of *LYCLC* yet published: a monument of painstaking scholarship.

15. *Ch'ung k'an LYCLC* of Hsü Kao-juan (special publication no. 42 of the Institute of History and Philology, Academia Sinica Taipei, 1960), is a good edition superseded before publication by the better ones of Chou Tsu-mo and Fan Hsiang-yung. Index of personal and place names.

A Japanese translation by Iriya Yoshitaka is included in *Rakuyō garanki, Suikei chū*, vol. 21 of Heibonsha's *Chūgoku koten bungaku taikei*, Tokyo, 1974.

Appendix II

The problem of the Great Market

The location and size of the Great Market in the western suburb, and its relation to the wards where the tradespeople and merchants who worked there lived, present problems that will not be finally settled until more ground surveys and spadework can recover the layout of this part of the city.

Yang gives some figures for east–west distances relating to this market in chapter 4 of the 'Record' which are apparently irreconcilable unless we take such figures as '3 *li*' to mean 'in the 3rd *li*'. He tells us that the distance from the Ch'ang-ho Gate of the inner city wall to the Chang-fen Bridge over the north–south waterway that marked the city's western limit was 7 *li*. That this waterway and the inner city wall ran virtually parallel is visible from a modern map. Within these 7 *li* we have to fit the Pai-ma Monastery 3 *li* (or in the 3rd *li*) from the Hsi-yang Gate and south of the highway, the market 4 *li* (or in the 4th *li*) from the gate and also south of the highway, the Yen-ku ward west of the market, then the Princes' Quarter which was 2 *li* wide. If we have to allow a full *li* for the width of the Yen-ku ward, that leaves a *li* for the market's dimension from east to west.

Yang also locates the market by reference to some other landmarks from Han times that are also mentioned by his contemporary Li Tao-yüan in *Shui ching chu* as places past which the Ku River flowed in its southward course outside the inner city's west wall.[1] Yang tells us that to the north-west of the market were the remains of the artificial mountain and pond constructed for the immensely rich Liang Chi.[2] This 'mountain' was on an earthen slope 3 *li* to the east of the Ch'ang-ho Gate. Su Pai's 1978 sketch-map shows the ground beginning to rise about 1.5 kilometres west of the gate. If Li's '3 *li*' measures the distance to the beginning of the slope, not to the structure on it (which might well have been a *li* or two further away) this would fit in with Yang's statement that it was north-west of the market.

---

[1] *SCC* 16, pp. 3/76–7.
[2] On this see also Hans Bielenstein (1976), p. 73.

Yang tells us that south of the market were two wards inhabited by musicians, and the Princess Tower (Huang-nü t'ai), which Li identifies with the P'ing-lo kuan of Han times and places south of the Pai-ma Monastery but not as far south as the Hsi-ming Gate.[3] Now the distance between the Hsi-yang and Hsi-ming Gates is some 1,400 metres.[4] This means that the north–south length of the market has to be fitted into some 1,100 metres at most. Were there no other evidence to take into account, we could posit a market of about 500 × 1,000 metres, or 1 × 2 *li*.

But Yang also tells us, in words open to various interpretations, that the market '*chou-hui pa li*'. Ho Ping-ti takes this as meaning that there were eight wards (*pa li*) *within* its perimeter (*chou-hui*).[5] This is a rather forced interpretation of an expression that more naturally means either 'the perimeter (of the market) was 8 *li*', using *li* as a linear measure, or else 'around (the market) there were eight wards', taking *li* as 'ward'. A perimeter of 8 *li* could not fit in with the other indications of distance Yang gives; so we are left with the last meaning. The difficulty here is that the wards of Loyang were supposed to be 300 *pu* square, and there would not have been enough room for eight wards of that size and shape.

A hypothetical solution can be reached by making two assumptions. One is that, like the markets in T'ang Ch'ang-an and Loyang, the Great Market was not residential. The other is that the wards market people lived in were much smaller than standard wards. In T'ang Loyang there was a group of half-sized wards next to the city's biggest market, the West Market.[6] It would also fit in with the aristocratic values that gave Northern Wei Loyang its form if merchants were required to live in much more crowded wards than princes and officials. On this basis we can posit a market of about 1 *li* from east to west, and 1 *li* or a little more from north to south, and surrounded by wards much smaller than standard ones, in the belt of land 2 *li* wide between the Pai-ma Monastery 3 *li* from the inner city wall and the Princes' Quarter beginning 5 *li* from it.

[3] On this see also Bielenstein, p. 61.

[4] Chung-kuo k'o-hsüeh-yüan k'ao-ku yen-chiu-so Lo-yang kung-tso-tui (1973), p. 200 and map on p. 199.

[5] Ho Ping-ti (1966), p. 101.

[6] On these T'ang cities and their markets see Hiraoka (1957); Chung-kuo k'o-hsüeh-yüan k'ao-ku yen-chiu-so (1961), pp. 96–7; Chung-kuo she-hui k'o-hsüeh-yüan k'ao-ku yen-chiu-so (1978); Su Pai (1978/3).

Appendix III

The Grain-processing Machinery in the Ching-ming Monastery

The water-powered grain-processing machinery installed in the Ching-ming monastery and described by Yang Hsüan-chih at the beginning of chapter 3 of the 'Record' raises some important and tantalizing questions.

First, the meaning of the four characters that identify the machines: ?*nien* 礴, *wei* 磑, *ch'ung* 舂, *po* 簸. The first of these is not found in dictionaries; but the general view of commentators that it was a variant of *nien* 碾 can be accepted.[1] The combination *nien wei* is used elsewhere to refer to water-powered milling machinery in Eastern Wei times,[2] as it often was in T'ang times. (T'ang usage of the term *nien-wei* was, however, not consistent.[3] Japanese lawyers in the ninth century took it to refer to water-powered *shui-tui* tilt-hammers.[4] They may have been confused in discussing foreign technical equipment, or they may have been following late T'ang usage: some Tun-huang texts appear to confuse *tui* and *wei*, possibly because both mills and hammers were powered by the same stream.[5])

Although *nien* and *wei* are sometimes used in combination as a generic term for milling machinery,[6] their separate meanings are distinct.[7] *Nien* has referred in recent centuries to the edge-runner mill,[8] and a pottery model of one remarkably similar to the *nien* mills turned by animals or people in Chinese villages today was found in a Sui tomb in Anyang.[9] The Yuan agronomist Wang Chen describes and illustrates *nien* powered both by animals and water.[10]

---

[1] In the following pages ?*nien* and *nien* are used as here to distinguish between the two characters.

[2] *PCS* 18, p. 236.

[3] On the various meanings given the term see Amano Motonosuke (1962), pp. 901–4.

[4] Twitchett (1957), pp. 533–5.

[5] As Amano points out, loc. cit. He also deals with an even later change of usage in legal texts of *nien* and *wei* as referring to the upper and lower stones of a rotary grinding mill.

[6] As Gernet suggested in discussing this passage (1956, p. 140).

[7] As Amano, Liu Hsien-chou, and Needham have shown.

[8] Following Needham's translation of this term, as of most of the others in this appendix (1954– , vol. 4, part 2, especially table 56.)

[9] Illustrated in Liu Hsien-chou (1963), p. 79, fig. 173.

[10] *Nung shu* 26, p. 285; 19, p. 406. The latter type is also found in Hsü Kuang-ch'i's *Nung-cheng ch'üan shu* 18, p. 364.

All the early pictures of water-powered *nien* (*shui-nien*) show the power source to be a horizontally-mounted water-wheel. A revolving upright pole, at the bottom of which the water-wheel was mounted, turned with its top end a radial shaft that made an edge-roller grinding-wheel go round its circular channel. This could have been used either to husk millet and other grain or else to make flour.

Wei must refer to a rotary millstone grinding above a grooved surface. Amano quotes a T'ang Buddhist dictionary to show that *wei* was then the northern term for what southerners called *mo*.[11] Other sources show *wei* being used as the equivalent not only of *mo*, a stone for grinding wheat to flour, but also of *lung*, a bamboo frame packed with dried mud used for husking.[12] As Loyang was in north China, it probably refers to a stone flour mill. At least one Northern Wei pottery model of a small hand-turned quern has survived,[13] and on the evidence of such models Twitchett has suggested that the *wei* was always a hand implement.[14] But as several 'tens' of *shui nien-mo*— water-powered *nien* and *mo* mills—were installed at Ts'ui Liang's suggestion on the embankment of the Ku river outside Northern Wei Loyang to the tenfold profit of the state,[15] in addition to the water-powered ?*nien* and *wei* of the Ching-ming Monastery, it is clear that water-powered *mo* or *wei* were known at this time, as they were later. Illustrations of a water-powered *mo*, along or in combination with a *nien* roller-mill and a *lung* husker can be seen in the *Nung shu*;[16] and references to water-powered *nien-wei* equipment are not uncommon in T'ang and earlier sources.[17]

Ch'ung, now as in antiquity, basically means to pound (grain) with pestle and mortar when used as a verb.[18] For this process to be water-powered either tilt hammers or trip-hammers would be needed. Of these, the tilt or 'spoon' hammer (*ts'ao-tui* or *shao-tui*) is the simpler: water is led along a channel to fall into a spoon-shaped container at one end of a large hammer mounted on a pivot until the dish descends, lifts the hammer, empties itself of water, and lets the raised hammer drop into a mortar filled with grain.[19] A more advanced alternative is the trip hammer (*shui-tui*), or series of trip hammers

---

[11] Op. cit., p. 868.

[12] Citations in Amano, loc. cit.; Liu Hsien-chou, pp. 74–5. Descriptions and illustrations of modern *lung* and *mo* in Needham, op. cit., pp. 185–202.

[13] e.g. Liu Hsien-chou, op. cit., p. 75.

[14] 1957, p. 535.

[15] *WS* 66, p. 1481.

[16] 19, pp. 401–2, 408–9.

[17] See Needham, pp. 396 ff., and Amano, pp. 868 ff.

[18] *Shuo wen chieh tzu*, p. 148.

[19] See *Nung shu* 19, p. 416; Needham, op. cit., p. 364.

worked by lugs on a shaft either directly connected to a vertical water-wheel or geared to a horizontal one. As *shui-tui* had been known since Han times they are probably meant here.[20]

Po here probably refers to bolting to sift flour from chaff. A simple modern household bolter from Shantung is essentially a sieve pushed to and fro along parallel runners (*po-lo*) so that the flour falls through into a container underneath.[21] A water-powered version of such a device being used in a water mill with a *mo*-type mill is illustrated in a tenth-century painting by Wei Hsien, 'Cha-k'ou p'an-ch'e t'u-chüan' (The Water Mill), the earliest surviving picture of water-powered *mo* and bolter either separately or together.[22] That some such techniques of converting rotary to longitudinal motion as those shown in this picture[23] were known to Northern Wei craftsmen is likely as reciprocating devices were needed for the water-powered bellows that fed oxygen into the furnaces that produced cast iron in Han times.[24]

It is thus clear that the monastery was equipped with remarkably sophisticated grain-processing machinery. There are some indications that some of it was a recent innovation. Not the pounders: water-powered trip-hammers had been used in Chin Loyang.[25] Chin mills, however, appear to have been powered by men or animals, not water.[26] The earliest clear reference to water-mills in China tells how the great inventor Tsu Ch'ung-chih erected water-powered trip (or tilt) hammers and mills (*shui tui mo*) in an imperial park in the southern capital between 483 and 492. This equipment was thought worthy of an inspection by the emperor, an indication of its novelty.[27]

In the decades following Tsu Ch'ung-chih's achievement the few water mills that are known to have been built in north China were evidently thought very remarkable, and their use was virtually a royal prerogative. The Ching-ming Monastery was an imperial foundation; Ts'ui Liang's mills just outside Loyang belonged to the

[20] See the evidence from *TPYL* 762 and other sources and the illustration in Needham, op. cit., pp. 391 and 393–6. On Han-Chin *shui-tui* see also Jan Chao-te (1941).

[21] Liu Hsien-chou, p. 83.

[22] Reproduced in *Wen wu* 1966, 2, with analysis and diagrams of the machinery by Cheng Wei on pp. 17–25.

[23] See Needham (1970), p. 186.

[24] Needham (1954–), vol. 4, part 2, pp. 392–3. For later illustrations of water-powered bolters see *Nung shu* 19, p. 414, and P. Dutton (1932).

[25] See the references in Amano, pp. 880 ff. I am inclined to regard those T'ang and Sung writers who refer not to *lien-chi shui-tui* (multiple water-powered trip-hammers) but to *lien-chi shui-wei* as making careless substitutions of the machinery of their own day.

[26] See Amano on Tu Yü's *pa-mo*, 'eightfold mill', probably eight small querns powered by an ox.

[27] *Nan Ch'i shu* 52, p. 906.

state; and only two other sets of water-mills are known to me to have existed in the north before Sui times. One set was installed on the banks of the new channel of the River Chang after the move of the capital to Yeh;[28] and a single *shui-nien* was included in the list of very generous presents given the last Eastern Wei monarch on his abdication in 550.[29] All of these could have been built by one small group of engineers, possibly including captives or émigrés from the south. It thus appears that the water-mills of Loyang and Yeh in the first half of the sixth century were the prototypes, reserved for the most privileged minority, of the water-mills that were to be in such widespread use in T'ang China.[30]

[28] *PCS* 18, p. 236.

[29] *PCS* 4, p. 51; *WS* 12, p. 313.

[30] On these later developments see Needham, pp. 400 ff.; Gernet, pp. 141–6; Kenneth Ch'en (1973), pp. 151–6; Twitchett (1957/2); and the references in Amano, pp. 905–7.

References

Only works cited in this book are listed. A fuller bibliography may be found in the Oxford D.Phil. thesis on which this book is based. No titles solely relating to the journey of Sun Yün and his companions are included here. Until my commentary on Yang's account of the journey is published, the interested reader may consult the thesis.

The principal editions of the *Lo-yang ch'ieh-lan chi* are listed and discussed in Appendix I above.

OTHER PRIMARY SOURCES IN CHINESE

Chan kuo ts'e, ed. Shang-hai ku-chi ch'u-pan-she (Shanghai, 1978).

Ch'i min yao shu, by Chia Ssu-hsieh: reference to *Ch'i min yao shu chin shih*, ed. Shih Sheng-han (Peking, 1958).

Chin shu, ed. CHSC (Peking, 1974).

Chou li, in *Shih-san-ching chu-shu* (Shanghai, 1935 repr.).

Chou shu, ed. CHSC (Peking, 1971).

Ch'u hsüeh chi, ed. CHSC (Peking, 1962).

Ch'üan shang-ku San-tai Ch'in Han San-kuo Liu-ch'ao wen, ed. Yen K'o-chün, CHSC repr. (Peking, 1962).

Han shu, ed. CHSC (Peking, 1962).

Han Wei Nan-pei-ch'ao mu-chih chi-shih, ed. Chao Wan-li (Peking, 1956).

Hou Han shu, ed. CHSC, Peking, 1965. (The numbering of *chüan* in this edition differs from that of most earlier ones.)

Hsü kao seng chuan, modern printing from blocks cut in Nanking in 1890. (This edition bears the misleading title *Hsu kao seng chuan erh-chi*, although it is in fact the first and only *HKSC*. The numbering of *chüan* differs from the Taishō Tripitaka's version.)

Jou-jan tzu-liao chi-lu, ed. Chung-kuo k'o-hsüeh-yüan li-shih yen-chiu-so (Peking, 1962).

Kuang hung ming chi, Ssu-pu pei-yao edition.

Liang shu, ed. CHSC (Peking, 1973).

Nan Ch'i shu, ed. CHSC (Peking, 1972).

Nan shih, ed. CHSC (Peking, 1975).

Nien-erh shih cha-chi by Chao Yi, Ssu-pu pei-yao one-volume edition.

Nung-cheng ch'üan shu, by Hsü Kuang-ch'i, CHSC (Peking, 1956).
Nung shu: see *Wang Chen nung shu*.
Pei Ch'i shu, ed. CHSC (Peking, 1972).
Pei shih, ed. CHSC (Peking, 1974).
San kuo chih, ed. CHSC (Peking, 1959).
Shang shu (*Shu ching*), in *Shih-san ching chu-shu* (Shanghai, 1935 repr.).
Shih chi, ed. CHSC (Peking, 1959).
Shih-liu kuo ch'un-ch'iu chi-pu, reconstructed by T'ang Ch'iu, Basic Sinological Series edition (Shanghai, 1958 repr.).
Shui-ching chu, by Li Tao-yüan, Basic Sinological Series edition (Shanghai, 1933). (See also *Shui-ching chu shu* by Yang Shou-ching and Hsiung Hui-chen, Peking, 1975.)
Sui shu, ed. CHSC (Peking, 1973).
Sui shu ching-chi chih, Commercial Press (Shanghai, 1955).
Sung shu, ed. CHSC (Peking, 1974).
T'ai-p'ing yü-lan, CHSC four-volume reprint of Sung edition (Shanghai, 1960).
T'ung tien, Commercial Press reprint in Shih t'ung series (Shanghai, 1935).
Tzu-chih t'ung-chien, ed. Ku-chi ch'u-pan-she (Peking, 1956).
Wang Chen nung shu, Wan-yu wen-k'u edition (Shanghai, 1963 repr.).
Wei shu, ed. CHSC (Peking, 1974).
Wen hsüan, Basic Sinological Series edition (Hong Kong, 1960 repr.).
Yen-shih chia-hsün, by Yen Chih-t'ui, in *Chu-tzu chi-ch'eng* (1959).
Yi-wen lei-chü, ed. CHSC (Shanghai, 1965).
Yüan Ho-nan chih, Ou-hsiang ling-shih edition, as reprinted in Hiraoka Takeo, ed., *Tōdai no Chōan to Rakuyō, shiryō-hen* (Tokyo, 1956).

SECONDARY WORKS IN CHINESE AND JAPANESE

Amano Motonosuke, *Chūgoku nōgyō-shi kenkyū* (Tokyo, 1962).
Chang Chi, 'Ho-pei Ching-hsien Feng-shih mu-ch'ün tiao-ch'a chi', *K'ao-ku t'ung-hsün* (1957), 3.
Chang Kuan-ying, 'Liang Chin Nan-pei-ch'ao shih-ch'i min-tsu ta pien-tung chung te Lin-chün Man', *LSYC* (1957), 2. 67–85.
Ch'en Hsüeh-lin, 'Pei Wei Liu-chen chih p'an-pien chi ch'i ying-hsiang,' *Chungchi Journal*, 2. 1 (1962), 26–50.
Ch'en Yin-k'o, *Sui T'ang chih-tu yüan-yüan lüeh lun kao* (Peking, 1963 repr.).
——, 'Tu *Lo-yang ch'ieh-lan chi* shu hou', repr. in *Ch'en Yin-k'o hsien-sheng lun chi* (Special Issue no.3 of *ASBHIP*) (Taipei, 1971), 385–8.
Cheng Ch'in-jen, *Pei Wei Chung-chu-sheng k'ao* (Taipei, 1965).
Cheng Wei, 'Ch'a-k'ou p'an-ch'e t'u-chüan,', *Wen wu* (1966), 2. 17–25.

Ch'eng Shu-te, *Chiu ch'ao lü k'ao* (Peking, 1963 edn.).

Chou Yi-liang, *Wei Chin Nan-pei-ch'ao shih-lun chi* (Peking, 1963).

Chung-kuo k'o-hsüeh-yüan k'ao-ku yen-chiu-so, *Hsin Chung-kuo te k'ao-ku shou-huo* (Peking, 1961).

——, 'Ho-nan Yen-shih Erh-li-t'ou yi-chih fa-chüeh chien pao', *K'ao-ku* (1965), 5. 215–24.

——, Erh-li-t'ou kung-tso tui, 'Ho-nan Yen-shih Erh-li-t'ou tsao-Shang kung-tien yi-chih fa-chüeh chien-pao' *K'ao-ku* (1974), 4. 234–48.

——, Lo-yang kung-tso-tui, 1973/1, 'Han-Wei Lo-yang ch'eng ch'u-pu chen-ch'a', *K'ao-ku* (1973), 4. 198–208.

——, 1973/2, 'Han-Wei Lo-yang-ch'eng yi-hao fang-chih ho ch'u-t'u te wa-wen', *K'ao-ku* (1973), 4. 209–17.

Chung-kuo she-hui k'o-hsüeh-yüan k'ao-ku yen-chiu-so Lo-yang kung-tso-tui, 1978/1, 'Han-Wei Lo-yang-ch'eng nan-chiao te Ling-t'ai yi-chih', *K'ao-ku* (1978), 1. 54–7, pls. I to III.

——, 1978/2, ' "Sui T'ang Tung-tu ch'eng-chih te k'an-ch'a ho fa-chüeh" hsü chi', *K'ao-ku* (1978), 6. 361–79.

Feng Ch'eng-chün, *Hsi-yü Nan-hai shih-ti k'ao-cheng lun-chu hui-chi* (Peking, 1957).

——, *Hsi-yü Nan-hai shih-ti k'ao-cheng yi-ts'ung*, vol. 6 (Peking, 1956); vol. 7 (Peking, 1957).

Gotō Kimpei, 'Ozai Seishū kō', *Tōyō Gakuho*, 44. 3 (1961), 3–60.

Hamaguchi Shigekuni, *Shin Kan Zui Tō shi no kenkyū*, 2 vols. (Tokyo, 1966).

——, *Tō ōchō no senjin seido* (Kyoto, 1966).

Han Kuo-p'an, *Pei-ch'ao ching-chi shih-t'an* (Shanghai, 1962).

——, *Nan-ch'ao ching-chi shih-t'an* (Shanghai, 1963).

Hatanaka Jōen, *Rakuyō garanki to sono keito'*, *Otani gakuhō* 30. 4, 39–55.

Hattori Katsuhiko, *Hoku-Gi Rakuyō no shakai to bunka* (Kyoto, 1965).

——, *Zoku Hoku-Gi Rakuyō no shakai to bunka* (Kyoto, 1968).

——, *Kodai Chūgoku no toshi to sono shūhen* (Kyoto, 1966).

Hiraoka Takeo, *Ch'ang-an yü Lo-yang* (Chinese translation of *Chōan to Rakuyō* by Yang Li-san) (Sian, 1957).

Ho Tzu-ch'üan, *Wei Chin Nan-pei-ch'ao shih lüeh* (Shanghai, 1958).

Ho-nan-sheng po-wu-kuan and Lo-yang-shih po-wu-kuan, 'Lo-yang Sui-T'ang Han-chia-ts'ang fa-chüeh', *Wen wu* (1972), 3. 49–62.

Ho-nan sheng wen-hua-chü wen-hua kung-tso-tui, 'Lo-yang Pei Wei Ch'ang-ling yi-chih tiao-ch'a', *K'ao-ku* (1966), 3. 155–8.

——, *Kung-hsien shih-k'u ssu* (Peking, 1963).

Hori Toshikazu, 'Hoku-Gi kinden hōki o meguru shomondai', *Tōyō Bunka Kenkyūjo kiyō*, 28 (1962), 54–131.

——, 'Kindensei no seiritsu', *Tōyōshi kenkyū*, 24. 1 and 2 (1965), 30–53 and 177–93.

——, *Kindensei no kenkyū* (Tokyo, 1975).

Hsia Nai, 'Tsung-shu Chung-kuo ch'u-t'u te Po-ssu Sa-sa-ch'ao yin-pi', *K'ao-ku hsüeh-pao* (1974), 1. 91–109.

Huang Chan-yüeh, '1955 nien Lo-yang Han Ho-nan hsien-ch'eng fa-chüeh pao-kao', *K'ao-ku hsüeh-pao* (1957), 4. 21–4.

Ikeda On, 'Kindensei: rokuseiki chūyō ni okeru kindensei o meguru', *Kodaishi kōza* 8 (1963), 137–74.

Ishida Yoshiyuki, 'Kozoku seiken to kanjin kizoku: toku ni Seika Saishi no ba-ai' in *Yamazaki sensei taikan kinen Tōyō-shigaku ronshu* (Tokyo, 1967), 27–37.

——, 'Kozoku seikenka ni okeru kanjin kizoku: futatabi Sai Kō hichū jikan o chushin ni shite', *Rekishigaku kenkyū*, 333 (1968), 45–51, 57.

Jan Chao-te, 'Shui-tui hsiao shih', *Wen-shih tsa-chih*, 1. 12 (1941), 64–7.

Kamata Shigeo, 'Namboku-chō Bukkyō shisōshi gairon', *Tōyō bunka* 57 (1977), 171–94.

Kaneko Hidetoshi, 'Hoku-Gi zenki no Bukkyō, in *Asiatic Studies in Honour of Dr. Jitsuzō Tamura on the Occasion of his Sixty-fourth Birthday* (Kyoto, 1968), 221–34.

——, 'Hoku-Gi zenki no seiji', *Tōyōshi kenkyū* 19. 1 (1960), 24–36.

Kao Kuan-ju, *Li-tai feng-chien wang-ch'ao yü Fo-chiao shih-wu*, vol. 1, mimographed and published by the San-shih hsüeh-hui, n.d. (bought in Peking in 1965).

Kawachi Jūzō, 'Hoku-Gi-ōchō no seiritsu to sono seikaku ni tsuite: shimin seisaku no tenkai kara kindensei e', *Tōyōshi kenkyū* 12. 5 (1953), 394–422.

Koga Noboru, 1965/1, 'Hoku-Gi no hōroku sei shikō ni tsuite', *Tōyōshi kenkyū* 24. 2 (1965), 152–76.

——, 1965/2, 'Hoku-Gi sanchō kō, *Tōhōgaku*, 31 (1965), 59–76.

Kuo Chien-pang, 'Lo-yang Pei Wei Ch'ang-ling yi-chih tiao-ch'a', *K'ao-ku* (1966), 3. 155–8.

Kuo Pao-chün, 'Lo-yang ku-ch'eng chen-ch'a chien-pao', *K'ao-ku t'ung-hsün*, 1. 1 (1955), 9–21.

Lao Kan, 'Lun Wei Hsiao-wen chih ch'ien-tu yü Han-hua' *ASBIHP* 8. 4 (1939), 485–94.

——, 'Pei Wei hou-ch'i te chung-yao tu-yi yü Pei Wei cheng-chih te kuan-hsi', *ASBIHP*, Extra vol. 4. 1 (1960), 229–69.

——, 'Pei Wei Lo-yang ch'eng-t'u te fu-yüan', *ASBIHP* 20 (1948), 229 ff.

Li Ch'ang-nien, *Ch'i min yao shu yen-chiu* (Peking, 1959).

Li Chien-jen, *Lo-yang ku-chin t'an* (Loyang, 1936).

Li Chien-nung, *Wei Chin Nan-pei-ch'ao Sui-T'ang ching-chi shih-kao* (Peking, 1963 repr.).

Li Shao-ming, 'Kuan yü Ch'iang-tsu ku-tai shih te chi-ko wen-t'i', *LSYC* (1963), 5. 165–82.

Li-shih yen-chiu pien-chi-pu (ed.), *Chung-kuo li-tai t'u-ti chih-tu wen-t'i t'ao-lun chi* (Peking, 1957).

Lin Lü-chih, *Hsien-pei shih* (Hong Kong, 1967).

Lin Shou-chin, 'Tung Chin Nan-pei-ch'ao shih-ch'i k'uang-yeh chu-tsao-yeh te hui-fu yü fa-chan', *LSYC* (1955), 6. 111–23.

Liu Hsien-chou, *Chung-kuo ku-tai nung-yeh chi-hsieh fa-ming shih* (Peking, 1963).

Liu Ju-lin, *Tung Chin Nan-pei-ch'ao hsüeh-shu pien-nien*, 2nd edn. (Changsha, 1940).

Lo Ch'ia-tzu, *Pei-ch'ao shih-k'u yi-shu* (Shanghai, 1955).

Lo-yang po-wu-kuan, 'Lo-yang Pei Wei Yüan Shao mu', *K'ao-ku* (1973), 4. 218–24, 243.

——, 'Ho-nan Lo-yang Pei Wei Yüan Yi mu tiao-ch'a', *Wen wu* (1974), 12. 53–55.

Lo-yang po-wu-kuan and Huang Ming-lan, 'Lo-yang Pei Wei Ching-ling wei-chih te ch'üeh-ting ho Ching-ling wei-chih te t'ui-tse', *Wen wu* (1978), 7. 36–41, 22.

Lu Yao-tung, 'Pei Wei P'ing-ch'eng tui Lo-yang kuei-chien te ying-hsiang', *Ssu yü yen* (Taipei), 5. 5 (15 Jan. 1968), 1389–1395, 1407.

Lü Ssu-mien, *Liang Chin Nan-pei-ch'ao shih* (Shanghai, 1948).

Lung-men pao-kuan-so, *Lung-men shih k'u* (Peking, 1961).

Ma Ch'ang-shou, *Wu-huan yü Hsien-pei* (Shanghai, 1962).

Maeda Masana, 'Hoku-Gi kan-ei bōeki ni kansuru kōsatsu: Sei-iki bōeki no tenkai o chūshin to shite', *Tōyōshi kenkyū* 13. 6 (1955), 476–504.

——, 'Hoku-Gi Heijō jidai no Orudosu sabaku nanenro', *Tōyōshi kenkyū*, 31. 2 (1972), 215–243.

Mao Han-kuang, *Liang Chin Nan-pei-ch'ao shih-tsu cheng-chih chih yen-chiu*, 2 vols. (Taipei, 1966).

Matsumoto Yoshimi, 'Hoku-Gi ni okeru kinden, sanchō ryōsei no seitei o meguru shomondai', *Tōyō Bunka Kenkyūjō kiyō*, 10 (1956), 85–177.

Matsunaga Masao, 'Hoku-Gi santō, *Tōyōshi kenkyū*, 29 (1970–1), 129–159 and 297–325.

Meng Chao-lin, 'Chi Hou Wei Hsing Wei mu ch'u-t'u-wu chi Hsing Luan mu ti fa-hsien', *K'ao-ku* (1959), 4. 209–10.

Miao Yüeh, *Tu shih ts'un k'ao* (Peking, 1963).

Miyakawa Hisayuki, *Riku-chō shi kenkyū: siiji-shakai-hen* (Tokyo, 1956).

——, 'Riku-chō jidai no doreisei no mondai', *Kodaigaku*, 8. 4 (1960), 339–49.

Miyazaki Ichisada, *Kyūhin kanjinhō no kenkyū: kakyo zenshi* (Kyoto, 1956).

——, 'Rikuchō shidai Kahoku no toshi', *Tōyōshi-kenkyū*, 20. 2 (1966), 53–74.

Mizuno Seiichi, *Unkō sekkutsu to sono jidai* (Tokyo, 1939).

Mizuno Seiichi and Nagahiro Toshio, *Ryōmon sekkutsu no kenkyū*, (Tokyo, 1941).

——, *Unkō sekkutsu*, (*Yun-kang: The Buddhist Cave-temples of the Fifth Century A.D. in North China*) (Kyoto, 1951–).

Mori Shikazō, 'Hokugi Rakuyō-sei no kibo ni tsuite', *Tōyōshi-kenkyū*, 11. 4 (1952), 317–31.

Moriya Mitsuo, 'Nanjin to hokujin', *Tōa ronsō*, 6 (1948), 36–60.

Nagasawa Kazutoshi, 'Iwayuru Sōun kōki ni tsuite', *Kodaigaku*, 14. 2 (1968), 93–107.

Nishijima Sadao, 'Gi no tondensei' *Tōyō Bunka Kenkyūjo kiyo*, 10. 1–84 (Tokyo, 1956).

——, 'Hokusei kasei sannen denryō ni tsuite', in *Wada Hokushi koki kinen Tōyō-shi ronsō* (1961), pp. 685–96.

Nishimura Genyū, *Chūgoku keizai-shi kenkyū: kinden seido hen* (Kyoto, 1968).

Nishiyama Buichi and Kumashiro Yukio, *Kōtei yakuchū Seimin yojutsu*, 2nd edn. (Tokyo, 1969).

Ochō Enichi (ed.), *Hoku-Gi Bukkyō no kenkyū* (Kyoto, 1970).

Okazaki Fumio, *Gi Shin Nambokuchō tsūshi* (1968 repr., Tokyo).

——, *Nambokuchō ni okeru shakai keizai seido* (1967 repr., Tokyo).

Ōsawa Terumichi, '*Rakuyō garanki* no jidai: josho', *Ritsumeikan bungaku*, 219 (1963), 44–54.

Shan-hsi sheng Ta-t'ung-shih po-wu-kuan and Shan-hsi sheng wen-wu kung-tso wei-yüan-hui, 'Shan-hsi Ta-t'ung shih-chia-chai Pei Wei Ssu-ma Chin-lung mu', *Wen wu* (1972), 3. 20–33.

Shan-hsi-sheng wen-wu kung-tso wei-yüan-hui and Shan-hsi Yün-kang shih-k'u wen-wu pao-kuan-so, *Yün-kang shih-k'u* (Peking, 1977).

Shan-hsi Yün-kang ku-chi pao-yang-so, *Yün-kang shih-k'u* (Peking, 1957).

Shan-pei wen-wu tiao-ch'a cheng-chi tsu, 'T'ung-wan-ch'eng yi-chih tiao-ch'a', *Wen wu* (1957), 10. 52–5.

Shih Nien-hai, *Ho shan chi* (Peking, 1963).

Shih Sheng-han, *Ts'ung Ch'i min yao shu k'an Chung-kuo ku-tai te nung-yeh k'o-hsüeh chih-shih* (Peking, 1957).

Sogabe Shizuo, 'Toshi ri-bō-sei no seiritsu katei ni tsuite', *Shigaku Zasshi*, 58. 6 (1946), 519–36.

——, *Kindenhō to sono zeieki seido* (Tokyo, 1953).

——, 'Nitchū no kinai seido', *Shirin*, 47, no. 3 (1966), 367–90.

Su Pai, 'Sheng-lo, P'ing-ch'eng yi-tai te T'o-pa Hsien-pei-Pei Wei yi-chi—Hsien-pei yi-chi chi-lu chih erh', *Wen wu* (1977), 11. 38–46.

——, 1978/1, 'Yun-kang shih-k'u fen-ch'i shih-lun' *K'ao-ku hsüeh-pao* (1978), 1. 25–38.

——, 1978/2, 'Pei Wei Lo-yang-ch'eng ho Pei-Mang-shan ling-mu—Hsien-pei yi chi chi-lu chih san', *Wen wu* (1978), 7. 42–52.

——, 1978/3, 'Sui-T'ang Ch'ang-an-ch'eng ho Lo-yang-ch'eng', *K'ao-ku* (1978), 6. 401–25.

Su P'ing-ch'i, 'Kuan yü Yang-shao wen-hua te jo-kan wen-t'i', *K'ao-ku hsüeh-pao* (1965), 1. 51–82.

Sun T'ung-hsün, *T'o-pa shih te Han-hua* (Taipei, 1962).

Ta-t'ung-shih po-wu-kuan and Shan-hsi-sheng wen-wu kung-tso wei-yüan-hui, 'Ta-t'ung Fang-shan Pei Wei Yung-ku-ling', *Wen wu* (1978), 1. 29–35.

T'ang Chang-ju, *Wei Chin Nan-pei-ch'ao shih-lun-ts'ung* (Peking, 1955).

——, *Wei Chin Nan-pei-ch'ao shih-lun-ts'ung hsü-pien* (Peking, 1959).

T'ang Chang-ju and Huang Hui-hsien, 'Shih lun Wei-mo Pei-chen chen-min pao-tung ti hsing-chih', *LSYC* (1964), 1. 97–114.

T'ang Huan-ch'eng, *Chung-kuo ku-tai ch'iao-liang* (Peking, 1957).

T'ang Yung-t'ung, *Wei Chin Nan-pei-ch'ao Fo-chiao shih* (Peking, 1963 repr.).

Tanigawa Michio, 'Hokugi-matsu no nairan to jōmin', *Shirin*, 41. 3 (1958), 177–97; 41. 5 (1958), 411–27.

——, 'Kindensei to rinen to dai tochi shoyū', *Tōyōshi kenkyu*, 25. 4 (1967), 439–60.

——, 'Hoku-chō kizoku no seikatsu rinri', in Chūgoku Chūseishi Kenkyūkai ed., *Chūgoku chūseishi kenkyū: Riku-chō Zui Tō no shakai to bunka* (Tokyo, 1970).

——, *Zui Tō teikoku keisei shiron* (Tokyo, 1971).

T'ao Hsi-sheng, *Chung-kuo cheng-chih chih-tu shih*, vol. 3 (Taipei, 1973).

T'ao Hsi-sheng and Wu Hsien-ch'ing, *Nan-pei-ch'ao ching-chi shih* (Shanghai, 1937).

Ts'en Chung-mien, *T'u-chüeh chi-shih* (Peking, 1958).

Tseng Wu-hsiu, 'Chung-kuo li-tai ch'ih-tu kai-shu', *Li-shih yen-chiu* (1964), 3.

Tsukamoto Zenryū, *Shina Bukkyōshi kenkyū: Hoku-Gi hen* (Kyoto, 1942).

——, *Gishō Shakurōshi no kenkyū* (Kyoto, 1961).

Uchida Gimpu, 'Hokuchō seikyoku ni okeru Senpi oyobi shohokuzoku-kei kizoku no chii', *Tōyōshi kenkyū*, 1. 3 (1936), 209–25.

——, 'Hoku-Gi sozei seido no hensen', *Rekishi kyōiku*, 17. 6 (1969), 33–9.

——, *Kita-Ajia shi kenkyū: Senbi Juzan Tokketsu hen* (Kyoto, 1975).

Utsonomiya Kiyoyoshi, *Kandai shakai-keizai shi kenkyū*, rev. edn. (Tokyo, 1967).

Wan Kuo-ting, 'Lun *Ch'i min yao shu*: wo-kuo hsien-ts'un tsui tsao te wan-cheng nung-shu', *LSYC* (1956), 1. 79–102.

Wan Sheng-nan, 'Wei-mo pei-chen pao-tung shih chieh-chi tou-cheng hai shih t'ung-chih chieh-chi nei-pu te tou-cheng?', *Shih-hsüeh yüeh-k'an* (1964), 9. 25–8.

Wang Ch'e and Ch'en Hsü, 'Lo-yang Pei Wei Yüan Yi mu te hsing hsiang t'u', *Wen wu* (1974), 12. 56–60.

Wang Ch'ing-cheng, 'Shih-wu nien yi-lai ku-tai huo-pi tzu-liao te fa-hsien ho yen-chiu chung te jo-kan wen-t'i', *Wen wu* (1965), 1. 26–36.

Wang Chung-lo, *Wei Chin Nan-pei-ch'ao Sui ch'u-T'ang shih*, vol. 1 (Shanghai, 1961).

Wen-wu ch'u-pan-she, *Kung-hsien shih-k'u ssu* (Peking, 1962).

Wu Ch'eng-lo, *Chung-kuo tu-liang-heng shih*, rev. by Ch'eng Li-chün (Shanghai, 1957).

Wu Ju-tso, 'Kuan-yü Hsia wen-hua chi ch'i lai-yüan te ch'u-pu t'an-so, *Wen wu* (1978), 9. 70–3.

Yang Hsien-yi, *Ling mo hsü chien*, privately printed (Peking, 1950).

Yang K'uan, *Chung-kuo li-tai ch'ih-tu k'ao* (Shanghai, 1955, repr. of 1938 edn.).

Yang Shou-ching, *Li-tai yü-ti t'u* (1903).

Yang Yao-k'un, 'Pei Wei mo-nien Pei-chen pao-tung fen-hsi', *LSYC* (1978), 11. 63–70.

Yano Chikara, 'Tō-sho no kizoku seiji ni tsuite', *Tōhōgaku*, 9 (1954), 12–18.

Yao Wei-yüan, *Pei-ch'ao Hu hsing k'ao* (Peking, 1962).

Yen Keng-wang, *Chung-kuo ti-fang hsing-cheng chih-tu shih, chüan chung: Wei Chin Nan-pei-ch'ao ti-fang hsing-cheng chih-tu* (Taipei, 1963).

Yen Wen-ju, 'Lo-yang Han Wei Sui T'ang ch'eng-chih chen-ch'a chi', *K'ao-ku hsüeh-pao* 9 (1955), 117–36.

Yin Wei-chang, 'Erh-li-t'ou wen-hua t'an-t'ao' (1978), 1. 1–4.

Yoshida Torao, *Gi Shin Nambokuchō sozei no kenkyū* (Tokyo, 1943).

Yoshikawa Tadao, *Kō Kei no ran shimatsu ki: Nanchō ni okeru kizoku shakai no meiun* (Tokyo, 1974).

Yuan Chia-hua et al., *Han-yü fang-yen kai-yao* (Peking, 1960).

WORKS IN WESTERN LANGUAGES

Amano Motonosuke, 'Dry Farming and the *Ch'i Min Yao Shu*', in *Silver Jubilee Volume of the Zimbun Kagaku Kenkyūsyo* (Kyoto, 1954).

E. Balazs, *Le Traité économique du 'Souei-chou'*, (Leiden, 1953).

——, *Le Traité juridique du 'Souei-chou'* (Leiden, 1954).

Hans Bielenstein, 'Lo-yang in Later Han Times', *Bulletin of the Museum of Far Eastern Antiquities* (Stockholm), 48 (1976), 1–142.

Lawrence P. Briggs, *The Ancient Khmer Empire* (Transactions of the American Philosophical Society, vol. 41, part 1) (Philadeophia, 1957).

Chang Kwang-chih, *The Archaeology of Ancient China*, 3rd edn. (New Haven, 1977).

E. Chavannes, *Mission archéologique dans la Chine septentrionale* (Paris, 1911–).

Kenneth Ch'en, *Buddhism in China: A Historical Survey* (Princeton, 1964).

——, *The Chinese Transformation of Buddhism*, (Princeton, 1973).

Cheng Te-k'un, *Archaeology in China*: Vol. 2, *Shang China* (Cambridge, 1961)..

——, *Archaeology in China*: Vol. 3, *Chou China* (Cambridge, 1963).

G. Coedès, *Les États hindouisés d'Indochine et d'Indonésie* (Paris, 1948).

——, *Les Peuples de la péninsule indochinoise: histoire, civilisations* (Paris, 1962).

Edward Conze, *Buddhism: Its Essence and Development* (Oxford, 1960).

——, *Buddhist Thought in India*, London, 1962.

H. G. Creel, *The Origins of Statecraft in China*: Vol. 1, *The Western Chou Empire* (Chicago, 1970).

P. D. Dutton, 'Yü Tao Ho', *The China Journal*, 16, 6 (June 1932), 331–4.

Wolfram Eberhard, *Das Toba-Reich Nord Chinas* (Leiden, 1949).

Patricia Buckley Ebrey, *The Aristocratic Families of Early Imperial China: A Case Study of the Po-ling Ts'ui Family* (Cambridge, 1978).

Gabriel Ferrand, 'Ye-tiao, Sseu-tiao et Java', *Journal Asiatique*, XIᵉ série, 8, 3 (1916), 521–32.

Fujita Toyohachi, 'Sur Yeh-t'iao, Szu-t'iao et Szu-he-t'iao', *Memoirs of the Faculty of Literature and Politics, Taihoku Imperial University*, 1. 1 (1929), 1–41.

J. Gernet, *Les Aspects économiques du Bouddhisme dans la société chinoise du Vᵉ au Xᵉ siècle* (Saigon, 1956).

Ho Ping-ti, 'Loyang, A.D. 495–534: A Study of the Physical and Socio-economic Planning of a Metropolitan Area', *HJAS* 26 (1966), 52–101.

Jennifer Holmgren, 'Empress Dowager Ling of the Northern Wei and the T'o-pa Sinicization Question', *Papers on Far Eastern History*, 18 (1978), 123–70.

E. R. Hughes, *Two Chinese Poets: Vignettes of Han Life and Thought* (Princeton, 1960).

Leon Hurvitz (tr.), Wei Shou, *Treatise on Buddhism:* An English translation of the original Chinese Text of Wei-shu CXIV and the Japanese annotation of Tsukamoto Zenryū (repr. from *Yün-kang, the Buddhist Cave Temples of the fifth century A.D. in north China*, vol. xvi, supplement) (Kyoto, 1956).

David G. Johnson, *The Medieval Chinese Oligarchy* (Boulder, Colorado, 1977).

Bernhard Karlgren, 'Glosses on the Book of Documents', *Bulletin of the Museum of Far Eastern Antiquities*, 20 (Stockholm, 1948) and 21 (1949).

——, 'The Book of Documents', *Bulletin of the Museum of Far Eastern Antiquities*, 22 (1950).

——, *Grammata Serica Recensa* (Stockholm, 1964 repr.)

Arnulf Kollautz and Miyakawa Hisayuki, *Geschichte und Kultur Eines Völkerwanderungszeitlichen Nomadenvolks: Die Jou-jan der Mongolei und die Awaren in Mitteleuropa*, 2 vols. (Klagenfurt, 1970).

Kumashiro Yukio, 'Recent Developments in Scholarship on the *Ch'imin yaoshu* in Japan and China', *The Developing Economies*, 9.4 (1971), 422–48.

Owen Lattimore, *Mongol Journeys* (London, 1941).

Berthold Laufer, 'Asbestos and Salamander', *T'oung Pao* 16 (1915), 299–373.

Liu Mau-ts'ai, *Die Chinesischen Nachrichten zur Geschichte der Ost-Türken (T'u-küe)*, (Wiesbaden, 1958).

Colin Mackerras, *The Uighur Empire (744–840) According to the T'ang Dynastic Histories* (Canberra, 1968).

Joseph Needham, *Science and Civilisation in China* (Cambridge, 1954–).

——, *Clerks and Craftsmen in China and the West* (Cambridge, 1970).

Paul Pelliot, 'Le Fou-nan', *BEFEO* 3 (1903).

E. G. Pulleyblank, 'Chinese and Indo-Europeans', *Journal of the Royal Asiatic Society* (1966), 9–39.

——, 'The Consonantal System of Old Chinese', *Asia Major*, N.S. 9 (1962), 58–144, 206–65.

Michael C. Rogers, *The Chronicle of Fu Chien: A Case of Exemplar History* (Berkeley and Los Angeles, 1968).

Shih Sheng-han, *A Preliminary Study of the Book 'Ch'i Min Yao Shu'*, 2nd edn. (Peking, 1962).

Teng Ssu-yü (ed. and tr.), *Family Instructions For the Yen Clan: Yen-shih chia-hsün by Yen Chih-t'ui* (Leiden, 1968).

Tsukamoto Zenryū, 'The Dates of Kumārajīva and Seng-chao re-examined', *Silver Jubilee Volume of the Zimbun Kagaku Kenkyūsyo* (Kyoto, 1954), 568–84.

—— (translated by Sargent), 'The Śramana Superintendent T'an-yao and his Time', *Monumenta Serica* 16 (1957).

D. C. Twitchett, 1957/1, 'The Monasteries and China's Economy in Mediaeval Times', *BSOAS* 19 (1957), 526–49.

——, 1957/2, 'The Fragment of the T'ang "Ordinances of the Department of Waterways" discovered at Tunhuang', *Asia Major*, N.S. 6 (1957), 23–79.

——, *Financial Administration Under the T'ang Dynasty*, 2nd edn. (Cambridge, 1970).

Arthur Waley, 'Loyang and its Fall' in *Secret History of the Mongols and Other Pieces* (London, 1963), 47–55.

Wang Yi-t'ung, 'Slaves and Other Comparable Social Groups during the Northern Dynasties (386–618)', *HJAS* 16 (1953), 293–364.

A. G. Wenley, *The Grand Empress Dowager Wen Ming and the Northern Wei Necropolis at Fang-shan* (Freer Gallery of Art Occasional Papers, vol. 1, no. 1) (Washington, D.C., 1947).

Paul Wheatley, *The Golden Khersonese: Studies in the Historical Geography of the Malay Peninsula before A.D. 1500* (Kuala Lumpur, 1961).

——, *The Pivot of the Four Quarters: A Preliminary Enquiry into the Origins and Character of the Ancient Chinese City* (Chicago and Edinburgh, 1972).

Yang Lien-sheng, 'Notes on the Economic History of the Chin Dynasty', *HJAS* 9 (1945–7).

E. Zurcher, *The Buddhist Conquest of China* (Leiden, 1959).

Index

compiled by Eileen Jenner

297

83

5